MW01119540

# SHAKESPEARE'S SENSE OF CHARACTER

# Studies in Performance and Early Modern Drama

## General Editor's Preface

### Helen Ostovich, McMaster University

Performance assumes a string of creative, analytical, and collaborative acts that, in defiance of theatrical ephemerality, live on through records, manuscripts, and printed books. The monographs and essay collections in this series offer original research which addresses theatre histories and performance histories in the context of the sixteenth and seventeenth century life. Of especial interest are studies in which women's activities are a central feature of discussion as financial or technical supporters (patrons, musicians, dancers, seamstresses, wigmakers, or 'gatherers'), if not authors or performers per se. Welcome too are critiques of early modern drama that not only take into account the production values of the plays, but also speculate on how intellectual advances or popular culture affect the theatre.

The series logo, selected by my colleague Mary V. Silcox, derives from Thomas Combe's duodecimo volume, *The Theater of Fine Devices* (London, 1592), Emblem VI, sig. B. The emblem of four masks has a verse which makes claims for the increasing complexity of early modern experience, a complexity that makes interpretation difficult. Hence the corresponding perhaps uneasy rise in sophistication:

> Masks will be more hereafter in request,
> And grow more deare than they did heretofore.

No longer simply signs of performance 'in play and jest', the mask has become the 'double face' worn 'in earnest' even by 'the best' of people, in order to manipulate or profit from the world around them. The books stamped with this design attempt to understand the complications of performance produced on stage and interpreted by the audience, whose experiences outside the theatre may reflect the emblem's argument:

> Most men do use some colour'd shift
> For to conceal their craftie drift.

Centuries after their first presentations, the possible performance choices and meanings they engender still stir the imaginations of actors, audiences, and readers of early plays. The products of scholarly creativity in this series, I hope, will also stir imaginations to new ways of thinking about performance.

# Shakespeare's Sense of Character
## On the Page and From the Stage

YU JIN KO
*Wellesley College, USA*

and

MICHAEL W. SHURGOT
*South Puget Sound Community College, USA*

ASHGATE

Published by
Ashgate Publishing Limited
Wey Court East
Union Road
Farnham
Surrey, GU9 7PT
England

Ashgate Publishing Company
110 Cherry Street
Suite 3-1
Burlington, VT 05401-3818
USA

www.ashgate.com

**British Library Cataloguing in Publication Data**
Shakespeare's sense of character: on the page and from the stage. – (Studies in performance and early modern drama)
1. Shakespeare, William, 1564–1616 – Characters. 2. Shakespeare, William, 1564–1616 – Dramatic production. 3. Characters and characteristics in literature.
I. Series II. Ko, Yu Jin, 1961– III. Shurgot, Michael W.,
1943–
822.3'3—dc23

**Library of Congress Cataloging-in-Publication Data**
Shakespeare's sense of character / edited by Yu Jin Ko and Michael W. Shurgot.
    p. cm.—(Studies in performance and early modern drama)
  Includes bibliographical references and index.
  ISBN 978-1-4094-4066-6 (hardcover: alk. paper)—ISBN 978-1-4094-4067-3 (ebook)
  1. Shakespeare, William, 1564–1616—Characters. 2. Shakespeare, William, 1564–1616—Dramatic production. 3. Characters and characteristics in literature. I. Ko, Yu Jin, 1961– II. Shurgot, Michael W., 1943–
  PR2989.S57 2012
  822.3'3—dc23

2012014865

ISBN 9781409440666 (hbk)
ISBN 9781409440673 (ebk)
ISBN 9781409472148 (epub)

Printed and bound in Great Britain by the
MPG Books Group, UK.

# Contents

# List of Illustrations

# Notes on Contributors

**Diego Arciniegas** was the Artistic Director of The Publick Theatre Boston from 2001 to 2011. He is a Senior Lecturer in Theatre Studies at Wellesley College. Born in Bogota, Colombia, educated at Williams College, he trained in theatre at the British and European Studies Group London (BESGL).

**James E. Berg** is Visiting Assistant Professor of English at Middlebury College. His current interest is in literary character, particularly as it developed during the English Renaissance, but also in other eras. He is currently working on a book, *The Character of Shakespeare's Plays.* His publications include "The Properties of Character in King Lear" in *Shakespeare and Character: Theory, History, Performance, and Theatrical Persons,* ed. Paul Yachnin and Jessica Slights (2008).

**Michael Bristol** is Greenshields Professor Emeritus at McGill University, where he is a member of the Shakespeare in Performance Research Team. He is the author of *Carnival and Theatre; Shakespeare's America / America's Shakespeare*; and *Big-Time Shakespeare*. His current research is on character and moral agency.

**Travis Curtright** is Associate Professor and Chair of the Literature Department at Ave Maria University. He is author of *The One Thomas More*, forthcoming from The Catholic University of America Press, co-editor of *Shakespeare's Last Plays* (2002), and professionally trained in acting at the American Shakespeare Center in Staunton, Virginia. His articles on Shakespeare and character have appeared in *Literary Imagination, Logos: A Journal of Catholic Thought*, and *English Language Notes.*

**Dan Donohue** has been a company member at the Oregon Shakespeare Festival since 1994, performing in over 30 productions in such diverse roles as Hamlet, Iago, Mercutio, Caliban, Mark Antony, and Hal in *Henry IV Parts 1 & 2,* and *Henry V.* On Broadway he played Scar in *The Lion King* and has performed major roles at other theatres such as Long Wharf Theatre, Portland Center Stage, Seattle Repertory Theatre, Intiman Theatre, Arizona Theatre Company, Utah Shakespeare Festival, Asolo Repertory Theatre, and elsewhere. He is an inaugural recipient of the Lunt-Fontanne Fellowship. He received a B.A. in Theatre Arts from Whitman College and an M.F.A. in Acting from Pennsylvania State University.

**William Flesch** is Professor of English at Brandeis University. His publications include *Comeuppance (*Harvard University Press, 2008) and *Generosity and the Limits of Authority: Shakespeare, Herbert, Milton (*Ithaca: Cornell University Press, 1992). His articles have appeared in *Critical Inquiry, Studies in Romanticism,* and *ELH.*

**Brett Gamboa** is Assistant Professor of English at Dartmouth College where he teaches courses on dramatic literature and performance. He is currently at work on a book about doubling roles in Shakespeare's plays.

**Yu Jin Ko** is Professor of English at Wellesley College. He is the author of *Mutability and Division on Shakespeare's Stage* as well as numerous articles on Shakespeare, especially Shakespeare in performance.

**Cary M. Mazer** is Associate Professor of Theatre Arts and English at the University of Pennsylvania. He writes about Shakespeare performance history, Victorian and Edwardian theatre, and contemporary dramaturgy, acting, and rehearsal practices. His response to Tiffany Stern's article can be downloaded at: http://www.english.upenn.edu/~cmazer/ResponsetoStern.pdf

**Eunice Roberts** trained at Bristol Old Vic Theatre School and continues to work as a professional actor. She was Visiting Director of Theatre at Vassar College, New York and regularly teaches for BADA in the UK. She is also an assessor for the internationally prestigious Trinity/Guildhall scheme of drama and performance evaluations. Her work as an Associate Director of Actors From The London Stage, which tours the US with productions of Shakespeare, led her to undertake postgraduate research into approaches to acting at the University of Kent and this forms the basis of her article in this volume.

**Michael W. Shurgot** retired from South Puget Sound Community College in Olympia, WA in 2006, where he received four distinguished faculty awards. He is the author of *Stages of Play: Shakespeare's Theatrical Energies in Elizabethan Performance* (Delaware, 1998), and editor of *North American Players of Shakespeare: A Book of Interviews* (Delaware, 2007). He reviews Shakespearean performances in Seattle for *Shakespeare Bulletin*, and the Oregon Shakespeare Festival and Globe plays for *The Upstart Crow*.

**Tiffany Stern** is Professor of Early Modern Drama at Oxford University. Her books are *Rehearsal from Shakespeare to Sheridan* (2000), *Making Shakespeare* (2004), *Shakespeare in Parts* (with Simon Palfrey, 2007) and *Documents of Performance in Early Modern England* (2009). She is a general editor of the New Mermaids play series and has produced editions of the anonymous *King Leir* (2002), *Sheridan's Rivals* (2004) and *Farquhar's Recruiting Officer* (2010). She is currently editing Richard Brome's *Jovial Crew* and embarking on a monograph about theatres and fairgrounds.

**James Wells** has published several essays on Shakespeare's plays and is the editor of *The Second Part of Henry the Fourth* and *The Merry Wives of Windsor* for The New Kittredge Shakespeare. He also writes about composers of contemporary classical music, Broadway musicals, and film scores for BMI's *Music World* magazine. He is Assistant Professor of English at Muskingum University.

**Lina Perkins Wilder** teaches courses on Shakespeare and the early modern period in English literature at Connecticut College. She is the author of *Shakespeare's Memory Theater* (Cambridge, 2010) as well as numerous articles in journals such as *Shakespeare Quarterly*.

**Bruce Young** teaches English at Brigham Young University, including courses on Shakespeare, C. S. Lewis, and world literature. He is the author of *Family Life in the Age of Shakespeare*.

# Acknowledgements

This collection evolved over a number of years and has received invaluable help and input from many sources, both individual and institutional. The editors would first like to thank the Shakespeare Association of America for providing the opportunity to pursue the topic of character in a seminar at the SAA Conference in 2008. Additional contributors came on board as papers continued to circulate at conferences organized by the American Society for Theatre Research and the British Shakespeare Association. An immense debt of gratitude is owed to Wellesley College and the Newhouse Center for the Humanities at Wellesley College for supporting a symposium in 2010 ("Shakespearean Character on Trial") that provided a venue for scholars and theatre practitioners to engage in a dialogue about character.

To more individuals than we can name here we also owe deep gratitude, but we would be horribly remiss without acknowledging the following: Ben Evett and his late father Dave Evett, Diego Arciniegas, Carol Dougherty, Nora Hussey, Carey Perloff, Tina Packer, Vilma Silva, Curt Tofteland, Hal Cobb, and our editor at Ashgate, Erika Gaffney. And most of all, our families.

# Introduction

## Yu Jin Ko

Character-based approaches to Shakespeare have been the targets of some of the most disparaging academic criticism in the past century. To think of fictional characters as real people—and thus to ponder what hidden motives or untold backstories might drive their actions—has been the surest way to earn the label of being naive. Yet no approach has been as persistent, especially in the theatre and in the interpretive practices of the broader public. This divide in critical orientation is beginning to be bridged, however, as scholars start to rethink the importance of character as a critical category, particularly in light of postmodern ideas that have dominated academic thinking in the past quarter century. This book participates in this incipient but powerful resurgence of interest in character by bringing scholars and theatre practitioners together to think about and demonstrate why character continues to matter.

To start, we can look at a theatrical experience that will be familiar to many in the audience at a Shakespeare play today: the fresh line reading that reveals motivation and character. Regular playgoers could probably cite numerous examples from Shakespeare productions that they happened to have seen most recently. The following moment is such an example. In an *Othello* staged by Shakespeare and Company (Lenox, Massachusetts) in 2008, the issue of race was about as downplayed at it could be. Cassio, for example, was played by an African-American actor, which had the effect of deflecting some of the focus from Othello's race and giving the impression that in this Venice the color of one's skin could be overlooked. Certainly this Othello (John Douglas Thompson) gave the impression that he was not preoccupied with race, even if some others may have been. The production made it clear that it wanted principally to tell a love story about sublime enthusiasms and new discoveries of powerful emotions that go tragically awry. However, as Othello began his celebrated speech recounting his course of wooing, he turned to Brabantio and delivered the half line "Her father loved me" (1.3.127) with pained remembrance, as if to say, "Don't you remember?" This served as Othello's first direct response to the various accusations and racist slurs, both direct and indirect, that Brabantio had previously hurled at him. After a pause, Othello completed the line—"oft invited me"—as another reminder of their past while expressing profound disappointment. One sensed that the disappointment concerned Brabantio's racial slurs, but the precise nature of that disappointment was not entirely clear. Was it that Brabantio turned out to harbor such revulsion toward Moors, or that he confirmed Othello's fears and suspicions that he did?

Ambiguous as that moment was, it highlighted and provided a window into a paradox that is very easy to overlook, especially in a production that minimizes the importance of race. Othello's public pronouncements in response to questions about his marriage suggest supreme confidence in his stature and no anxiety at all about his race:

> I fetch my life and being
> From men of royal siege, and my demerits
> May speak unbonneted to as proud a fortune
> As this that I have reached. (1.2.21–24)

In fact, he never refers to his race until the temptation scene (3.3). But this does lead to the question of why Othello marries Desdemona in secret, with neither her father's knowledge nor consent. Wouldn't a man of such heroic stature and dignity choose to marry openly? (John Douglas Thompson certainly played up Othello's dignified bearing, which only pressed the question more urgently.) One could imagine, nonetheless, that Othello and Desdemona had a conversation about their marriage plans, during which they might have mentioned race as a reason for eloping. If so, what was Othello's reaction? Did he try to reassure Desdemona that her father would come around? Deny the importance of race even as he went along with Desdemona's plans? Determine not to let the issue ruin his marriage? Repress his rage? His sense of humiliation?

One might suggest that the canon of Shakespeare criticism in the past century was formed in the effort to find ever new objections to analyzing Othello in this way—in the way associated above all with A.C. Bradley and his classic study *Shakespearean Tragedy*. "The center" of Shakespearean tragedy, Bradley wrote in oft-quoted words, lay "in action issuing from character, or character issuing in action."[1] In revising Aristotle by subordinating action to character, he made character the force behind, rather than the product of, action, and further made the "inward struggle" (26) of the characters the principle locus of interest. Whatever "outer" (25) conflict or struggle the tragic hero may engage in—whether against personal enemies, circumstances or even cosmological forces—"the concentration of interest" (26) remained on the drama of inner conflict. If Shakespeare's heroes experienced this conflict in "magnitude" (27) and "scale" (26) beyond what is to be found in "real life," they were still, however, fundamentally "made of the stuff we find within ourselves" (26). In this, as has frequently been pointed out, Bradley was following the Romantics and their passion for encountering life-like individuality in Shakespeare's plays. For Coleridge, this encounter was defined by something in particular: "The characters of the *dramatis personae*, like those in real life, are to be inferred by the reader;—they are not told to him."[2] Indeed, this creative endeavor to infer or discover the hidden recesses of character came

---

[1]    *Shakespearean Tragedy* (1904; New York: Fawcett Premier, 1965), 20.
[2]    *Selected Poetry and Prose of Coleridge*, Donald A. Stauffer, ed. (Random House, 1951), 436.

to define Bradley's work, as evidenced in part by the titles given to some of the appendices of *Shakespearean Tragedy*: "Where was Hamlet at the time of his father's death?" "Did Emilia suspect Iago?" "'He has no children'."

But we have been reminded countless times, perhaps most memorably by L.C. Knights in his famous response to Bradley, that fictional characters are not actual people.[3] More importantly, we were told that focusing on individual personalities obscured the view of the artistic whole—of the unity of aesthetic and philosophical vision that more formalist modes of analysis, like New Criticism, would reveal. Hence we were told not to ask how many children Lady Macbeth might have had but what the metaphor of the child in *Macbeth* could reveal about the play's ethical and metaphysical vision.[4] Historically-minded critics also warned us about the limits of universality—the assumption that Shakespeare's creations would mirror people in our world—by delineating the differences between their world picture and ours.[5] Some theatre historians joined the chorus to suggest that Elizabethan stage conventions were incompatible with the psychological realism assumed by character analysis.[6] Even more punishing jolts came with the tidal wave of postmodernist criticism in a variety of forms: deconstruction, feminism, new-historicism, materialism, postcolonialism, to mention the most prominent. Each sought in one form or another to deconstruct, or expose the constructedness of, our idea of character by historicizing our understanding of subjectivity—our sense of self. Subjectivity became above all an insidious though cherished illusion—the effect of ingrained metaphysical residues in language, of ideology, of a misbegotten and oppressive essentialism. It became routine for many to qualify the features associated with subjectivity—individuality, inwardness, autonomy—with pejoratives such as "bourgeois," "humanist," and "patriarchal." True selfhood was to be understood as a contingent construct produced by the interplay of social and material forces, of power, of discursive practices. Indeed, we were told that focusing on character in the old, humanist sense would occlude our understanding of the real issues raised by a play.[7] At the same time, new

---

[3]  See *How many children had Lady Macbeth? An Essay in the Theory and Practice of Shakespeare Criticism* (Cambridge: G. Fraser, The Minority Press, 1933).

[4]  The representative work might be Cleanth Brook's "The Naked Babe and the Cloak of Manliness" in *The Well Wrought Urn* (New York, Harcourt Brace, 1947).

[5]  See, for example, E.M.W. Tillyard, *The Elizabethan World Picture* (New York: Macmillan, 1944) and *Shakespeare's History Plays* (New York: Macmillan, 1946).

[6]  One could always start with M.C. Bradbrook, *Elizabethan Stage Conditions: A Study of their Place in the Interpretation of Shakespeare's Plays* (Cambridge: Cambridge University Press, 1932).

[7]  Influential critics of post-modernism (broadly defined) are of course too numerous to cite. Here are some representative critics: Stephen Greenblatt, *Renaissance Self-Fashioning* (Chicago: University of Chicago Press, 1980); Francis Barker, *The Tremulous Private Body* (New York: Methuen, 1984); Jonathan Dollimore, *Radical Tragedy* (Chicago: University of Chicago Press, 1984); Catherine Belsey, *The Subject of Tragedy* (London and NY: Methuen, 1985); Ania Loomba, *Gender, Race, Renaissance Drama* (NY and Manchester:

attempts were made to "defamiliarize" Shakespeare's characters by, for example, arguing anew that original stage practices like the use of boy actors in female roles were antithetical to a drama of psychological naturalism but in ways that helped to reveal the constructedness of gender.[8] Taken altogether, one important result was that readings of character principally became value judgments about whether Shakespeare's plays subverted or perpetuated oppressive notions of identity.

Yet character-based approaches to Shakespeare in the Bradleyan vein never disappeared. Certainly in the theatre they thrived, and continue to thrive, especially in the form of Stanislavskian practices. Here is the actor-narrator of Stanislavski's *Creating a Role* reflecting on Othello after being told to go "deeper down into the *subtext* where the writer has concealed the motives which prompted him to create the play" (emphasis in original):

> One knows something of his earlier life, the period of his first acquaintance with Desdemona, his falling in love, the abduction ... . But how much more the author left unsaid concerning what happened before the play begins, also in the intervals between scenes .... It was what Shakespeare left unsaid that ... I undertook to fill out.[9]

Despite the influence of theatre revolutionaries and visionaries like Brecht, Artaud, and Grotowski—who all tried in their various ways to break free from what they saw as the restrictive conventionalities of realist theatre—this kind of psychological realism that relies on what Coleridge would call inferential imagination has remained the underlying norm. Academics have generally been more apologetic, or sheepish, about engaging in Bradleyan practices, but there have been notable exceptions who have mounted spirited defenses of Bradley, in particular by revalidating the act of inferential reading. For A.D. Nuttall, for example, Bradley was the supreme example of a "transparent," as opposed to an "opaque," critic—someone for whom the formal devices of literary representation (like metaphors) became "windows" into the internal reality of characters. Indeed, literary representation, being necessarily allusive and therefore incomplete, demanded the use of "inference," not only at the most reductively absurd level of inferring that Hamlet has legs even though "Shakespeare never mentions them," but more fundamentally so that we can "submit" fully to the "mimetic enchantment" of make-believe realities.[10] To infer is willingly to suspend disbelief.

---

Manchester University Press, 1989); Frederic Jameson, *Postmodernism, or, The Cultural Logic of Late Capitalism* (Durham: Duke University Press, 1991); and a far more recent book that takes into account the ideas of all the cited works, Margareta de Grazia, Hamlet *without Hamlet* (Cambridge: Cambridge University Press, 2007).

[8]     See, Laura Levine, *Men in Women's Clothing* (Cambridge and New York: Cambridge University Press, 1994) and Lesley Anne Soule, "Subverting Rosalind: Cocky Ros in the Forest of Arden," *New Theatre Quarterly* (May 1991): 126–36.

[9]     *Creating a Role*, Elizabeth Reynolds Hapgood, trans. (New York: Theatre Arts Books, 1961), 261, 263.

[10]    A.D. Nuttall, *A New Mimesis* (London and New York: Methuen, 1983), 80–82.

More recently, and most outlandishly, Harold Bloom has championed Bradley in a way that makes the capacity to infer itself the defining feature of the form of inwardness that Shakespeare is said to have invented and bequeathed to us. If Shakespeare's characters seem uncannily real to us, as though they could "get up and walk out of their plays,"[11] it is because, rather circularly, Shakespeare inaugurated "personality as we have come to recognize it"[12] and invented our deepest sense of what it is to be human. In particular, the characters are (borrowing Hegel's formulation) "free artists of themselves," continually overhearing themselves and reinventing themselves with an "introspective consciousness"[13] in a seemingly ceaseless process of individuation. In the case of Hamlet, his "freedom can be defined as *the freedom to infer*, and we learn this intellectual liberty by attending to Hamlet;" naturally, "inference becomes the audience's way to Hamlet's consciousness." The suggestion here (in the typically gnomic phrasing of Bloom) is that inference—as the imaginative practice of searching beyond the given, which in Hamlet assumes "sublime" and prophetic forms ("O my prophetic soul!")—is the defining cognitive capacity behind crucial forms of artistry, including self-creation and imaginative reading.[14] Without inference, there is no self as we know it, much less literary character. Bloom's central argument about inference is thus a defense of fiction: the act of relating fictive reality to our reality through inference "enlarges" and in some sense creates our idea of "what makes the self authentically human."[15] In the end, then, a character approach to drama is an effort to articulate, and in that sense give reality to, the struggles and possibilities of selfhood.

The Bradleyan and anti-Bradleyan lines of criticism might thus be conveniently divided into approaches that privilege either the private or the social, the inner or the outer. If this introduction has given far more space to the Bradleyans, it is merely an attempt to counterbalance the overwhelming prominence given to postmodernist critics in academia during the past several decades. However, if there is one insight driving this book, it is that inferential readings of character are not incompatible with the rich variety of concerns—from aesthetic ones concerning structural unity and dramaturgical practices to sociopolitical ones about power relations—that have engaged critics for the past century. If genuine dialogue between the two camps has been difficult, it is partly the effect of rhetorical excesses. The willful hyperboles of Bloom have their counterparts, for example, in the postmodernist caricature of the supposedly reigning, essentialist view of dramatic character as a pre-social, inviolate, transcendent subjectivity that precedes the lines on the page and supersedes the actions of the play. Indeed, if we turn back to the theatrical

---

[11]   Bloom, *The Western Canon* (New York: Harcourt Brace, 1994), 72.

[12]   Bloom, *Shakespeare, The Invention of the Human* (New York: Riverhead Books, 1998), 4.

[13]   *Western Canon,* 73

[14]   *Invention of the Human,* 419.

[15]   *Invention,* 9, 17.

example of Shakespeare and Company's *Othello* cited earlier, we will be able to see why dialogue between character criticism and seemingly antithetical forms of criticism is—and has been in limited form—possible.

In that short moment when he addressed Brabantio with the half line "Her father loved me," Othello provided a fleeting glimpse of what lay inside, beneath the combination of dignified, soldierly calm and irrepressible passion for Desdemona that defined him: the untold backstory behind the narrated backstory of the wooing. The untold story belonged, not to the world of epic adventure and exotic climes, but to the decidedly social world of Venice in which not only marriage but social advancement more generally for a racial other includes careful negotiation and some complex mixture of denial, determination and repression. Whatever may or may not have passed between Desdemona and Othello as they settled upon the idea of a secret marriage, it became clear that this Othello was highly aware, just below the surface, of how judiciously he needed to navigate the social world of Venice. In that short moment of addressing Brabantio, even in a production that sought to be principally a tragic story of epic love, Othello also told the story of so many powerful public figures who are black, both past and present. That is to say, at the moment when the actor invited inferential reading into the deepest recesses of his character, he also gestured most pointedly to the formative power of cultural practices.

This theatrical moment also pointed, then, to some of the reasons behind the most recent twist in the annals of character criticism: a resurgence of interest in character in a small but growing circle that includes scholars who have tried to rehabilitate character criticism by updating it—by incorporating as well as contesting the insights of postmodern thought in particular to open up the boundaries of character criticism. Representative of this group of scholars is one of our contributors, Michael Bristol, who, in his essay titled "How many children did she have?," comes out of the character closet, as it were, but as a committed materialist. If, he argues, asking inferential questions of the kind mocked by L.C. Knights is a way of engaging in "Shakespeare's make believe," that engagement can be "part of a larger commitment to ethical and political reflection."[16] As he later explains in an essay in the volume *Presentist Shakespeares* (2007), the act of filling in the gaps of a narrative using inference and one's knowledge of the world is an "indispensable" form of "presentism"—of "combining premises taken from a fiction with premises taken from the actual world;" this form of presentism can, however, be further mixed with what we now call "historicism"—"historical research into the collective belief systems of the author's world"—to "engage our views about very basic and even universal ethical concerns."[17] Put another way, treating characters as people you know or might meet is also a way of engaging

---

[16] "How many children did she have?" in *Philosophical Shakespeares*, John J. Joughlin, ed. (London and New York: Routledge, 2000), 18–33; 33.

[17] Bristol, "… And I'm the King of France," in *Presentist Shakespeares*, Hugh Grady and Terence Hawkes, ed. (London and New York: Routledge, 2007), 46–63; 50–53.

seriously with them as ethical agents who, like Othello, struggle with and are shaped, or misshaped, by the enormous pressures—emotional to ideological—that their particular worlds impose upon them.

Indeed, the most serious way in which one can treat characters as ethical agents with a bearing on us is to consent to the one "indispensable" operation required by fiction—imagining characters as living beings who bear an important, ontological relationship to us. Giving this consent has been made easier by critical writing that has countered some of the principal assertions of post-structuralist thought regarding the distance between modern and early-modern understandings of selfhood. Seminal works like *Inwardness and Theater in the English Renaissance* by Katharine Eisaman Maus and *Sources of the Self* by Charles Taylor, as well as a more recent study of William Blake by Laura Quinney (*William Blake on Self and Soul*), have demonstrated significant continuities in, for example, modern and earlier notions of inwardness and individual consciousness.[18] Theatre historians like Tiffany Stern (who contributes an essay to this volume) have reinforced this sense of continuity by re-examining the very conditions of Shakespeare's theatre that have often been used as evidence that naturalistic characterization in the Bradley-Stanislavski vein could not have existed. Countering the idea that the short rehearsal time precluded character building, Stern (along with co-author Simon Palfrey) argues in *Shakespeare in Parts* that, as obliquely suggested in Hamlet's hendiadyc formulation "the motive and the cue for passion" (2.2.561), Shakespeare manipulates cues to supply his actors with the kind motives that modern actors would routinely associate with the term motivation: "cues can help achieve the 'psychological' sophistication, and that almost tangible reality of feeling, for which Shakespeare has been so often celebrated."[19] In this connection, the critical shibboleth that character criticism as we understand it began with the early Romantic writers, or alternatively, with the advent of eighteenth-century humanism, has been challenged by critics like John Lee, who has persuasively argued that there is "no sharp break" between the Restoration criticism of Margaret Cavendish and John Dryden and the Romantic Coleridge's reading of Shakespearean character. All are said to be concerned with the question "Who's There?", and to engage in a fundamentally similar character criticism in search of answers.[20] The editors of the recent *Shakespeare and Character* have gone even further to suggest that character has been central to the history of Shakespeare criticism from the beginning for the simple reason that character is the central "organizing principle" of Shakespeare's plays. "Shakespeare tends to overturn," they argue, "the Aristotelian ranking of plot and character... so that character

---

[18]   *Inwardness and Theater in the English Renaissance* (Chicago: University of Chicago Press, 1995); *Sources of the Self* (Cambridge: Harvard University Press, 1992); *William Blake* (Cambridge: Harvard University Press, 2009).

[19]   *Shakespeare in Parts* (Oxford and New York: Oxford University Press, 2007), 110.

[20]   *Shakespeare's Hamlet and the Controversies of Self* (Oxford: Oxford University Press, 2000), 128.

displaces plot as the center of interest."[21] One could go even further still: if Michael Bristol and others have found ways of reconciling character criticism and some of its traditional adversaries in a "new character criticism,"[22] it is only because we—including the fiercest opponents of character criticism—have ineluctably been character critics all along, though in various states of being closeted.

Even a cursory glance at the history of twentieth-century Shakespeare criticism will bear this out. Harry Levin's *Question of Hamlet* (1959), for example, is a brilliant piece of humanistic formalist criticism that retains (even as it goes well beyond) some of the core New Critical principles that underlie L.C. Knights's critique of character criticism; the book is, as Levin spells out clearly at the outset, an effort to counter the tradition of thinking of "Hamlet without *Hamlet*,"[23] of Hamlet in isolation from the larger vision and context provided by the play. Some of the most compelling passages in the book could, nonetheless, come directly out of Bradley or Coleridge and speak to character in a way that is intended to resonate with us: he says of Hamlet of Act 5, "Since we cannot altogether arrange our lives, we are constantly seeking some principle of arrangement in the universe, whether it be the finger of deity or the determination of chance" (105). Consideration of the world of *Hamlet* and its perplexities, both social and cosmological, leads back to what Bradley would call Hamlet's inner struggle—just as focus on Hamlet's inner struggle leads out into his world in a continually revolving dynamic.

Levin's reading of Hamlet's existential or spiritual dilemma is further not incompatible with some readings of character that Jonathan Dollimore offers in his landmark *Radical Tragedy* (1984), a materialist critique of Hamlet without *Hamlet*, as it were, in which social context becomes the defining ground of character, or selfhood. Though the target of the book is "essentialist humanism," its reading of Lear's descent into madness and self-loss shares key elements of the twentieth century's humanist understanding of selfhood (represented in important respects by Harry Levin) as precariously informed by contingencies:

> More important than Lear's pity is his "madness"—less divine furor than a process of collapse which reminds us just how precarious is the psychological equilibrium which we call sanity, and just how dependent upon an identity which is social rather than essential. What makes Lear the person he is—or rather was—is not kingly essence (divine right), but, among other things, his authority and his family.[24]

---

[21]    Paul Yachnin and Jessica Slights, *Shakespeare and Character: Theory, History, Performance and Theatrical Persons* (New York: Palgrave Macmillan, 2009), 6–7.

[22]    *Shakespeare and Character*, 1. One could add Christy Desmet's work from 1992, *Reading Shakespeare's Characters* (Amherst: University of Massachusetts Press) to the list of "new" character criticism.

[23]    Harry Levin, *The Question of Hamlet* (New York: Oxford University Press, 1959), 5.

[24]    *Radical Tragedy*, 250, 195.

What we see in this analysis is an understanding of character that has affinities with the ideas behind the essays by Bruce Young and William Flesch in this volume: that, inasmuch as Shakespeare's plays always present characters as social beings in interaction with others, we find at the heart of Shakespearean character a web of relationships, or selves formed, and fractured, in their relationship with others. To assert that Shakespearean character is fundamentally relational is not to repudiate character criticism and the many conceptual terms associated with it—inwardness, personality, motivation, backstory, journey—but to extend the boundaries of what a character is and thereby reaffirm the continuing importance of character criticism.

Similar points could be made about many prominent scholars whose work one wouldn't immediately associate with character criticism. The feminist psychoanalytic work of Janet Adelman, for example, is driven by a "vernacular"[25] presentist outlook—the view that a character like Lear is violently dysfunctional in ways that are familiar to families even today and thus can provide insights into damaging pathologies that wreck families. Perhaps ironically, Adelman provides some of her most penetrating insights into Lear when she suggests that Cordelia changes from a "subject" with seeming "inwardness" and "flesh-and-blood being" in the first Act to an "object" or "creature of Lear's need" who is essentially emptied of "subjectivity" and "motivation" in her return in the later Acts; Shakespeare is said to be "complicit" in flattening out Cordelia's character to fulfill the desperate and despotic need in Lear for the "kind nursery" of a purified Cordelia to cleanse his being of the corruption that is associated deep within the patriarchal imagination with mortality and the sexualized maternal body.[26] The play becomes in Adelman's reading a tragic object lesson in reducing others to objects because of deep and misrecognized psychic needs. Despite significant differences, important continuities exist between this reading and Dan Donohue's reading of Iago in this book as a character whose destructive rage is driven by the need to be needed.

One could go on listing the numerous scholars whose work contains crucial elements of character criticism, but let two final examples serve. Michael Neill's *Issues of Death* (1997) is a rich, literary-historical account of how death was understood and confronted in Renaissance England. Neill's readings of Renaissance tragedy develop from a detailed study of cultural matters from the loss of Purgatory in the Protestant dispensation to "the strain of adjusting the psychic economy of an increasingly individualistic society to the stubborn facts of mortality."[27] Of revenge heroes like Hamlet, Neill writes, "Alternately disabled

---

[25] The word "vernacular" is from Bristol's essay "How many children did she have?" (19), and is intended to mean something like "broadly practiced in the culture."

[26] Janet Adelman, *Suffocating Mothers* (New York and London: Routledge, 1992), 124–25.

[27] Michael Neill, *Issues of Death: Mortality and Identity in English Renaissance Tragedy* (Oxford: Oxford University Press, 1997), 30.

by their inability to forget, and driven by their violent compulsion to remember, revenge heroes must wrestle to redeem their dead from the shame of being forgotten, even as they struggle to lay these perturbed spirits to rest, and thereby free themselves from the insistent presence of the past" (246). Readings of cultural practice and psychological motivation come together here in a way that reflects what actual actors have to say about Hamlet, as in the following comment by Ethan Hawke in his "Introduction" to the screenplay of Michael Almereyda's film version of *Hamlet*: "[T]he play is the story of a father reaching out from beyond the grave and corrupting and burdening the mind of his child with the baggage of his own vengeful anger and lust for power."[28]

Finally, Margreta de Grazia's Hamlet *without Hamlet,* as the inversion in its title indicates, is an attempt, once and for all, to rid the play *Hamlet* of the "Hamlet" that is argued to be the product of Coleridge and Romantic, anachronistic notions of psychology. De Grazia's focus is on what "critical tradition" has "ignored": Hamlet's "hamlet" (44)—land, and all the material and immaterial inheritances he is deprived of and which, she argues, stand behind Hamlet's famous melancholy. It should be noted in passing that others, including Dover Wilson in 1935, have also argued for the centrality of Hamlet's lost inheritance. But more to the point, the thematic focus on land finds its theatrical analogue in the focus on non-representational conventions, like that of the Vice, which, following Robert Weimann, de Grazia sees at the root of Hamlet's antic disposition. She takes issue with Weimann, however, for asserting that Shakespeare employed the Vice convention ultimately to create "a more poetically unified individuality" (196) in Hamlet. Nonetheless, her analysis, for example, of Hamlet's Vice-like "retributional excess" (192–93) in his desire to kill Claudius while the latter is in the heat of sin beautifully articulates the kinds of genre-eluding complexities and inconsistencies that have been seen as hallmarks of Hamlet's singular character: "In uttering the devil's sentiments, Hamlet crosses the divide between the natural and the unnatural, the human and the monstrous, in egregious violation of the 'special observance' he has imposed upon the Players to 'o'erstep not the modesty of nature'" (193). She could not have made the point any better that naturalistic and non-naturalistic elements combine in volatile ways in Shakespeare's dramaturgy to create uniquely shaped individual characters on stage.

The theatrical element in De Grazia's comment will serve here as well as a transition back to the world of the stage. Assertions to the contrary and her deep knowledge of theatrical history notwithstanding, de Grazia places herself squarely in the end on one side of the critical tradition that divides acting styles into the opposing poles of "naturalism" and "formalism," though other related binaries like "representation" and "presentation" are often interchanged for them.[29]

---

[28]   *William Shakespeare's Hamlet* (London: Faber and Faber, 2000), xiv.

[29]   Some representative critics in this tradition include, Muriel Bradbrook (*Elizabethan Stage Conditions: A Study of their Place in the Interpretation of Shakespeare's Plays* [Cambridge: Cambridge University Press, 1932]), Marvin Rosenberg ("Elizabethan

More specifically, her emphasis on non-naturalistic practices proceeds from the position—as much ideological as theatre-historical—that such practices are incompatible with the host of qualities associated with psychologized personhood, like inwardness and life-like forms of inner disunity. The performance-oriented essays in this volume will more often follow the alternative path set forth previously by scholars like S. L. Bethell, J. L Styan, Robert Weimann, and Meredith Anne Skura to explore how multiple theatrical practices combine to create character.[30] In this, the essays will join other scholarly efforts in this volume in continuing the work of expanding our notions of what Shakespearean character is and initiating new ways of talking about character across critical boundaries. They will all join very consciously, in other words, in the growing dialogue that extends the range of critical vocabularies that character criticism can work in. To reclaim character criticism we must, after all, move forwards, not backwards. However, one of the most important things that this book does in the spirit of moving the dialogue forward is to include voices from the theatre—essays written by theatre professionals who experience character first-hand in literally embodying characters onstage. The history of the stage is also a history of what has been possible, and in this crucial respect, characters live only in the moment of their physical embodiment in performance. The question of whether the cultural history of death, or our understanding of the capacity to infer, or the persistence of patriarchal anxieties, can inform our sense of character is, in a very practical sense, a question of whether an actor can perform a specific action or motivation that reflects larger issues. Actors are, to twist a phrase, the living abstract and brief chronicles of character.

Many academics will no doubt resist this last thought, and continue the tension—and sometimes the war of mutual suspicion—between theatre practice and criticism that is as old as Plato and Aristotle. As one might remember, even in his defense of tragedy against epic in *The Poetics*, Aristotle takes recourse

---

Actors: Men or Marionettes?", *PMLA* 69 [1954]: 915–27), B. L. Joseph (*Elizabethan Acting* [Oxford: Oxford University Press, 1964]), Peter Hyland ("'A Kind of Woman': The Elizabethan Boy-Actor and the Kabuki Onagata," *Theatre Research International* 12.1 [1987]: 1–8), Edward Burns (*Character: Acting and Being on the Pre-Modern Stage* [New York: St. Martin's Press, 1990]), and Peter Thompson ("Rogues and Rhetoricians: Acting Styles in Early English Drama," in *A New History of Early English Drama*, ed. John D. Cox and David Scott Kastan [New York: Columbia Univ. Press, 1997], 321–35).

[30]   The works alluded to are: S.L. Bethell (*Shakespeare and the Popular Dramatic Tradition* (Westminster: P.S. King & Staples, 1944); J.L. Styan, *The Shakespeare Revolution* (Cambridge: Cambridge University Press, 1977); Robert Weimann, *Shakespeare and the Popular Tradition in the Theater: Studies in the Social Dimension of Dramatic Form and Function* (Baltimore, Md.: Johns Hopkins University Press, 1987) and, with Douglas Bruster, *Shakespeare and the Power of Performance: Stage and Page in the Elizabethan Theatre* (New York: Cambridge University Press, 2008); and Meredith Anne Skura, *Shakespeare the Actor and the Purposes of Playing* (Chicago: University of Chicago Press, 1993).

to an argument that is still familiar today; he acknowledges that tragedy can be ruined by performers, but denies that this makes tragedy inherently inferior to epic, because "tragedy produces its effect even without movement, just as epic does, for a reading makes its nature quite clear."[31] The idea that performance is an incidental, and potentially corrupting, adjunct to the literary essence or "nature" of drama is also of course at the heart of Romantic appreciation of Shakespeare. As Charles Lamb (in)famously declared, "[T]he plays of Shakespeare are less calculated for performance on a stage than those of almost any other dramatist whatever," because, even with "great performers," "we find to our cost that instead of realizing an idea, we have only materialized and brought down a fine vision to the standard of flesh and blood."[32] Ironically, then, the very poets and thinkers who are most often held responsible for initiating the kind of character criticism that we have inherited have arguably had the greatest hand in ushering in the practice of treating the play as a poem, and with it the *longue durée* of high literature. The still visible hegemony of New Critical practices is only one manifestation of this *longue durée*, as is the ascendancy of literary study as an institutional discipline.

It is of course true that miserable performances simply come with the territory. Many scholars, moreover, have written wonderfully illuminating works about Shakespeare in performance, especially in the past quarter century, so what's to follow needs to be modulated to reflect this fact. But the larger fact is that suspicion between the theatre and academia persists, and does so because, as has been the case from the beginning, a high/low distinction operates that has many elements and cognates, including the distinction between theory and practice. On one side, the text still retains for so many the quality of a near-Platonic, metaphysical Form, to which performances remain shadowy and inadequate replicas.[33] Additionally, superior status is granted, or self-granted, to academic and theoretical, as opposed to theatrical and practical, knowledge. On the other side, a competing claim for priority is made based on the fact that Shakespeare's plays were first and foremost scripts for performance. Accordingly, the tables are turned to value practice and to dismiss academic knowledge as airy abstractions that are irrelevant to the living heart of drama—namely, performance.[34] Hence the impasse that academics and theatre practitioners often face, though of course a multitude of other issues are also involved. This book tries to take a small step toward stimulating more dialogue between scholars and theatre practitioners by neutralizing the priority of

---

[31]   *Ancient Literary Criticism: The Principal Texts in New Translations*, D. A. Russell and M. Winterbottom, ed. (Oxford: Oxford University Press, 1972), 131–32.

[32]   *The Romantics on Shakespeare*, Jonathan Bate, ed. (New York: Penguin, 1992), 113.

[33]   On the "essentializing rhetoric" (4) that enters into discussion of texts, by both scholars and practitioners, see W.B. Worthen, *Shakespeare and the Authority of Performance* (New York: Cambridge University Press, 1997).

[34]   Even a man with an academic background like John Barton is not beyond mocking academic discourse as just so much "jargon" (101) in *Playing Shakespeare* (London: Methuen, 1984). Perhaps it's *because* he has an academic background.

competing claims and starting from the premise that a fruitful and genuine sharing of knowledge can take place precisely because different forms of knowledge are involved. Put more bluntly, it is simply, self-evidently absurd for scholars to think that a full account of Shakespearean character can exclude perspectives from the theatre; by the same token, it would be self-defeating for people in the theatre to think scholars have little to offer when dealing with scripts that are over four hundred years old. To put it more positively, performances in their breathing, embodied reality can enlarge our sense of character in ways that critical writing can't, while scholarly essays can illuminate aspects of character that an actor might never have considered in the hurly burly of rehearsal and performance.

It is also important to keep in mind, as the essays will amply demonstrate, that neither scholars nor actors belong to monolithic categories. Contrary to common assumptions, not all people of the theatre are, for example, Method actors who follow familiar psychological-realist models. The set of reflections by Eunice Roberts (of Actors From The London Stage) on how character, actor and self do and do not come together in the moment of performance will prove to be as theoretically dense and challenging as any contribution by a scholar. In recounting his journey as Antonio in *The Merchant of Venice*, Diego Arciniegas will certainly map out a psychological trajectory with some familiar paths, but he will proceed through the entire play as if encountering the mind of Antonio and the world of Venice for the first time in an actorly mode that Michael Davies would call "processional"—by allowing, that is, the sense of character to develop as the consequence of, and not the pre-given impetus for, the series of actions and interactions that unfold over time.[35] On the flip side, some of the scholars in this volume will try to understand characters' inner journeys anew, as though they were in the space of the rehearsal room rather than the study. At the same time, many of the scholars will offer divergent and even conflicting perspectives. Cary Mazer will challenge Tiffany Stern's reading of what original stage practices imply about characterization in Shakespeare's theatre, while James Wells and Lina Wilder will examine character from non-naturalistic viewpoints. But perhaps most importantly, some of the scholars and theatre professionals will respond to each other in their essays. In bringing scholars and theatre professionals together, this book tries to embody the dialogue that is necessary for the common endeavor of sustaining the vitality of Shakespeare's characters.

Nonetheless, it must be acknowledged that scholars and practitioners do often use vocabularies that appear to be at odds with each other. In Michael Bristol's analysis of Helena's character in *All's Well That Ends Well* in this volume, he engages in the kind of Stanislavskian speculation that is common in the theatre as he wonders what exactly transpired in the bedroom during the bed trick. His imaginative musings lead him to suggest that Helena follows the affective dictates of a radical sexual economy that identifies her inner being with a particular virtue:

---

[35] See *Hamlet*, Character Studies Series (New York: Continuum Books, 2008), esp. 22–4.

the capacity to deliver a sexual gift that, in its superfluity, possesses the ability to transform the other. It would not be hard to imagine that an actress writing about Helena would come up with something rather different, focusing not on how the discourse of a radical sexual economy might enter into one's own sense of self, but on, for example, how her own experiences with irrational forms of passion might help her understand Helena's enduring passion for Bertram. One might find a similar dynamic if an actor's account of playing Henry V were paired with James Wells's analysis of how Shakespeare constructs Henry's moral character by exploiting the theatrical paradox that the palpable reality of the actor's body can render the fictional character of Henry unreal. However, as (my colleague) Diego Arciniegas likes to point out in conversation and in rehearsal when academics are present, this divide in perspective and vocabulary recalls the aphorism attributed to Bernard Shaw that England and America are countries separated by a common language. More specifically, and as Arciniegas intimates in his piece in this volume, the sense that actorly and scholarly analyses pull in opposing directions is sometimes simply the result of actors and scholars using an overlapping vocabulary but from first-person and third-party perspectives. If Henry appears problematically fictive, that is the result of a third-party reading of the first-person enactment by an actor of specific motivations and choices. If T.S. Eliot had magically appeared (via the kinds of fantasies seen in film and fiction) at the performance of *Othello* cited at the start of this Introduction, he might indeed have thought that Othello's final speech exposed Othello's "Bovarysme,"[36] but the actor John Douglas Thompson would certainly have been playing a far simpler motivation or action (at least for some of the lines): set the record straight. Were Thompson to offer an account, it would surely differ from Eliot's, but if one took the underlying differences between first and third-person perspectives fully into account, the differences would appear not necessarily as incompatible but complementary.

In this spirit, this Introduction will conclude by examining one more instance of the kind of unexpected line delivery in performance that was cited at the outset. This will be a trivial instance, though it will both reveal the moment-to-moment motivations that actors must consider, and, as in the *Othello* example, take the audience deeper not only into the character but also the character's social world. It involves the clown Launcelot in 2.5 of a performance of *The Merchant of Venice* (2008) by a Boston-based company called The Actors' Shakespeare Project, when Shylock is instructing Jessica on what to do at home while he goes out to supper with Bassanio. At this point in the play, Launcelot has already switched masters and is acting as go-between for not only Shylock and Bassanio, but also for Lorenzo and Jessica as the latter two plot their elopement. Shylock, played as a cross between an avuncular jokester with Woody Allen-ish antics ("the ewes being rank/ In the end of autumn turned to the rams," 1.3.80-81) and a gruff businessman who harbors rage with the clear-sightedness earned in the blood sport of business

---

[36]     See "Shakespeare and the Stoicism of Seneca," in *Selected Essays* (New York: Harcourt, Brace, 1950): 107–120; 120.

("Hath a dog money?", 1.3.121), delivered the following lines as though he was about to change his mind about leaving his house:

> Jessica, my girl,
> Look to my house. I am right loath to go;
> There is some ill a-brewing towards my rest,
> For I did dream of money-bags to-night. (1.5.15–18)

With comic precision, however, Launcelot jumped in rather too abruptly and urgently with, "I beseech you, sir, go," before catching himself and delivering an impromptu explanation with elaborate, hammed-up casualness: "My young master doth expect your reproach" (19). The actor furnished his two simple sentences with a concrete motivation (get Shylock to leave the house so that Lorenzo can steal Jessica away) while crystallizing Launcelot's character as a cynical scrounger of sorts whose actions nonetheless revealed an endearing weak spot for Jessica and youthful love.

Calling Launcelot a cynical scrounger is of course a simplification. Launcelot is a "clown," and was played with the slap-stick antics and the *shtick* that convention allots to clowns. However, as was fitting for what J.L. Styan has called a theatre of "non-illusory illusion,"[37] the non-naturalistic forms of theatrical clowning served in part to enlarge our sense of the character—who he is in his totality as an onstage presence. Further, in the way that a funny comedian can make audiences feel an affective connection to him by making them laugh, this Launcelot also established a connection with the audience with the whole of his persona. Hence, if any in the audience found his choice to help Jessica out to be an endearing expression of character in the simplest Bradleyan sense, that response also carried with it the emotional energy that had been vested in him as a clowning figure. Establishing this kind of layered, sympathetic identification with Launcelot's character was not without serious consequence in this production of the play, however.

The production's way of acknowledging what the director called "the dark and problematic cultural history" associated with the play was to be guided by the thoughts of James Shapiro quoted in the program: "*The Merchant*'s capacity to illuminate a culture is invariably compromised when those staging it flinch from presenting the play in its complex entirety." This meant that the production would do nothing overt to tip the balance in favor of Shylock by, for example, sentimentalizing him or demonizing the Christians. It was determined to "discomfit" the audience by staging a comedy that triumphs over a Jew who brandishes all the qualities written into the part, including those that are deemed to reflect the anti-Semitic fantasies of the Renaissance. This Shylock stated with relish, as though the sentiment should be self-evident, that he hated Antonio, not only because "he is a Christian" (1.2.42), but "more" because he "lends out money gratis, and brings down/ The rate of usance" (1.2.42–45). His furious lament about the ducats that Jessica stole and spent in Genoa ("Fourscore ducats at a sitting,

---

[37]   *The Shakespeare Revolution*, 7.

fourscore ducats!" 3.1.110–111) was not, for example, displaced pain about the loss of his daughter; it was about the ducats.

However—and here another layer of complexity was introduced—this compulsive preoccupation with "thrift" (1.3.90) did not seem out of the ordinary in the world of this production. This world was awash in money, with wads of cash or caskets of gold constantly changing hands (including between Shylock and Tubal), and everyone venturing or gambling in some way (including shooting craps). One could not but follow the ducats in this production, including of course the three thousand that began circulating with Shylock's loan to Antonio so that Bassanio could venture, or gamble, for Portia. Simply put, economic, ethnic, gender and personal relations were so intertwined in this hectic world of exchanges, ventures and dependencies that separating them out became impossible. (In this respect, this production anticipated in spirit some of the features of the New York Public's production of the play in Central Park in 2010 with Al Pacino as Shylock that Brett Gamboa reviews in this volume.) Each character thus appeared compromised in some way, which is also to say that each appeared a product of social and material forces; and yet each character, by the same token, also appeared individuated as characters with inner lives who were negotiating, often unawares, those very forces. Hence any analysis of the outward conditions led inevitably to inferential ventures into the inner life of a character and vice versa. Concomitantly, the anxieties and the complexities of the play became most palpable when the characters appeared most fully realized as individual selves. In the very minor case of Launcelot, if one inferred that helping Jessica was a free choice and not just an errand done for a big tip (another wad of cash) from Lorenzo, this perception could have led to a sympathetic affiliation with Launcelot. But that affiliation would have aligned the audience member with the forces of anti-Semitism and could have ever so slightly tipped the balance of sympathy against Shylock. In this production that highlighted bonds, cultural identities and sectarian loyalties, it was when one entered into such affiliations that the play became, as the director had hoped, the most "unsettling." To conclude, then, the production offered another case in which the analysis of character inevitably entailed broader social analysis of the playworld.

This last conclusion is again, however, not a program for this volume. By no means will all the essays concern themselves with demonstrating this Introduction's argument about the intertwined nature of character study and social analysis. A wide array of concerns will drive the essays and thereby demonstrate the compatibility of character analysis and other discourses. All the essays—from scholars and theatre professionals alike—will share a common interest, nonetheless, in revitalizing character as a central focus of exploration.

# PART 1
## Shakespearean Persons

# Chapter 1
# How Dark Was It in That Room? Performing a Scene Shakespeare Never Wrote

## Michael Bristol

What do Shakespeare's characters do when they're offstage where we can't see them? Ellen Terry wondered how the boy in *Henry V* learned French.[1] And how did Mariana get away with tricking Angelo into thinking she was Isabella in *Measure for Measure*?[2] If you think these are naïve questions, you may not want to read any more of this essay because it will just annoy you. But before you move on to the next chapter you may want to consider that Shakespeare deliberately provokes your curiosity by organizing his stories around incidents that happen offstage. These are the scenes Shakespeare never wrote, structuring absences indispensable for understanding what goes on in the scenes he did write.[3] Elizabeth Inchbald thought that Mariana and Isabella didn't actually succeed in fooling Angelo, which would account for his exacerbated vindictiveness towards Claudio.[4] Maybe Helena, in *All's Well That Ends Well*, didn't fool her mean begrudging husband either. I once met a flight attendant who thought Lady Macbeth had a child out of wedlock with Duncan, which helps explain her murderous hatred of the King.[5] You have to read with a lot of imagination to come up with stuff like this, but why would you want to suppress your imagination when you read a Shakespeare play? Ellen Terry, Elizabeth Inchbald, and the flight attendant were all actresses; this is exactly what they might do in order to perform one of these roles. It is difficult to

---

[1]    Ellen Terry, *Four Lectures on Shakespeare* (London : M. Hopkinson, 1932), 119–120. For revealing her curiosity about this, Ellen Terry was ridiculed by L. C. Knights in "How Many Children Had Lady Macbeth?" in *Explorations: Essays in Criticism, Mainly on the Literature of the Seventeenth Century* (London: Chatto and Windus, 1946), 2.

[2]    Elizabeth Inchbald, "Remarks." *Measure for Measure; A Comedy, in Five Acts; As Performed at the Theater Royal, Covent Garden.* (London: Longman, Hurst, Rees, and Orme, 1773), 4.

[3]    Michael Bristol, "Vernacular Criticism and the Scenes Shakespeare Never Wrote." *Shakespeare Survey* vol. 51 (Cambridge: Cambridge University Press, 2000), 37–51.

[4]    Inchbald, 4.

[5]    Bristol, 38.

see what it would mean for them to "play a part" without having a robust sense of a dramatic character as a complete person.[6]

It is said that there are married couples who like to meet in a singles bar and make believe they are strangers. They have a drink and then check into a hotel room where they have a one night stand or else the wife pretends to be a call girl. While I have no personal experience with such doings, I have read about it in magazines, so it must be true. Shocking. I know. This is not exactly what happens in *All's Well That Ends Well*, although what does happen is just as shocking. Bertram, the husband, is ordered by the King to marry Helen. He refuses to consummate the marriage and runs off to war, without so much as kissing her good-bye, leaving Helen with nothing but a brief letter.

> HELEN   Look on his letter, madam; here's my passport.
>     *She reads the letter*
> 'When thou canst get the ring upon my finger which never shall come off, and
> show me a child begotten of thy body that I am father to, then call me husband.
> But in such a 'then' I write a 'never'.
> This is a dreadful sentence.[7]

Helen eventually succeeds in performing both these impossible tasks through the same strategic device. When Bertram makes an assignation with another woman, Helen substitutes herself in the bedroom, where she finally enjoys his embrace, becomes pregnant, and acquires the ring all at the same time. Later, when the truth of the matter comes to light, Bertram has a profound change of heart and all is well in the end—or is it?[8] A lot of disapproval has been expressed about the means Helen uses to achieve her purpose. Some critics, mostly men of my own generation, are really bothered by what they see as the "shotgun wedding" scenario and they condemn Helen for the deception of Bertram. Others have concluded that the sex must have been joyless and demeaning. But is there anything really wrong with the means or its relationship to the end? Is the sex in the story crassly instrumental or does it have other valences? The encounter in that darkened room is crucial to the story. But how can anyone perform a scene Shakespeare never wrote? The text

---

[6]   Bert O. States, *Hamlet and the Concept of Character* (Baltimore: Johns Hopkins University Press, 1992). For States the notion of character as the representation of a coherent self is essentially the art of theatrical performance. This is the art form that Shakespeare understood very well.

[7]   3.2.56–61. All textual references are to Susan Snyder, ed., *All's Well That Ends Well* (Oxford: Oxford University Press, 1994).

[8]   This essay is based on Snyder's edition of *All's Well That Ends Well*. Her edition is an exemplary work of textual scholarship and I am deeply indebted to her critical intelligence throughout my discussion of the story. Her treatment of the issues raised by this play is the most sensible and the most imaginative that I have encountered and I would recommend that anyone truly interested in understanding this often obscure work to consult her admirable introduction and notes.

gives us no specific instructions for how the scene ought to be performed. We can only imagine why it might have worked in the performances of the two characters.

### I could never do that!

First of all, how did she get away with it? Is it really possible for a woman to convince a man he's going to bed with someone else? I suppose—hypothetically— that my wife could really get me going by playing the role of an expensive call-girl if she did it with enough conviction and dramatic art. But that would be consensual making believe. What would happen if I called an escort service, set up a rendezvous, and my wife showed up at the place of the assignation? What on earth would I be thinking just at that moment? "Oh my God, I'm busted" is one possibility. "So that's what she's been up to when I've been off at work" is the other. It would be next to impossible to actually go through with it. Of course if one had sufficient aplomb and presence of mind it could be exciting to play along, enjoy the experience, and, at the end of the evening pay the agreed upon fee along with a generous tip. This would be taking consensual make believe to a much more intense level. Nobody would actually be fooled, and a whole lot of significant questions would remain unanswered, but there could be an interesting bond of complicity as long as no one was to cop out. On balance, however, the bed trick would appear to be a non-starter. Nevertheless, it is definitely true in the fiction that Helen succeeds in getting into bed with Bertram, even though he has gone to considerable lengths to avoid just exactly that, and so it must also be true in the fiction that some effective means were employed to accomplish this end.

Jacob was beguiled by his Uncle Laban into marrying Leah when she took the place of Rachel on their wedding night. How this was done is not explained in scripture, but it must have been very dark on the wedding night, because Jacob only found out the next day: "in the morning, behold, it was Leah." Perhaps Helen's trick was accomplished by a similar combination of darkness and not much talking. In fact this is the general outline of the proposition Diana makes when she agrees to surrender to Bertram's soliciting.

> DIANA   When midnight comes, knock at my chamber window.
> I'll order take my mother shall not hear.
> Now will I charge you in the band of truth,
> When you have conquered my yet-maiden bed,
> Remain there but an hour, nor speak to me. (4.2.55–8).

In addition to the time limit, there are two other circumstances working in Helen's favour. First, Bertram has no idea that his detested wife is anywhere nearby and so he does not even consider the possibility that the woman he will embrace could be Helen. Second, the intensity of Bertram's desire for Diana, matched paradoxically by the intensity of his aversion to Helen, actually facilitates the deception. Since he is so swept up in his own fantasy he may not notice all that much about his actual partner. Even under these evidently favourable circumstances Helen will have to play her part with real conviction and dramatic art. But she is an accomplished dissembler, performing the role of a grieving daughter, a learned doctor, and a devout pilgrim. Performing the character of the about-to-be-conquered-and-willing-maiden ought to be a snap for her. On stage it would even be possible for the actress playing the role of Helen to appear as "Diana" in the scene just cited to test out the credulity of Bertram. Besides, she really doesn't have all that much to lose.

There are some ways for Helen to avoid being discovered; partners don't have to be face to face to have sexual intercourse, for example. One time when I raised these possibilities with colleagues at an academic conference I was told that Helen was confident she could get away with it because she knew that it was the sort of thing that's possible in a fairy tale. In other words, the relevant background knowledge for *All's Well That Ends Well* is recognizing what kind of story is involved rather than indiscreet speculation about what goes on in bedrooms.[9] Different kinds of stories have different conventions—interstellar travel is a convention of science fiction just as bed tricks are a convention of romance. To inquire into the actual circumstances of its execution is to exhibit vulgar and deplorable curiosity. I think there are theoretical problems with these arguments in the case of *All's Well That Ends Well*, since it is true in the fiction that Helen succeeds with the bed-trick, but it is not true in the fiction that she thinks she is a character in a fairy-tale. On the contrary, she has some definite ideas about how to make her scheme work, so our vulgar curiosity is really entirely justified as an effort to account for her sexual exploits in more explicit detail.

The bed trick is fundamental to understanding the story of *All's Well That Ends Well*. Helen takes advantage of Bertram's sexual fixation with Diana to get herself into bed with her husband. And in the fiction Helen intends for her deception to succeed. For Helen the question of the bed trick is anything but a "convention of the genre." To the contrary, the bed trick is the *only possible solution* to her difficulties. Of course I understand perfectly well that there are narrative conventions that require suspension of disbelief.[10] But with Shakespeare things are generally not that simple. His stories often disrupt conventional narratives by

---

    9    David Lewis, "Truth in Fiction," in *Philosophical Papers, Vol. I*. (Oxford: Oxford University Press, 1983), 268 ff.

    10    I always had trouble understanding why "suspending disbelief" would nullify any further curiosity I might have about how something as involved as the bed trick actually gets done. Suspension of disbelief is not just passive or unthinking acceptance of literary convention; it amounts to a basic understanding of what is true in the fiction and how it makes sense even when it seems implausible. If Helen has been able to carry it off, does this not imply that she has given some thought to the conditions that would make such a scheme possible, whether it would be worth trying in light of its anticipated pay-offs, and what means might be used to guarantee its success? Working out a detailed explanation for how she got away with it would then be a way to gain deeper insight into Helen's character. And it would be an even more robust instance of suspending disbelief.

including details that require us to take things more literally. And, as I will show later in this discussion, *All's Well That Ends Well* goes even farther, bringing out some of the actual details of what happened in that darkened room as a way to suggest why things turn out the way they do.

The resistance of my colleagues eventually led me to realize that asking how Helen was able to succeed with the bed trick is not an adventitious question. In fact the character of Helen is defined by her boldness in conceiving such an outlandish scheme and by the resources she can draw on to carry it off.[11] The complexity of the situation, however, can only be fully understood through a consideration of the motivational scenarios involved in Helen's fixation on Bertram and on Bertram's equally compulsive rejection of her. Helen is the heiress of a famous doctor, who has passed on to her the secrets of his practice. Although she seems to be grieving over her father's death, in fact she is consumed with sexual desire for a man who has no interest in her

> HELEN     My imagination
> Carries no favor in't but Bertram's.
> I am undone. There is no living, none,
> If Bertram be away. . . .
>           'Twas pretty, though a plague,
> To see him every hour, to sit and draw
> His arched brows, his hawking eye, his curls,
> In our heart's table—heart too capable
> Of every line and trick of his sweet favor.
> But now he's gone and my idolatrous fancy
> Must sanctify his relics. (1.1.84–100)

For Helen, Bertram is a fantasy constituted by her visual imagination. She is not the only one of Shakespeare's heroines to look at a man, to construct the object of her desire by means of that looking, and to make an active attempt at staging the erotic *mise-en-scene* she has imagined. What distinguishes Helen from other Shakespeare characters who actively pursue a man is the boldness and the reckless perversity of her act.

Within the normative horizons suggested by this play, marriage is a bond or obligation sealed between two men in which a young woman (sometimes supplemented by substantial material property) is "the gift." In *All's Well That Ends Well*, Helen's medical knowledge is the stake that puts the King of France in her debt. She travels to the court and introduces herself as the healer of the King's infirmity. Helen's proposition is that if she fails at curing the King's sickness she will be publicly humiliated, tortured and killed. If she is successful, however, she expects a lavish reward.

---

[11]  Eileen Z. Cohen, "'Virtue is bold': The Bed-trick and Characterization in *All's Well That Ends Well* and *Measure for Measure,.*" *Philological Quarterly* 65 (1986): 176–77, 184–85.

HELEN   … Not helping, death's my fee,
        But if I help, what do you promise me?

KING    Make thy demand.

HELEN                   But will you make it even.

KING    Aye, by my sceptre and the hope of heaven.

HELEN   Then thou shalt give me with thy kingly hand
        What husband in thy power I will command. (2.1.188–93)

The pay-off in this bargain is that a nobleman of her own choosing will be given to her as a husband. The key point is that a *man* will be made a gift to her in a bond of mutual loyalty between a man and a woman. When she is successful, she chooses Bertram from among all the lords of France and the King, a man of his word, fulfils his part of the bargain by declaring them to be husband and wife. Bertram, however, refuses to accept.

KING    Why, then, young Bertram, take her. She's thy wife.

BERTRAM   My wife, my liege! I shall beseech your Highness,
          In such a business give me leave to use
          The help of my own eyes. (2.3.106–109)

Bertram's refusal to accept Helen is obviously connected with pride over his aristocratic standing, but it is also an expression of shame over his sexual abjection. The real insult is to Bertram's masculinity, the denial of the autonomy of his own sexual will and the shamefulness of being disposed of as an object *in front of his own peers*. The King has made a bargain with a woman here that nullifies the central principle of the masculine sexual economy, an economy in which the positions of looking and of being looked at define the respective sexual positions of men and women. Helen is utterly captivated and undone by the way Bertram looks. Bertram, by contrast, can't stand the sight of Helen—or maybe it's even worse—he won't even look at her.

   In order to make the bed trick seem more plausible, the actresses who play the two women should probably have a strong similarity in complexion, size and physical proportions. The more they look like each other the easier it is for an audience to suspend their disbelief. But this would make Bertram's insistence on choosing with his own eyes a matter of considerable ambiguity, to say the least. If I want my girlfriend to be somebody who looks exactly like Scarlett Johanssen, why would I refuse the offer of a date with Scarlett Johanssen herself? But then, come to think of it, why would I agree to a date that only lasts an hour, takes place in utter darkness, and we don't even get to speak to each other? On the other hand, if the casting were to suggest a strong physical contrast between the two women, then the idea of Bertram's preference seems more credible, but the success of the bed trick much more puzzling. If I am extremely besotted with Scarlett Johanssen, I might be entirely unmoved by the attractions of Natalie Portman. You would perhaps understand why I would have a strong preference, even if your own were very different. But then you might wonder how on earth I would fail to notice the substitution no matter how dark it was in that room. Either way it would seem that Bertram's sexuality is strangely disembodied, much less a matter of his actual object choice than of his imagination. His assertion of male sexual autonomy is thwarted when he agrees to an assignation under conditions of darkness and silence. But the defeat of masculine sexual will goes even farther, because what happens in that dark room is that Helen enjoys Bertram sexually without obtaining his consent.[12]

The question of how Helen managed the bed-trick is something I would often ask graduate students to consider in their analysis of *All's Well That Ends Well* and *Measure for Measure*. At more or less this point in the discussion one year, one young woman suddenly exclaimed, "Well, I could never do that!" It was not because she didn't think she could ever accomplish such an action in a practical sense. Her response was provoked by the thought that it might actually be possible for her to succeed.[13] "Do you mean you wouldn't have the nerve to try it, or do you mean that you wouldn't feel right tricking someone like that?" She was admirably candid: "For me it's not a performance. I want to be loved for who I really am—or not at all." Getting away with it was hardly the problem. The bed-trick was about a deeper question of self-acknowledgment and self-respect. At the heart of the matter is moral agency, or what is now generally referred to as a person's character. The crucial problem for my student was in being constrained to deny who she really was or to deform her character to be more pleasing for someone else. To be rejected by someone you love would be bad, but faking your way through a sexual encounter to attain a token of that love would be a whole lot worse.

Saying "I could never do that" means that my student possesses a strong sense of her own virtue, where virtue has the sense of strength of character, of being fully answerable to one's own self. Virtue can refer to abstinence from certain bad habits like overeating, or cheating on exams, or turning tricks in bedrooms. It can also refer to enduring qualities like courage or generosity or prudence that we reveal in actions. But there is a much more robust sense of virtue as *rapport a soi*, the value I have for myself. My virtue is that set of properties I cherish because they define who I am and function as the internal source of my actions. Virtues are capabilities understood in relation to how we choose to express them

---

[12]   David MCandless, "Helen's Bed-Trick: Gender and Performance in *All's Well That Ends Well.*" *Shakespeare Quarterly* 45 (1994): 450.

[13]   Michael Bristol, "'A System of Oeconomicall Prudence': Shakespearean Character and the Practice of Moral Inquiry," in *Shakespeare and the Eighteenth Century*, ed., Peter Sabor and Paul Yachnin. (Aldershot: Ashgate, 2008), 22.

and to what ends they are applied.[14] Asking how Helen got away with the bed trick is partly about how she solved a problem of sexual logistics: Should I wear a wig? What kind of perfume does she wear? How does she do that little movement with her left shoulder? Knowing how to perform another person's identity is certainly a capability; done skillfully it is a great art. But what virtue can there be in theatricality and dramatic arts?[15] Some people have thought that Helen's performance with Bertram is meretricious and obscene. In my view the situation is not so obvious. Helen's "performance" in the bedroom is the expression of deeper honesty, with herself and with Bertram. The bed-trick poses a complicated moral question; it's really asking how it is possible for Helen to reconcile her actions with her sense of who she really is.

## The Character Issue

"Who can find a virtuous woman? For her price is far above rubies." (*Proverbs*: 31:10). The King of France admonishes Bertram for refusing to see that "virtue and she is her own dower." Bertram's mother, the Countess of Roussilon, has a similar opinion, as do some of the other Lords of France. But not everyone really admires Helen. Katherine Mansfield was scandalized by the bed trick.

> I must say Helen is a terrifying female. Her virtue, her persistence, her pegging away after the odious Bertram (and disguised as a pilgrim—so typical!) And then telling the whole story to that good widow woman. And that tame fish Diana. As to lying in Diana's bed and enjoying the embraces meant for Diana— well, I know nothing more sickening. It would take a respectable woman to do such a thing . ...*What* a cup of tea the widow and D. must have enjoyed while it was taking place.[16]

This, I think, gets at the discomfort we are likely to feel about the working out of this tale. But the trouble here goes much deeper than Mansfield's reflections on the self-serving banality of Helen's strategy. The whole future relationship between Bertram and Helen is based on lies and deception. Bertram lies to Helen to get her out of the way, he lies to Diana about his intentions, and then, when he is caught he lies about what he has done. Helen, on her side, pimped herself out to a man who doesn't love her, hoping somehow to "make her marriage work."

The fictional universe in Shakespeare's plays represents a libidinal economy that differs in important respects from our own. In this economy sexuality is a gift

---

    [14]   Martha C. Nussbaum. *Women and Human Development: the Capabilities Approach.* (Cambridge: Cambridge University Press, 2000), 5–15, 70–96.

    [15]   Kent R. Lehnhof, "Performing Woman: Female Theatricality in *All's Well, That Ends Well*," in *All's Well That Ends Well: New Critical Essays*, ed., Gary Waller. (New York: Routledge, 2007), 115–118, 121–22.

    [16]   Katherine Mansfield, *Journal of Katherine Mansfield*. ed., J. Middleton Murry (New York: Alfred A. Knopf, 1927), 274.

rather than an instrumental value. Sex, rather than its restraint, can be a virtue in and of itself. *All's Well That Ends Well* is saturated with the codes of this sexual economy, which results in the seemingly bizarre and contradictory tangle of motives that make the play's narrative action hard to understand. The poignancy of Helen's situation is expressed in her impassioned confession to the Countess of Rousillon, Bertram's mother:

> HELEN                              I love your son.
> My friends were poor, but honest, so's my love.
> Be not offended, for it hurts not him
> That he is loved of me; I follow him not
> By any token of presumptuous suit,
> Nor would I have him till I do deserve him,
> Yet never know how that desert should be.
> I know I love in vain, strive against hope;
> Yet in this captious and intenible sieve
> I still pour in the waters of my love,
> And lack not to lose still. (1.3.194–204)

The sieve is "captious" a word that means that something is likely to entrap or ensnare or deceive. Susan Snyder renders the word as cap'cious to bring out the additional sense of "capacious" or capable of receiving, though not of holding a large volume of water. But the captious, or capacious sieve, is also intenible or untenable, which can mean something that can't be occupied, something that can't be defended, or literally something that can't hold or be held. Snyder also points out that the image of carrying water in a sieve has other valences as well. The Danaids were sisters forced to marry against their will. They killed their husbands on their wedding night and their punishment was to pour water into a sieve for eternity. Members of Shakespeare's audience might also have known of the vestal virgin, Tuccia, who was accused of unchastity. To prove her virtue she carried water in a sieve from the River Tiber to the temple.[17]

The image of the sieve that actually contains fluid is an image of the intact, virginal body. But Helen's sieve is "captious" and "intenible." Like an ordinary sieve it has no power of containment. She still pours out the "waters of her love." There is a literal reference here to the physiology of continuous sexual arousal. Helen acknowledges that she is open, vulnerable, and even unchaste in that she is already given over to an ardent sexual desire for Bertram even though her body is in fact still virginal. Helen's virginity is, however, a mere technicality. She knows what sexual resources she has and how she would like to use them. She also understands what value they have both for her and for others. The problem is finding a way to participate fully in the sexual economy without surrendering agency or personhood. As a married woman she will become the exclusive sexual property of her husband. As a courtesan she would retain limited agency as the

---

[17]    Snyder, *All's Well*, Notes, 104.

vendor of sexual goods and services, but the actual sex is reduced to the status of a commodity. Neither situation looks very promising. Is there any way to get something in return for this capacity for lavish "pouring out?"

The relationship of sexual pleasure to commerce or trafficking is foregrounded in an exchange between Helen and Paroles on the paradoxical value of virginity.

> PAROLES   Are you meditating on virginity?
>
> HELEN   Aye. You have some stain of soldier in you. Let me ask you a question. Man is enemy to virginity. How may we barricado it against him?
>
> PAROLES   Keep him out.
>
> HELEN   But he assails, and our virginity, though valiant, in the defense, yet is weak. Unfold to us some warlike resistance.
>
> PAROLES   There is none. Man, sitting down before you, will undermine you and blow you up.
>
> HELEN   Bless our poor virginity from underminers and blowers up! Is there no military policy how virgins might blow up men?
>
> PAROLES   Virginity being blown down, man will quicklier be blown up. Marry, in blowing him down again, with the breach yourselves made you lose your city. It is not politic in the commonwealth of nature to preserve virginity. Loss of virginity is rational increase, and there was never virgin got till virginity was first lost. That you were made of is metal to make virgins. Virginity by being once lost may be ten times found. By being ever kept, it is ever lost. 'Tis too cold a companion. Away with 't! (1.1. 112–133)

Paroles maintains that virginity is indefensible in military terms. It is actually a commodity whose selling price declines over time. On this account a wife and a courtesan are in the same situation, only the conditions of sale are different. Virginity is a pure exchange value in that its worth can be realized only in its expenditure. As a commodity it is frequently over-rated and over-priced, but its loss represents the possibility of "rational increase." It makes no sense to think of preserving virginity; it is more prudent to think of it as an investment. Virginity is "metal," coinage or currency, but it is also "mettle," the stuff a person is made of, courage, strength of character, or, quite simply, virtue.

Helen would like to pour out the water of her love as a gift to someone who will appreciate her sexual generosity, her willingness to lose her virginity under the right circumstances.

> HELEN   How might one do, sir, to lose it to her own liking?
>
> PAROLES   Let me see. Marry, ill, to like him that ne'er likes it. 'Tis a commodity will lose the gloss with lying; the longer kept, the less worth. Off with't while 'tis vendible. Answer the time of request. (1.1.152–157)

Paroles's advice—to find someone who doesn't like virginal women—is basically what Helen already understands. Gains in sexual knowledge are the principal compensation for the expenditure of virginity. Unlike virginity, sex is a renewable resource or an endowment that can remain in the control of its possessor. Guided partly by Paroles's instruction, Helen's virtue emerges in her increasingly candid sexual self-awareness. What she understands better than Paroles, however, is that finding a man who will really appreciate what she has to offer is more complex than the simple buying and selling he recommends. In the case of Bertram she will have to teach him what sex is.

What does Helen know? The bed-trick is not the only important scene that Shakespeare never wrote in this play. The healing of the King's fistula is the action that makes the bed-trick a possibility. Frank Whigham has discussed the social and erotic significance of Helen's therapeutic knowledge: "Helena must risk shame to work her way through to her cross-class marriage through arcane efforts in the bedroom."[18] Both scenes hint at some very deep level of knowing that confers an equally mysterious power on its possessor. What Helen knows, evidently, is the male body, in its aspects of openness and vulnerability, as well as in its capacity to give and to receive pleasure. In sixteenth-century usage fistula was an ulcer that perforates a "hollow organ." Today it is most often used in connection with a persistent lesion in the anal region. The fistula is in an important sense something secret, hidden, and obscene. The idea of a perforated ulcer, or sore that cannot heal, is not only debilitating and possibly deadly; it is also shameful in the way it violates the integrity of the body, especially the male body. In the healing scene, Helen restores the damaged body of the King by the skilful closing of this adventitious bodily orifice, an action that restores the King's virility by re-establishing the functions of containment and control of bodily fluids.

In the bed-trick, Helen assures a socially permissible use of male virility by assuming the burden of sexual knowing for both partners.[19] But the act is paradoxical and even preposterous in the contradictory relations of ends and means, intentions and actual deed.

> HELEN     Why then to-night
> Let us assay our plot; which, if it speed,
> Is wicked meaning in a lawful deed
> And lawful meaning in a wicked act,
> Where both not sin, and yet a sinful fact:
> But let's about it. (3.7.43–8)

---

[18]   Frank Whigham, "Reading Social Conflict in the Alimentary Tract: More on the Body in Renaissance Drama," *ELH* 55 (1988): 338.

[19]   Janet Adelman, "Bed Tricks: On Marriage as the End of Comedy in *All's Well That Ends Well* and *Measure for Measure*," in *Shakespeare's Personality*, eds., Norman Holland, Sidney Homan, Bernard J. Paris. (Berkeley and London: University of California Press, 1989), 152–58. See also William Babula, "The Character and the Conclusion: Bertram and the Ending of *All's Well That Ends Well*." *South Atlantic Review* 42, no. 2 (1977): 98.

When Bertram conquers Helen's yet-maiden bed he is consummating his marriage, even though he intends to commit adultery with Diana. Helen intends to consummate her marriage, but in order to accomplish this she has to prostitute herself. Everything is all right, objectively speaking, but everything is all wrong— an expense of spirit in a waste of shame. There is, however, a second level of paradox in Helen's action. She accomplishes her purpose by virtue of a skillfully executed performance, acting the part of Diana with conviction and dramatic art. But the sexual response isn't faked. Helen is herself the "cap'cious sieve"— captious in the way she ensnares Bertram for her husband, but also capacious not only in giving him what he wants sexually but also in conceiving his child. It's not clear how she was able to accomplish this, but Helen is Doctor She. If she can cure the King's fistula, it's reasonable to think she knows how to get herself pregnant.

There is, however, yet another paradox in the bed-trick. In describing her encounter with Bertram in that dark room to Diana and the Widow, Helen recalls the excitement of sex with a "perfect stranger:"

> HELEN               But O strange men!
> That can such sweet use make of what they hate,
> When saucy trusting of the cozened thoughts
> Defiles the pitchy night: so lust doth play
> With what it loathes for that which is away. (4.4.21–5)

This is a common Shakespearean motif of erotic "indifference" where sexual pleasure is in some sense independent of a specific object. The odd thing about this situation, of course, is that the "sweet use" that Bertram makes of Helen is, from his point of view, inseparable from his fantasy or delusion of scopic power over the sexual object. The pleasure he gives her is connected at some very deep level with the contempt he feels for both his actual and for his imaginary partner. The idea of "faking an orgasm" is part of our sexual culture. We are prepared to believe in the sexual dishonesty of women. Helen's speech makes reference to the much less well-known phenomenon of faking an erection. Men occasionally laugh at such a notion, because they have internalized the self-serving belief that an erection cannot be faked. But forced and unfeeling arousal on the part of men is extremely common, and this is what Helen's speech refers to. Bertram "used" her in the sense that he paid for the enjoyment of her body. But her comments also suggest that she enjoyed being used by him even though there is an element of hatred in her partner. Men "make sweet use of what they hate." Still, does she mean that Bertram hates his actual partner—herself—but is making sweet use of her because he thinks she is Diana? In that sense she is just "enjoying the embraces meant for Diana." Or does she mean that he actually hates his imagined partner— Diana—but makes sweet use of her because it gives him pleasure to prostitute her. Are human beings in some way interchangeable? In that case what are we to make of that groundless and compelling partiality we call love? What is the meaning, finally, of substitution or for that matter of performance?

Helen's virtue—her character, as we might say—lies in a quality of alacrity, a willingness and a capability of acting to shape her world. Used in relation to the properties of certain herbs or gem-stones, virtue means efficacy arising from physical qualities, specifically the power to affect the human body in a beneficial manner; strengthening, sustaining, or healing properties (*OED*). As Doctor She, Helen would certainly know the virtues or healing properties of gems and of various herbs, but she is also identified with such healing objects.[20] The King calls her a "jewel." Lafeu thinks "we may pick a thousand sallets ere we light on such another herb." And the clown compares her to sweet marjoram—"an excellent remedy for the rain"—and then more specifically to "the herb of grace." Rue, also known as herb of grace, is known for its unpleasant bitter or sour taste, and also for its virtue as an antidote for poisons. Helen is rueful both in the sense of sorrowful and also in the sense of compassionate, even if she is in other ways also ruthless in her pursuit of Bertram. Helen "wears her rue with a difference." She makes herself vulnerable and her "rue" keeps the poison of Bertram's hatred from killing her. And, at the same time, she makes him rue or repent his own actions in rejecting her love.

## Was Bertram Fooled?

A lot of people have trouble with the idea of Bertram having a change of heart when he eventually learns the truth about what happened in that dark room. Katherine Mansfield, as we have seen, thinks he is just odious. Susan Snyder rightly points out that the actor who plays Bertram isn't given a whole lot to work with to express his profound transformation.[21] She also summarizes a long critical tradition of skepticism about the play's "happy ending" that sees Bertram as a jerk and Helen as both a sneak and a slut.[22] This is a play in which normative gender positions of giving and receiving, of sexual domination and sexual submission, are reversed or at least significantly altered. But how "well" does all of this end? Does a sadder-but-wiser Bertram really love Helen at the end of the play and for that matter what does it mean to say that Helen loves Bertram?

> HELEN   O my good lord, when I was like this maid,
>         I found you wondrous kind. There is your ring;
>         And look you, here's your letter. This it says:
>         "When from my finger you can get this ring
>         And are by me with child," etc. This is done.
>         Will you be mine, now you are doubly won?
>
> BERTRAM   If she my liege, can make me know this clearly,
>         I'll love her dearly, ever, ever dearly. (5.3.309–315).

---

[20]   Catherine Field, "'Sweet practicer, thy physic I will try': Helen and Her 'good receipt' in *All's Well, That Ends Well*," in *All's Well That Ends Well: New Critical Essays*, ed., Gary Waller (New York: Routledge, 2007), 194–95, 205–206.

[21]   Snyder, *All's Well*, Introduction, 27.

[22]   Snyder, *All's Well,* Introduction, 17–18, 40–52.

All well and good, and, as the King says, "All yet seems well, and if it end so meet, / The bitter past, more welcome is the sweet" (5.3.333–34). But what, one is prompted to ask, does Helen expect to do with this male sexuality that doesn't know what it wants? What is happy about this ending, and who is making "sweet use" of whom? We can speak of Bertram's capitulation to Helen's sexual will, if that is what the play's ending is showing us. And we can say that Helen has what she wants, if what she wants can be summed up as something like this: "He's rich, he's handsome, and he's pretty good in bed. It's true he doesn't have much of a personality but you can't have everything."

This rather sour response to how it all works out is how a lot of people have seen the story. Bummer. But if I can suspend my disbelief in the bed-trick, either because this is a fairy tale or because I can figure out how she got it to work, then why can't I suspend my disbelief in Bertram's change of heart? So—what if Bertram wasn't exactly fooled? What if his "dreadful sentence" was not, as Snyder sensibly observes, an absolute casting off but rather a set of instructions for a difficult and perverse game or consensual make-believe? He sets up an assignation—calls the escort service, if you will—and his wife shows up in the hotel room. He doesn't cop out. She thinks to herself, "He knows it's me" but she doesn't cop out either. They don't speak; they can hardly see each other, they have to rely on touch and scent and maybe taste. Their embrace is a dissolution of identities. An hour later she's gone, but he is wearing her token and she is wearing his.

Actually, not even I can really believe in this scenario even though, as Snyder also points out, the word "sentence" can mean "imposition of tasks" rather than something like "condemnation."[23] And in fact "imposition of a task" is the way Helen actually construes Bertram's letter. The bed-trick is not just a far-fetched contrivance possible only in fairy tales; it is a trope for what commonly happens in sexual encounters, even monogamous ones. Sex is a strange affair. In one way it is just physiology, body parts fitting together, stimulus and response. Anyone will do. In another way it is all sheer fantasy. And no one is ever really sure what—or who—their partner is actually thinking about or what their experience has been like. That's why sometimes we ask "Was it good for you?" even if it would be better not to cop out. If I'm right about this then I don't necessarily need to believe that Bertram dreamed up an elaborate consensual make-believe and Helen boldly played along. I only have to believe that Helen had some intuitive understanding of what he really wanted, even if he didn't have a clue himself.

Bertram was fooled but he wasn't cheated; there was no deception in Helen's act. In French "deception" means disappointment. In that sense all of the deception is on Bertram's side in denying Helen the loves she so ardently craves. Bertram's rejection of Helen is a lack of willingness to trust in the possibility of goodness. The problem with Bertram is not that he's a snob. The larger problem is that he will not put himself under an obligation to another, not even his King. Bertram

---

[23]   Snyder, *All's Well,* Notes, p. 148.

refuses to give love, and he refuses to return the love he is given. The point he has missed is that love is not really all that easy to find, and that it can take us by surprise. His "utter casting off" of Helen is like a rejection of God's grace: something we can't explain but also something we would be wise not to refuse.[24] The *virtue* of theatricality is that assuming a role can be a creative way to enrich and deepen a personal relationship.[25] It can even be a transformative moral action that helps another person grasp their own deeper aspirations or discover a more authentic *rapport a soi*.

What's going to bother some people about this discussion is that the agency of grace and transformation in *All's Well That Ends Well* is anonymous sex in a darkened hotel room—a one night stand, not to put too fine a point on it. Other people are going to object that what looks like an episode of casual sex is really just a contrivance devised by Helen to enforce the social constraints of heterosexual monogamy on a man who prefers the company of his male friends. He didn't like her because of her social position, he didn't like her because her erotic persistence took away his masculine independence, he didn't like her because he was more comfortable with same-sex companionship, and maybe he didn't like her because both his mother and his King insisted he should marry her. He didn't like her, in other words, until he went to bed with her. Could the sex be so fantastic that it would be enough for him to have a complete change of heart? While I personally have no experience with such doings, I can at least try to suspend my disbelief on that one. But Helen's character would have to be performed with great conviction and dramatic art.

I once made the claim in a conference presentation that knowing what went on in those scenes Shakespeare never wrote was important for understanding what the characters involved might mean for each other. Afterwards someone in the audience got up and publicly told me I was "perfectly idiotic" to suggest that sex was in any way important for understanding how two people really felt about each other. Honestly, my feelings were hurt. The person who called me an idiot in front of several hundred colleagues was herself someone I admired and liked. As a matter of fact I do understand that sex is not necessarily all that important for people who love each other and that what goes on in other people's bedrooms is none of my business. But—with all due respect—I really do think that sex is a powerful and transformative element in the fictional universe of Shakespeare's plays: not sexuality, not gender, not homo-social bonding, just sex. The fictional characters in plays like *Romeo and Juliet*, *Othello*, and *All's Well That Ends Well* are grown up people who are profoundly affected by sexual desire and its expression, not always in self-actualizing ways.

---

[24]  Cynthia Lewis, "'Derived Honesty and Achieved Goodness': Doctrines of Grace in *All's Well That Ends Well." Renaissance and Reformation* 14 (1990): 151–56.

[25]  Tzachi Zamir, "Love as Performance," in *Double Vision: Moral Philosophy and Shakespearean Drama* (Princeton: Princeton University Press, 2007), 132–35.

Helen's virtue is what's known as chastity. This is exactly what Katherine Mansfield found so objectionable in her—that she was a "respectable woman." But Helen did not go to Florence with the idea of staging a phony one-night stand with Bertram. She went to Florence with the intention of renouncing her claims on him, hoping in that way to preserve his life by persuading him to give up his military adventures. The Diana situation was a more risky way to accomplish her purpose without finally abandoning her hopes.

> HELEN   Oft expectation fails and most oft there
> Where most it promises, and oft it hits
> Where hope is coldest and despair most fits. (2.1.140–143)

Helen was "objectively" chaste when Bertram conquered her "yet-maiden" bed. And Bertram's "embraces" were not "meant for Diana" because they were meant for Helen, even if he really "meant" to give them to another woman. But the virtue of chastity is not about not having sex or only having sex with someone you are married to. Chastity is about taking responsibility for your own sexuality.

The bed trick is preposterous—it's really a crazy idea. Personally I wouldn't have the nerve to try it. But sometimes, at least in Shakespeare, crazy ideas and preposterous schemes really work out. In *All's Well That Ends Well,* marital fidelity is expressed as casual sex; monogamy is experienced in the form of promiscuity. I definitely think it is possible to perform the scene that Shakespeare never wrote for that darkened room as a radically transformative experience if the role of Helen is enacted with sufficient strength of character. It's possible—but not easy. Most of the people who are ever going to think about this play or see it performed are going to be skeptical about the value of marriage and even more skeptical about the liberating possibilities of chastity. Does anyone believe in the radical value of sex as the expression of moral agency, or is that just another focus of our skepticism? All things considered it's probably a lot more plausible to perform the play ironically. The more difficult challenge would be to perform the scene Shakespeare never wrote as the expression of secular grace.

## Chapter 2
# Shakespearean Characters and Early Modern Subjectivity: The Case of *King Lear*

Bruce W. Young

For moderns, the idea of dramatic character is inextricably connected with the idea of subjectivity, of what it means to be a self—or, more precisely, what it means to experience one's own existence as something unique and substantial. A dramatic character is perhaps only an imaginary or fictional person, but to be recognized as a person in any sense, a dramatic character must resemble the people we are surrounded by, even the people we experience ourselves to be. Dramatic characters seem to act, speak, even think (sometimes out loud). They often, though not always, display something of the unpredictability and elusiveness we associate with the people we encounter. The actors who impersonate these characters lend them a bodily presence and visible continuity that together constitute something resembling personal identity. Whether enacted on the stage or imagined by readers, such characters appear to sustain a variety of relations with each other, arising from and producing what appear to be such emotions as desire, compassion, anger, contempt, loathing, and delight—emotions we are conscious of experiencing. It is hard, therefore, not to imagine these characters as experiencing something like our own sense of self, of inner awareness and particularized identity.

Nonetheless, it has been claimed that what we would recognize as subjectivity did not exist in the early modern period, that though people may have been conscious of the social roles they were expected to perform, they did not think of themselves as possessing substantial and individualized personal identity. This claim invites us to read Shakespeare's characters as something quite different from ourselves, to see them as essentially social performances rather than personalities. Beatrice Gottlieb, while not excluding a degree of emotional content in early modern social and especially family relationships, argues that "[t]he relationships most commonly depicted were almost never treated as dynamic interactions of individual personalities. Rather, they were performances—good, bad, sincere, perfunctory." Relationships consisted of people "following or not following appropriate role patterns."[1] According to Gottlieb, what an individual of the period was normally aware of was not inward experience but social obligations.

---

[1]    Beatrice Gottlieb, *The Family in the Western World from the Black Death to the Industrial Age* (New York and Oxford: Oxford University Press, 1993), 262.

Some have gone further to suggest that the very concept of an inner life did not exist in Shakespeare's time. Francis Barker, for instance, contrasts bourgeois subjectivity, which supposedly did not arise until the later 1600s, with "[p]re-bourgeois subjection," which "does not properly involve subjectivity at all, but a condition of dependent membership in which place and articulation are defined not by an interiorized self-recognition ... but by incorporation in the body politic."[2] Others argue that, while solitary experience was possible, it was viewed as correlative to public realities and did not provide a sense of private identity. In Patricia Fumerton's formulation, "the 'self'"—at least the early modern self—"was void."[3]

Alternatively, it has been claimed that the early modern period saw the emergence of modern subjectivity. This claim has the advantage of providing a transition between an earlier era when subjectivity as we know it was presumably unavailable and a modern one in which it is full blown. Yet this view still depends on oppositions that seem to me too stark and absolute. I offer yet another view: that, though the concept and even the experience of subjectivity have certainly changed over time, subjectivity is a useful notion for understanding human experience in any period, that it has never been either the self-contained and mastering entity imagined in the modern period nor merely (as more recent thinkers have suggested) the product of impersonal forces, and that agency has never been either entirely unfettered or simply an illusion.

The idea that there are only two alternatives—either self-contained subjectivity or something approaching the emptiness of pure space—is itself perhaps symptomatic of a way of thinking that would have been foreign to the early modern period. Both of these ways of viewing subjectivity tend to posit it as an absolute, either as something capable of existing entirely on its own or as a function with no distinguishing contents whatever. Neither captures the ambiguity that being a person apparently held in early modern thought—the way being oneself implied difference from yet connection with others, the way being a person thus involved having a distinctive character and location while at the same time being fundamentally dependent on the world as a whole, in all its social, natural, and spiritual dimensions. On the one hand, the discourse of the period and in particular the drama it produced present persons and dramatic personages concerned with the state of their souls or with their personal advancement. On the other hand, the pervasive concern with obligations, loyalties, and roles suggests that being a person (or a character) always involved the presence and expectations of others. Of course, those living in the early modern period would not have used modern philosophical language to describe their condition. Yet if being a person was conceived as necessarily involving relationships with others (as I believe

---

    [2]    Francis Barker, *The Tremulous Private Body: Essays on Subjection* (London and New York: Methuen, 1984), 31.

    [3]    Patricia Fumerton, *Cultural Aesthetics: Renaissance Literature and the Practice of Social Ornament* (Chicago: University of Chicago Press, 1991), 130.

it was in Shakespeare's period), then—to use the current idiom—subjectivity already implied intersubjectivity.

Attuned as it is to the nuances of subjectivity, contemporary philosophy may be helpful as we seek to understand the status and relationship of selves and dramatic characters in the early modern period. Among recent thinkers who have discussed what it means to be a person, Emmanuel Levinas in particular has emphasized the intersubjective dimension of all subjectivity, arguing that "[c]oncrete life is not the solipsist's life of a consciousness closed upon itself," but instead that "[i]n the very idea of concrete being is contained the idea of an intersubjective world." Hence, our understanding of consciousness requires more than the "egological reduction," the attempt to describe individual consciousness in pure isolation; "We must also discover 'others' and the intersubjective world."[4] Furthermore, this intersubjective world is from the start ethical, since the presence of others "puts into question the happy spontaneity of the self" and invests the self's freedom with an ethical dimension by showing it to be potentially "murderous and usurpatory."[5] Yet the primacy of others does not extinguish the inner life. In fact, according to Levinas, the inner life arises precisely in response to the presence of others.

Though Levinas's analysis arguably applies to any experience we would recognize as human, it has, as I have suggested, a particular relevance to Shakespeare's time and thus to our understanding of Shakespeare's characters. To understand the relevance of Levinas's thought, however, requires us to place both it and Shakespeare's period in the larger history of subjectivity, a history that encompasses changes in how subjectivity has been conceived as well as in how it has been experienced. Levinas is often classed among the postmodern thinkers who have critiqued notions of the isolated self that took hold during the seventeenth century, shortly after Shakespeare's time, and that flowered over the next two centuries or more. Like other contemporary thinkers, Levinas seeks to reinterpret subjectivity as something other than the exercising of autonomous powers capable of mastering the world. Yet at the same time he resists the postmodern tendency to reduce subjectivity to a nonentity or to something essentially impersonal.

To make my approach to Shakespeare's characters clear—and especially to clarify why I have turned to Levinas for assistance—I offer here a brief history of subjectivity. This history, of course, is complicated, and what follows must be considered no more than a provisional sketch. We may start by noticing that the age of Shakespeare was a period during which the modern sense of self was developing in a variety of ways, influenced in particular (as Charles Taylor has pointed out) by neo-Stoic thought and the intense spiritual self-examination that came in the wake of the Reformation and the Counter-reformation. Taylor acknowledges that the sense of selfhood we commonly take to be obvious and natural is an invention of

---

4     Emmanuel Levinas, *The Theory of Intuition in Husserl's Phenomenology*, trans. André Orianne (Evanston: Northwestern University Press, 1973), 150.

5     Emmanuel Levinas, "Signature," in *Difficult Freedom: Essays on Judaism*, trans. Seán Hand (Baltimore: The Johns Hopkins University Press, 1990), 293–94.

the modern Western world. Yet he sees the roots of that sense in much older habits of thought and traces its development at least as far back as Augustine, "who introduced the inwardness of radical reflexivity and bequeathed it to the Western tradition of thought."[6] At the same time, Taylor points out an important distinction between Augustine's and modern versions of inwardness: while moderns tend to view the inner life as entirely private, for Augustine, we turn inward in order to know God and enter into deeper relation with him; we thus always remain in relationship with and under obligation to someone other than ourselves.

Of course, Augustine's attitude did not necessarily coincide in every respect with the ordinary experience of Shakespeare and his contemporaries. Yet Augustine's influence was pervasive, and it became even stronger after the Reformation. Other influences cooperated during the sixteenth and seventeenth centuries to produce a particular kind of subjectivity. Montaigne heightened the sense that one's inner experience is unique and particular. As many have pointed out, Descartes's insistence, several decades later, on a split between thought and bodily existence moved yet further toward the idea of the self as self-contained and self-governing. The result, according to Taylor, was a "new conception of inwardness, an inwardness of self-sufficiency, of autonomous powers of ordering by reason" (1989, 158). "[B]y the turn of the eighteenth century," he concludes, "something recognizably like the modern self is in process of constitution, at least among the social and spiritual elites of northwestern Europe and its American offshoots" (1989, 185). This modern view includes the sense of *being* and *having* a "self," a self one can somehow examine and also control, a self in which images or conceptions of the "outside" world reside as ideas, a self in which also reside moral sentiments and the freedom and responsibility to act in accordance with those sentiments. This view of the self prepared the way for the idea of social life as a contract entered into by pre-existing selves.

Here, at least, in this view of social life that became dominant in the eighteenth century, we have a strong contrast to the very different view that prevailed in Shakespeare's time: namely, that social and moral relations bind us to others whether we want them to or not. Society, for early modern England, and indeed for the premodern world in general, is more like a body than an agreement between conscious agents. Individual people are like organs in that body, naturally and inextricably connected to each other and dependent on the life that sustains the entire body. In *King Lear*, Shakespeare has Kent refer to such social bonds as "holy cords .../ Which are t[oo] intrinse"—too intricately interconnected—"t' unloose," and has several characters (Albany and Lear, among others) use corporeal images to describe interpersonal relations.[7] Albany, for instance, compares Goneril to a branch and her father to the trunk which provides life-giving sap (4.2.32–36). Lear

---

    [6]    Charles Taylor, *Sources of the Self: The Making of the Modern Identity* (Cambridge, MA: Harvard University Press, 1989), 131.

    [7]    2.2.74–5. All Shakespearean quotations are from *The Riverside Shakespeare,* 2nd ed., ed. G. Blakemore Evans, J.J. M. Tobin, et al. (Boston: Houghton Mifflin, 1997).

calls his daughters his "flesh" and "blood" and sees the connection as so physically intimate that an offending daughter is "a disease that's in my flesh, / Which I must needs call mine" (2.4.221–23). Yet the very fact that such statements are made points to the efforts several of the play's characters carry out to wrench themselves free from their bonds with others and become self-sufficient agents in charge of their own existence. In the Shakespearean text itself, it appears, we have evidence of both the older and the emerging views.

The modern conception of self continued to develop from the eighteenth century onward, reaching a kind of zenith in some romantic strains of thought (especially in German idealism) that made the self equivalent to the absolute. Robert Solomon traces these developments and their aftermath in a book subtitled *The Rise and Fall of the Self*, indicating that, following the self's apparent triumph, the move during the nineteenth and twentieth centuries, at least among philosophers, has been to diminish the self and its pretensions.[8] Certain strains of what we call postmodern thought critique the self—or more properly the "subject"—even more radically and argue that, in contrast to the controlling *cogito* that moderns had come to imagine, the subject is instead a function or even an illusory effect of discourse, of linguistic or cultural practices, or of the structures of power. The subject is certainly not the autonomous, self-contained, self-sufficient "self" that had arisen in Western thought by the eighteenth century. It might better be described as a space or site where various forces are at play. Furthermore, the subject envisioned in this way apparently lacks agency, individual particularity, and even an inner life, at least one separated from a realm of exteriority. If this description does not match actual experience, some strict postmodernists might argue that what appear to be agency, particularity, or an inner life are simply reflections of cultural and linguistic practices.

Much can be said for the postmodern deflation of the self. But perhaps postmodern thought has gone too far. As Solomon points out, there is "very little difference" in the end "[b]etween the self as absolute Spirit and the self as nothing" (1988, 202). In both cases, the plurality of concrete existence has been effaced, replaced by a kind of absolute monism. And the person thinking of the world in either way is in effect taking his or her consciousness as coextensive with the totality of what is, so that, paradoxically, a pervasive and solipsistic subjectivity is reintroduced by the very attempt to deconstruct the subject.

For a way out of this bind, we may wish to turn again to Levinas, who represents another side of postmodern thought and whose importance it would be hard to overrate, given his influence on thinkers ranging from Sartre and Beauvoir to Derrida and Irigaray. Levinas's way out of the all-or-nothing bind is to conceive of the self as genuinely separate from what is other than the self and yet also as primordially and inevitably involved in relationship with others. In order to think about this remarkable situation, a situation in which Levinas argues we always

---

[8]    Robert Solomon, *Continental Philosophy since 1750: The Rise and Fall of the Self* (Oxford and New York: Oxford University Press, 1988).

necessarily find ourselves, we must set aside our habitual tendency to take a panoramic view of human experience, as if we were outside of it, and, as we do so, to interpret human interaction as a dialectical process within a totality. According to Levinas, the relationship of the self and the other is *not* dialectical and cannot be viewed from the outside. Self and other are not opposing or interchangeable entities within a system that consciousness can encompass.

In Levinas's words, "The same [that is, the self's identification with itself and its experience] and the other can not enter into a cognition that would encompass them; the relations that the separated being [the self] maintains with what transcends it are not produced on the ground of totality, do not crystallize into a system."[9] Rather, consciousness arises precisely in response to the other person, and that encounter takes place face to face, that is, in a way that is irreducible to the totalizing vision of an outside observer. Hence, "the primordial multiplicity [of self and other] is observed within the very face to face that constitutes it. It is produced in multiple singularities and not in a being exterior to this number who would count the multiples" (1969, 251). Though I can name myself and the other together, "[h]e and I do not form a number. ...Neither possession nor the unity of number nor the unity of concepts link[s] me to the Stranger [i.e., the other person] ..., the Stranger who disturbs the being at home with oneself" (1969, 39). Since "the other, despite the relationship with the same, remains transcendent to the same," "[e]ven when I shall have linked the Other to myself with the conjunction 'and,' the Other continues to face me, to reveal himself in his face" (1969, 39, 80–81). Therefore, "[t]he same and the other at the same time maintain themselves in relationship and *absolve* themselves from this relation, remain absolutely separated" (1969, 102). Subjectivity, as Levinas understands it, requires this situation of simultaneous separation and relationship. Separation and relationship are not oppositions within a dialectic but rather constitute the very *way* in which being is produced. Subjectivity involves the activity of maintaining one's identity with oneself but also of transcending oneself, since relation with the other is an inescapable, even grounding, condition of that activity of self-identification.

Levinas's ideas and terminology provide what seem to me useful tools for approaching Shakespeare's characters. While we certainly ought to distinguish the postmodern from the early modern, insights such as those articulated by Levinas may help us see things about Shakespeare's characters that would remain obscure if we held naively to certain concepts about the "self" that have intervened between Shakespeare's time and ours. Levinas can help in clearing away much that would otherwise be misleading or irrelevant in the view of selfhood that dominated from the late seventeenth into the early nineteenth century—a view that may appear something of an aberration when compared to the socially grounded view of self of earlier periods. While constituting something other than a return to the past, recent thinkers can help us appreciate and enter imaginatively into that earlier view. In

---

[9]    Emmanuel Levinas, *Totality and Infinity: An Essay on Exteriority,* trans. Alphonso Lingis (Pittsburgh: Duquesne University Press, 1969), 80.

particular, Levinas's emphasis on intersubjectivity may open our eyes both to what is familiar and to what is unfamiliar in Shakespeare's images of personhood and personal interaction. I propose, then, to use Levinas's ideas as an aid as we consider whether and to what degree we can properly think of Shakespeare's characters as possessing subjectivity—as we consider, in fact, what we could possibly mean by "subjectivity" in connection with Shakespeare's fictional persons.

Any number of plays could be used as test cases for such a study. I choose to examine *King Lear* in part because it is a text in which competing ideas of subjectivity are at play. To an extent—though with many qualifications—the play supports the idea that personal identity is mainly a matter of social roles, not of self-sufficient subjectivity as moderns would understand it. The characters are emphatically identified in terms of such roles as king and subject, master and servant, parent, child, and sibling—and in the case of Edmund, his socially determined status as bastard. The play begins with Lear's expectation that his daughters and his subjects generally will fulfill their prescribed roles. I have already cited the view expressed by several of the play's characters that compares human beings, especially in their familial and political relationships, to parts of a single body. Lear views Goneril as his flesh and blood, or more precisely, as a disease in his flesh (2.4.221–22). Albany is sure Goneril will come to "deadly use" since she is trying to "sliver and disbranch" herself from "her material sap"— that is, from her father, viewed as the life-giving origin of the familial organism (4.2.34–6). This view, with its organic imagery and its assumption that roles are natural and necessary, confirms the primacy of social function in establishing the characters' identities.

Yet this view is repeatedly contested. Cordelia and Edgar are disowned and stripped of their familial roles, and Kent similarly finds himself socially naked and rootless. Lear asks if Regan and Goneril are indeed his daughters and whether (being treated as he is) he is truly a king and father. Edmund objects to the status that has been imposed on him and announces his allegiance to Nature as the primal source of being and identity in opposition to the superficialities of social convention. In various ways, the play poses the question, "What would a character (or a person such as a character represents) be if deprived of all social roles?" The question appears most directly in Lear's famous words: "Who is it that can tell me who I am?" (1.4.230). It is implied in Lear's question in the hovel, where he wonders what is left when a person is deprived of shelter, clothing, reason, and social status: "Is man no more than this?" (3.4.102–103). The ready-made identity supposedly provided by social roles appears to be an inadequate response to such questions.

At the same time, virtually all the characters seek identity in some kind of social role. After displacing his father, Edmund acquires a new status as the Earl of Gloucester. The characters whose roles are taken from them resume these roles, or something like them, not by social enforcement but by choice. The disguises adopted by Kent and Edgar provide them with temporary identities and allow them to fulfill the roles of servant and son even if they are not recognized as such. Roles thus continue to be important, but they are not simply imposed or accepted without question. They may be rejected or adopted in some oblique or modified form.

Cordelia and Lear are especially complicated sites for the establishing and contesting of identity. Cordelia apparently views herself as a loving daughter yet refuses to perform that role in the way Lear demands. Then, though explicitly stripped of familial identity, she nevertheless chooses to returns in her role as a daughter, even kneeling to ask her father's blessing and choosing to forgive him, despite his not feeling worthy of her acts. Lear finds validation in the renewed relationship with his daughter, yet he hesitates to take on the full trappings of father and king, kneeling to Cordelia rather than standing to give the blessing she requests. In the reunion scene, he is at first unsure of Cordelia's and Kent's identity—in fact, it is unclear whether he ever fully recognizes Kent. He is unsure of his own status as well: Is he alive or dead? Where is he? Where have his clothes come from? He is even vague about his age. He complains, "Would I were assur'd / Of my condition!" (4.7.55–6), and despite the reconciliation with Cordelia, he never receives a completely adequate response to his complaint.

Having put the social sources of identity in question, the play presents alternative sources and puts them to the test as well. Nature is a source that seems to transcend human society, yet the precise meaning of the word *Nature* proves hard to pin down. Most often the word refers to a creative power transcending yet sustaining the visible world, having endowed the characters with individual qualities and provided the moral and physical structure within which they operate. Yet the characters persistently fail to meet the expectations presumably set by Nature. Such a failure is indicated in Lear's question, "Is there any cause in nature that make these hard hearts?" (3. 6.77–8). Apparently beyond and in charge of nature are the gods, to whom several characters appeal, Lear especially when stripped of social status (for instance, when he says, "You see me here, you gods, a poor old man" [2.4.272]). But the gods' active role in responding to such appeals is notoriously uncertain.

The self-assertive individualism of Goneril, Regan, and Edmund stands in contrast to the uncertainty about identity that afflicts so many others. This individualism can, in fact, be interpreted as these more masterful characters' response to a condition in which all roles are contested and unstable. It is as if, in a world where identity is grounded neither in nature nor in social convention, one must forge one's own identity. The stance that Goneril, Regan, and Edmund take resembles the one Søren Kierkegaard attributes to the Renaissance prince Caesar Borgia, whose motto was "Either Caesar or nothing"—either a self-fashioned identity or no identity at all.[10] These characters, though early modern, are vivid examples of the sort of self-contained and self-governing ego that Taylor and others associate with modern subjectivity, the kind of subjectivity that came to dominate and seem "natural" only after Shakespeare's time.

---

[10]    Soren Kierkegaard, *Fear and Trembling* and *The Sickness unto Death,* trans Walter Lowrie (Princeton: Princeton University Press, 1954), 152.

It is telling that in *King Lear* the characters who seem most modern in their sensibilities are the villains. Goneril says, "The laws are mine, not thine" (5.3.159), and her actions support the notion that she sees herself as an autonomous, controlling ego. Her alliance with Regan is one of expedience on both sides, and they end up competing to the death for Edmund. Edmund's case is more complicated. He argues that he would be what he is whatever stars oversaw his conception. Still, he points to "Nature"—in some sense a divine entity—as his mistress and the source of his energies and qualities (1.2.1–22). But Nature as Edmund conceives it apparently expects nothing from him but the pursuit of his own desires and so seems something of an alter ego, a repository of amoral energy and splendor from which he derives his own character. In obeying Nature, he but obeys himself. Edmund prefigures the modern sense of self in viewing anything and anyone other than himself as an obstacle or an object to be possessed and in seeing himself as unconstrained by any external moral structures. It appears that his actions proceed from attitudes expressed in such statements as these: "Let me, if not by birth, have land by wit: / All with me's meet that I can fashion fit" (1.2.183–84); "my state / Stands on me to defend, not to debate" (5.1.68–9); and "The younger rises when the old doth fall" (3.3.25). Even if Edmund's dramatically represented sense of self is a construction of language, that language (e.g., the emphatic use of "I," "me," and "my") seems to proceed from, or to have produced, an awareness of himself as separate from everyone else and as capable of, almost compulsively bound to, promoting his interests and his power over others.

Lear, on the other hand, pursues his interests and power over others while using the traditional language of social roles and obligations, even language that evokes an organic view of society. His daughters ought to love him, and their failure to do so resembles a mouth tearing the hand that lifts food to it (3.4.14–16). It is easy for us to view Lear as a victim of his own massive egotism. But apparently he views himself (or so his language leads us to imagine) as the victim of daughters failing to act in accordance with the proper nature of things. That is why this family dispute seems to him to involve the ripping apart of the entire cosmos. As a result of this cosmic disintegration, Lear finds himself in a position to experience something like modern subjectivity. That is, he feels himself to be isolated—even nature and the gods seem to have abandoned him—and he becomes aware at least of the possibility of viewing himself as a being who exists apart from roles and relationships. I take that to be the import of such words as these: "Does any here know me? This is not Lear" (1.4.226). Yes, these words are sarcastic: he is berating Goneril for not treating him in accordance with his social position. Yet the passage also verges on panic: if he is not treated like a king and father, who is he? The breakdown of social roles thus leads to the question, "Who is it that can tell me who I am?" (1.4.230), and at least to the possibility of imagining Lear as an entirely isolated self. Self-reflective early modern spectators might even be led to see themselves, at least momentarily, in the same way.

Whether presented in terms of the villains' ruthless self-advancement or Lear's tortured isolation, what we might call modern subjectivity undeniably plays a significant role in *King Lear*. Yet however engaging to spectators and readers, this sort of subjectivity seems just as unsatisfactory in the play's dramatic world as mere subjection to a social role. Indeed, the self-created and self-sustaining subjectivity aimed at by Goneril, Regan, and Edmund turns out to provide an identity no more stable—perhaps less stable—than the identity that social roles provide. The final scenes reveal a serious flaw in this kind of mastering subjectivity: it pits those who practice it against each other so that eventually, as they compete for dominance, all are destroyed. More subtly and significantly, the play also suggests that those who promote themselves at the expense of others cannot do so in good conscience and therefore cannot properly sustain the kind of subjectivity they seek to practice. After all his efforts at self-promotion have failed, Edmund attempts something like repentance. Goneril's efforts lead to despair, which—as a kind of self-loathing, or more precisely, a loathing of the very condition of being a self—marks the breakdown of subjectivity. When we witness Goneril about to kill herself, exposed and deprived of all hope of succeeding in her aims, we may interpret her as choosing the only way to avoid further humiliation. But we may also view her suicide as an attempt at self-annihilation, as if she feels compelled to escape not just from her situation but also from herself. Kierkegaard's analysis of despair aptly fits Goneril's condition. According to Kierkegaard, the person who seeks heroic mastery is already seeking to escape himself, and if he fails in his quest (as such figures ultimately do), "he now cannot endure to be himself." "Essentially he is equally in despair in either case," for either he "despairingly wills to be ...a self which he is not," or failing that, he wishes not to exist at all (1954, 152–53).

Levinas describes this sort of subjectivity as "alienable" (*Totality,* 245): paradoxically, the very focus upon self, the compulsion to satisfy one's own needs and promote one's personal status at the expense of others, prevents the attainment of genuine identity, prevents one from being oneself in the most significant sense. This is so, according to Levinas, because the self—at least, the ethical self, the self that can be itself in good conscience—comes into being in responding to others: "To utter 'I,' to affirm [one's] irreducible singularity ..., means to possess a privileged place with regard to responsibilities for which no one can replace me and from which no one can release me. To be unable to shirk: this is the I.... The accomplishing of the I qua I and morality constitute one sole and same process in being: morality comes to birth ...in the fact that infinite exigencies, that of serving the poor, the stranger, the widow, and the orphan, converge at one point of the universe"—namely, here where the "I," the singular self, is situated (*1969,* 245).

In contrast to characters for whom the pursuit of personal power and enjoyment seems to be the ultimate project, characters such as Edgar, Cordelia, Kent, and the Fool can be read as exemplifying an older kind of subjectivity, that of being subjected to obligations. The Fool not only stays with Lear, at least during the first part of the play, but argues—in a passage much complicated with irony—against self-interest. The "wise man" (the Fool may be thinking of Goneril, Regan, and Edmund, among others) will abandon his loyalties when they contradict his interests, for he may break his neck if he hangs on to a great one, like Lear, who is on his way down. Yet the Fool insists on remaining true to Lear despite the dangers and would have "none but knaves" practice the wisdom of self-interest, which (it appears) will turn them into fools of a different sort (2.4.67–85). The risks of loyalty evoked by the Fool are amply demonstrated by what happens later in the play, to Kent, Edgar, Cordelia, perhaps the Fool himself, and also to Gloucester, who is blinded after giving aid to Lear. The loyalty of Kent and Edgar exposes them to danger and suffering. Cordelia, of course, dies. And though we don't know for sure what happens to the Fool, we learn he "hath much pin'd away" (1.4.74). Along with Lear, he endures the storm, and he apparently ends up homeless or worse. As for Gloucester, even before being blinded, he knows he has put his life at risk: as he goes to help Lear, he tells Edmund, "If I die for't (as no less is threat'ned me), the King my old master must be reliev'd" (3.3.17–19).

Yet it is hardly adequate to read these characters as simply representing the older view that exalts the primacy of social bonds. Like Cordelia, Kent is banished for refusing to submit to Lear, and though his refusal may constitute loyalty of a truer kind, he seeks his own way of being loyal to Lear, even creating an alternative identity as he serves him in disguise. Similarly, Edgar and Cordelia both fill and fail to fill their expected roles. The very characters who most authentically affirm the value of social bonds are also agents who actively choose particular ways of fulfilling their social obligations, even if that means risking or sacrificing their social identities. For this and other reasons, it is difficult to attribute to these characters anything but a complicated sense of subjectivity.

Edgar, like Lear, experiences isolation because others have turned against him. His isolation does not produce the mastering subjectivity of an ego that is in charge of itself and its world but something like the opposite. He is evacuated of substance and identity: "Edgar I nothing am" (2.3.21), a phrase capable of being read either as "I am no longer Edgar" or as "I Edgar am nothing." These two readings come down to much the same thing: to be deprived of his name and of his social roles and relationships is in effect to become nothing, to become something like the empty space that postmodern thought associates with subjectivity.

Yet this very recognition of his loss of self is also an act of self-awareness. The rest of the play shows Edgar very much an agent, more so perhaps than he would have been if he had remained in a comfortable social and familial context. He creates an identity of his own—Poor Tom. He accompanies and serves his father. And then, though nameless and faceless, he acts something like the part of an assertive ego when he challenges and defeats his brother. On the other hand, he performs all these assertive acts in a spirit of submission. The identity he chooses is the most vulnerable he can imagine, mad, poor, naked, and exposed to the elements ("Poor Tom's a-cold"). Even speaking in his own voice, to himself, he presents himself as emotionally vulnerable ("Who is't can say, 'I am at the worst'? / I am worse than e'er I was"; "O thou side-piercing sight!"; "my heart breaks" [4.1.25–6; 4.6.85, 142]) and as subject to necessity ("I cannot daub it further. … And yet I must" [4.1.52–4]). He advises patience and tells his father, "Men must endure / Their going hence even as their coming hither" (5.3.9–10). Even his most assertive acts—killing Oswald and Edmund—are done in the service of others, and he hints that he does the latter of these as an instrument of the gods. He ends the play speaking of the "weight" that he and others "must obey" (5.3.327)—that is, he speaks of himself not as a mastering agent but as one subjected to external forces and responsibilities.

The text invites us to view Cordelia as a similarly complicated example of subjectivity. Her words and behavior in the first scene combine submissiveness and self-assertion. In saying that she loves her father "according to [her] bond, no more nor less" (1.1.93), she both acknowledges her social role and sets limits to how far she will submit to it. Lear claims that what she calls "plainness" is really "pride" (1.1.129). Even if that is putting it too strongly, we can see in her judgment of her sisters and her refusal to yield to expectations that seem demeaning a desire to preserve her sense of her own integrity and virtue. In other words, given the text, we would have to exercise extraordinary ingenuity not to see Cordelia as possessing a *sense of self*—an awareness of, or an image of, herself as a substantial entity with a particular character that she has some degree of power over and that she wants to preserve, even in the face of obligations others would press upon her.

But Cordelia, like Edgar and Lear, undergoes a stripping of identity: she is disowned, disinherited, and banished. The King of France is presented as extraordinary in taking her with "nothing"—a word, of course, that reverberates through the play. Like Edgar, she appears to be something of an empty site, exposed, vulnerable, and void of substance. On the other hand, France's statement, "She is herself a dowry" (1.1.241), suggests that, even without social status, she has substantial identity, perhaps identity grounded in what we like to call "moral character." Interestingly, she seems most truly and substantially herself at the very moment she is stripped of social identity. Yet the play makes it hard to draw with confidence even that much significance from France's statement.

France's statement, though it seems simple enough, is especially difficult to read if we are trying to understand its place in the history of subjectivity. Is France in fact saying that Cordelia has a determinate character even apart from social status, even without a home, a family, or any material means? If she has such a character, does that mean the play is inviting us to view subjectivity as self-contained, independent of social roles and relationships, even independent of changing circumstances? If it does so, that view amounts to a momentary glimpse, since Cordelia is quickly married to France and disappears from the play for the next two acts. We never really see her as an isolated self. And in fact, despite her self-assertion and despite France's praise of her virtue at the very moment she becomes a social nonentity, Cordelia never appears to aim at a radically self-created identity.

When she returns, it is in the service of her father. Her motive ("love, dear love" [4.4.28]) and her reunion with Lear suggest that she remains a dutiful daughter. She seems, that is, to confirm the view that early modern subjectivity amounted to "subjection," to "a condition of dependent membership" (Barker 1984, 31).

Some modern readers of the play have, in fact, betrayed their modernity by in effect condemning Cordelia (or Shakespeare or the play) for her return. According to Carol Thomas Neely, readers must learn not "to be Cordelia."[11] Janet Adelman argues that Cordelia's death effects "the ultimate silencing of her subjectivity" and that, "[a]t the end, ... having evacuated Cordelia's subjectivity, the play takes even her death from her."[12] For such readers, the play ends with Cordelia as an iconic or otherwise lifeless figure, deprived of subjectivity—suggesting of course that she was previously in possession of it and that she would have been better off if allowed to stay in France.

To be sure, the subjectivity imagined by such readers is not one of complete isolation, but it is one of self-control and self-preservation—something like the modern sense of self that some say existed only in nascent form, if at all, in the early modern period. It seems to me that readers who see subjectivity of this kind in the play are not entirely mistaken. For if the play itself is taken as a guide, a modern sense of self appears to have been powerfully present in the period. It is simply that Shakespeare tends to associate it with such characters as Goneril and Edmund.

What kind of subjectivity, then, does *King Lear* associate with characters like Edgar and Cordelia? The play presents them as moral agents, capable of assertive action, capable of resisting expectations. Yet it also places them in a moral and social context, with obligations to others, and shows them as willingly and actively submitting to those obligations, at least when they judge the obligations to be genuine. These characters are *subjected* to roles and relationships, yet they appear at the same time to have an inner life of reflection, emotion, and choice, and they appear to exercise volition. Unlike Goneril, Regan, Edmund, and Cornwall, though, they do not seek to exercise that volition in a moral vacuum and do not act with an eye primarily to their own interest. Perhaps the most startling moments in the play (if we are thinking about subjectivity) are the moments of stripping or self-emptying when characters like Edgar, Cordelia, and Lear seem to be without identity in either the traditional or the modern sense. Yet these moments, though presenting the characters as almost nothing and as supremely vulnerable, are also the moments at which they acquire something like real significance and particularity, because they are not simply performers of social roles.

Paradoxically, these are also moments that impel them, either immediately or eventually, to recognize the otherness of others. In one of his exchanges with his father, Edgar calls himself a "most poor man, made tame to fortune's blows, / Who, by the art of known and feeling sorrows, / Am pregnant to good pity" (4.6.221–23). His identity—what we might call his "character" in one sense of

---

[11]   Carol Thomas Neely, "Epilogue: Remembering Shakespeare, Revising Ourselves," in *Women's Re-Visions of Shakespeare,* ed. Marianne Novy (Urbana and Chicago: University of Illinois Press, 1990), 248.

[12]   Janet Adelman, *Suffocating Mothers: Fantasies of Maternal Origin in Shakespeare's Plays, Hamlet to The Tempest,* (New York and London: Routledge, 1992), 127.

that word—has arisen in response to being subjected to what is other than himself. When he speaks these words, of course, Edgar is playing a role, pretending to be "someone else." Yet he acts on what he has said and continues to show compassion to his father. Edgar's self-emptying and exposure have apparently led him to care for others and to exercise his moral agency on their behalf. By losing himself, he has in a sense become himself.

In Edgar—in this imaginary person we call a dramatic character—we may discern subjectivity of a kind hard to classify as either premodern or modern, or postmodern, for that matter. His identity and the sort of experience we imagine him having are not merely socially imposed, nor is he a self-created ego. Nor is he merely a space in which language or power relations manifest themselves. His apparently contradictory condition of self-emptying and ethical agency seems to me most adequately described by Levinas, for whom subjectivity is necessarily linked with ethics. Levinas agrees with other contemporary thinkers that the masterful *cogito* is an illusion, though an illusion to which we are all subject. Yet he points to another kind of subjectivity intimately involved with being human, a subjectivity that "[starts] from [the] position or deposition of the sovereign I in self consciousness, a deposition which is precisely its responsibility for the Other."[13] In a richly suggestive passage, Levinas writes: "I am defined as a subjectivity, as a singular person, as an 'I,' precisely because I am exposed to the other. It is my inescapable and incontrovertible answerability to the other that makes me an individual 'I.' So that I become a responsible or ethical 'I' to the extent that I agree to depose or dethrone myself—abdicate my position of centrality—in favor of the vulnerable other." He goes on to make it clear that he does not intend to "preserve … the idea of a subject who would be a substantial or mastering center of meaning, an idealist, self-sufficient *cogito*" and in fact opposes ethical subjectivity to what he calls "[t]hese traditional ontological versions of subjectivity."[14] Perhaps it is a mistake to read back into *Lear* Levinas's postmodern conception of "ethical subjectivity." Yet Levinas was himself influenced by Shakespeare and would probably not object to the linkage.

Cordelia seems to me, in fact, an especially potent image of the kind of ethical subjectivity Levinas has in mind. Cordelia's return can be viewed as expressing her willingness to expose herself to risk and even death in the service of the other. Her reunion with Lear can be read as her acknowledgment and welcoming of the other as other even when that other has persecuted her. According to Levinas, such acknowledgment and welcoming does not mean deliberately letting oneself be abused or destroyed, for to serve and respond to the other requires that one have resources from which to serve. To serve the other means to treat the other as other; among other things it means—as it does for Cordelia—to command and

---

[13]     Emmanuel Levinas, *Ethics and Infinity: Conversations with Philippe Nemo,* trans. Richard A. Cohen (Pittsburgh: Duquesne University Press, 1985), 101.

[14]     Emmanuel Levinas and Richard Kearney, "Dialogue with Emmanuel Levinas," in *Face to Face with Levinas,* ed. Richard A. Cohen (Albany: SUNY Press, 1986), 26–7.

to teach. Yet it also means to put the other before oneself, to take the attitude Cordelia expresses when she says, "For thee, oppressed king, I am cast down, / Myself could else out-frown false Fortune's frown" (5.3.5–6). It is also an attitude that Lear himself at least begins to adopt as he focuses on Cordelia rather than on himself.

From a Levinasian point of view, it is by offering herself and sustaining the other that Cordelia attains authentic subjectivity, that she lives (that is) the only kind of life worth living. Her sisters, on the other hand, may be identified with "the alienable subjectivity of need and will, which claims to be already and henceforth in possession of itself, but which death makes mockery of." The call to responsibility transfigures this subjectivity, bringing it to its final reality and keeping it from being "reduced to [a] place within a totality"; this transformation "does not consist in flattering [the self's] subjective tendencies and consoling him for his death, but in existing for the Other" (1969, 245–46). Paradoxically, subjectivity in its richest sense—personal identity and experience that may be described as significant and substantial—arises in "being for the other," in being (in a sense) beyond oneself. It is as responsible to the other that I am unique and irreplaceable, and it is as I shift the center of my concern outside of myself that my subjectivity may, in some sense, be called good: "The I, which we have seen arise … as a separated being having apart, in itself, the center around which its existence gravitates, is confirmed in its singularity by purging itself of this gravitation, purges itself interminably, and is confirmed precisely in this incessant effort to purge itself. This is termed goodness. Perhaps the possibility of a point of the universe where such an overflow of responsibility is produced ultimately defines the I" (*1969*, 244–45).

Of course, Cordelia as presented on the page or in performance cannot be summed up in a few sentences. Through the course of the play, different dimensions of what we call her "character" are revealed—perhaps that character even changes in some respects. The sort of subjectivity it makes sense to attribute to her comes close at some moments to dutiful subjection; at others, to proud self-assertion; at others, to discomfort and uncertainty. As I read it, the play's first scene presents Cordelia as actively trying to cope with difficult circumstances, making choices that arise from a complicated and changing set of desires, and stumbling as she tries to fulfill her role as a daughter while at the same time maintaining her sense of her own integrity, what we might call her "self." In the course of the play, it appears that her desires do not change radically. Yet her strategies for achieving them change, and perhaps her willingness to sacrifice even her sense of superior virtue deepens as she focuses less on herself and more on her father. To account for all of the evidence the play provides, we should perhaps view France's claim that "she is herself a dowry" not as pointing to a complete and self-contained character of the sort modern ideas of selfhood would assert but instead to a way of being—and not even to a finished way of being, but rather to desires for that way of being, desires that we may imagine Cordelia as actively pursuing, desires that lead moment by moment to words and actions that more or less effectively fulfill them. The strongest and most persistent of Cordelia's desires can be summed up in one of the phrases I have borrowed from Levinas: "being for the other." This desire is focused especially on her father but extends to others as well, as her general goodwill and even her judgment of her sisters (since she would like them to be better) indicate.

What makes Cordelia Cordelia, then, is not a substance such as we could define in a static list of characteristics. Rather, it is an activity, the activity of "being for the other." In a sense, her identity, especially in the latter part of the play, consists paradoxically of emptying her identity, giving up her self-possession in favor of a continual sacrificing of identity on behalf of the other. If we are caught up in the spirit of the play, we may feel inclined to join with Lear in saying, "Upon such sacrifices, …/ The gods themselves throw incense" (5.3.20–21). His words likely refer to the sacrifices involved in imprisonment and the loss of social position. But these are in essence sacrifices of one self on behalf of another—sacrifices of comfort, status, and all else involved in the egoistic gravitation.

*King Lear* presents a world in which neither social roles nor self-assertion seems to provide secure identity. Neither what some consider the premodern condition of subjection without subjectivity nor the modern condition of self-contained and self-mastering selfhood seem to provide a satisfactory grounding for personal identity. Yet the play does more than deconstruct all possible foundations for identity; in its images of "being for the other," it also hints at a positive approach to the issue. The sort of subjectivity we can attribute to Cordelia, Edgar, and Kent is obviously from the start intersubjective—that is, it arises in their concern for and efforts to serve others. Yet even the villains' subjectivity must be viewed as intersubjective: their competition with each other and their efforts to manipulate and dominate those who stand in their way would make no sense if the villains were in fact isolated egos. The absurdity and insatiability of evil, as Levinas points out, lie in the very fact that the person who seeks to eliminate the otherness of others finds himself without anyone to celebrate his triumph if those others are indeed turned into objects. Every character in *King Lear*, however we might want to classify them, is constituted by his or her orientation toward others; every moment of the play consists of words and actions representing various ways the characters respond to each other.

In a book titled *Reading Shakespeare's Characters*, Christy Desmet notes that "[r]ecent literary theory has successfully discredited the notion of a transcendent, coherent self"—or as I prefer to put it, a static and self-contained self.[15] Freed from having to align Shakespeare's characters with this problematic and anachronistic view of self, she goes on to show how these characters are "constructed through language" (1992, 13). It may be tempting to take this formulation as asserting that the characters are mere linguistic constructs, nothing more than signs at play with other signs, and that we should dismiss as illusions any sense we have that they

---

[15]    Christy Desmet, *Reading Shakespeare's Characters: Rhetoric, Ethics, and Identity* (Amherst: University of Massachusetts Press, 1992), 3.

possess of agency or self-consciousness. But as the details of Desmet's project make clear, the fact that characters and their relationships are produced through the medium of language in no way deprives them of agency or inwardness. Language indeed is the means by which action, relationship, and self-awareness are effected. But as Levinas argues, language always already involves relationship with others—one reason subjectivity is always intersubjective. Certainly the impression most readers and playgoers have is that the characters consist of more than just language, at least if language is understood as nothing more than a structure of signs or a set of rhetorical strategies. In fact, though dramatic characters unavoidably possess linguistic and social dimensions, these not only do not prevent us from viewing the characters as having an inner life of emotion and reflection but virtually demand of us such a view.

If we take *King Lear* as our example (and the same could be said for many other plays), the subjectivity we imagine the characters to possess, though conveyed through language, depends on more than language in its narrower sense. To begin with, it involves bodily presence and a range of emotions and intentions. In addition to these, the text itself points to several other sources of personal identity and character, including family and other social relationships, the stars, and "nature." Arguably, each of these—along with language—plays its part. Yet I would argue that something even more powerful and pervasive than any of these is at work. More than anything else, *King Lear*'s vision of subjectivity is tied either to self-offering (i.e., being for the other) or to self-aggrandizement. In both cases, even when a character seems in hot pursuit of his or her own interests, the characters act out these versions of subjectivity in a context of already existing and unavoidable relationships.

I believe it makes sense to view Shakespeare's characters as imaginary persons for whom a degree of subjectivity and agency can be posited. Yet despite evidence at times of something approaching a modern sense of self-contained, self-sufficient selfhood, these characters are best understood in relational terms—not as beings to whom we should ascribe static or substantial (and essentially isolated) "personalities" that could be analyzed separately from other characters, but rather as locations for a dynamic activity of offering and response requiring us to take into account multiple characters in order to think about any one of them. The characters' imagined subjectivity is always from the start intersubjective. If we acknowledge that fact, I believe our encounters with them will yield a richer sense of the plays and of the plays' past and present relevance, despite whatever changes have taken place since Shakespeare's time.

# Chapter 3
# What Makes Someone a Character in Shakespeare?

## William Flesch

Discussions of the characters of Shakespeare's plays tend to be vertically self-referential: Bradley or Coleridge or Hazlitt or Pope or Johnson or Bloom or Keats admires how true to life a character is, how the character seems to step straight up off the stage (or leap off the page) and become like some integral or complete individual *we* know—we who are real people.[1] Such characters are characters *for us*. Of course this kind of criticism has always risked opposition from philologists, who think of it as a sloppy way of dismissing the careful and minute analysis that establishing and interpreting the details of the text requires. Character is merely the projection of the critic, who, like a bumptious biographer, can only find in Shakespeare what he or she is capable of imagining, not what Shakespeare did imagine. Johnson and Hazlitt and Bloom are hardly bumptious, but their appeal to large categories of common experience seems to purchase grandness at the expense of subtlety. Their Shakespeare risks being wise at the expense of being smart. (The naive philosophical skepticism that certain deconstructive practitioners of the last generation brought to *their* study of Shakespeare is an interesting mirror image of their forebears: they projected their own smartness onto Shakespeare, which is the flip side of the way the character critics tended to find their own wisdom reflected in him.)

But what was Shakespeare's own view of character? How do the plays themselves treat the question? This is one of a number of questions that can profitably be asked about Shakespeare, for example: what does internal evidence show about Shakespeare's own views about the nature of theater (an obvious

---

[1]   See, most obviously, A.C. Bradley, *Shakespearean Tragedy: Lectures on Hamlet, Othello, King Lear, Macbeth* (1904; repr., New York: Penguin, 1991); Samuel Taylor Coleridge, *Coleridge's Writings on Shakespeare*, ed., Terence Hawkes (New York: Capricorn Books, 1959); William Hazlitt, *Characters of Shakespeare's Plays* (1817; repr., Oxford University Press, 1916); Alexander Pope, *The Works of Shakespeare: In Six Volumes* ( 1725; repr., Nabu Press, 2010); Harold Bloom, *Shakespeare: The Invention of The Human* (New York: Riverhead, 1999); John Keats, *Selected Letters*, ed., Robert Gittings (New York: Oxford University Press, 2009); and Samuel Johnson: *The Complete Works of Shakespeare: The Dr. Johnson Edition* (1765; repr., Philadephia: Gebbie, 1896). I discuss Keats's relation to Shakespeare's characters in "The Ambivalence of Generosity: Keats Reading Shakespeare," *ELH* 62:1 (1995): 149-169.

question), or textual accuracy (a question I've treated elsewhere),[2] or character? Obviously all these questions are related and thinking about one is a way of thinking about the others, and about how they were connected for Shakespeare. The question of character is probably the most central question of all, since it's the robustness of character that is essential to Shakespeare's range, depth, and power. That robustness is not a crude contradiction of a sense of their endless subtlety, but a tribute to it, since the coherence of his characters can withstand the most extreme variations in impulse, situation, and reaction to which they are submitted during the developing and increasing stresses of the unfolding story. Their deep coherence is in a relation of reciprocal support with the robustness of the meaning of what they say, even if the textual accuracy of words and lines may be contested. To take a simple example, "Last not least" (*Quarto*) and "Last and least" (*Folio*) mean the same thing in *King Lear*, despite their semantic (and even syntactic) differences, because it's Lear who says these lines, and because they're about Cordelia.[3] Yes, indeed, the *Folio*'s tweak does bring her fragility out a little more, and helps set

---

[2]    "The bounds of the incidental: Shakespeare reading by his own light," in *Something Understood: Essays and Poetry for Helen Vendler*, ed., Stephen Burt and Nick Halpern (Charlottesville: University of Virginia Press, 2009), 83–104.

[3]    Any variorum edition will flag this difference (as well as the difference between Cordelia's "What shall Cordelia do?" in the *Quarto* and "What shall Cordelia speak?" in the *Folio*, which alerts us to the way that for *Cordelia* speaking and doing are one; the *Folio* revision underscores her silence at the end.) I don't give a citation to a particular edition of Shakespeare here, because it has become a matter of principle to me not to cite any particular edition of Shakespeare in my writing on him, except where I am addressing the specifics of that edition, for the reasons I've just summarized here. I give these reasons more fully in "The Bounds of the Incidental" by way of endorsing Johnson's comment (highly relevant to my argument here as well) that "It is not very grateful to consider how little the succession of editors has added to this author's power of pleasing. He was read, admired, studied, and imitated, while he was yet deformed with all the improprieties which ignorance and neglect could accumulate upon him; while the reading was yet not rectified, nor his allusions understood; yet then did Dryden pronounce, 'that Shakespeare was the man who, of all modern and perhaps ancient poets, had the largest and most comprehensive soul'" (2:cxxxvii); I admire and agree as well with Johnson's bracing formulation about Shakespeare's language that "Shakespeare regarded more the series of ideas, than of words; and his language, not being designed for the reader's desk, was all that he desired it to be, if it conveyed his meaning to the audience" (2:cxxix). My polemic is thus against what I regard as a false and harmful idea that one should cite from a particular edition of Shakespeare when I believe instead that to be a decent critic of Shakespeare, as to be a decent director or actor of Shakespeare, means that one must also make one's own editorial decisions about contested lines. Obviously if I were to offer novel editorial suggestions, I'd flag them; but in general I am opposed to unnecessary consistency in citing Shakespeare, as if my acceptance of one reading by Harold Jenkins (for example) would commit me to taking a stand on why I don't accept another reading of his when these readings seem generally non-controversial. "Generally non-controversial": the point of this footnote, and of this essay, is to make a claim for the currently underdefended importance of generality in thinking about Shakespeare, his texts, and his characters.

up the end of the play, but it's *her* fragility that it brings out: the dramatic meaning of the lines in context is the same—and it's the same because the dramatic conflict is between the characters of Cordelia and Lear. This is why it doesn't matter that much whether an actor is word perfect as long as that actor conveys some general aura of stability to an audience. It's the nature of all drama—of all conversation— that variation in what people say doesn't really change who they are for us, though it may help change (deepen, darken, lighten, soften, sadden, rejuvenate, energize, depress) our relation to them. We're interested in the person first, and then because we're interested in the person we are interested in what he or she says. If part of the trick of drama is to show who a person is through what she says, it's also the case that as a play progresses the function of speeches alters from such establishing of character to becoming the primary ways that those established characters take action (and as we'll see also suspend action for something like mutual presence). But this is true early on as well, since the characters are created by actors, and the audience has a sense of their presence, which makes *what* they say what *they* say.

Then an obvious answer to the question what makes characters robust in Shakespeare is: actors do. One way that they do helps illuminate Shakespeare's dramaturgical practice and dramatic vision. In a small and highly successful company like the King's Men, where the leading actors are well-known, there is some inevitable continuity between roles (as there is more recently for Cary Grant, say, or Katharine Hepburn, or Fred Astaire or Meg Ryan), so that Burbage's Hamlet can allude to having played Brutus, and having stabbed the actor playing Polonius when he played Caesar. The recalcitrant theatrical fact of the importance of the individual and individualized actors to the production, a fact that neither Shakespeare nor his audience can dissolve, is also a general human experience and one that Shakespeare thematizes, especially in the late plays.

One way to describe what *The Tempest* says about what it means to grow older is that when you are young you think that the world is full of novel people; but when you are old you discover that the only people there are to work with and form your life around are the people who've been there all along. The great hope that both theater and life create and inevitably disappoint is the endless promise of human novelty. But in the end both playwright and person discover that the people they interacted with and made interact with each other early on are not the cohort of the moment but the people they'll deal with till the end. Younger characters in Shakespeare, and the characters in early Shakespeare, imagine an endless stream of new and interesting people in their lives. It's as though they have a lot of great Shakespeare plays left to see for the first time. But older characters in Shakespeare, and especially older characters in late Shakespeare, come to realize that there is no new friend after Polixenes, no new king after Alonzo. The forgiveness so often celebrated or deplored in the Romances is not the point of the plays, but the manifestation of the fact that if you want to interact with people at all, these are the only people with whom you get to interact. The people who represent the time of life one thought to leave behind are the people who are there at the end. Their human history is not to be put by, either by Prospero or by Shakespeare's audience. The robustness of character is at once the enabling condition of drama and the bittersweet lesson that Shakespeare's characters learn more and more often in his drama, a lesson counter to the promise of meeting new people that drama always makes to both its characters and its audience, a lesson with which both characters and audience must come to terms. Character is destiny: not one's own character so much as that of the settled group of others who will always be the context for one's life. You meet new people when you're young, but only when you're young. The people you meet then are the people you still have to deal with in old age.

That last sentence is one way to give a short summary of *Macbeth*, and of many of the *Macbeth*-like plays. The tyrants in those plays—Macbeth, Richard III, etc. (even Henry IV)—thought that becoming King would open up a new world for them, but it doesn't. Like Richard II, it turns out that they "need friends" (3.2.176), and that the only friends available are their old friends. Kill them—kill Banquo or Buckingham—or exile Cordelia and Kent, and who's left?

I think Shakespeare felt this most strongly in his late plays: not surprisingly since the late plays describe this discovery as one made longitudinally, after having the same friends for many years; and Shakespeare himself could only have made this discovery longitudinally, partly by writing for the same actors for many years. So let's consider a late tyrant: Leontes. His tyranny (and its fate) clearly indicates a spendthrift prodigality in giving up human relationships. He dispenses with Polixenes, and that act of rash wastefulness leads immediately to Camillo's departure and (for Leontes) good riddance; he sends Perdita out to die of exposure; he is willing to see Hermione die in his presence; and he even throws away, perhaps most surprisingly, all reverence for the Oracle. Yet at the end, who surrounds him? Nearly the same people—older, sadder, different, guilt-inducing, but the same people—as those he thought he was abandoning or dismissing at the start.[4]

The crucial moment that sets the tone for the way the play, or fate, or other people, thwart Leontes's attempt to free himself of the people who surround him and define his world is the moment when Paulina comes to expostulate with him about his tyranny. Her sternly fearless rebuke is all too much for him, and he responds:

> Away with that audacious lady!—Antigonus,
> I charg'd thee that she should not come about me:
> I knew she would. (2.3.42–4)

The exasperation of that last line is wonderful. He *knows* her, knows (as Antigonus is about to confirm) that character trumps even his tyrannical control. He's given the order, but even as he gave it he *knew* that it wouldn't be effective. He knew this because he knew her—knew what kind of person Paulina was: knew her character.

---

[4]  Like most of Shakespeare's plays, *The Winter's Tale* conforms to the trajectory towards convergence of all the remaining characters of any importance that Dan Decker identifies as the central story arc of the most successful genre of narrative ever practiced: the standard Hollywood movie. See his *Anatomy of a Screenplay* (Chicago: The Screenwriters Group, 1998).

That expression of exasperation is also his first and crucial concession that he too is defined by others. Drama being what it is, characters are defined by their interactions. Plays show how much what we are is essentially governed by what we know, and what we know is mainly each other. We know others and because what we are is a function of what we know, the others that we know define us and make us known.

Dan Decker is very interested in the type of character that screenwriters call the window. The idea of the window extends and generalizes the older function of the confidant. The window may be but need not be a confidant—only someone whose dramatic presence causes a main character to reveal aspects of herself or of her thinking. Windows are an essential part of drama, since they allow an audience to understand a central character better. But Shakespeare makes a character's selection of and relation to his or her windows an explicit dramatic issue: not only a means but also a subject of representation.[5] By their windows shall characters be known, and so their windows determine them. This is because windows define the perspective or frame the field in which a character has its being. This is a fact of drama: it's how dramatists work. In Shakespeare, characters sense how much they are determined by what others know about them. And so, should they wish to be different people from what they are known to be, they must change who their windows are.

Banishment, as suggested above, is an attempt, perhaps the most frequent in Shakespearean tragedy, by a powerful figure to change the window he's seen through, and sees himself through. Hal first takes Falstaff as a window, and is who he is through his capacity to know Falstaff and the others: "I know you all…" (*1 Henry IV*, 1.2.195). But at the end of *Part II*, he changes who he is by no longer knowing the window character, by banishing Falstaff as window: "I know thee not, old man, fall to thy prayers" (*2 Henry IV*, 5.5.47). This banishment, of course, is correlated with Henry IV's death—that is the closing of another determinative window. What after all puts as much pressure on a character as a parent's censorious judgment? Both Hal and Hamlet reveal themselves through

---

[5]    Diego Arciniegas will argue something similar below about the relation of Salerio and Solanio to Antonio in *Merchant of Venice*. I am also struck by the way Tubal acts as a window for Shylock when he gives him (and us) the information about what Jessica is doing in 3.1: Tubal *also* tortures him, with some relish, in conveying his own *Schadenfreude*, and so is not *merely* a window but someone who has entered into a dramatic relation with Shylock, though his main structural function is to shed light on Shylock's character and motives. In the trial scene Portia will also function as a window onto Shylock ("My deeds upon my head! I crave the law" [4.1.213]), even as Antonio serves as a window to Bassanio's erotic preference-rankings. This is by no means the most important function of Portia or Antonio, but it is *a* main function, since the central thing that Shakespearean drama dramatizes is the revelation of character—to others and to the character himself. This revelation is dramatic because it has the effect of changing action, so just as drama is always about the dynamism that the progressive illumination of character brings with it, window characters are almost always dramatic in Shakespeare: the drama in Shakespeare is the revelation of character under the situational stress of being around others whose characters are likewise being revealed.

their interactions with their fathers by determining their own actions through the revelatory parts they insist on playing in their dynamic relations to those windows.

Acts of banishment are ways by which Shakespeare's characters attempt to take control of their lives; thus, their selection of and their relation to their windows track their motivations. They seek to select their windows, and not just appear through the windows that are a background feature of all drama. So Macbeth rejects (at first) the witches as windows ("I think not of them," 2.1.22) and has to choose between Banquo and Lady Macbeth. Claudius banishes Hamlet—one window—and Hamlet effectively banishes the ghost; what Macbeth says about the witches really is true about Hamlet: from the end of Act 2, when he begins distancing himself from the ghost ("The spirit I have seen / May be a devil," 2.2.598; "death, / The undiscovered country, from whose bourn/ No traveller returns," 3.1.77–9), and certainly after the closet scene, he thinks not of him at all. But Hamlet never turns against his sense of Horatio as window. Othello falls when he selects Iago rather than Cassio as his window. (His courtship of Desdemona had used Brabantio as his window.) Richard III falls when he banishes Buckingham. Lear banishes Kent, his window, but Kent stays with him. Gloucester is saved, his character is saved, when Edgar becomes his window, or when he accepts Edgar as his window.

In other plays, Shakespeare experiments with the converse of banishment, when the window defects: Cressida betrays Troilus; Enobarbus betrays Antony, which makes Antony different and more intense, now that he has no Roman window but only Eros and Cleopatra. Hers are Charmian, and to some extent Iras: Dolabella too, after Antony is gone, but he fails her, fails to understand the truth of what she says about Antony, which is the point: only Antony is an adequate window on Cleopatra. This marks a kind of converse situation from *Romeo and Juliet*: Romeo is banished and Romeo and Juliet no longer frame and save and limit each other. In *The Winter's Tale* Leontes banishes his windows, but then: enter Paulina. Ariel is of course Prospero's window, and Prospero loses Ariel. Contrast this with a comedy like *Twelfth Night*, where the Duke marries Viola, whom he had thought of as a window.

Characters are who they are through their sociological relations: we are determined by our friends, and by what they know about us. When we try to change our friends, we try to change who we are by changing how we are known. The fact that we know them says something about us; the fact that they know us also says something about us; and what we know about each other is in large part the very fact that we know each other the way we know each other. In drama we see who characters are through *their* friends. When they try to banish their friends, they are trying to change who *they* are. Our characters are mutually determined by those whom we really know, whose subjectivity matters to us.[6] Shakespeare saw how telling this dramatic fact was and put it to use.

---

[6]   I hope it's obvious here how much this essay offers moments of practical criticism consistent with Bruce Young's Levinasian argument above, particularly with his central claim that "the primacy of others does not extinguish the inner life. In fact, according to Levinas, the inner life arises precisely in response to the presence of others."

One can note (in a moderately Cavellian way) that what sets Leontes off is Hermione's questioning of Polixenes about him, as though he is becoming too hemmed in by being known.[7] He depends, throughout, on the judgment of others (which is why he is so anxious not to be thought a tyrant), but he also seeks to transcend that judgment and be free of it. So when he says "I knew she would," the slightly sardonic helplessness of those words characterizes him for us and for those around him as someone who can't get around Paulina, and knows that he can't, even after charging his most obedient vassal to keep her away. (Note too that we don't quite think of Antigonus as craven, though he certainly comes close, because he is saved by being used or needed by Paulina and the dream-Hermione as well.)

I think Shakespeare is most explicit about this kind of defining familiarity in his later plays, though I think he's been thinking about this dynamic, or making use of it intuitively, from the start. Take another fairly late moment, from *Antony and Cleopatra*. Antony is raging against Cleopatra's dalliance with Thidias's offers, and he rails against Cleopatra through a series of ranting speeches, which she checks with half-lines, knowing that she "must stay his time" (3.13.155). She knows this because she knows him. Finally, as he is running out of steam, she asks:

> Cleopatra:                    Not know me yet?
> Antony:   Cold-hearted toward me? (57–8)

It's here that finally he does know her, and so becomes himself again:

> Cleopatra:                    It is my birthday:
> I had thought t'have held it poor; but since my lord
> Is Antony again, I will be Cleopatra. (184–86)

He is Antony when he knows her, and then of course she is Cleopatra, even reborn as Cleopatra, when he knows her.[8] Antony is himself sublimely well-known: past the size of dreaming, as she will say (against Dolabella's incredulity), and as Enobarbus will confirm (against a soldier's incredulity). When Antony sends Enobarbus's treasure after him, the soldier assumes that his report of this fact cannot be believed:

> Soldier:                    Enobarbus, Antony
> Hath after thee sent all thy treasure, with
> His bounty overplus: the messenger
> Came on my guard; and at thy tent is now
> Unloading of his mules.

---

[7]   See Stanley Cavell, "Recounting Gains, Showing Losses: Reading *The Winter's Tale*," in *Disowning Knowledge in Seven Plays of Shakespeare* (Cambridge: Cambridge University Press, 2003), 193–221, esp. 212.

[8]   Laura Quinney makes a similar argument in "Enter a Messenger," in *William Shakespeare's Antony and Cleopatra*, ed., Harold Bloom (New York: Chelsea House, 1988), 151–67.

| | |
|---|---|
| Enobarbus: | I give it you. |
| Soldier: Mock not, Enobarbus. | |
| I tell you true. (4.6.19–24) | |

But Enobarbus is not mocking. He recognizes immediately that Antony has done this, and he recognizes this because he knows Antony. He knows Antony's character. Such knowledge goes very deep, being the stuff of the love between Antony and Cleopatra, but also the nature of what both he and Antony have most deeply become. If characters are essentially defined by what they know about others, defined that is by what they *can* know about others and therefore what they have to know about others, their most intense experiences are always mediated by such knowledge, sometimes very explicitly.

I want to stress what might seem to be the obvious importance of the fact that dramatic characters exist in and through their interaction because this is an essential feature of Shakespeare's depiction of character and of his sense of what character is, and not merely a means to such depiction. The line that runs from Coleridge to Bradley to Bloom sometimes risks losing sight of this essential social point: no character, even when alone, is alone. Shakespeare's characters are more essentially characters for each other before they are characters for us. They can be characters for us only because they are already characters, because they already know each other, and create themselves and each other out of the knowledge of others that organizes the soul of each.

This is another way of pressing the idea of recognition in the plays. Everything I say here applies in an obvious way to the comedies as well: in our reliance, for example, on Portia to understand, to *get*, Bassanio well enough to manipulate him into choosing the right casket and to give up the ring, and well enough to see what can be made of him despite his fecklessness, or (in a different mode) our reliance on Beatrice to understand that Hero could not have done what she's accused of, or (in a still different mode) on Petruchio to really get Kate, to see what she really is.

Or consider the nice and complex way that Theseus woos Hippolyta in Act V of *A Midsummer Night's Dream*, when he describes how he understood why the great clerks became "tongue-tied" (5.1.104) around him. They couldn't remember or recite the speeches that they thought would show their devotion, but this was all to the good: "Trust me, sweet, / Out of this silence yet I pick'd a welcome" (99–100). She *can* trust him now, because the very fact that he is capable of understanding silence as welcome, proved in his ability to understand and give this very account, underwrites the trust he desires. She'll trust him because he knows what the clerks mean beyond what they manage to say—and also because he knows of her that this is just the thing to win her trust. Hermione's sorrow for Leontes touches on the same trust: "I never wish'd to see you sorry, now / I trust I shall" (2.1.123–24). She knows that he's not himself—not himself because he does not know her. The trust that Theseus hopes and rightly anticipates from Hippolyta is the trust that Hermione still has in Leontes: in what she knows he really is, in what she knows (rightly) about him more than he knows about himself. Such a moment is an essential feature of the reciprocal effects of knowledge that I am trying to bring out: that much of what she is displays itself at this moment where she understands much of what he is.

I can't imagine that this argument is really controversial, so I would like to identify and give two clear examples of a different scenic dynamic that I think is to be found in some form or other throughout Shakespeare's work, from *The Comedy of Errors* through the Romances: a kind of subliminal recognition scene. It is a scene and dynamic that Falstaff claims as his own but of course fails to live up to when he tells Hal that he's seen through his disguise: "I knew ye as well as him that made ye" (*1 Henry IV*, 2.4.267–68). Knowing others even when they are disguised speaks to one's own character. Beatrice recognizes the disguised Benedick, and that makes her Beatrice. (Lear does not quite recognize the disguised Kent, and that makes him pitiable.) My first example is (as usual) from *The Winter's Tale*: Paulina rebukes Leontes for praising Perdita's beauty:

> Florizel:  Step forth mine advocate; at your request
>            My father will grant precious things as trifles.
> Leontes:   Would he do so, I'd beg your precious mistress,
>            Which he counts but a trifle.
> Paulina:   Sir, my liege,
>            Your eye hath too much youth in't: not a month
>            'Fore your queen died, she was more worth such gazes
>            Than what you look on now.
> Leontes:   I thought of her,
>            Even in these looks I made. (5.1.221–28)

How did Florizel come to ask Leontes (of all people!) for help? Well, Florizel knows his father. He knows his father loves Leontes still. We think the better both of Florizel and of Polixenes because of this fact, especially after Polixenes has himself shown his own tendencies towards petty tyranny in his oppression of Florizel and Perdita. One reason we think the better of Polixenes is that Florizel does know this of him—of him and of the Leontes he has learned about from his father. But the center of this scene, of course, is Leontes's response to Perdita. He recognizes her as precious to him. Everyone sees the faint family-romance suggestion here, which recurs in the Romances. Indeed Paulina underlines it. (Does she know who Perdita is? Not yet, according to the plot, but I think the answer is: of course she does.) More important than the Oedipal hint is the *gentleness of knowledge* it now shows in Leontes, whose knowledge had failed so abysmally. He recognizes Hermione's daughter in Perdita: "I thought of her / Even in these looks I made." In contrast to his earlier relation to Mamillius, who makes him think of himself, Perdita makes him think of his wife. He recognizes something deep and important there, without knowing it. We recognize him recognizing it, and that is a further and major step towards his rehabilitation in our eyes.

An even more complex interaction of a very similar sort occurs in *King Lear*. After his blinding, Gloucester is poorly led into Edgar's presence. He asks the old man who is there, and the old man leading him replies that it's poor Mad Tom. Gloucester's response is to recall seeing a similar beggar the night before—though he doesn't realize that this is the same person:

> I' the last night's storm I such a fellow saw;
> Which made me think a man a worm: my son
> Came then into my mind; and yet my mind
> Was then scarce friends with him: I have heard more since. (4.1.32–5)

I find these lines very haunting. Gloucester is not merely the sum of his plot-functions, one of which is to be the deceived father. He has given up on Edgar, renounced him and felt himself forced into being an autonomous agent, even if a sad one. (His autonomy is shown in his willingness to succor Lear on the heath, against Regan's and Cornwall's orders.) But then he thinks of Edgar, not to any purpose or with any result. It's not even that he recognized him subliminally; that formulation (which I suggested above) is itself a crude simplification. It's rather that the absent Edgar was present to him at that moment, as he is present to him at this one. The deep and crucial effect of this scene is that Gloucester isn't mourning an absent person, a scenario with which we are familiar since the dawn of elegy. Edgar's absence or evanescence or irreality is more profound than that. His *presence* brings out the extent to which what Gloucester is is Edgar's father. He stands against the claim that character is a function of dramatic interaction, the claim that people do what they do for the purposes of advancing scene and plot. Mourning the absent is just as much a mode of interaction as speaking to an interlocutor who is present. But Gloucester does neither. Edgar is there, but not for Gloucester, and yet Edgar turns out to be everywhere for Gloucester. His character is ultimately built on his love for Edgar. (Again, this is what enables us to forgive his brutality, as we will forgive Leontes's.) Edgar's presence has nothing to do with this, not even in the attenuated mode of absence. Rather it is Edgar who defines Gloucester: for Gloucester what it means to be human is for Edgar to come into his mind; and for everyone what it means to be human is to know other people. This is the reason that Gloucester's greatest depth of character is shown in those scenes where he and Edgar are together without his knowing it.[9]

I think this scene is a particularly intense example of a more general aspect of the deepest dramatic experiences Shakespeare makes possible, the experience of the characters' fullness rather than their actions. Screenwriters talk about the "lost point," the place in the script where the main character seems completely blocked from reaching the goal the story has established. This moment is one of the most interesting crises or inflection points in the story. Decker, one of the best critics of Shakespeare I have read (though he never mentions him) says that this is one of the likeliest points for the main character's goal to change—sometimes to become

---

[9]    I discuss this relationship beyond presence and absence, in terms I more or less learned from Levinas's close friend Maurice Blanchot, at some greater length in *Generosity and the Limits of Authority: Shakespeare, Herbert, Milton* (Ithaca: Cornell University Press, 1992), 183–86.

enriched, perhaps by becoming more subtle or evincing more understanding. In Shakespeare that enrichment tends to take the form of a pause—usually a long one—in which original, plot-driving goals are suspended and we get to share just the presence of characters (to our minds, to each others' minds: "my son / Came then into my mind") without their being functions or agents of plot at all any more. I think it's the fact that we are given these experiences in Shakespeare, these long spells of resignation to the world as it is, that makes it seem so right to discuss and analyze Shakespeare's characters as though they had real psychologies and depths rather than being vehicles of the plot. We spend an inordinate amount of time with them when they are just being themselves—whether in tragedy (Hamlet after the shipwreck, Lear or Edgar and Gloucester after the storm) or in comedy (in the Forest of Arden or near the Bohemian seacoast or in the prison of Vienna). These scenes are wonderful when decently staged. We feel that we've passed into another world, made the transition from motives we must decode to a world where the characters are at home with each other, no longer want anything from each other because there's no more to want. I think this tends to happen about two hours into a play, when we have come to know the *actors*, when the real people on stage have become familiar to us. It's a sort of Indian Summer feeling in the plays—seasonless even as time grows short. I keep wondering about something that theater people must know: how long does it take to get to that time in a play? How long, how much stress, must we experience before we feel at home in this strange syncope of homelessness? Somehow Shakespeare times it perfectly (Fellini too, I'd say), but what does that timing consist of? I'd imagine it has something to do with the audience's effort of sustained attention. When we are attentive to others for a long time, we ascribe the same attentiveness to them—otherwise we wouldn't stay attentive to them. And after an hour or two, we expect that the masks will fall. That's when Shakespeare has his characters start speaking directly, seriously, without manipulation. That's when time slows and characters start feeling real, as though time is a wave moving through the medium of character, focusing attention on the medium and not what's moving through it. We become aware of Shakespeare's characters as modulations of our own attentiveness, and so we're aware of them as aware of each other's awareness of each other, with all that this means of shared introspection, of a sense of the other's subjectivity. It's an amazing thing, the deference to full humanity that they earn. And it has everything to do with the time we've spent with them in the theater. It is always Indian Summer in Ilyria, and that's one reason why we want convergence at the end: the feeling that everyone we've shared this experience with, all the actors and all the characters, are there at the end.

This does not prevent endings from being surprising. But the way characters surprise—from the Abbess in *The Comedy of Errors* to Paulina and Hermione in *The Winter's Tale*—always has to do with confirming depths or aspects of their characters that we recognize, *re*-cognize, notice and note again, and not for the first time. They surprise but they don't startle, and the surprise is that we still haven't quite recognized this last depth in them, even as they come into our minds, even as we know in general terms what they will do.

I want to conclude by citing one other example of the constitution of character through recognition and understanding, one other example of the way characters are most deeply defined in the moment that they recognize other characters. I cite *Richard II* here, partly because Bradley doesn't like Richard, and thinks that he fails to be a great tragic figure (1991, 38 n.1). But Bullingbrook disagrees, and it's Bullingbrook's recognition of Richard as a tragic figure that makes both him and Richard as great and moving as they are. At Flint Castle, for example, it's Bullingbrook who most understands what Richard is doing, and most sympathizes with him. The strange, austere, and immaterial sympathy that Bullingbrook shows Richard throughout the second half of the play is what makes the play so compelling. Bullingbrook's regret at what he fully intends to do to Richard, and Richard's insistence on helping Bullingbrook do it, make for a scene of mutual understanding that allows us to see in their relationship something like the quickness of understanding between Antony and Cleopatra, or even between Claudius and Gertrude. One of the most moving surprises of *Hamlet* is the moment when Gertrude begins telling Claudius of the death of Polonius: "Ah, mine own lord, what have I seen tonight!" (4.1.5). Her tenderness towards him, and his tender reception of her tenderness, minister to a deep sense of their characters. So too is Bullingbrook tender to Richard, and Richard is most moving as a figure when he both recognizes and expects that tenderness, when he knows that Bullingbrook will fetch him a looking-glass if he asks for one, just as he expects tenderness from Bullingbrook in the moment of shared recognition of the outcome of their conflict:

| Richard: | What you will have, I'll give, and willing too; |
| | For do we must what force will have us do. |
| | Set on towards London, cousin, is it so? |
| Bullingbrook: | Yea, my good lord. |
| Richard: | Then I must not say no. (3.3.206–209) |

Richard is forced to give up his kingdom, but also and more profoundly he is willing to do it. He and Bullingbrook have, strangely, become friends: hence the hauntingly sorrowful "Yea, my good lord." For Richard to be human is (as I quoted him saying before) to "need friends." Bullingbrook is such a friend, his opaque character finally defined in the spectral friendship he has for Richard (just like Gloucester's spectral friendship for Edgar)—"I ... love him murdered" (5.6.40)—just as Richard's is finally defined in his recognition and participation in this spectral friendship. (It is a similar friendship that Iago attempts and parodies.) We could sum up this argument by saying that a proper recognition of the nature of character, in literature and in life, is that character is irreducibly social, irreducibly arises between people. But we should stress, equally, that the fact that the human world is irreducibly social means that character and personality form themselves out of the recognition of character and personality. To be human, in Shakespeare as in life, is to recognize other humans, and to recognize them as the people who will and should define one's own life.

# Chapter 4
# Wopsle's Revenge, or, Reading Hamlet as Character in *Great Expectations*[1]

James E. Berg

"How did you like my reading of the character, gentlemen?" Mr. Wopsle, the ridiculous former clergyman from Pip's childhood, the Polonius-figure who has decided to take up acting by assuming the role of Hamlet, asks this question in the thirty-first chapter of *Great Expectations*, which tells the story of a failed performance of Shakespeare's best-known play.[2] Pip and his friend Herbert, ushered backstage by Wopsle's costume designer, respond with a mixture of amusement and pity, inviting Wopsle home for a long *post-mortem* over supper. What to make of the little episode, which seems of minor consequence to the plot of the novel, has long preoccupied critics.[3] The chapter first appeared in *All the Year Round* (the magazine in which *Great Expectations* was published in serial form) just as a performance of *Hamlet* starring a favorite of Dickens, the renowned Shakespearean actor Albert Fechter, opened in London. Perhaps, despite elaborate theories to the contrary, it was merely inserted for the nonce. George J. Worth thinks the broad resemblances it brings to mind between *Hamlet* and *Great Expectations*

[1]     Special thanks to Mark Bayer and Gretchen Minton, the directors of the 2006 Shakespeare Association of America seminar on "Shakespeare's Literary Afterlives" for providing an occasion for the original draft of this essay and for their subsequent suggestions. Thanks also to Yu Jin Ko, Edward Tayler, and Martha Woodruff for offering encouragement and suggestions.

[2]     Charles Dickens, *Great Expectations* (1861; repr., London: Oxford University Press, 1953), 242. All subsequent references to the novel are from this edition.

[3]     See, for instance, John Hagan Jr. "Structural Patterns in Dickens's *Great Expectations*," *ELH* 21, no. 1 (1954): 54–66, esp. 62; William Axton, "'Keystone Structure' in Dickens' Novels," *University of Toronto Quarterly* 37, no. 1 (1967): 31–50, esp. 48–50; Robert F. Flessner, *Dickens and Shakespeare: A Study in Histrionic Contrasts* (New York: Haskell, 1965); James D. Berry, "Wopsle Once More," *Dickensian* 64 (1968): 43–7; A.L. French, "Beating and Crying: *Great Expectations*," *Essays in Criticism* 24 (1974): 147–68, esp. 147–48; William A. Wilson, "The Magic Circle of Genius: Dickens's Translations of Shakespearean Drama in *Great Expectations*," *Nineteenth-Century Fiction* 40 (1985): 154–74; esp. 159; George J. Worth, "Mr. Wopsle's Hamlet: 'Something Too Much of This'," *Dickens Studies Annual: Essays on Victorian Fiction* 17 (1988): 35–46. Among the most recent entries into this conversation, and one of the most interesting, occurs in Alexander Welsh, *Hamlet in His Modern Guises* (Princeton and Oxford: Princeton University Press, 2001), 102–39.

are more "accidental" than "essential."[4] But even if the installment was merely a stalling for time—a topical interlude designed to keep *Great Expectations* going and Pip "alive" through March, 1861—there is something worthy of pause in Wopsle's choice of the phrase "my reading of the character." The episode has much to tell about Dickens's sense of the nature of literary "character," and what *does* keep "a character" such as Hamlet, or Pip, "alive," rendering "him" more than mere reading material, more than the mere sign or semblance of a person.

Or to put that another way, the episode has much to tell about what it means, for Dickens, to make character seem like *more* than character This becomes obvious if we stick rigorously to the most precise, current critical usage of "character," which designates "person in story" or "role in play." For insofar as this term "character" names (as Stephen Orgel puts it) the "elements of a linguistic structure, lines in a drama, and, more basically, words on a page" that represent persons, it serves, in itself, as a reminder that the persons on stage or in a novel are artificial, that they are constructed out of signifying material—reading material.[5] Today, for rhetorical reasons probably pertaining to the aesthetic values assumed to be implicit in character criticism, the term "character" is occasionally conflated with what should really be called "a certain *kind* of character": the "three-dimensional," "complex," "lifelike" character who seems to have an inner psyche—the kind often preferred because it actually hides the nature of character as figure designed to be interpreted, or, in the broadest sense, *read*.[6] In my view (and in Dickens's usage) this is actually the kind of character that makes us *forget* it is character, and certainly *not* the only kind of character there is. Hence, when Wopsle says, "How did you like my *reading* of the character," he inadvertently reminds his interlocutors that Hamlet *is* character, in the sense of *reading material*.

Wopsle's phrase "reading of the character," in fact, signals his *inability* to render character more than character, his inability to make Hamlet himself more than mere "text," in the broadest sense, to be deciphered. It suggests continuity between the "character" as known to Shakespeare, resonant as this word was with the ancient Greek, χαρακτήρ (as in "writing" or "engraving") and a modern novelist's sense of "character." When Shakespeareans study the *dramatis personae* in the plays, we often seek, for fear of the charge of anachronism or essentialism, any name for literary figures of persons ("subject position," "impersonation," etcetera) other than that notorious c-word, banishing that to the territory of the novel, or to the realm of method acting. We may concede that sixteenth- and seventeenth-

---

    4    Worth, "Mr Wopsle's Hamlet," 38.

    5    Stephen Orgel, "What is a Character?" in *The Authentic Shakespeare and other Problems of the Early Modern Stage* (London: Routledge, 2002), 8.

    6    Alan Sinfield's chapter "When is a Character Not a Character?" which is in many ways a profound contribution to Shakespeare criticism, features a prominent example of such tendentious (and, I believe, questionable) usage. See *Faultlines: Cultural Materialism and the Politics of Dissident Reading* (Berkeley: University of California Press, 1992), 153–79.

century uses of the term "character" were frequently associated, as in the ancient Theophrastan tradition, with the features and behaviors of persons.[7] But they did not, we explain, encompass what the term "character" has come to imply: a complex, "three-dimensional," "inward psyche" who undergoes "growth" and "change," who seems to have a presence above the page or between the lines. They implied a rigid and unchanging signifying mark, or stamp, or seal, or handwriting expressive of some unchanging, readable aspect of a person.[8]

The *Hamlet* episode in *Great Expectations* challenges a common assumption to which this valid point has often given rise, an assumption that critics continue to make despite occasional demonstrations of its inaccuracy: that the old, figural understanding of character is alien to the concept of character as it applies to nineteenth-century novelistic personification, which so often seeks to provide the illusion that literary characters transcend text as if they were people one might

---

[7]     The first English version of Theophrastan charactery appeared in 1608 in Hall's *Characters of the Virtues and Vices*, but there were Latin and even Greek versions available in England during the sixteenth century as well. As Donald Beecher observes, "Editions of Theophrastus containing up to fifteen of the characters started appearing as early as 1517, with new editions-at least one each decade-thereafter," and adds, "Theophrastus' *Characters* was decidedly present throughout the century, although principally as a philological challenge. It was not until late in the century that scholars began to 'read' him in relation to social data carried in his portraits." (See *Sir Thomas Overbury [And Others], Characters* [Ottowa: Dovehouse Editions, 2003].) Still, the concept of character as something to be associated with personhood would have been prevalent early, as well as late, in Shakespeare's career. Recruiting Theridimas, Marlowe's Tamburlaine asks, in 1588, "Art thou but captain of a thousand horse, /That by characters graven in thy brows,/ And by thy martial face and stout aspect,/ Deserv'st to have the leading of an host?" (1.2.167– 70). (Irving Ribner, ed. *The Complete Plays of Christopher Marlowe* [New York: Odyssey Press, 1963]). In Nashe's *Unfortunate Traveller* (first published in 1594), a combatant in the Earl of Surrey's joust has a mountain-like mount, "under" which, we are told, "did he *characterize* a man desirous to climb to the heaven of honour, kept under with the mountain of his prince's command, and yet had he arms and legs exempted from the suppression of that mountain" (*The Unfortunate Traveller and Other Works*, ed. J. B. Steane [London: Penguin Books, 1985], 320–321). Shakespeare's Sonnet 108, speculating that all creation, including people, was originally pre-scribed, conjures the image of the beloved appearing in an "antique book" written when "mind at first in character was done." *Shakespeare's Sonnets*, ed., Stephen Booth (New Haven and London: Yale University Press, 1977).

[8]     The work of Peter Thomson is eloquent in articulating this perspective—and quite reasonable insofar as it uses the concept of character as signifying mark to distinguish between early modern acting techniques and Stanislavskian method acting. But insofar as it views literary character as something "internal," it is symptomatic, I think, of what has caused critics to miss out on opportunities that might be afforded by a return to character study. See "Rogues and Rhetoricians: Acting Styles in Early English Drama," in *A New History of Early English Drama*, eds., David Scott Kastan and John D. Cox (New York: Columbia University Press, 1998), 321–35.

meet.[9] The modern literary imitation of person, which provides the illusion that the person in the text can be encountered as a "thou," a *meetable person*, rather than an "it" (a mere collection of signifying materials) does not, in my opinion, require a concept of character radically transformed from "character" in its more literal early modern sense.[10] Indeed, as I shall suggest with an examination of the *Hamlet* episode, truly understanding how such a novelist as Dickens achieves a sense of personhood for characters may *require* something closer to Shakespeare's sense of character than one might think.[11] For Dickens dramatically reveals, in this episode, that he has either absorbed or rediscovered the fundamentals of a Shakespearean magic of characterization, the neglect of which would render a Hamlet figure utterly "flat," utterly recognizable as mere character.[12] He apparently grasps the Shakespearean insight that, in the world of the text, one of the most effective ways to make characters seem more than character is to arrange circumstances so that the readers of the text encounter them as characters-in-the-midst-of-reading— characters reading other characters, or even reading themselves as characters.[13]

It might be objected that in exploring what makes characters seem like people one could meet, I am forgetting the context of dramatic performance—forgetting the obvious facts that Shakespeare wrote for the theater and Dickens loved the theater. A good actor can lend liveliness to any character, and an imaginative reader can do the same for any character in a novel. But this fails to explain why certain

---

[9]   One such demonstration, now over twenty years old, but still quite timely and worthy of study, occurs in Harold Fisch's "Character as Linguistic Sign," *New Literary History,* 21, no. 3 (1982): 592–606. More recent is Christy Desmet's *Reading Shakespeare's Characters: Rhetoric, Ethics, and Identity* (Amherst: University of Massachusetts Press, 1992), 36–58, in which Desmet observes resemblances between seventeenth-century Theophrastan characters and modern novelistic characters.

[10]   The language is Martin Buber's, quoted in Fisch, 605 and n. 24. See *I and Thou*, trans., Ronald Gregor Smith (Edinburgh: T. and T. Clark, 1959).

[11]   Such older identifications of "character" with person or personal attribute derive, perhaps, from a sense of creation itself, including human creatures, as a collection of signifying *figures*. The idea of the *figura* is famously discussed by Erich Auerbach in his essay "Figura," in *Scenes from the Drama of European Literature* (New York: Meridian Books, 1959), 11–76; and, most recently, in Lisa Freinkel, *Reading Shakespeare's Will: The Theology of Figure from Augustine to the Sonnets* (New York: Columbia University Press, 2002). The related conceit of the world as a book of characters is discussed in Ernst Robert Curtius, *European Literature and the Latin Middle Ages*, trans., Willard R. Trask (Princeton: Princeton University Press, 1953), 319–47.

[12]   It is not my purpose to determine the extent of Shakespeare's "influence" on Dickens in this respect. But it is interesting to note how thoroughly Dickens was steeped in Shakespeare. For a discussion of his remarkable memory for Shakespeare's plays, see Valerie L. Gager, *Shakespeare and Dickens: The Dynamics of Influence* (Cambridge: Cambridge University Press, 1990).

[13]   For a brilliant discussion, in terms of post-structuralist reader-response and rhetorical theory, of how *Hamlet* fosters identification with characters through the activity of reading, see Desmet, 10–34.

characters encountered in *reading* appear to be more than character, while others appear merely to be characters. Hamlet leaps off the *page*, and even if this leaping depends largely on decisions by readers and actors, the decisions must take place at some point during the readings of the text.[14] Certainly in the nineteenth century, it was the Hamlet readers read, as much as the Hamlets they saw on the stage, who came across as the paragon of the textual character, who seemed like more than text, and of whom Hazlitt was famously inspired to say, "It is *we* who are Hamlet." "It may seem a paradox," remarked Charles Lamb when writing of *Hamlet*, "But I cannot help being of the opinion that the plays of Shakespeare are less calculated for performance on a stage than those of any other dramatist whatever."[15] Even nineteenth-century drama critics tended to see Hamlet as a soul emergent from text, prior to being acted—one whom the player of Hamlet needed to mimic, rather than produce. James Hackett, in his pan of Macready's Hamlet (published in 1863), insisted, "a great artist owes it to his own pretensions to study closely, discern and try to penetrate, and to develop with fidelity in his portraiture, the most delicate recesses in Hamlet's mind."[16] And G. H. Lewes, lauding Fechter's performance, observed that the actor was "lymphatic, delicate, handsome, and with his long flaxen curls, quivering sensitive nostrils, fine eye, and sympathetic voice. [sic] perfectly represents the graceful prince."[17] Remarkably Lewes seems to read and interpret Fechter's physiognomy as if Fechter were a character and Hamlet a human being.

Dickens's Wopsle upends Fechter's humble reduction of himself to a character representing the person of Hamlet. Wopsle's Hamlet is the caricature of the three-dimensional personage flattened into something read. So emphatic is this caricature that, for Edward Said, the *Hamlet* episode anticipates the Derridean challenge to the "privilege given by Western metaphysics to voice over writing."[18] Said argues

---

[14]    It is worth considering too that, as Lukas Erne has suggested, Hamlet was as much written for reading as it was performance, and early performances of Hamlet may have made do with "flatter" characters than did the early readings. See Erne's *Shakespeare as Literary Dramatist* (Cambridge: Cambridge University Press, 2003), 240–44. Oddly enough, Erne's hypothesis may be compatible with the insights of Leslie Wade Soule, which cast the actor as subverter of the character: in the theater, the character may have come across as flat in part because the actor rendered himself round at the character's expense. See *Actor as Anti-Character: Dionysus, the Devil, and the Boy Rosalind* (Westport, CT: Greenwood Press, 2000).

[15]    *Critical Responses to* Hamlet, Volume 2: 1790–1838, ed., David Farley-Hills (New York: AMS Press, 1996), 101.

[16]    "William Charles Macready as Hamlet, New York, 1826 and 1843" in *Critical Responses to* Hamlet, *1600-1900, Volume Three: 1839-1854*, ed., David Farley-Hills (New York: AMS Press, 1996), 29.

[17]    G. H. Lewes, "Fechter in Hamlet and Othello." *Blackwood's Magazine* 40 (December 1861), 745.

[18]    Edward Said, "The Problem of Textuality: Two Exemplary Positions," *Critical Inquiry* 4, no. 4 (1978): 673–714, esp. 688.

that the episode makes the text itself of *Hamlet* loom large as something without intrinsic authenticity. Remarkably, this argument complements the violence Wopsle does to the nineteenth-century illusion of Hamlet as person. Hamlet is exposed as text, read as character, reduced to the status of signifying mark, what "we" are *not*. Instead of bringing Hamlet alive as one of us, Wopsle's performance employs, as Pip observes, "elocution … very slow, very dreary, very uphill and down-hill, and very unlike any way in which any man in any natural circumstances of life or death ever expressed himself about anything" (1953, 241). Again, this is precisely the opposite of Fechter's purported achievement: "Our sympathies are completely secured. And as he endeavours to *act*, not to *declaim* the part, we feel that we have Hamlet the Dane before us." By contrast, Wopsle is prone to slip back to his days of scriptural sermonizing, as his designating the performance a "service," as opposed to a "representation" (the word with which he immediately corrects the slip), suggests (1953, 243). His forgetting any pretense of realism—his dusting his hand with a pocket handkerchief after holding Yorick's skull—suggests a presentation of a character to be read, rather than met, to spectators demanding to meet Hamlet rather than read him. Wopsle has reduced the great foundation of Romanticism, Hamlet the "real" person, to hieroglyph. Rather than a realistic illusion easily mistaken for what it represents, the very dishevelment accompanying Hamlet's antic disposition is now a sartorial pictogram pointing away from itself: Wopsle's Hamlet appears wearing the emblem of a disordered stocking, "its disorder expressed, according to usage, by one very neat fold in the top" (1953, 240).[19] Here Wopsle comes near to seeming extra-textual himself by doing spectacular violence to the extra-textual "nature" of Hamlet (the notion of Hamlet as "real person"), everywhere flattening Hamlet—even Hamlet on stage—into text.

Such flattening into text is possible, even though the reading character (in this case, Wopsle) and the character to be read (in this case Hamlet) are both text in the first place, because, of course, there is more than one "layer" or "level" of text. There is text represented as text within text. The *Hamlet* episode is Wopsle's "reading" of Hamlet, in turn read by Pip, and Pip's reading of Wopsle-as-Hamlet, in turn read by me. But if this layering and the enlivening effect I am discussing are to occur, if we are to feel we meet, in the text, a reading character *in the act of reading*, it is not only the interpretation of *text* that must be represented but the *process* of interpretation. Comprehension must not seem immediate; the character-reader must *struggle* to read: once a character has reached comprehension and is therefore no longer reading, there is nothing to get in the way of our recognizing him as reading material, as character, rather than as reading companion. In *Great*

---

[19]   Such a neat fold representing Hamlet's madness may be found in the illustration for *Hamlet* in Nicholas Rowe's 1709 illustrated edition of Shakespeare's plays. See *Hamlet, Prince of Denmark* in *The Works of William Shakespear: in six volumes, adorned with cuts*, vol. 5. (London: Jacob Tonson, 1709). Perhaps this is where Dickens got the idea. If so, the fold in the stocking is emblematic of the idea of a Hamlet confined to a book, a Hamlet who is, through and through, reading material, despite the fact that he is also, as in the illustration, on stage.

*Expectations*, as in *Hamlet*, making a struggle out of reading entails a significant expansion of how we conventionally define "text" and "reading" (unless the character is barely literate enough to grasp this printed or written matter as text, and so gets the chance to struggle with what, to a novel-reader, would seem elementary). The novel conjures, accordingly, a world more immediately familiar to Shakespeare than to us—a world that *is* a text but not so immediately decipherable as text that the reading of it can be taken for granted. Such is the world in which Shakespeare's Vincentio can mystify Angelo by saying, "There is a kind of character in thy life/That to th'oberver doth thy history fully unfold"; or in which Fluellen, citing "figures in all things," can (in struggling to read) absurdly suggest that Henry V and Alexander, with their respective friends Falstaff and Clytus, were signifiers with related meanings; or in which Hamlet can provoke our doubts about his reading skills by calling his sinful father "a combination and a form indeed,/Where every god did seem to set his seal/To give the world assurance of a man."[20] It is a world in which, as Sir Thomas Browne puts it, "[t]here are mystically in our faces certaine characters ... wherein he that cannot read A, B, C, may read our natures"—a world in the process of being recognized as a tissue of signs to be parsed syntactically, *figured out*.[21]

Browne perhaps makes such reading sound easier than it is. Reading *things* is slow and hard, if not impossible, except to God and perhaps the gifted soothsayer, who at best can boast, "In nature's infinite book of secrecy/A little can I read."[22] As sixteenth-century theologian Andreas Hyperius warned, "truly to marke things that happen in this uisible worlde ... to examine what signification they have as touching the power, the righteousnesse, or goodnesse, of God ... is a thing verie difficult." But like Polonius in Shakespeare's play, Wopsle's Hamlet is a figure never struggling through such a process of reading. He is frozen and immovable, or in Herbert and Pip's words, "massive and concrete" (1953, 242). There are of course reasons for this as pertinent to Pip's narrative as to Wopsle's incompetence. But I take these as the narrative's way of parodying Wopsle's approach. I also take them as a negative indication of what kinds of structural devices are conducive to the emergence of characters who do come across as readers.

It is significant in this regard that Pip omits from the account any hint of a *revenge* plot. As Alexander Welsh demonstrates, the revenge plot is what *Hamlet* and *Great Expectations* have most pervasively in common, so the absence of it from the most extended explicit reference to *Hamlet* in the novel warrants some attention.[23] Presumably, Pip remains silent about revenge in his discussion of

---

[20]   These quotations, from *Measure for Measure*, 1.1.27–9; *Henry V*, 4.7.22–39; and *Hamlet*, 3.4.60–61, are taken from *The Riverside Shakespeare*, 2nd ed., G. Blakemore Evans (New York: Houghton Mifflin, 1997). All subsequent quotations from *Hamlet* are from *The Riverside Shakespeare*.

[21]   Sir Thomas Browne, *Religio Medici and Other Works*, ed., L.C. Martin (1643; repr., Oxford: Clarendon Press, 1964), 57.

[22]   Antony and Cleopatra, in *The Riverside Shakespeare* (1.2.10–11).

[23]   Welsh, 102–139.

Wopsle's performance because the plot of *Hamlet* is common knowledge among the literate. But the omission also suggests that the context that is Hamlet's situation is so taken for granted in Wopsle's performance as to go unnoticed—that it is in performance as well as summary, too obvious, too easily read, too tired to be remembered. What with the distracting behavior of the actors and the laughing audience bent sarcastically on taking lines out of context, the *Hamlet* Pip describes amounts to a taking-for-granted of the very theme that makes *Hamlet Hamlet*. Tellingly, Pip's summary begins not with the mysterious appearance of the ghost (the author of the revenge) but with the holding of court by the king and queen. Then it jumps without delay from episode to episode. Even the descriptions of what we know to be motives and cues for, as well as acts of, revenge are emptied of any sense of struggle, and therefore any attention to process, as in this summary of the events occurring between Ophelia's funeral and Hamlet's killing of Claudius:

> The arrival of the body for interment (in an empty black box with the lid tumbling open), was the signal for a general joy which was much enhanced by the discovery, among the bearers, of an individual obnoxious to identification. The joy attended Mr Wopsle through his struggle with Laertes on the brink of the orchestra and the grave, and slackened no more until he had tumbled the king off the kitchen-table, and had died by inches from the ankles upward. (1953, 240)

The passage, like the narration of the rest of the episode, strongly implies that the revenge process missing from the account of the performance was also unnoticeable in performance itself. Ophelia's funeral procession did not, in the performance, plausibly prompt the vengeful quarrel between Hamlet and Laertes; instead, it "was a signal for" the spectators' joy; nor *was* the death of Hamlet apparently Laertes's revenge for the death of Polonius (which is never mentioned in the summary); rather, it *was*, likewise, a cue for merriment. The result is a sequence of poses that gives the characters posed no challenge in figuring out their meaning in the plot—no opportunity to struggle to read themselves and each other.

This is crucial, if so obvious as often to be overlooked. Revenge as represented in *Hamlet* is an emphatically readerly event, so that its absence from Wopsle's performance dries up a well-spring for the acts of reading that pervade the play. As Frederick Kiefer points out, Elizabethan revenge has deep associations with images of books and writing—or, I would add, with the reading material that is character in the Shakespearean sense. Emblematic of these associations is Hamlet's entrance "reading upon a book" just after he has sworn to take vengeance with "wings as swift as meditation or thoughts of love."[24] Nor did Shakespeare

---

[24]   Chapter 5 of Frederick Kiefer's *Writing on the Renaissance Stage: Written Words, Printed Pages, Metaphoric Books* (Cranbury, NJ: Associated University Presses, 1996), deftly unpacks theological, literary, and theatrical associations between revenge and writing in *The Spanish Tragedy* and in the context of the Elizabethan stage. Chapter 4 on "metaphoric books" is also of interest for this essay. See also Eve Rachele Sanders's discussion of reading in *Hamlet*, "Enter Hamlet reading on a booke" in *Gender and Literacy on the Shakespearean Stage* (Cambridge: Cambridge University Press, 1998), which implicitly associates Hamlet's reading with revenge.

invent the readerly dimension of revenge. A Renaissance emblem for revenge entitled *vindicta divina* consisted of a winged book flying over the earth, open for declamation.[25] It harks back to the Book of Revelation, in which, before opening the fifth seal of the Book of Judgment, the Lamb of God hears those martyred for his sake ask, "How long, Lord ... doest not thou judge and avenge our blood on them, that dwell on the earth?"[26]

Revenge, as so conceived, is the reading of a past act, the forcible recitation of a past injury (etymologically, the word "revenge" derives from the Latin *vindicare*, which combines *vim* [force] and *dicare* [to proclaim, the root *dic* also connoting speech or telling, as in *dicere*, "to say"]).[27] Revenge *signifies* precisely that for which it serves as retribution, relating, in *deed* (not just in word) an injury already done. An economical example: through revenge Laertes hopes to *relate to* Hamlet his *reading* of Hamlet's killing of Polonius: "Thus didst thou" (4.7.57): you, Hamlet, killed Polonius—"thus."[28] The revenge process, then, is also the process of forcing the victim to see himself reduced to mere *character* to be read: in communicating what Hamlet has done, in "saying" "thus didst thou" by reciting a past action *with* action, in declaiming the story, as it were, Laertes would have the satisfaction of seeing Hamlet recognize himself as a signifier representing the dead Polonius. Of course, revenge, in this regard, is a suicide mission: the revenger too becomes a signifier, Laertes becoming a character representing the Hamlet who has killed Polonius. Both persons are to be reduced to *signs* in the Augustinian

---

[25]   The image may be found in Henry Peacham's emblem book, *Minerva Britanna* (1612). I owe my citation of the image to Kiefer, who reproduces it in the context of his discussion of *The Spanish Tragedy* (241). *Hamlet* of course mimics that play's association of revenge with reading, though also altering it in many ways. Thus Hamlet's entrance with a book at a significant moment recalls and transforms Hieronymo's appearance "with a book in his hand" and uttering the biblical phrase "*vindicta mihi.*" Thomas Kyd, *The Spanish Tragedy, or Hieronimo is Mad Again,* in *The First Part of Hieronimo and The Spanish Tragedy,* ed., Andrew S. Cairncross (Lincoln: University of Nebraska Press, 1967), 3.13.1.

[26]   Revelation 6:10, in The Bible, Translated from the Hebrew and Greek (London, 1599).

[27]   "Avenge, *v*" and "vindicate, *v*" *Oxford English Dictionary*, 2nd Edition, 1989, *OED Online*, 2 February, 2008   <http://dictionary.oed.com/cgi/entry/50015404> and <http://dictionary.oed.com/cgi/entry/50015404>, respectively.

[28]   In the first or "bad" quarto of *Hamlet*, published in 1603, Laertes at one point anticipates killing Hamlet with "thus, he dies." Some editors therefore emend "thus didst thou," as it occurs in the *Second Quarto* (1605) and *Folio* (1623) to "thus diest thou." It is quite possible that the printer misread the manuscript ("d"s in secretary hand can often look like "e"s). But there is nothing other than the line in the *First Quarto* that corroborates this possibility. I find "didst" preferable, particularly insofar as it anticipates the fates of Laertes and Hamlet, who, in exchanging swords by accident, ultimately realize the meaning of "thus didst thou" in their fencing match, as well as in Laertes's revenge for Polonius's stabbing. In any case, the emendation happened in the twentieth century, so Dickens would not have encountered it.

sense of the term: things that point *beyond* themselves to more important things.[29] But the very process of all this reduction to character is also a process of *reading*— living, after all, is also a process of dying. In reducing himself to character, the revenger also asserts himself as a reader, a declaimer, of what is being related, and in so doing, he even makes a dying reader out of the revengee, *to whom*, perhaps among others, he is reciting "out loud"—reading *forcefully*. Laertes actively reads past events *to* Hamlet, establishing intimacy with him so that Hamlet is in on the reading, too: "thus didst *thou*." Likewise, in Hamlet's revenge on Claudius, it is in the struggle by characters to reduce each other *to* character that the illusion of character-as-reader, character as more-than-character, comes to life. Such struggle produces seeming readers out of the characters of the play—and especially out of Hamlet himself—through the redundant device of showing characters dying *into* character in a telling by force. In short, revenge in *Hamlet* produces characters who are both character and more than character, both character and readers-of-character—seemingly "dynamic" as opposed to merely "semantic" characters, to borrow William Dodd's terminology.[30]

But with the suppression of the revenge plot that characterizes Wopsle's performance, such reading never occurs. Never is Wopsle's Hamlet captured struggling to figure out what the ghost's presence means ("What may this mean," asks Shakespeare's Hamlet, / "That thou, dead corpse, again in complete steel,/ Revisits thus the glimpses of the moon ...?" [1.4.53]). As he comes across in *Great Expectations*, he never reads the ghost's commandment in the "book and volume" of his brain, never "falls to perusal" of Ophelia's physiognomy (2.1.87), never rivets his eyes to his uncle's face during the performance of *The Mousetrap*, never scans the scenario of killing his uncle while his uncle is praying, never seeks to interpret his own responses to the news, from the ghost, of his father's murder. Pip's account of the performance—and by implication the performance itself— omits the moments that make Hamlet what Leroy Searle calls "an exemplary reader."[31] All this serves to embarrass Wopsle for flattening a character who, even in most direct encounters with *texts* of Hamlet, comes across as a person.

However, I sense in Pip's response to Wopsle's reading of the character a perspective from which the character Wopsle seems to emerge, Hamlet-like, as alive and sympathetic as the reader to whom the book itself is directed. A bad actor, a *reader* who cannot be one with the character he plays, Wopsle also distinguishes himself, for Pip, from character generally and identifies himself as one whom a reader might actually meet—a fellow reader, even if he is a character.

---

[29]    Augustine defines a sign as "a thing which in itself makes some other thing come to mind, besides the impression that it presents to the senses." *On Christian Teaching*, trans., R.P.H. Green (Oxford: Oxford University Press, 1997), II.1.

[30]    See William Nigel Dodd's "Character as Dynamic Identity: From Fictional Interaction Script to Performance," in *Shakespeare and Character: Theory, History, Performance and Theatrical Persons*, eds., Paul Yachnin and Jessica Slights (Basingstoke, U.K.: Palgrave, 2009), 62–82.

[31]    Leroy F. Searle, "Hamlet, Oedipus, and the Problem of Reading," *Comparative Literature* 49. no. 4 (1997): 316–43, esp. 335.

Pip's fearful comment after the performance, "Let us go at once, or perhaps we will meet him" (1953, 241), indicates as much; to "meet" the humiliated person of Wopsle is to meet his humiliation, to live it, whereas to read him is to remain separate enough from it to make sense of it. But there is a way in which Pip has already met Wopsle during the performance. The person of Hamlet (never named during the account of the performance proper) never occupies the stage, but certainly Pip's "gifted townsman" Wopsle does (1953, 238). And if the phrase "gifted townsman" abounds in irony, it also indicates the empathy that allows Pip to identify with Wopsle's point of view, to feel "very keenly for him" (1953, 241), and compels Pip, ultimately, to invite him to supper.

Pip's very suggestions that Wopsle is reading and not acting—performing a homiletic "service" and not a representation—give pause in this regard, eliciting a second look. If these suggestions satirize Wopsle's acting, they also indicate a readerly attunement to him, a *knowing what Wopsle is getting at in his reading*. While the rest of the audience refuses to read Wopsle's neatly folded stocking in the context of the revenge plot, commenting instead on the paleness it reveals in his leg, Pip knows what it means to "express." While the rest of the audience treats Wopsle's use of the handkerchief during the gravedigger scene as a failing in an actor's representation ("even this innocent and indispensable action did not pass without the comment, 'Wai-ter!'" [1953, 240]), Pip perceives the innocence of the unplanned reflex that comes with being Wopsle, that has nothing to do with the intended reading. Even Pip's criticism of Wopsle's elocution suggests that he has read along with his townsman, admittedly while laughing at him:

> I laughed in spite of myself all the time, the whole thing was so droll; *and yet* I had a latent impression that there was something decidedly fine in Mr Wopsle's elocution—not for old associations' sake, I am afraid, but because it was very slow, very dreary, very up-hill and down-hill, and very unlike any way in which any man in any natural circumstances of life or death ever expressed himself about anything. (1953, 241; emphasis mine)

With regard to what immediately follows, the phrase "something decidedly fine in Mr Wopsle's elocution" of course suggests satirical irony; what first looks like praise for Wopsle's performance turns out to be a devastating comment on the unnaturalness of Wopsle's declamatory reading, the surprise illustrating Pip's perception of how "droll" this reading is. Without the "and yet" immediately after Pip's confession and justification of his laughter, that interpretation would work perfectly, the voice of the narrator taking a brutally Swiftian tone. But the "and yet" suggests that the "something fine" about Wopsle's elocution may indeed have struck a chord in Pip, that it could somehow be viewed as contrary to the drollness of the "whole thing." Dickens could not have let the passage stand without "and yet"; omitting it would have removed Pip too far from Wopsle, rendering his expressions of sympathy with the failed actor, and his fear of meeting him, implausible. Perhaps that was Dickens's immediate reason for adding it. In any case, it is effective as a qualifier for the satire precisely because of a readerly connection it sets up between Wopsle and Pip: though Pip recognizes the artificiality of Wopsle's "reading" as ineffective, he must know more than the mass of spectators who witness the performance along with him about what Wopsle is getting and not getting in his reading of Hamlet.

But though Pip's narrative articulates sympathy for Wopsle, selecting him as a fellow-reader, it is nevertheless at least in the process of violently reducing him—as Wopsle has reduced Hamlet—to the status of character. It is rendering Wopsle the caricature of the reading character (caricature always emphasizes the character-ness of a character), so that Pip emerges as the reader with whom the readers of the novel identify: the "three-dimensional" character, the "person" with an "inner life," the Hamlet of the story. From the start, the *Hamlet* episode insists on eliminating differentiation between the performers of the play-within-the-text and the characters in that play:

> On our arrival in Denmark, we found the king and queen of that country elevated in two arm-chairs on a kitchen table, holding a Court. The whole of the Danish nobility were in attendance; consisting of a noble boy in the wash-leather boots of a gigantic ancestor, a venerable Peer with a dirty face who seemed to have risen from the people late in life, and the Danish chivalry with a comb in its hair and a pair of white silk legs, and presenting on the whole a feminine appearance. My gifted townsman stood gloomily apart, with folded arms, and I could have wished that his curls and forehead had been more plausible (1953, 239).

Crushing together the readers with the parts they "play," the narrative begins with what the narrator identifies as his and his companion's "arrival in Denmark," rather than their arrival in the theater. And instead of identifying the actors pretending to be the characters "holding a court," it treats the performers as indistinct from the characters they are playing. Even where the narrator identifies his "gifted townsman" as opposed to "Hamlet," the setting of *Denmark*, rather than the stage, becomes the textual burial-ground in which Pip submerges Wopsle. The result is delightful in its irony: what we have is emphatically not what one might expect from the player's burying himself in his part (a life-like character Hamlet in a scene so verisimilar as to make one forget that one is in a theater, or that the character is a product of a play-text) but flattened-out Wopsle-as-reader-of-Hamlet—the forced burial of Wopsle into the character Hamlet. As for the problems in verisimilitude that make the production a reading of characters rather than a representation of persons—the kitchen table supporting the king- and-queen character, the ill-fitting boots on the boy-playing-Osric-and-gravedigger-and-clergyman character, the unwashed face of the Polonius character, the singleness and effeteness of the chivalry-of-Denmark character, and of course the artificiality of the curls and forehead on the Wopsle-as-reader-of-Hamlet character—these become absurd insertions into the very text of *Hamlet*, deflating anticipations, which the play seems to invite from the intelligently perverse, of the vengeful swallowing-up of readers into character. If Wopsle figures Hamlet out into text, Pip's narrative does the same to Wopsle, despite Wopsle's status as reader.

Unquestionably, the flaws in verisimilitude could, through a different narrative approach, render such bad actors' *readings* of characters more immediate, thus allowing us to identify with the bad actors as readers. Consider Joe Gargery, doing his pathetic best to play the gentleman when visiting Pip and Herbert in their London lodgings. Unaccustomed to a top hat, he treats it like a "bird's nest with eggs in it"; he repeatedly pronounces "architectural" "architectooralooral"; he attempts, unsuccessfully, to conceal his dropping of food while eating (1953, 210). The result is to make him look like one in the process of figuring things out, like a reader and interpreter of his own prescribed role as visitor and relation of a gentleman, and of Pip-and-friend as gentlemen, and thus momentarily to threaten Pip's status as *the* reader, rather than *a* character. At moments such as these, the emergent reader, despite all the advantages at his disposal, can find himself submerged into text, as another character may turn tables on him, giving us glimpses of him as mere signifier to be read in the contexts of other signifiers. In the *Hamlet* episode, I have the sense, as I read Wopsle's post-performance account of the spectator in the front row who has cast aspersions, that I have just missed such a moment. But Pip never depicts Wopsle *struggling* to interpret this spectator's behavior. Polonius-like, Pip's Wopsle determines the meaning instantly: the unruly spectator was a plant by the rivalrous player of the part of Claudius. Wopsle's explanation is thus not a reading in process but a reading already completed, a marginal trace to be read. Even here, Wopsle's reading is, as Herbert and Pip put it, "massive and concrete," already immovable and hard, figured out. Pip's reading of the same figure, however, is in process. With skilful hypallage in his description of this "sulky man who had been cooling his impatient nose against an iron bar in the front row of the gallery" (1953, 240), he emerges as reader by reducing this reading character to caricature. But in Pip's narrative, the full significance of the sulky man is never completely figured out.

Much later, however, Wopsle's penchant for reading does allow him to emerge from the text, a momentary "thou" whom I, as reader, can meet. This happens during Pip's account of a *second* Wopsle performance, in which Pip describes the very moment of Wopsle's recognition of him among the spectators. Wopsle is now cast not as Hamlet but as a wizard in a Christmas Pantomime:

> The business of this enchanter on earth, being principally to be talked at, sung at, butted at, danced at, and flashed at with fires of various colours, he had a good deal of time on his hands. And I observed with great surprise, that he devoted to staring in my direction as if he were lost in amazement.

> There was something so remarkable in the increasing glare of Mr Wopsle's eye, and he seemed to be turning so many things over in his mind and to grow so confused, that I could not make it out. I sat thinking of it, long after he had ascended to the clouds in a large watch-case, and still I could not make it out. (1953, 364)

Wopsle turns tables, becomes the reading character, by virtue of which status he seems momentarily illegible ("I could not make it out," Pip repeats). Readerly activity, as it turns out, is what allows Wopsle to recognize the convict Compeyson, behind Pip, among the spectators. It is marked not by an image of easy and direct comprehension but by the image of struggle, confusion, uncertainty, "amazement" that comes with the parsing of a difficult text with an unexpected meaning. As Wopsle explains to Pip, his recognition might not have occurred except for the syntactical proximity—as in the pairing of elements in a sentence or letters in a syllable ("Whether I should have noticed him at first but for your being there ... I can't be positive" [1953, 364]). Even at this point, Wopsle has not completed his figuring out of the meaning of the character behind Pip (and he never does), but he is, nevertheless, in the midst of a readerly feat, a feat of recollection: by collecting (reading together) signifiers, Wopsle at least begins to figure out the person behind Pip, a person he has glimpsed only once in the dark many years previously, when he, Pip, and others were chasing two convicts through the marshes near Pip's childhood home. Wopsle adds to this feat a haunting, though crucially incomplete, interpretation that suddenly does render him worthy of comparison to Hamlet. He echoes Hamlet's experience, shared by spectators and readers, though not by Gertrude, in the Queen's bedchamber: "I had the ridiculous fancy that he must be with you, Mr Pip, till I saw that you were quite unconscious of him, sitting behind you there, like a ghost" (1953, 364).

Quite unconscious. What happens to Pip in this description is telling: he becomes a character submerged in text, a character to be read, rather than a conscious reader; that this could happen to our narrator is perhaps what is most terrifying about the scene—more terrifying than the particular threat posed by Compeyson. Yet in being forced by Wopsle to read himself as a character in syntactical relation to Compeyson ("I could not doubt ... that he was there, because I was there, and that ... danger was always near and active"[1953, 366]), Pip again comes alive as a fellow reader, whose terror I share. Pip reads Wopsle reading him ("I saw that you saw me," he says, immediately, on meeting him [1953, 364]). I see this event as Wopsle's revenge, and, though it occupies a minute portion of the novel, I submit that it is as formidable as any piece of retribution represented in the text.

True, figurative as it is, that designation needs qualification. Wopsle's moment of reading Pip may be understood as Wopsle's revenge only if it is viewed in a way that allows the witness or reader of the spectacle of vengeance to claim ownership. Wopsle cannot be the author of Pip's reduction to mere character; his discernment is, unlike that of a true revenger's plot, unfinished. His account suggests that his "figuring out" is incomplete, that he does not *fully* know what it means that Compeyson is sitting behind Pip—as indeed he does not. And if he has reason to feel himself vindicated for having been treated, by Pip, as mere character, he does not know this either, since he presumably does not know Pip sees him in this way. Nevertheless, Wopsle's moment of subjectivity has about it the feel of revenge. Wopsle's analogy to a "ghost" suggests readerly satisfaction, on his part, at the spectacle of Pip's past returning to haunt him—not, perhaps, the satisfaction of an injured party authoring the downfall of his adversary, but the satisfaction of a witness to an act of retribution—of a Hamlet, say, watching Pyrrhus's destruction of Priam. More to the point, exchanges of readership for characterhood conform to a pattern of injury and retribution, though neither character seems fully conscious of this pattern. Pip finds himself the victim of Wopsle's verbal aggression—his

likening of the boy Pip to swine—early in the story. And at that point in the
narrative, as well as at every other point, up to that of the *Hamlet* episode, Pip,
in return, satirizes him, reads him as caricature. At this instant, for just an instant,
surrounded as he is by the setting of the ridiculous show in which he finds himself
acting, Wopsle is free from the stigma of caricature, free to see Pip as a character
of one haunted by a ghost from the past, and Pip is, for the first time, utterly
dependent on his reading for information.

That Wopsle's reading has the feel of vengeance is consistent with what we can
infer from the scene, that an act of vengeance is indeed in the offing: the author
of the revenge is not Wopsle (as indeed the author of revenge in *Hamlet* is not
Hamlet) but the "ghost," Compeyson, whose enemy, Magwitch, Pip has aided,
and who therefore fittingly, is shadowing Pip to find him out and destroy him.
What makes this revenge plot interesting is its capacity (like that of *Hamlet*) to
produce a multiplicity of reading characters—characters who are in the process
of reading each other and themselves, thus treating each other and themselves *as*
character, and so coming across, momentarily, as more than character. Indeed, the
effect of Wopsle's relating his reading to Pip is finally to turn Pip into a reader of
himself as character, and to face him with a "peculiar terror," terror that he should
be "so unconscious," as he puts it (1953, 366), as to forget his adversary and
his position in an unfolding revenge plot. So finally the revenge plot creates the
paradoxical impression of subjectivity in a character by virtue of the fact that this
character is in the process of reading himself as *mere* character. If the revenge plot
is Compeyson's to write, it is, at this moment, Pip's (as well as Wopsle's) to read,
despite the fact that Pip is one of its characters being read.

The novel is thick with the theme of revenge, which facilitates such tricks in
virtually every installment. Miss Havisham, Orlick, and Compeyson's extended
revenge plots are obvious. But even Magwitch's mock-Spenserian gesture of
fashioning Pip as gentleman is tinged with what he calls the "low" motive of
vindicating his unfair treatment, resulting from his crude origins, at the hands of
Compeyson and the courts, by showing that he can *make* the very kind of character
he has been punished for not being. Repeatedly, such plots mimic the gesture of
turning persons—Estella, Pip, Jaggers, Herbert, Mr. Pocket, Joe, etcetera—into
characters, marks left by the finger of the revenger on the world described in the
text of *Great Expectations*, and marks read by some of these characters themselves
and—always—by the victims. If Dickens took inspiration for *Great Expectations*
from the revenge plots of *Hamlet*, for him perhaps the archetypal revenge story,
then it seems likely that he found in *Hamlet*'s production of readers among its
characters, and particularly in its production of Hamlet as the reader-revenger, the
importance of reading as a way of making characters seem more than character.

But my argument is not that Dickens learned from *Hamlet* in particular to
produce seemingly meetable literary characters; such an argument is unprovable
and misses what is truly at stake in the way in which Dickens uses Hamlet in his
novel. The technique does not depend on *Hamlet per se*, but rather on a sense
of human character that Dickens still had in common with Shakespeare. Hence,
it can occur without reference to *Hamlet*. Pip's first reading teacher, Biddy, for

instance, is also consistently a reader of Pip, always in the process of interpreting and judging him, but never quite arriving at a conclusion; though she appears infrequently, and also briefly becomes more than character through her reading, which does not allude directly to anything in *Hamlet*. The point is that, to turn characters into "subjects," Dickens has to turn them into readers, which usually means understanding character in itself as signifying mark, even where it applies to persons in life. What is truly remarkable is that Dickens's reading of the character of Hamlet is so accurately Shakespearean in its implicit conception of what a character must be, and that it fits so well with his regular method of making characters seem more than character: emphasizing the textual nature of his artificial persons so that readers of these persons can emerge as reading characters within the novel itself. I conclude from the pervasiveness of the technique that the sense of literary character on which Dickens depended for the illusion of personhood still had a deep kinship with the sense of literary character prevalent in Shakespeare's time, the sense of character as thing to be read. In installment after installment, Dickens creates circumstances in which his impersonations are emphasized as things to be read—and read only with great difficulty—thus also producing characters in the process of reading.

The logic of this technique—that an effective way to camouflage the character-ness of a character is to make that character look like the reader, the entity who must at some point in the process distinguish him- or herself from the thing read—does not absolutely require that the character to be read serve as an impersonation. What is important is that the text be difficult enough to recognize as text or at least difficult enough to decipher that the process of reading becomes apparent. Hence, Joe Gargery's struggle to read Pip's letter (40–43) makes him look as meetable to me as does his more sophisticated, and tortured, reading of his wife (and Pip's sister) as "a—fine—figure—of—a—woman." "A little redness, or a little matter of Bone, here or there," he significantly adds, "what does it *signify* to me?" (1953, 43, emphasis mine). Indeed, the whole first part of *Great Expectations*, which tells the story of Pip's emergence into literacy, allows Pip from the start to be *in the process of reading*, of recognizing characters as *literal* characters, letters indicating things beyond themselves. Upon starting to read the novel as Pip is starting to read, I share with Pip the trials and errors of encountering text the meaning of which is deferred, of knowing that everything I encounter signifies, but not knowing what its significance is or how that significance is being conveyed. That is the effect of the novel's opening with an account of Pip's struggle with the writing on his parents' tombstones: "the shape of the letters on my father's grave gave me the odd idea that he was a square, stout dark man, with curly hair. From the character and turn of the inscription, *Also Georgiana Wife of the Above*, I drew the childish conclusion that my mother was freckled and sickly." It is Pip's *struggle* with reading that lets him share my ontological status as reader.

Like Shakespeare, then, Dickens replicates this struggle for the *literate* character by setting him up as a reader of what no one is very good at deciphering—the text of life itself, in which people themselves are characters. Even on the first page of the novel, in showing Pip's reading of the tombstones themselves as if they were people, Dickens sets Pip up in precisely this way. Because Pip has no memory of his parents before their deaths, because he cannot separate them from the concrete text signifying them, he has only a sense of them as human beings who are also characters to be read. Throughout the novel, this treatment of human being *as text* elevates Pip's status to my own—to the status of the person in the process of reading. It is still performing this function when Magwitch reappears in Chapter 39. Consider the moment Pip comes to recognize his mysterious benefactor, the convict whom as a young man he encountered while reading the tombstones:

I read with my watch upon the table, purposing to close my book at eleven o'clock. As I shut it, Saint Paul's, and all the many church-clocks in the City – some leading, some accompanying, some following – struck that hour. The sound was curiously flawed by the wind; and I was listening, and thinking how the wind assailed and tore it, when I heard a footstep on the stair.

What nervous folly made me start, and awfully connect it with the footstep of my dead sister, matters not. It was past in a moment, and I listened again, and heard the footstep stumble in coming on. Remembering then, that the staircase-lights were blown out, I took up my reading-lamp and went out to the stair-head. Whoever was below had stopped on seeing my lamp, for all was quiet.

'There is some one down there, is there not?' I called out, looking down.

'Yes,' said a voice from the darkness beneath.

'What floor do you want?'

'The top. Mr Pip.'

'That is my name. – There is nothing the matter?'

'Nothing the matter,' returned the voice. And the man came on. I stood with my lamp held out over the stair-rail, and he came slowly within its light. It was a shaded lamp, to shine upon a book, and its circle of light was very contracted; so that he was in it for a mere instant, and then out of it. In the instant, I had seen a face that was strange to me, looking up with an incomprehensible air of being touched and pleased by the sight of me.

Moving the lamp as the man moved, I made out that he was substantially dressed, but roughly; like a voyager by sea. That he had long iron-grey hair. That his age was about sixty. That he was a muscular man, strong on his legs, and that he was browned and hardened by exposure to weather. As he ascended the last stair or two, and the light of my lamp included us both, I saw, with a stupid kind of amazement, that he was holding out both his hands to me. (1953, 299–300)

This account of Magwitch's return is a continuation of Pip's reading of his book, for though Pip closes his book at eleven, the faulty stroke of the bell only marks the continuation of his readerly activity. Tellingly, he gradually comprehends the convict by the light of his reading lamp, which is so weak as to create the same unfolding effect that one might feel in parsing an involved sentence or paragraph. Pip experiences a truly penitential reading, a struggle from beginning to end, far too convoluted and drawn out, in its entirety, to fit within the compass of this essay. By the end of the passage that will have to suffice, he has not yet even reached the level of comprehension to be achieved by Wopsle from the vision of Compeyson among the spectators at the play. Confronted with a confusing arrangement of signs, Pip begins parsing them haltingly—first, erroneously connecting figure's footstep with the figure of his sister (an understandable misreading, since the two figures share the context of Pip's childhood home); then, tangentially, if correctly, interpreting the figure's stumble on the stairs as a reminder of the blown lamps; then, pertinently, discovering the figure's destination to be himself, and the reading light having finally caught the figure's face, interpreting the figure's state to be joyous; then, with admirable and correct attention to detail, reading his age and associating his "browned and hardened" state with exposure to weather; and then observing an expression of greeting. At this point, Pip, still stupidly amazed in the labyrinth of three-dimensional text in which Magwitch is a character, has barely begun to grasp what the old man signifies. Through his difficulty in figuring it out, comes, of course, that indispensable element of suspense. But even more importantly, the episode synchronizes Pip's reading—his progress towards comprehension— with my reading, so that I feel myself meeting him, a companion in the semiotic struggle, as a *character*, in the true sense of the term, comes up the stairs.

As critics have shown, the re-entrance of Magwitch reverberates distinctly with the ghost scenes in the first act of *Hamlet*. How central these reverberations are to Dickens's planning of the episode is ancillary to my point. Perhaps the determination to echo *Hamlet* is the effect, and not the cause, of his presenting this recognition as readerly. Perhaps even the wonderful characterization of Pip as not only the object of Magwitch's gratitude but also a Hamlet-like instrument of his ghostly revenge was an afterthought. The technique I am describing by no means depends everywhere on allusion to *Hamlet*. It recurs in virtually every installment, in one way or another, continually elevating Pip, and occasionally others, to the status of "thou." What is more, the "thou"-ness established through reading in *Great Expectations* undoubtedly serves different social agendas than does the similarly established "thou"-ness in *Hamlet*, agendas reflective of the vastly different historical moments of the two works. Where Pip's nineteenth-century emergence as reading character might serve as a meditation on what it means to forget one's own place and meaning in a world divided by economic and social class, Hamlet's seventeenth-century emergence as reading character can be understood as a meditation on what it means to forget one's place in God's providential scheme. But where echoes of *Hamlet* do occur in *Great Expectations*, I take them as signs that Dickens's technique of making characters look like more than character has something startlingly in common with Shakespeare's— something that reminded Dickens of *Hamlet*, if not something that he learned from *Hamlet*: namely the portrayal of characters in the process of reading, which demands the recognition of persons *as* characters—as reading material.

# PART 2
## Character in Action

# Chapter 5
# Historicizing Spontaneity:
# The Illusion of the First Time of
# "The Illusion of the First Time"

## Cary M. Mazer

If there is, indeed, a gap between personness in early modern dramatic writing on the one hand, and the idea of subjectivity in "character criticism" from the nineteenth to the twenty-first century on the other, this gap is erased, if not eradicated altogether, in modern theatrical practice.

Theatre artists read scripts through the spectacles (to borrow Bernard Beckerman's phrase) of the theatrical aesthetics of their time; and theatre audiences experience and comprehend the theatre event they are witnessing according to the same tacit codes.[1] Nowhere is this more evident than with regard to dramatic character. However successfully historicist scholars have destabilized notions of early modern subjectivity, modern actors (in the mainstream Anglophone theatre at least) still "build" their "character" as coherent, psychologized, and interiorized entities, impelled by a web of biographical causality, drawn towards "goals" and "objectives," by using the shared vocabulary and tools of a highly articulated system of acting first codified at the end of the nineteenth century. And that's the way audiences perceive character, constructing a sense of a coherent person from their experience of witnessing the actor's performance, according to what Alan Sinfield has called, disapprovingly, the "character effect."[2] Mainstream theatre artists today create characters on stage from old scripts in ways they are confident contemporary audiences will perceive and understand them; and contemporary mainstream audiences perceive and understand dramatic character according to ways the actors perform them, having constructed their characters from a shared set of rehearsal practices. Mainstream histrionic practice is where "character criticism" lives ... so much so that most actors are surprised when they learn that theatre scholars—whether early modern historicists or postmodern performance theorists—declare character criticism dead, and suggest alternative models of personal subjectivity or theatrical mimesis.

---

[1]    Bernard Beckerman, *Dynamic of Drama: Theory and Method of Analysis* (New York: Knopf, 1970), 3.

[2]    Alan Sinfield, "When is a Character Not a Character? Desdemona, Olivia , Lady Macbeth, and Subjectivity," in *Faultlines: Cultural Materialism and the Politics of Dissident Reading* (Berkeley: University of California Press, 1992), 52–79: esp. 58.

So pervasive is the character-based approach to acting in contemporary theatrical practice that it surfaces in some unlikely places. One of the least likely places is in the body of theatrical activity that identifies itself as "Original Practices" (or "O.P." for short), an approach to staging the plays of Shakespeare and his contemporaries that purports to bypass modern playhouse architecture, actor–audience relations, stage conventions, acting techniques, and even rehearsal methods in order to return to the conditions and conventions of the scripts' original performances. And yet here, too, one can find the theatrical equivalent of "character criticism" at work, in the discourses of O.P. if not in the practices themselves.

To demonstrate this, it is useful to look at one of the cornerstone properties of O.P.: spontaneity. In *Acting from Shakespeare's First Folio*, Don Weingust, the O.P. movement's most articulate and perceptive scholarly chronicler, describes the theatrical effect generated by Patrick Tucker's Original Shakespeare Company, in which the actors learn their roles from sides and perform the play with minimal rehearsal:

> Because none of the players knows [sic] how any of the others will react, speak or move, nor what they will say save their brief cues, there is no need to manufacture an "illusion of the first time." [...] Everyone in the building, whether on stage or off, becomes part of a "real," as opposed to "realistic" event, occurring in space and time immediately before his or her eyes and ears. The audience is hearing for the first time what the actors are also, and the energy generated in this immediate encounter is nothing short of electric.[3]

What interests me about Weingust's brief critical observation are two things: the distinction he is drawing between the genuinely "real" and merely "realistic" (to which I will return shortly); and, more tellingly, his citation of the phrase "the illusion of the first time." For the concept of "the illusion of the first time" (and indeed the phrase itself) is not a universal and eternal property of theatre, but rather a concept (and a phrase) that arose from a precise period of theatrical activity, and—I'd like to suggest—belongs to that particular period and not necessarily to any other.

There are some aspects of theatre—and specifically of representational acting—that can be regarded as perennial and axiomatic: that an actor stands in for a character, that language bears some correspondence to thought and emotion, etc. But many other aspects of representational acting, including things we often take for granted, are geographically or temporally specific. Theorists and practitioners of Original Practices, along with the scholars who write about them, often confuse the perennial and the specific when they define several aspects of early modern character and acting. These include how the actor generates passion, how passion gets expressed through language, what constitutes "character"—consciousness, subjectivity, interiority, biography, etc.

---

[3]     Don Weingust, *Acting from Shakespeare's First Folio: Theory, Text, and Performance* (New York: Routledge, 2006), 171.

There is an irony to putting O.P. folk to the test of historicity, for the primary argument of Original Practices is, above all, historicist, in all three areas with which they are legitimately obsessed: language and text, stage and auditorium, and rehearsal practices. Recapture these period conditions, they argue, and you recapture how the scripts were designed to work in performance. But though the O.P. folks' argument depends upon the temporal specificity of early modern performance, in fetishizing "spontaneity," and in invoking "the illusion of the first time," they are, I suggest, merely substituting one historical period for another, ascribing to the early modern period the terms, values, and assumptions of the period I choose to call "the long Stanislavskian century," beginning in the late nineteenth century and extending through the twentieth, and possibly, into the twenty-first, centuries. My interest here is not in whether the advocates of O.P. are right or wrong about the importance of spontaneity in early modern acting, but in when, where, and how spontaneity, as the O.P. folks use the term, is defined, and how these definitions are shaped by the histrionic values of the late nineteenth century and those of today. Like Richard Paul Knowles (writing about Shakespeare and voice teachers), I am "less interested in how well the methods 'work' than in *what* ideological work they *do*."[4]

Let's begin with the distinction Weingust draws between the "realistic" and the "real." My own preferred terms, following philosophers of art like Suzanne Langer, are the "virtual" and the "actual": an object in space is "actual"; the image of that object reflected in a mirror, which appears to exist in the same distance beyond the plane of the mirror that the actual object is from the mirror, is "virtual."[5] Unlike painting, which employs pigment on canvas to create a virtual image of an actual person, object, or place, the theatre employs as its material for creating the virtual the same substance as the actual: people doing are represented by people doing. And so the project of theatrical "realism" has always been to make the virtual asymptotically approach the status of the actual.

The phrase Weingust uses—"the illusion of the first time"—originated in a 1913 lecture, "The Illusion of the First Time in Acting," by the American playwright and actor William Gillette. Gillette's lecture comes at the end of a thirty or forty year period during which theatre practitioners, critics, and theorists struggled to account for the tensions between the virtual and the actual in acting.[6]

---

[4]    Richard Paul Knowles, "Shakespeare, Voice, and Ideology: Interrogating the Natural Voice," in James C. Bulman, ed., *Shakespeare, Theory and Performance* (London: Routledge, 1996), 92–112: esp. 93; see also W. B. Worthen, "Shakespeare's Body," in *Shakespeare and the Authority of Performance* (New York: Cambridge University Press, 1997), 95–105; and Sarah Werner, "Performing Shakespeare: Voice Training and the Feminist Actor," *New Theatre Quarterly* 12. no. 47 (Aug 1996): 249–58.

[5]    See in particular Suzanne Langer's The Dynamic Image" in *Problems in Art: Ten Philosophical Lectures* (New York: Scribner, 1957), 1–12.

[6]    This began, in England, with the publication in English of Talma's "Reflections on Acting" in the British monthly *The Theatre* in 1877, at the insistence of Henry Irving (the magazine's unstated owner), and the publication of a translation of Denis Diderot's *The*

These late nineteenth-century essays, lectures, and books were stumbling, insufficiently-articulated, inchoate, and often wrong headed, applying pre-late-nineteenth-century terms and categories to phenomena theatergoers simply could not account for: Constantine Stanislavski (as John Gillies has documented) simply could not explain why he found Tommasso Salvini so astonishingly present, nor could Bernard Shaw figure out how Eleanora Duse blushed. What was needed was not an existing set of terms and categories—e.g. Shaw describing Duse as having connected a series of histrionic "points"—but a new vocabulary altogether, what Joseph R. Roach, borrowing from Thomas Kuhn, calls a paradigm.

Stanislavski's "system," articulated in the first decades of the twentieth century and published in a series of books (aimed at American readers) in the 1920s, was nothing less than the codification of a new paradigm of acting, replacing practices based on recitation and imitation with one based on units of action: the actor breaks the role into units in which the character *does*; and by doing these things him- or herself—"doing real things in imagined circumstances"—the actor is perceived by the audience to be the character. Independent of, and apart from, the virtuality of the character, the actor's action is actual, collapsing the distance between the virtuality of stage representation and the actuality it seeks to achieve.

The transformation of Stanislavski's "system" into the "Method," by Richard Boleslavsky and Maria Ouspenskaya at the American Laboratory Theatre in the 1920s, and then by the members and alumni of the Group Theatre in the 1930s and '50s, represents a further fetishizing of the actual. Lee Strasberg endorsed "affective memory" as a tool for the actor to experience the actual on the stage, drawing upon his or her own life ("the actor, therefore, uses the 'objective correlative' of his own experiences to find a means of expressing the emotion the actor needs to express on stage"), while using the words and the situation of the script, using "sense memory" as a means of triggering an "emotional memory" which, as in Proust, can be re-experienced.[7] Sanford Meisner, who routinely began his acting classes with the axiomatic declaration, "The foundation of acting is the reality of doing,"[8] used what he called the "word repetition game," in which the actor begins by responding to the immediate reality of sensation and the exercise-partner's words, to help the actor create a foundation of genuine response to genuine stimulus—to shorten the distance between what Meisner called "the pinch and the ouch," that could, later in the actor's training, be expanded to include the imagined circumstances of the role. "Don't do anything unless something happens to make you do it," he insisted (1987, 34): something in the world changes, which

---

*Paradox of Acting*, with a disapproving introduction by Irving, six years later. The central question raised by Diderot's *Paradox*—whether or not the actor really feels, in the moment of the performance—was taken up in a series of articles by Constant Coquelin, Irving, and Dion Boucicault in 1887, and by William Archer in *Masks or Faces?* in 1888.

    [7]    Lee Strasberg, *A Dream of Passion: The Development of the Method* (New York: New American Library, 1988), 121.

    [8]    Sanford Meisner, *Sanford Meisner on Acting* (New York: Vintage, 1987), 16.

causes you to change; and if the actor has established the foundations thoroughly, the change that happens is, in his words, "spontaneous" (1987, 30).

Like Meisner's word repetitions, theatre games were a means of grounding behavior in the actual, of the actor learning to trust to stimulus and response. Viola Spolin, who, with her son Paul Sills, inspired several generations of improv comedy in Chicago, writes in her encyclopedic *Improvisation for the Theatre*, "Spontaneity is the moment of personal freedom when we are faced with a reality and see it, explore it, and act accordingly. In this reality the bits and pieces of ourselves function as an organic whole."[9] For Strasberg, improvisation is neither a verbal exercise nor a license to paraphrase the author's words; "Improvisation," he writes, "is essential if the actor is to develop the spontaneity necessary to create in each performance 'the illusion of the first time'" (1987, 107). The key phrase— the cliché of method acting—is that the actor is always "in the moment." Note the importance, here as in Gillette, of the factor of time: the "reality" of the actor (i.e. the apparent representational completeness of the virtual) rests in the apparent truthfulness of the performer's and the performance's existence in the perpetual present tense. The actor, doing real things in imagined circumstances, does them in "real"—i.e. in the audience's—time.

The theorists and practitioners of Original Practices, coming at the latter end of the Long Stanislavskian Century, inherited the "reality" of "present-tense-ness" from the Stanislavskian paradigm. Their source for this, I'd like to suggest, is the somewhat monolithic dogma about Shakespearean verse speaking that emerged in the 1970s, which has been most eloquently articulated by Cicely Berry, John Barton, Kristin Linklater, and Patsy Rodenburg.

All of these voice gurus argue that "naturalism"—which they identify as the aesthetic of contemporary acting that is well-suited to contemporary dramatic writing and the media of film and television—is not equivalent to the acting aesthetics of the early modern period, and is not by itself ideally suited to handling the demands of Shakespearean characterization, emotional expression, or heightened language. John Barton, in the first episode of his widely disseminated television series *Playing Shakespeare*, calls these "the two traditions," and argues that, to act Shakespeare, a contemporary actor must draw upon both: "Playing Shakespeare is to do with marrying the two traditions. And in saying that I'm not suggesting that one's more important than the other. They are both vital."[10]

When the voice gurus describe "naturalism,"—which Barton defines as "The deliberate attempt to make everything as natural and lifelike as possible" (1984, 11)—they unmoor it from its associations with a specific mid-nineteenth-century literary and theatrical sub-movement of realism (along with its informing scientific program) and assign it instead to mid-twentieth-century Method-based (and American) acting, and its clichéd mannerisms: grunts, pauses, and scratches.

---

[9]   Viola Spolin, *Improvisation for the Theater* (Evanston: Northwestern University Press, 1963), 4.

[10]   John Barton, *Playing Shakespeare* (New York: Methuen, 1984), 23.

Barton asks David Suchet to perform Salerio's first long speech to Antonio in *The Merchant of Venice* "naturalistically"—the transcription adds the stage direction to the printed speech, "with many grunts and pauses"—and then concludes, "We've just been listening to what is sometimes called the 'naturalistic fallacy'" (1984, 17–18).

For all four of the voice gurus, the differences between contemporary "naturalism" and contemporary Shakespearean acting is neither emotions nor the dynamics of a character's actions and objectives, but whether or not the actor and the character act between the words or on the words. In real life, Linklater argues, "The adult voice is, in most instances, conditioned to talk *about* feelings rather than to *reveal* them."[11] For Berry, what distinguishes Shakespeare from "naturalism" is that, in Shakespeare, "our feelings and thought have to be released at the moment of speech." The crucial factor in the 1970s and 80s codification of Shakespearean verse speaking is time—not time as a theme, as in Barton's much-parodied fetishizing of that word, but time as theatrical phenomenon. When we act "naturalistically," Berry argues, "in our concern to get the motive right, we sometimes think the thought slightly before we say it—we plan our thinking to an extent—and so we do not live through the thought as it happens."[12] But when acting Shakespeare, Berry suggests,

> the thought and feeling must be instinctive and must be let go unambiguously with the words, for there is no time for naturalistic consideration: it is always explicit. When, with the character, there is consideration of feeling or ambiguity or thought, these are expressed in the choice of word itself and the rhythm of the speech, and happen with it. ... The way language happens always begs the question: which comes first, the thought or the word. And because the speech is direct, it is the physical movement of the thought. (1992, 47)

"Heightened language," Barton argues,

> must be something that the actor, or rather the character he's playing, *finds for himself* because he *needs* those words and images to express his intentions. [...] We can put this idea in various ways: we can say you've got to *find* them or *coin* them or *fresh-mint* them. We can use any word we want to describe the idea of inventing a phrase at the very moment it is uttered. The vital thing is that the speaker must *need* the phrase. He must not think of such phrases as simply words that pre-exist the text. They have got to be words that he finds as he utters them. (1984, 17; Barton's emphases.)

The actor "must *find* the language and make his listeners feel the words are coming out for the very first time" (1984, 86–7).

---

[11]   Kristin Linklater, *Freeing Shakespeare's Voice: The Actor's Guide to Talking the Text* (New York: Theatre Communications Group, 1992), 6.

[12]   Cicely Berry, *The Actor and the Text* (New York: Applause Books, 1992), 19.

In drawing a distinction between what they call "naturalism" and the heightened language of early modern dramatic writing and acting, and in relegating "naturalism" to a style and set of expressive conventions rather than to a distinctive paradigm, the voice gurus are appropriating for Shakespearean acting the one feature that arguably distinguishes proto-Stanislavskian and Stanislavskian acting from the paradigms that preceded it: being spontaneous and "in the moment." As Patsy Rodenburg observes, in acting Shakespeare, "Your existence is in the moment and on the word and thought. It fires through your mouth and is made real through the word."[13] Note Rodenburg's phrase "made real." For the voice gurus, speech opens up the metaphysical possibility of the actual. Berry famously quotes Peter Brook, who said, when she was assisting him in rehearsing *A Midsummer Night's Dream* in 1970, "words change both the situation, the speaker and the listener. After words are spoken, nothing is quite the same." Language makes something happen, and what happens is here, now, and, above all, *real*.

There is a direct line between the voice gurus and the Folio-script fetishists of the Original Practices movement.[14] Like the voice gurus, the O.P. polemicists Neil Freeman and Patrick Tucker knowingly or unconsciously meld the "two traditions." On the one hand, as with the voice gurus, everything the actor needs is in the language, and the structures and rhythms of the verse are effectively Shakespeare's stage directions; Freeman takes this one step further, ascribing the same type of authorial/directorial intentionality to the irregular spelling, punctuation, capitalization, and lineation of the *First Folio*. On the other hand, Freeman is explicitly Stanislavskian in many of his suggestions to actors: for example, he urges the actress playing Juliet, returning to feelings of love for Romeo after calling him a fiend, to recall people she has loved, and to "hear their voice," "smell their perfume," "remember what the person felt like when you held them, and breathe the touch throughout your body," etc., calling such an exercise "sense memory."[15] In addition, he speaks of Viola's emotional "journey" and of Lady Macbeth balancing "costs and rewards" (1999; 174, 193). And, in a suggestion not unlike the acting theories of the Group Theatre veteran Morris Carnovsky, he invites the actor to envision a sequence of visually concrete mental images (1999, 47–8). In describing the insights the early published scripts gives the actor, he even uses the word "subtext" (1999, 59).

---

[13] Patsy Rodenburg, *Speaking Shakespeare* (New York: Palgrave Macmillan, 2002), 5–6.

[14] Neil Freeman acknowledges Kristin Linklater and her one-time partner at Shakespeare and Company, Tina Packer, in *Shakespeare's First Texts* and his three-volume workbook, *Once More Unto the Speech, Dear Friends* (and Linklater returns the favor, dedicating a significant part of a chapter to Freeman and the First Folio in *Freeing Shakespeare's Voice*); and Patrick Tucker acknowledges John Barton in *Secrets of Acting Shakespeare*.

[15] Neil Freeman, *Shakespeare's First Texts* (Vancouver: Folio Scripts, 1999), 46.

Above all, Freeman inherits from the voice gurus the proto-Stanislavskian ideal of time, of acting as though in the present. His goal is to get the actor to "think like an Elizabethan," by which he means, as Barton, Berry, Linklater, and Rodenburg do, that thought and speech are simultaneous. Speech, he suggests, is "the mind in action" (1999, 44). *"Do not consider a speech as a 'set' speech,"* he advises; *"It is a series of thoughts, with no predicted end; there is no end until the end is actually reached. Stay in the ever-changing present,"* a phrase he credits to the twentieth-century actor, director, and movement artist Jean-Louis Barrault (1993, 43; Freeman's emphasis). Much of his introduction to each of the three volumes of his workbook, *Once More unto the Speech, Dear Friends*, is dedicated to cataloguing the different relationships the actor and the character have to time in the present tense—whether the character's thoughts are under control (what he calls "ice-cold"), or the character is working them through ("Einstein Shakespeare"), whether the character is volatile ("Russian Shakespeare," though he appears to be alluding, not to Stanislavski and Chekhov, but to extremities of emotional affect), or explosive ("volcanic"), with each variant further subdivided between instances where the character expects the given situation, or is surprised and emotionally challenged by the unexpected.[16]

In valuing above all the unfolding of simultaneous thought, emotion, and speech, and in joining the voice gurus in fetishizing language as the expression of the character's need to find (or, as Barton would say, to "coin," to "fresh mint") the word and phrase to express the emotions of the moment—the concept by which the voice specialists adhere most closely to the Stanislavskian paradigms of being "in the moment"—Freeman faces the same paradox that faced William Gillette nearly a century earlier. "Now it is a very difficult thing," observed Gillette, "—and even now an uncommon thing—for an actor who knows exactly what he is going to say to behave exactly as though he didn't; to let his thoughts (apparently) occur to him as him as he goes along, even though they are in his mind already; and (apparently) to search for and find the words by which to express those thoughts, even though these words are at his tongue's very ends."[17] Here is Freeman on the same phenomenon: "Of course, it's very easy to say to an actor/reader, 'the character must seem to have spontaneous and new thoughts, even though, in the case of the actor, you have been rehearsing the play for week!'. The question is, how?" (1999, 44). Freeman answers his own question: "So how is spontaneity, freshness of thought maintained? ... Simply by letting go," by moving from image from image, from *Folio* punctuation mark to punctuation mark, letting yourself be changed, via the language, by the "ever-changing present" (1999, 46). Freeman's elusive proto-Stanislavskian goal is, as it is for Strasberg, Meisner, Spolin, et. al.,

---

[16]   Neil Freeman, *Once More unto the Speech, Dear Friends:  Monologues from Shakespeare's First Folio with Modern Text Versions for Comparison* (New York: Applause Theatre Books, 2006),vol I, 6–7.

[17]   William Gillette, *The Illusion of the First Time in Acting*, Publications of the Dramatic Museum of Columbia University, 2nd Series (1915), 132.

spontaneity. And he proposes to achieve this by asking the actor to concentrate on each moment of the text, to move from moment to moment, to always ask (in what he calls the "inner dialogue" game) "what happens next?"

Freeman accepts that spontaneity is, as in Gillette, an illusion. But for Patrick Tucker, spontaneity is actual: to create the appearance of spontaneity, he suggests, be genuinely spontaneous. His program is, of course, to act without rehearsal from cue scripts. On the one hand, everything the actor needs to know is in the text, as it is for the voice gurus and for Freeman. But, unlike Freeman and the voice gurus, Tucker is most interested in what the cue-script doesn't tell the actor: what the context for the action is, what the action or objective of the other characters in the scene are, even who the speaker is who provides the cue for the actor's next line. Tucker's book, *Secrets of Acting Shakespeare: The Original Approach*— less a manifesto than a set of documents and anecdotes about productions by his theatre group, the Original Shakespeare Company—includes numerous examples of actors making discoveries in the moment, where the actor's confusions, uncertainties, and discoveries correspond to what the character is experiencing in the fictional situation: the quarreling lovers in *A Midsummer Night's Dream*, uncertain about the object of the affections they are expressing so passionately; Isabella surprised by her brother's reactions to Angelo's ultimatum; the Bastard's discovery, in *King John*, that his father is Richard Cordelion. The audience's delight in the apparent spontaneity of the event, Tucker suggests, is the experience of watching a discovery that is, to use Weingust's terms—not "realistic" but "real": the actor may only be representing the character, but the audience reads the "actual" discoveries of the actor for those of the character. Tucker even suggests that the plays' original audiences valued the actuality of spontaneity as much as the OSC's audiences do: early modern audiences, he speculates, were willing to pay double admission prices for first performances, not because they valued the novelty of new writing, but because they wanted to maximize their experience of the performance's spontaneity.[18]

In forsaking standard rehearsal processes in favor of an abbreviated rehearsal period with actors learning their lines from cue scripts, Tucker sets up a dichotomy between Shakespeare and "naturalism":

> So much modern acting is based on the idea that if only we can work out what is going on, and then work out how we ourselves would respond to that, then if we put all this into our acting, we will come over as truthful and real. Alas, this is not so for classic plays, where the writing is not based on some form of naturalism but on another basis altogether—on language as communication, on poetry as a form of subtext, and on the whole affecting an audience the way a wonderful painting or piece of music might, as a complete experience, not as a simple slice of life. (2002, 30)

---

[18]    Patrick Tucker, *Secrets of Acting Shakespeare: The Original Approach* (New York: Routledge, 2002), 146.

Like the voice gurus, who posit a false dichotomy between Shakespeare and "naturalism," defining "naturalism," not as an aesthetic paradigm but as a "style," co-opting on behalf of Shakespeare the quintessential Stanislavskian notions of being "in the moment," so too Tucker here establishes a false dichotomy between Shakespeare and naturalism based on erroneous definitions of naturalism, enabling him to co-opt aspects of the Stanislavskian paradigm and assign them to Shakespeare instead. Yes, the Moscow Art Theatre and the Group Theatre had long rehearsal periods, and the major Method Acting teachers advocated extensive and intensive biographical exploration. But although Tucker advocates abandoning intense preparation in favor of the free and spontaneous discoveries of performance, he is not abandoning character-based acting or dramatic "action" based on emotional objectives and emotional needs. He observes about the actress playing Isabella in her scene with Claudio: "she has to create the character who wants and needs to say those particular lines, not worry about what a supposed novice nun would feel or say" (2002, 91). Action and emotional objectives follow from the stimulus and response of the moment, Tucker seems to be suggesting, rather than from character biography and back story. Tucker's objections to intensive, introspective, Strasbergian biographical preparation, and his emphasis instead on the actor's response to the stimuli of the immediate situation, are valid. But these same objections are shared by many of the most interesting late-twentieth-century Stanislavski-based schools of acting, what I like to call "Stanislavski 2.0"—seen in Declan Donnellan's notion of the "Target," Charles Marowitz's "Other Way," Anne Bogart's "Viewpoints," David Mamet's "Practical Acting"—which similarly free the actor from biographical determinism in order to pursue no less Stanislavskian objectives.[19] For Tucker, acting is still shaped by the pursuit of objectives; poetry provides what Tucker calls "subtext"; and the actor and the character, "fresh-coining" the language as though in the moment, are acting upon what Rodenburg calls "The Need for Words." The truth of Tucker's theatre, like that of Sanford Meisner and Viola Spolin, depends above all on the truth of the spontaneous response to stimulus. Like Meisner, he is most interested in reducing the temporal distance between the pinch and the ouch. For Tucker, the truth of the performance is the ouch.

Many of the ideas that Freeman and Tucker discovered in practice have actually been borne out by the scholarship of Tiffany Stern (who, to be sure, is Tucker's niece). For example, Tucker found that several of his actors needed one-on-one verse work with a coach in preparing their roles from their cue-scripts, and so he accedes to what he calls "verse-nursing"; and he gathers his full company

---

[19]    See Declan Donnellan, *The Actor and the Target* (St. Paul: Theatre Communications Group, 2002); Charles Marowitz, *The Other Way: An Alternative Approach to Acting and Directing* (New York: Applause, 1999); Anne Bogart and Tina Landau. *The Viewpoints Book: A Practical Guide to Viewpoints and Composition* (New York: Theatre Communications Group, 2005). For my own experiments in asking actors to play action without biography, see "*Miss Julie* at the University of Pennsylvania: A Case Study in Shared Student-Faculty Theatre Research," *New England Theatre Journal* 20 (2009), 104–111.

for a single rehearsal of key moments—which he calls a "Burbage"—before the first performance, to coordinate difficult group entrances and the movement of larger props and set pieces. Stern found that both of these practices (though not the names) were standard practice in early modern playhouses.

Stern, like Tucker, seems almost obsessively fascinated by moments in which the situation for the actor waiting for a cue is congruent with the actions and emotions of the character. She notes in particular cases where the confusion generated by an ambiguous cue belongs to the character and the fictional situation as much as it does to the actors. In one example (which she cites in each of her books) Shylock, escorting the Jailer taking Antonio to prison, says "I will have my bond" numerous times before Solanio is able to speak his next line, for which "I will have my bond" is the cue: "Weighed down with the irritation and embarrassment of repeated false cues," she argues, "the actor playing Solanio will have been wrought to a pitch of uncompromising anger by the time he was actually permitted to speak. The interruption and the shouting down are provided for by the part, and the anger required, rather than being 'directed' in advance, is created in performance."[20] For Stern, the actuality of the actors' confusion creates the reality of the fictional scene, which, as Weingust says of Tucker's theatre pieces, ceases to be "realistic" and becomes instead "real."

Stern makes the phenomenon of early modern actors performing from cue-scripts—which forms small if significant components of *Rehearsal from Shakespeare to Sheridan* and *Making Shakespeare*—the centerpiece of her next book, *Shakespeare in Parts*, written with Simon Palfrey, who had previously written on character and language in the late plays. The historical scholarship of *Shakespeare in Parts* is, as in Stern's previous books, unimpeachable; but some of the interpretive implications she and Palfrey draw fall into some of the same patterns, and raise some of the same questions about methodology and aesthetic assumptions, as those of the O.P. practitioners and polemicists whose obsessions they share.

As in Stern's earlier work, the authors gravitate toward moments when ambiguous cuing or the surprise of the unexpected generate emotions in the actor that correspond to those of the character: they revel in Cordelia's first scene, Macduff's reaction to the news of his family's assassination, and Bertram's discovery of precisely whom he is marrying at the end of the play. Like Freeman, they emphasize Isabella's surprise throughout her encounters with Angelo, Claudio, and the Duke, and especially at the Duke's proposal at the end of the play.[21]

---

[20]   Tiffany Stern, *Rehearsal from Shakespeare to Sheridan* (Oxford and New York: Oxford University Press, 2000), 89.

[21]   It is useful to compare their emphasis on Isabella's making discoveries in real time to the observations of Juliet Stevenson about playing the role, and working in the RSC tradition of Barton and Berry, in Carol Rutter's *Clamourous Voices: Shakespeare's Women Today* (New York: Routledge, 1989), in which even the line "more than our brother is our chastity" is so sudden a discovery that it astonishes Isabella as much as it does the audience (51).

Palfrey and Stern are admirably cautious about the conclusions they can draw from their own examples about early modern character and acting. They are careful to state that "This is not to propose a straightforward contiguity between the actor's ego and emotions of the character."[22] And they pause as they begin to write about character to note:

> However—and this point is fundamental to our method and argument—we do not base our conclusion upon any preconceptions concerning what an actor's relationship should or must be to his parts; still less do we base our argument (as it were pre-emptively) upon expectations of actorly neuroses, or motivational techniques, or empathy exercises, of anything of the kind. Rather, as with everything in the book, we proceed 'inductively' from the particular instances—the evidence about contemporary practice of rehearsal/conning, and the evidence of Shakespeare's play-texts—generating conclusions from the accumulation of discrete phenomena. (2007, 78)

That said, here is their explanation of Cordelia's first scene:

> Shakespeare clearly wants his actors to share in the surprise and tentativeness of the experiences he unfolds for his characters. This is, indeed, the surest way of achieving the requisite immediacy of successful theatre. And a fundamental method Shakespeare uses for doing so is to make the information offered by the cued part tell a slightly differently-angled story from the simultaneous unfolding 'whole' scene […] Cues become almost the glands of the part, small nodal points that structure and serve the larger organism, synthesizing, secreting, distributing whatever chemistry is here at work. (2007, 100)

The glandular imagery aside, note how they identify a play's "chemistry" as its having achieved "the requisite immediacy of successful theatre." And note how they explain how an actor can recapture the spontaneity of the first performance at later performances:

> If the actor feels the dramatic rightness of a 'surprise', feels how this rightness originated in his own experience (of uncertainty, anger, shock, etc.), then his job in a subsequent performance will be to recover such feeling with as much freshness and gusto as he can muster. We might liken it to a small wound or trauma that *needs* to be repeated; it may even be that 'surprise' was itself an aid to memory, or at least to the memorable etching of *that* particular persona 'in' the actor's sense memory. Almost everything written about early modern actors attest to an aesthetic of seeming spontaneity, however calmly or even coldly arrived at. Hence the mother-lode of Shakespearean characterization: parts wherein the osmosis of actor and character is respected, and exploited, as never before. (2007, 154)

---

[22]    Tiffany Stern and Simom Palfrey, *Shakespeare in Parts* (Oxford and New York: Oxford University Press, 2007), 118.

Note here the selective emphasis on the early modern theatre's putative "spontaneity" (for which they offer no supporting evidence in support of their statement that "almost everything written" attests to it), and their truly astonishing invocation of the term and concept of "sense memory."

And so Palfrey and Stern soldier on, through several hundred pages of part-book-based character analysis, to a set of grand conclusions about early modern histrionic aesthetics and the phenomenology of early modern performance:

> [...] working from parts means that there is precious little chance to pre-emptively know what is coming; previous little of that practised, comprehensive foreknowledge that modern actors, rehearsing week after week from a full text, hope or expect to secure. Shakespeare's actors had to play their parts *now*, perilously in the present. Often they are left waiting for something yet to come; often they are exposed to surprise, accident and abruptness. Experience for these actors is repetitive *and* immediate: however haunted by memories or anticipations, however paralysed by fear or riddled with uncanny recapitulations, *this* particular thing has never happened before, just as *that* actor has never been exactly in this moment. We might know every last word, but still there is no securely predictive script. [...] The play is dead unless the actor is alive, and the actor is only alive if the part seems—to him and to the audience—to be happening for the very first time. If he once felt surprise and apprehension, it is precisely such feeling that he needs to recover, so that in acting the part he can always be a micro-moment 'before' any thought or movement, assuring the audience that his character, *now*, is the one who has the thought or makes the movement. (2007, 491–92)

Having disclaimed any preconceptions about the aesthetics of acting the enactment of character, Palfrey and Stern now conclude, on the basis of their character analyses, that the aesthetics of acting were, at the end of the sixteenth century and the beginning of the seventeenth, precisely what they were at the beginning of the long Stanislavskian century three hundred years later: aspiring to create a performance that exists in the perpetual present, as though for the first time. Faced with the conundrum that Gillette recognized a century ago—that an actor had to speak and behave as though for the first time what had been meticulously prepared beforehand—they eliminate rehearsal altogether, opting for a Spolin-like improvisational freedom, and a Meisnerian truth-of-the-moment that stems from a truthful response to an actual stimulus. And, as they state in their final paragraph, "In exploring something as lost and unfamiliar as actors' parts, we have nevertheless been led to perhaps surprisingly recognizable conclusions: that the actors were asked to act 'feelingly'" (2007, 484).

My main contention—that the polemicists and practitioners of Original Practices, while claiming that they are eschewing modernist and contemporary theatrical aesthetics and recapturing the lost aesthetics of Shakespeare's own theatre, are actually actively participating in the very aesthetics that they are renouncing—may ultimately rest on whether or not one is prepared to accept Palfrey and Stern's conclusions. And I will allow for the possibility that they may, indeed, be right. (At the very least, I certainly admire them for seeking to derive their conclusions from analysis of evidence rather than taking it all as axiomatic, as the O.P. practitioners do.) If they *are* right, then Gillette and the other semi-articulate early formulators of a stumbling and inchoate set of acting principles at the dawn of the Long Stanislavskian Century were not merely the products of the aesthetic and material assumptions of their day, but were in fact grappling with universal and eternal principles of theatre, principles that Shakespeare and his contemporaries had already discovered and put into practice. I must confess, though, that I remain unconvinced. And for me, the burden of proof rests with O.P.

What is most astonishing about Stern and Palfrey's scholarly exercise is what it says about the persistence of character criticism, even within a theatrical and historicist—or, more accurately, a theatre historicist—project. And it is noteworthy that such character criticism is not derived from the persistence of trends in literary criticism, but is rather due to the inescapability of contemporary paradigms of theatrical practice. Modern theatre practitioners, whose principal task is to create a theatre piece for their audiences, in their theatre, *now*, are freed from any obligation to replicate the complexities and ambiguities of early modern subjectivity in their original time, and so can embrace, explicitly or tacitly, the character-based histrionic paradigms of the Long Stanislavskian Century. O.P. practitioners, by contrast, work within the self-imposed restrictions of early modern culture and stagecraft, as they have reconstructed these things based on their historical studies; and yet, as I have shown, they read their history backwards, ascribing to Shakespeare's own theatrical practices the character-based principles of temporality, spontaneity, and subjectivity that derives from modern Stanislavskian histrionic paradigms, thereby practicing a uniquely theatrical version of the intentional fallacy.[23] O.P. scholars, exercising immense scholarly caution and meticulous attention to historical detail, derive a definition of dramatic character from early modern theatrical practices; but as their understanding of these early modern theatrical practices is, like the theatrical work of O.P. practitioners, unconsciously shaped by modern Stanislavskian paradigms of acting and character, it is hardly surprising that their conclusions are so proto-Stanislavksian. And so we are left, for better and for worse, with yet another form of traditional character criticism.

Et in Arcadia ego.[24]

---

[23]  See my "The Intentional-Fallacy Fallacy," in Lena Cowan Orlin and Miranda Johnson-Haddad, eds., *Staging Shakespeare: Essays in Honor of Alan C. Dessen* ( Newark: University of Delaware Press, 2007), 99–113.

[24]  An earlier version of this essay was presented at a working group on Shakespeare in Performance at the American Society for Theatre Research conference in San Juan in 2009; I am grateful for the comments and feedback of Andrew Carlson, Rebecca Johanssen, Yu Jin Ko, Andrew Sofer, W.B. Worthen, and above all the working group organizer, Don Weingust. This essay is part of an ongoing collegial dialogue with Weingust.

## Chapter 6
# (Re:)Historicizing Spontaneity: Original Practices, Stanislavski, and Characterization

### Tiffany Stern

The term "Original Practices" ("O.P.") was created in 1998 by actor and director Mark Rylance to address what was happening at the theater for which he was Artistic Director, "Shakespeare's Globe." It had little to do with characterization, though it did relate to spontaneousness. Defending the nature of Globe productions, Rylance said that his actors engaged in banter with the audience in a way that replicated "original practice."[1] Thus O.P. in its earliest definition was linked to a form of spontaneous response said to be the quintessence of early modern performance, a point to which I will return. For Cary Mazer (in his preceding essay in this volume), a disparate collection of people, some of whom stopped working, and some of whom started working, as the term O.P. came into being, are said to share O.P. aims: Patrick Tucker, a semi-retired director; Neil Freeman, an Emeritus academic and theater practitioner; and three current academics, Don Weingust, Simon Palfrey and me. All are seen by him as having "the same aesthetic assumptions as O.P.," although in fact none has ever used the term "Original Practice" to describe their work.[2] But, writes Mazer, these assumptions have their origins in 1970s ideas about verse speaking as articulated by one director and three voice coaches (called, collectively, by him, "voice gurus"). These 70s practitioners, he further claims, were actually putting into practice Stanislavskian or post-Stanislavskian precepts. Beliefs about how to create dramatic character expressed by the "voice gurus," and inherited by the "O.P. folks," are consequently erroneous: they are datable only to the 'Long Stanislavskian Century' and later.

This chapter will address some features of Mazer's reading of O.P. before supplying an analysis of early modern techniques for characterizing spontaneity that will suggest that "Stanislavskian" ideas of characterization, spontaneity and emotional realism have a considerably older heritage than has been proposed.

---

[1]   Mark Rylance, "Meet the Real Shakespeare," *The Times of London*, 14 August 1998.

[2]   "Original Practices" is in the index to Don Weingust's *Acting from Shakespeare's First Folio: Theory, Text, and Performance* (New York: Routledge, 2006), though the term does not appear to be used in the text.

There is a link that tenuously unites Mazer's "folk": all have a connection to Patrick Tucker, some through sharing his directing aims, some through promoting his beliefs about the First Folio, some through blood (I am his niece). As Patrick Tucker named his players "The Original Shakespeare Company" (OSC) in 1990, his ideas might be called the precursors of O.P.; indeed, Rylance may have taken the word "original," rather than, say, "authentic," from him. Tucker's "originalities," however, clashed with those of the Globe. He experimented with early modern rehearsal techniques, giving each of his OSC players only his or her own lines and cues to learn, and staging the result—boisterous, largely undirected, emotionally charged performances, that reconceived character as rooted in actors' eviscerated texts. Rylance was exploring alternative originalities at this time—gender, accents, clothes and, of course, space, but not method of production; "characterization" in Globe productions was still, in contemporary fashion, determined by a director's concept. In 1999 Rylance evicted the OSC from its yearly performances at the Globe, because, he wrote, their approach did not "serve the play"; the company folded the following year.[3] Cast out from the "home" of O.P. by the "inventor" of the phrase, Tucker is possibly the only practitioner in the world who is definitely not O.P. as defined by its originator.

Mazer's second claim is that the people he unites under the umbrella term "O.P. folks" are forever "fetishizing 'spontaneity'" in their concepts of character and performance. Yet, he argues, far from being early modern, the idea that actors should generate real emotions in the moment of performance is traceable to Stanislavski. He posits a trajectory in which Stanislavskian ideas were promulgated in the 1970s by a group of what he calls "voice gurus" and then haphazardly adopted by the "folks." The "gurus" are Royal Shakespeare Company (RSC) director John Barton; RSC voice coach Cicely Berry; and the British and British-trained Kristin Linklater and Patsy Rodenburg.

Mazer's useful definition of the background to the "method" supposedly adopted by the "gurus," however, raises some questions. "The method," as Mazer explains it, is made up of a series of books by Stanislavski published in the 1920s and aimed at American readers (the "system"), combined with further work undertaken by Richard Boleslavsky and Maria Ouspenskaya at the American Laboratory Theater in the 1920s, and added to by the members and alumni of the Group Theater, also in America, in the 1930s and 50s. As his definitions make clear, an obsessive interest in "the method" as a primary way of conceiving characters' emotions is American—so much so that while American actors have traditionally been taught "method acting" first and foremost, British actors have traditionally been taught "classical" (or what in America is sometimes called "English") acting, though twenty-first-century practice muddies this. Illustrative of the powerful divide that separated famous American and British actors in the 70s—the time in which Mazer locates the spread of Stanislavskianism by the British "voice gurus"—is the tale, often told, of the filming of *Marathon Man* (1976). Dustin Hoffman, an American

---

[3]        The letter is discussed in Weingust, *Acting from Shakespeare's First Folio,* 183–84.

"method actor," and Laurence Olivier, an English "classical actor," famous for his RSC performances of Macbeth, Coriolanus and Titus Andronicus, were to play a scene together. As the story goes, Hoffman, in preparation for being the dentist's sleep-deprived victim, spent two days without sleep, experiencing the suffering appropriate for his part. Olivier, seeing the state Hoffman was in as they arrived on set, is said to have exclaimed: "Dear boy! ... why don't you try acting?"[4]

Whether or not the story is true, British theater training offered by the RSC of the 70s was seldom Stanislavskian. The RSC's attitude to characterization and emotions, elegantly presented in Abigail Rokison's *Shakespearean Verse Speaking*, actually comes from an entirely different progenitor: the charismatic academic George ("Dadie") Rylands, who was a regular director of Cambridge University's "Marlowe Society" performances between 1929-66.[5] Rylands believed in generating character through speaking verse correctly. His notions were foundational to the RSC, for John Barton, Peter Hall and Trever Nunn all produced or acted under Rylands' tutelage while students; the RSC's tendency to beat out the iambics (which creates the need for voice coaches) is directly traceable to Rylands. Yet Rylands' ideas had descended ultimately from William Poel (1852–1934), the actor and theater manager who had founded the Elizabethan Stage Society in an attempt to recreate Elizabethan performance conditions. It was Poel's nephew, Reginald Pole, who had created the Cambridge Marlowe Dramatic Society in 1907, with a view to furthering his uncle's work in a university context; Rylands, intellectually and practically, "inherited" Poel and passed on his ideas.

Poel could be described as, in his nature, anti-Stanislavskian. Writing in 1923, before the works of Stanislavski had been published in English, and long before anything approaching "the method" had reached England from America, Poel maintained that modern performance should be artful rather than "real":

> We continually hear English teachers say to their pupils, "Fancy yourselves really in the position of the person whose character you have undertaken to represent, and let the inspiration of the moment do the rest." ... It is apparent that voices which have had no preliminary training, and which therefore possess no flexibility of the vocal organs, cannot support the continual strain of an impressive delivery of poetic eloquence.[6]

The RSC, and the Central School of Verse and Drama, which proudly embrace what Peter Hall has called the "Poel Principles," can certainly be said, as Mazer suggests, to have origins in a system "codified in the nineteenth century"—as

---

[4]  Alan Hamilton, "Laurence Olivier at Seventy-Five," *The Times of London*, 17 May 1982.

[5]  Abigail Rokison, *Shakespearean Verse Speaking: Text and Theatre Practice* (Cambridge: Cambridge University Press, 2009), 29–30.

[6]  William Poel, "What became of £12,000," *Shakespeare Journal* 9 (1923), 33–4, quoted in Stephen C. Schultz, "William Poel on the Speaking of Shakespearean Verse: A Reevaluation," *Shakespeare Quarterly* 28 (1977), 334–50 (335).

watered down through Rylands, and thence through Barton, Hall and Nunn. And Mazer is likely to be right, too, that some of his "O.P. folks" have inherited ideas essentially from RSC practice, for Tucker was assistant director for the RSC in the late 1960s, and worked for Barton; Weingust and Freeman could have received his thoughts through conversation and performance, and through admiring the productions. But it is hard to argue that this has much to do with Stanislavski. Rather, in a neat circle, the nineteenth century precursor to O.P. feeds into RSC performance, and thence back to Mazer's "O.P. folks."

Yet, though Mazer's idea about the RSC's Stanislavskian lineage is questionable, he is nevertheless right that spontaneity of one kind or another—often located in the character—*is* favored by scholars and directors of "original" performances. So the big question is whether this notion is Stanislavskian in its origin or whether it could have been acquired from elsewhere. Might "sponteaneous" emotions in performance have an early modern heritage? To explore this, it is necessary to summarize what has already been said of relevance to this debate, before providing some further "new" historical material.

Early modern actors received and learned their characters from "parts" ("parts" being the early modern word for what Mazer sometimes calls "sides," a Victorian term, and sometimes "cue scripts," a term adopted from the 1950s by Tucker). These parts contained all the lines the character was going to say, plus cues of, generally, one to three words in length. As actors would learn their parts and cues in advance of rehearsal or performance, any "characterization" they developed would be based on the words articulated by their fictional personae. Rehearsal practices merely made the divide between character and play more pointed: for in a process known as "study," actors would learn their parts at home, away from the rest of the text, though sometimes employing the help of an "instructor." Only once they had fully learned their roles would the individually-prepared actors rehearse ensemble; this they would do as many times as necessary to make a good performance. As rehearsal was unpaid, however, "as many times as necessary" tended to mean "one time" and could mean "no times."[7]

Of particular interest, with respect to actors experiencing texts in a "real" and "spontaneous" fashion, is the following tension. Given that the main aim of the actor in "study" was to isolate the "passions" his character went through and decide how to portray them using the appropriate gesture and emphasis, acting at the time seems to have been formulaic, fixed, and, though utterly based on the emotions, not spontaneous. Yet given that there was no "director," and that almost any instructions not on the part were picked up during the ensemble process of rehearsal or, more often, performance—a process made particularly vertiginous by its reliance on "cues" rather than deep knowledge of the full text—acting at the time was simultaneously filled with moments that were immediate and unpredictable. Mazer's sense is perhaps that the one negates the other: but it would seem that early modern performance was both prescribed and ungovernable, partly

7    Simon Palfrey and Tiffany Stern, "Rehearsal," *Shakespeare in Parts* (Oxford: Oxford University Press, 2009), 70–73.

because "passion," or emotion, was at the heart of what performance—and hence character—was; and partly because cues were.

Acting at the time was often called "passioning" or "passionating," because of its emotional burden; witness Samuel Nicholson's asking an actor "whose person did you passionate?"[8] So Hamlet, keen to determine how good the player is, demands as "a taste" of "your quality," "a passionate speech" (*Hamlet*, 2.2.306). He later instructs the player how to perform best in the "torrent, tempest, and, as I may say, whirlwind of your passions" (*Hamlet*, 3.2.5–6). A character, indeed, was on some level seen as a series of emotional units—just as, later, in Stanislavski's system, a character would be seen as a series of "units of action" (it could, indeed, be said that passion brings about action and vice versa). An actor seems to have scanned his text therefore for those moments when one passion gave way to another, indicated, in early modern parts, by change of vocabulary and rhetorical style—from prolix to specific, from lyrical to blunt, from prose to verse, etc; such emotional switches were, from the Restoration onwards, known as "transitions."[9] Yet as Joseph Roach brilliantly discusses, passions were thought to be physiological secretions within the body as well as feelings.[10] To perform a character well, an actor had to embrace both his own and his character's changing physiological state, for as Thomas Wright explains in *The Passions of the Minde in Generall*, "the passion which is in our brest is the fountaine and origen of all externall actions."[11] He could do this in two ways: by pretending (as, all those years later, "classic" actor Olivier would do), or by forcing himself into the position where he experienced "real feelings" (as, all those years later, "method" actor Hoffman would do).

It would be useful to be able, at this stage, to quote some early modern English acting manuals. Alas, there are none. What there are, instead, are translations, anecdotes, and redactions, written in the early modern period, but often about performance in the times of the ancient Greeks and Romans. These classical performances are, however, regularly said to be replicated in the early modern era, for humanists accepted and promoted many of the values of their Golden and Silver Ages forebears. The period preceding what Mazer calls the Long Stanislavski Century—what might be called the Long Early Modern Period—produces instances that sometimes seem interchangeable with Mazer's definition of the Stanislavskian "system" and the "method."

To begin with "affective memory": the practice of making performance "real" by drawing upon one's own life so as to experience, in Mazer's words, "the actual on the stage." Mazer traces this idea to Strasberg, but Strasberg, like the early modernists, thought it an ancient Greek theatrical practice, and he, like they,

---

[8]    Samuel Nicholson, *Acolastus* (London: John Baylie, 1600), G3b.

[9]    For more on this, see Palfrey and Stern, "Interpreting Parts and Emotions," *Shakespeare in Parts*, 311–327.

[10]   Joseph R. Roach, "Changeling Proteus: Rhetoric and the Passions in the Seventeenth Century," *The Player's Passion* (Ann Arbor: University of Michigan Press, 1993), 23–57.

[11]   Thomas Wright, *The Passions of the Minde* (London: Valentine Simmes, 1604), 174.

presented as a model a story first related by Aulius Gellius (ca. 125 AD—after 180 AD) concerning Polus (or Polo), the classical tragedian. Here is an early modern telling of the tale, together with its conclusion:

> Wee well remember, how Polo the tragedian, acting the part of Electra upon the Stage; and being mournefully to bring in the bones of her brother Orestes in a pot, hee brought in the bones of his owne Sonne lately buried, that the sight of them might wring forth true tears indeed; and by their passionate presentment of them, act it more feelingly: for objects of Ocular passion cannot chuse but worke in the actors person.[12]

Richard Brathwait, writing/translating the extract above, uses the story to offer advice: "Objects of Ocular passion" can be used to trigger emotions out of one's past life on the contemporary stage. Strasberg also drew conclusions from this story, which he saw as being a forerunner to his own beliefs: "Rather than mere acting, this was in fact real grief being expressed."[13]

Polus's method, however, was advisable only for performers who required "helps." Other writers maintained that sense memory could if necessary be extracted spontaneously from one's own mind or memory, with no objects required. The spokesman for this approach was originally Quintilian, whose *Institutio Oratoria* was a foundational rhetorical manual in the humanist educational curriculum of the early modern period. It was in the first century AD that Quintilian, who had "often seen actors, both in tragedy and comedy ... after going through some distressing scene, quit the theater weeping," advised orators to locate "truthful" emotions in their lives and then re-remember them when "performing" their speeches—or, as Mazer puts it, draw upon their own lives "using 'sense memory'" as a means of triggering an 'emotional memory'":

> The chief requisite, then, for moving the feelings of others is, as far as I can judge, that we ourselves be moved, for the assumption of grief, anger, and indignation will be often ridiculous if we adapt merely our words and looks, and not our minds, to those passions ... But by what means, it may be asked, shall we be affected since our feelings are not in our own power? I will attempt to

---

[12]    Richard Brathwait, *The Arcadian Princesse* (London: Th. Harper, 1635), 66–7; repeated 153–54. See also Charles Fitz-Geffry, *Compassion towards Captives* (London: Leonard Lichfield, 1636), 25; Justus Lipsius, *Two Bookes of Constancie* (London: Richard Johnes, 1595), 18; Fanciscus Junius, *The Painting of the Ancients* (London: Richard Hodginksonne, 1638), 62; George Benson, *A Sermon Preached at Paules Crosse* (London: H. Lownes, 1609), 61. Leofranc Holford-Strevens, "Polus And His Urn: A Case Study in the Theory of Acting c. 300 B.C. – c. A.D. 2000," *International Journal of the Classical Tradition,* 11 (2005), 499–523, considers the use made of the anecdote by theorists of acting and rhetoric from the Renaissance onwards, calling attention to a change during the eighteenth century from approval to disapprobation.

[13]    Lee Strasberg, in "The Art of the Theatre," *Encyclopaedia Britannica,* 15th edn (Chicago: Encyclopaedia Britannica, 1992), xxviii. 515–30 (525).

say something also on this point. What the Greeks call φαντασίαι (*phantasiai*) we call *visiones,* images by which the representations of absent objects are so distinctly represented to the mind that we seem to see them with our eyes and to have them before us. Whoever shall best conceive such images will have the greatest power in moving the feelings.[14]

Classical practice, propounded in the early modern period, promoted the exploitation of genuinely previous or imagined sources of emotion in order to create "real" moments that happened on stage as if for the first time—or even actually for the first time. As Lipsius wrote, comparing "vain glorious" people who pretended to care for their country (but who only really cared for their own private sorrows) with actors, "You play a Comedy, & under the person of your country, you bewail with tears your private miseries."[15]

An alternative was to identify so powerfully with the character one was performing as to experience not one's own feelings but the character's feelings: "no *Actor* well can play the *King,* / That is not one in his imagination."[16] This, however, was hazardous, for it meant losing oneself in a fictional role, risking being overtaken by the unreality altogether.[17] Just as, years later, "one of the byproducts of the Stanislavski method was a … fear that when method actors 'became' their characters, they [moved] precariously close to the madness that accompanies a loss of self,"[18] so early modern tales told of actors who became "stuck" and could not shake off their fictional personas. Clarimant in Carlell's *Passionate Lover* declares, "My care was such to do it to the life, / That I am really become what I did personate";[19] in "Against Aesop the Stage-player," John Davies relates how he:

> came to English Aesop (on a tide)
> As he lay tirde (as tirde) before to play:
> I came unto him in his flood of pride;
> He then was King, and thought I should obey.
> And so I did, …
> I, like a Subject (with submisse regard)
> Did him salute, yet he re-greeted mee
> But with a Nod, because his speech he spar'd
> For Lords and Knights that came his Grace to see.

---

[14]  John Selby Watson trans., *Quintilian's Institutes of Oratory* (London: Henry G. Bohn, 1856), 429, 427.

[15]  Lipsius, *Two Bookes of Constancie* (1595), 18.

[16]  Robert Aylett, *Divine and Moral Speculations* (London: Abel Roper, 1654), 93.

[17]  For more on this, see Palfrey and Stern, "'Becoming' the Part," *Shakespeare in Parts*, 45–50.

[18]  Jody Enders, "Of Madness and Method Acting" in *Death by Drama and Other Medieval Urban Legends* (Chicago: University of Chicago Press, 2002), 46.

[19]  Lodowick Carlell, *The Passionate Lover,* Part I (London: Humphrey Moseley, 1655), 20.

All this while, the English "Aesop" is, though offstage, performing being the king whose clothes he wears:

> I well knew him (though he knew not me)
> To be a player ...[20]

The problem was common enough; Brathwait, too, writes of "those Tragedians, who imitate the State of such persons they represented, after they have put off their Habits."[21] Other stories on the subject are, however, less jokey. One concerns actors who are so changed offstage by their onstage characters that only alcohol will return them to themselves—and even that does not always work:

> I have known my selfe, a Tyrant coming from the Scene not able to reduce himselfe, into the knowledge of himselfe, till Sack made him ... forget he was an Emperour ... and ... one most admirable Mimicke in our late Stage, so lively and corporally personated a Changeling, that he could never compose his Face to the figure it had, before he undertook that part.[22]

Somewhere between the two were the tales of actors who, on stage, experienced a burst of spontaneous emotion—either because they were summoning it from the past, or because they were "being" the character who had it. Again, warning stories from classical Greek practice are then shown to be happening in the early modern theater:

> in the times of the Auntients it oftentimes fell out, that the Stage players who acted some furious person as an Hercules ... have so acted ... their partes, as themselves in the midst of their sporte, have become truly and indeede furious, and have done actes of outrage and fury, even such as the parties did whome they represent.[23]

Amongst the early modern witnesses to this kind of acting is Hamlet. He is wrong-footed by the fact that the player cries real tears when speaking of a fictional death. As Mazer put it, summarizing Stanislavski, "Independent of, and apart from, the virtuality of the character, the actor's action is actual." And as Hamlet put it:

> ... this player here,
> But in a fiction, in a dream of passion,
> Could force his soul so to his own conceit
> That from her working all his visage wann'd,

---

[20]    John Davies, "Against Aesop the Stage-player" in *The Scourge of Folly* (London: Edward Allde,1611), 85.

[21]    Richard Brathwait, *A Survey of History* (London: N. and I. Okes, 1638), 370.

[22]    Edmund Gayton, *Pleasant Notes upon Don Quixote* (London: William Hunt, 1654), 144.

[23]    Pierre Le Loyer, *A Treatise of Spectres* (London: Val. Simmes, 1605), 116.

Tears in his eyes, distraction in's aspect,
A broken voice, and his whole function suiting
With forms to his conceit? And all for nothing!
For Hecuba! (*Hamlet*, 2.2.544–51)

That the "reality" of early modern performances was based on the reality of the "passions" felt enabled John Quarles to complicate the paradigm. He suggested that actual passion could seem paltry compared to actors' passions, at the very same time asserting that actors perform their passions "really" or "to the life": "Judge Ladies, judge, if ever grief could be / More acted to the life then 'tis in me."[24] Along similar lines, and using the same complicated phrase, "to the life," his *Virgin Widow* has the following exchange:

> *For.* *Comodus*, What eye did ere till now behold
> Folly and madnesse acted to the life?
> *Co.* I wonder *Formidon*, the King could bear
> Such sawcy passion with so clear a brow.[25]

"Sawcy passion" performed "to the life" was what, to Quarles, acting a character was.

As is clear from the above, any helps that might propel either the actor or his fictional character into the correct passion in the moment would be invaluable. The contention that Palfrey and I put forward in *Shakespeare in Parts* was that Shakespeare's use of cues and parts provided this assistance. We were intrigued, for instance, by the way cues themselves were so often associated with emotional switches—from Edmund's "my cue is villainous melancholy" in *King Lear* (1.2.135) to Hamlet's "motive and cue for passion" in *Hamlet* (2.2.554)—and we explored the way cues often contained emotion-laden words, "love," "hate," "joy," etc, wondering what this said for the loaded cue-space as well as for the cue and the text itself. We should perhaps have pointed out that the very word "cue" accrued meanings to do with the emotions it brought about. It is described in the *OED* as, variously, a "concluding word which is direction for speech," "a hint as to how to act," and "a humour or state of mind." That development of meaning shows a simple actors' prompt becoming connected to mood and mentality, as though cues ultimately create emotion and intellectual state.

As we were concentrating on proposing a form of "character criticism" through exploring the little-discussed medium of cues and parts, we did not supply additional information on the history of acting "spontaneity" more generally; that has been, briefly, rectified here. It should be remarked, however, that in the early modern period, as at every subsequent period, there were vexed and opposite statements made about what actors did, why and how; the potential slippage between "seeming" and "being," or "showing true" rather than "with true life"

---

[24] John Quarles, *The History Of the Most Vile Dimagoras* (London: J. M., 1658), 97.

[25] Francis Quarles, *The Virgin Widow* (London: R. Royston, 1649), B1a.

was, and still is, in a good performance, difficult to locate. Barry Lording's actors intend, confusingly:

> to show,
> Things never done with that true life,
> That thoughts and wits shall stand at strife,
> Whether the things now shewne be true,
> Or whether wee our selves now do
> The things wee but present.[26]

As it seems, the early modern theater may have had its fair share of Oliviers as well as Hoffmans.

For the next hundred years, the century preceding the "Long Stanislavskian" one, real emotion spontaneously produced on the stage continued to be identified as the pinnacle of good characterization. Aaron Hill advised eighteenth-century actors to locate their "real" feelings within themselves on the stage, complaining, at the same time, that contemporary actors were less likely to do this than their forebears:

> Wou'd but each *actor*, imitating *well*,
> Learn, from *himself*, another to *excel*:
> Search his *own* bosom; copy, from *within*,
> *Seize* your *attention*, and your *passions* win;
> *Then*, would the stage, of *no neglect*, complain,
> But *love*, and *grief*, and *pity*, charm, again.[27]

That same century, an actor emerged who was not fearful of tapping into his own emotions and "really feeling" on stage. David Garrick was famous for his whip-crack emotional "transitions"; he could switch "from one passion into another, with a consummate ease."[28] He explained his abilities by saying that he would be overtaken, on stage, by the heady combination of his own and his character's emotions; his internal "mine" would be "sprung" (exploded) by his character's passion with such immediacy that even he would be surprised:

> the greatest strokes of Genius, have been unknown to the Actor himself, 'till Circumstances, and the warmth of the Scene has sprung the Mine as it were, as much to his own Surprize, as that of the Audience.[29]

---

[26]   Barry Lording, *Ram-Alley* (London: G. Eld., 1611), A2a.

[27]   Aaron Hill, "Prologue, spoken by a young Gentleman, At a Play, called the Tuscan Treaty," *The Works* (London: n.p., 1753), 119–20.

[28]   John Hill, *The Actor* (London: R. Griffiths, 1750), 69.

[29]   David Garrick, *The Letters,* ed. David M. Little and George M. Kahrl, 3 vols (London: Oxford University Press, 1963), 2: 635.

Whatever was the source for Garrick's passionate acting, one word was regularly employed to describe it: "spontaneous." "'Tis thine," writes Robert Lloyd to Garrick,

> ... to lead with more than magic skill,
> The train of captive passions at thy will;
> To bid the bursting tear spontaneous flow
> In the sweet sense of sympathetic woe.[30]

Thus aspects of "the method" with respect to character, in particular, the idea of being spontaneous in performance through locating emotions in the "sense memory," or through really being "in the moment" on stage, did indeed precede the set of acting principles laid down at the dawn of the Long Stanislavskian Century. This is not to say, however, that William Gillette and others were "in fact grappling with ... principles that Shakespeare and his contemporaries had already discovered and put into practice"; as it seems, they were grappling with principles discovered classically and imitated in the early modern period— preceding Stanislavski, then, by several hundred years. Ideas of "emotional truth" and "spontaneity" in the performance of a character, "how the actor generates passion ... what constitutes 'character'—consciousness, subjectivity, interiority, biography, etc.," can indeed be relegated to the "perennial" rather than purely, as Mazer suggested, the "specific."

One reason the early modern stage embraced spontaneity so vigorously was because other aspects of its performance also happened starkly "in the moment." Unlike a modern production, where long-rehearsed actors can have a cinematic, if bloodless, perfection, early modern performances, so much less carefully prepared, showed all the flaws and strengths of their actors. There was more prompting on the stage, and there were more performers reduced, terrifyingly, to a "non-plus"; but there were also more moments of part-based "discovery" on the stage, when, as Thomas Dekker put it, "Plaudits, Showts and Acclamations" were given to players because they had "play'd good parts ... Bravely-well."[31]

For this was a theater of the "now." While a polite modern audience claps at the end of a production, early modern spectators would clap and hiss their way through individual actors' performances, judging the presentation of character as it happened. Casca in *Julius Caesar* describes a motley audience responding instantly to Caesar as though to an actor: "If the tag-rag people did not clap him and hiss him, according as he pleased and displeased them, as they use to do the players in the theater, I am no true man" (1.2.262–65). This response expressed, but also demanded, instant and spontaneous gratification. God, in one analogy, is even compared to a spectator who judges actors' performances while they take place: "He that sits in the Heavens will laugh them to scorn, and hisse them off

---

[30]   Robert Lloyd, *The Poetical Works* (London: T. Evans, 1774), 10–11.

[31]   Thomas Dekker, *The Blacke Rod, and the White Rod* (London: John Cowper, 1630), 3.

the stage, if they do not mend their action"[32]—"mending" performance, or exiting, were the actors' onstage choices, and, thrillingly, the spectators could observe which they chose. In other ways, too, spectators insisted on theatrical spontaneity. They might shout tags and phrases at clowns and other characters, goading them into giving immediate replies, so that there was often some sense of "improv" about drama in general.[33] Perhaps this was because performances seem often to have ended with what these days might actually be called "improv": a jig (a semi-improvised song and dance), or "themes" (an improvisational exchange in which the audience shouted out questions and the clown created rhymed responses to them). Jigs and themes connected performance with immediacy, while perhaps encouraging the actors concerned "to develop the spontaneity necessary to create in each performance "the illusion of the first time"," as Mazer quotes Strasberg as saying. This takes us, of course, back to Mark Rylance, who named O.P. after the actor-audience spontaneity that, to him, was at the heart of early modern production.

This chapter has suggested that the "O.P. folks" may indeed have inherited their ideas of characterization from the nineteenth century (though not from Stanislavski), but that behind that lies the beliefs of the early modern period, and behind that, the performance practices of Roman and, even before that, Greek theater. Confusingly, however, Mazer at one point stated that he was not really interested in the truth or otherwise of the claims made by the "O.P. folks," only in the nineteenth-century vocabulary they use. Of course, if their concepts are shown to date from the early modern period or earlier, their vocabulary is vocabulary which is made up of a conglomeration of words and phrases from different periods, some of which date from the Stanislavskian era, like "affective memory" (OED first recorded usage, 1895), and some of which date from the seventeenth century, like "spontaneous" (OED first recorded usage, 1656).

Although one is unable to be a spokesman for all "O.P. folks," an attempt has been made here to give a sample of the history upon which *Shakespeare in Parts* built its beliefs about character. Yet these accounts have redounded positively back onto the work of the other people adduced by Mazer. History has suggested that the "folks," the "gurus," the "polemicists" and the "obsessives" may well be, in all the contested meanings of the word, more "original" than Stanislavski. Or, at least, more "original" than the "Stanislavski folks."

---

[32] John Spencer, *Kaina kai Palaia: Things New and Old* (London: W. Wilson and J. Streater, 1658), 189.

[33] Examples of this are documented in Tiffany Stern, "Extemporisation by Clowns and Others," *Documents of Performance in Early Modern England* (Cambridge: Cambridge University Press, 2010), 245–50.

# Chapter 7
# Retracing Antonio:
# In Search of the Merchant of Venice

## Diego Arciniegas

As a species, we actors are a superstitious bunch. The very thought of writing about acting makes us quake in our *kothurnoi*. We are afraid of provoking Theatre gods, who long ago decreed performance should speak for itself. We worry about unintentionally revealing forbidden knowledge if we root around in the attic of our previous performance experiences searching for acting first principles. We fear stumbling upon and opening some Pandora's box whose evil might be to render the magic useless even as it is unleashed. Many of us believe we are not so much the possessors of any particular wisdom as its flawed conduits. We are never one hundred percent certain why anything works, even when it does, and we don't aspire to any such conviction. Certainty, we suspect, obliterates possibility in performance. Conversely stated, uncertainty makes anything possible on stage. This superstition, I dare not call it a philosophy, helps manage stage fright, and puts it to good use. But beyond living a fearful superstitious existence, we actors hate to be pinned down. We resist subjugation to any law from which we may need to deviate if circumstances change; and in the Theater, circumstances *always* change. Personally I avoid actors who talk at length about their process, because I invariably come away with the impression they are trying to convince themselves as much as anybody else.

So I will begin with a caution offered by someone who has written—or led a series of workshops that became the basis of a book—on the subject, and whom Professor Mazer (in this volume) rather disparagingly calls a "Voice Guru": John Barton. Towards the beginning of *Playing Shakespeare*, Barton writes that "we can hardly ever make any generalizations about acting without adding some sort of qualification," and warns us about jargon, which can lead to "*talking* about acting taking the place of actually doing it."[1] Nonetheless, partly as a result of receiving some of my theater training in England (and attentively watching the *Playing Shakespeare* series on TV in my bed-sit), I bring a fairly classical approach to Shakespearean performance and start with the verse: iambic pentameter, *de dum de dum de dum de dum de dum*[2] As I learn the lines, I explore how the words and

---

[1] *Playing Shakespeare, an Actors Guide* (1984; NY: Anchor Books, 2001), 8.

[2] I will reference specific verse scansion techniques as I examine Antonio's words, but leave a comprehensive examination of the practice to other, better sources. (See, for example, *Playing Shakespeare*, Chapter 2, "Using the Verse – Heightened and Naturalistic verse").

cadences resonate in my body. The approach feels tactile, reptilian, and precedes rational analysis. It more closely approximates singing than contemporary acting. Once I have followed the notes, half notes, rests, and quarter rests hard-coded into the language, once I believe I can "sing the tune" of the text, I ask myself how my character *feels* as I speak his lines. I try to probe deeply into the words I speak, and the images I employ, for the sensations they cause within me. My instincts apprehend better than my intellect comprehends. It also surpasses contemporary approaches for addressing Shakespeare's emotional demands because I have never murdered, raped, nor consumed my young. No amount of borrowing from my personal life can prepare me for Macbeth, or Chiron, or Titus. I have, on the other hand, tasted human behaviors while performing a character from Shakespeare that I would not ordinarily permit myself. By the time I am satisfied I have met the technical requirements of the text, any insight I may have gained seems more a self-evident truth to which I have been led than any interpretation I might have crafted.

But I should first address an issue raised by Professor Mazer, because he would undoubtedly place my approach to character among the modern techniques and methods he critiques. Professor Mazer's argument could be summed up in his contention that "the polemicists and practitioners of Original Practices, while claiming that they are eschewing modernist and contemporary theatrical aesthetics and recapturing the lost aesthetics of Shakespeare's own theatre, are actually actively participating in the very aesthetics that they are renouncing." I can see two significant problems here. First, in explaining contemporary theatrical aesthetics, he asserts that "modern actors (in the mainstream Anglophone theater at least) still 'build' their 'character' as coherent, psychologized, and interiorized entities, impelled by a web of biographical causality, drawn towards 'goals' and 'objectives,' by using the shared vocabulary and tools of a highly articulated system of acting first codified at the end of the nineteenth century." While this may be true of some actors, it is certainly not true across the board. As I hope my essay will make clear, my approach to character is predicated on the belief that Shakespearean character emerges in the moment to moment actions, reactions and interactions of the character throughout the entire play—that character is, as some scholars say, "processional." This approach to character permits us, for one, to challenge the tradition of a role (e.g. romantic Romeo, bitchy Lady M., "Dick the Shit"), or discover it fresh for ourselves. More importantly, if, after the fact, I analyze what my character needs and wants in terms of "goals" or "objectives," it is a retroactive and third-party perspective. In fact, it is often the audience member, critic, or scholar who builds a coherent, psychologized entity from the fragments of performance. What I try to give a sense of in the pages below are how the individual moments that, taken together, form a character get produced in the live space of rehearsal and performance.

Nonetheless, I would also disagree with one particular point that Professor Mazer's friendly adversary Professor Stern makes with reference to the way Shakespeare seems to exploit the use of parts to build surprise and spontaneity into performance. "If," she writes, "the actor feels the dramatic rightness of a 'surprise,' feels how this rightness originated in his own experience (of uncertainty, anger, shock, etc.), then his job in a subsequent performance will be to recover such feeling with as much freshness and gusto as he can muster." On the contrary. Certainly today, we encourage the actor to forget about last night's performance and endeavor not to compare his or her current efforts to those of the previous time. To do so is always to be reliving a previous performance rather than addressing the concerns of the current one. A part of what I have tried to do below is recapture the moments when the character I am playing is discovering his thoughts—or I am discovering him—as if for the first time, in the moment of the only performance that matters—the current one.

The following retraces the steps of a character I performed—Antonio from *The Merchant of Venice*—in a production that I directed in 2004 for Boston Publick Theatre. Antonio suits my purpose well, despite comparatively little stage time and even less dialogue; his relative taciturnity enables me to explore in considerable detail the quiet person around whom the lives of the more garrulous of the play's characters revolve. As a character, Antonio demands attention immediately, speaking first, and speaking of himself. He doesn't know why he's sad. Sadness makes him stupid. The condition has reached the point he doesn't "know himself." I ask myself who talks about not knowing himself without knowing himself. Antonio's reflection transports me, past Hamlet, right to the "mirror" scene in *Richard II*. "The shadow of your sorrow hath destroy'd/ The shadow of your face" (4.1.292). Will Antonio prove, like Richard II, to be the unwitting author of his own fate? Is he narcissistic like Richard II? I put the thought aside because decisions made too early can mislead. "Never fall in love with an idea," I remind myself, borrowing an important design principle from an architect acquaintance. "More will be revealed," my best friend and theatre colleague Susanne Nitter is fond of saying. As a director, I often annoy actors by responding to certain questions with "I don't know yet." We aren't permitted to know everything at once, as we start to slip into the world of a play. This refusal to jump to early conclusions about a character avoids generalizations, or the superimposition of our own personal baggage, or even a predetermined "through-line" that makes all the actions consistently cohere under one "arc." (Who actually behaves like that?)

Structurally, Antonio's first speech slows down to monosyllables, and contains a half line. Barton describes a line, or even a half line, composed of one-syllable words as the equivalent of taking a yellow marker and highlighting it. He argues that it is very difficult to say it quickly. Giving slow, equally strong stress to strings of monosyllables can pay dividends. "But how I caught it, found it, or came by it/ What stuff 'tis made of, whereof it is born/ I am to learn [short line]." With the exception of "Whereof," these two and a half lines are monosyllabic.[3] The lone polysyllable provides a rhythmic trampoline to catapult me into the suspension

---

[3]    "Whereof" can break down further into two monosyllabic prepositions if we don't have complete confidence in our typesetter.

caused by the pause in the half line "I am to learn." Whenever encountering a short line, the performer must decide whether to take the pause before, after, or at some specific point within the line. My favorite example comes from Hamlet: "For in that sleep of death what dreams may come/ When we have shuffled off this mortal coil/ Must give us pause. There's the respect..." The line containing "pause" is short. Whether to take the pause before or after the word becomes at that moment the most pressing existential question the interpreter of Hamlet must answer. Pause on "pause." Could text come with better instructions? One cup Shakespeare. Add breath. To my continual amazement, form and content dance together in this fashion throughout the canon. They form performative clues I can follow. In the case of Antonio, where to take the pause becomes self-evident. If he pauses at the end of the short line, his thoughts trail off for the remaining feet of the verse line. He snaps out of his reverie with the remaining mostly monosyllabic lines, "And such a want wit sadness makes of me/ That I have much ado to know myself."

Antonio's companions, the seemingly interchangeable Salerio and Solanio, go to great lengths to paint vivid pictures of Antonio's financially overextended sea-faring business, after which the question of love arises:

> SOLANIO: Why, then you are in love.
> ANTONIO: Fie, fie!

Monosyllabic, terse, and short, the tone shifts instantly from the colorful nautical pageantry of moments before. The sudden switch to two short lines indicates the presence of pauses. If the words from both lines were taken as a single shared one, it would still be hypometric. Something unspoken is happening. I opt not to share the lines, but to insert a pause before and after Antonio's retort. The suggestion Antonio is in love hangs in the air, as does the reply, an expression of contempt or impatience. Antonio doth protest too much, methinks.

When Ben Lambert, the actor playing Gratiano, matches my last monosyllabic half line, "And mine a sad one," with a monosyllabic and antithetical one of his own, I want to slug him. "Let me play the fool," he offers. His simplistic solutions insult my feelings. I can barely contain my resentment at his insinuation that the purpose of my "willful stillness" is "to be dressed in an opinion/ Of wisdom, gravity" and 'profound conceit'." He clearly misreads me. I stare him down, until he interrupts himself with "I'll tell thee more of this another time."

The much-needed change of subject seems to arrive in the persons of Bassanio, Lorenzo, and Gratiano, at which point characters start to excuse themselves at alarming rates, dragging the unwilling behind them. I feel something about to happen, but have no idea what it is. Gratiano grows increasingly annoying with his shallow diagnosis of my having "too much respect of the world." My next lines permit me to descend into the kind of morose circumspection that could glaze over the eyes of a Jaques. "I hold the world but as the world," I snap monosyllabically at Gratiano and through clenched teeth. I proclaim the world "a stage," as does my distant cousin from the Forest of Arden. In my version of the metaphor, "every man must play a part/ And mine a sad one." What has happened? Resignation replaces puzzlement. The arrival of my friends makes me feel worse rather than better.

I find myself exhausted by the time Bassanio, who, I have learned, has been looking for me, and I are alone together. This change from a group interaction to a private dialogue brings to mind, in retrospect, what William Flesch writes in his piece (in this volume) on what makes someone a character in Shakespeare. Flesch makes the general observation that "characters are defined by their interactions with each other," by which he means more specifically that "characters sense how much they are determined by what others know about them" because "what we are is essentially governed by what we know, and what we know is mainly each other." And so if characters "wish to be different people from what they are known to be, they must change who their friends are." Antonio doesn't break from his current friends, and Bassanio has been a long-time friend, but his turn to Bassanio in the dramatic sequence has the feel of an attempt to cast aside his earlier self and look to Bassanio for a new beginning. At any rate, when Bassanio presses on with the drollery at Gratiano's expense, I abruptly change the subject, feeling an impatience I thought I reserved only for Gratiano. "Well, tell me what lady is the same/ To whom you swore a secret pilgrimage/ That you to-day promised to tell me of." New information emerges: a secret pilgrimage, an unspecified lady, and a promise of additional news. I feel instinctively this news will address the unease plaguing me since the start of the play. I didn't mention Bassanio's secret pilgrimage to Solanio and Salerio. My discretion causes sadness, but I maintain it notwithstanding. Characterologically I feel reasonably secure observing Antonio is discreet, possibly secretive, and disturbingly dependent upon Bassanio's news.

Bassanio replies indirectly to my query, reminding me of the money he owes. It has left him "gag'd" to me, to whom he owes "the most in money and in love." Arden glosses "gag'd" to mean bound and pledged, but makes no reference to "engaged," the closest reading of the word.[4] The engagement doubles down: money and love. Bassanio reassures me of a plan to recoup his losses. I encourage him to continue, with the conditional assurance that if it be honorable, "my purse, my person, my extremest means" are "unlocked" to him. The alliteration of purse and person equates me with my money. Images of latches snapping open, trunks unlocking, and myself opening physically to Bassanio propel me towards him. I find my five foot seven self-aggressing Nat McIntyre's six foot four Bassanio, regardless of how silly I feel. Bassanio continues to evade, evincing an economic theory predicated upon archery. Neither Antonio nor I could miss the imprudence of such an analogy. Neither of us acknowledges it. The expression "Throwing good money after bad" comes to mind. Then, "In Belmont there is a lady...."

My tone changes immediately when I learn of the quest to vie for Portia. It becomes formal, correct, and professional. Am I hiding behind my now well-

---

[4]    Barton makes this very point while explaining the principles of verse, *Playing Shakespeare*, 39.

established discretion? Once I explain my overextended finances, a change occurs. It hinges on the word "therefore." I begin to speak in the imperative. "Go forth," "Try what my credit can in Venice do," "Go presently inquire." "Therefore" occurs in the middle of the verse line, following the caesura. If you are a believer in the technique of breathing only at the end of the verse lines, or "phrasing with the verse" as John Barton terms it, a small gift awaits you.[5]

> Neither have I money,/ nor commodity [*breath*]
> To raise a present sum,/ therefore go forth… [*breath*]

The front slashes above represent the caesurae. The decision to borrow on behalf of Bassanio occurs in the middle of the verse line. I call the technique of beginning a new thought without taking a new breath "speaking from the bottom of your gas tanks." We do it every day without giving it much thought. My lung capacity is overextended as I try to make my decision sound like a good one. It rings hollow. I can feel how bad this idea is, even as I give voice to it. I can't help noticing the violence of my imagery, when I vow to "furnish" Bassanio, despite having to stretch my credit on the rack. I am overcompensating. I notice my only mention of the lady's name occurs in the middle of its respective verse line. I say "to fair Portia" from the "bottom" of my "tanks" as well. I can barely bring myself to say her name. By the time I have reached the rhymed couplet that concludes the scene, I am more exhausted and disheartened than I was before.

Shylock and Bassanio are immersed in prose in the next scene into which I enter. The form suits Shylock's crafty, droning calculation as he runs a pun-peppered risk assessment on my merchant ventures. "Ships." "Rats." "Pi—rats." The groundlings are warming up. Shylock puns further on the double meaning of "assurance," reassuring Bassanio he has every intention of securitizing the financial transaction. The puns establish Shylock as a double-talker, a formidable business tactician. I get down to business immediately, calling him by his non-Christian first name. I declare my distaste for excessive borrowing and lending practices as preface to engaging in them. When he tries to tell me the parable of Jacob and Laban, I challenge the relevance of the story. "And what of him? did he take interest?" Shylock takes my word up, but replies indirectly. "No, not take interest, not as you would say/ Directly int'rest…" He parses the word "interest." Where is he going with this? Shylock invites me to pay close attention to Jacob's actions in the Bible story. He "peeled" certain "wands," and "He stuck them up."

---

      5    Barton, *Playing Shakespeare*, 42. This technique is the subject of considerable heated debate, and has caused normally rational people to become ridiculously dogmatic. Barton, I note, is surprisingly pragmatic on the subject, but gently insists people try it. "I myself believe that in Shakespeare's later verse it is still right more often than not to phrase with the verse-line. Some people would not agree with that, but I think such verse is in part a form of naturalistic writing by Shakespeare. That is to say, he catches our trick of often pausing in ungrammatical places and running on at full-stops. If you look at it in that way you will be surprised how often it works" (36).

That is the full extent of Jacob's actions in the parable. I am unclear as to what Shylock wants me to "mark" about Jacob's "peeling" and sticking up of "wands." Why is the moneylender recounting an improbable Biblical passage about visual stimulation during ovine coitus causing certain phenotypic outcomes? Visual stimulation in sheep may be the topic of conversation, but there is more here than meets the eye.

The verse structure provides some clues about the exchange. Shylock's story leads me to the precise moment when the sheep are "in the act," referring to it as the "doing of the deed of kind." The cadences and the alliteration of the phrase create a pulsating rhythm, which Shylock shatters with the brutally monosyllabic "He stuck them up." The language may be appropriate to animal husbandry, but his delivery is brutally graphic. Why is he rubbing my nose in fornicative imagery? Does the punning on the word "interest" refer to taking interest on loans, or taking an interest in copulation for increase? Shylock's sexual allusiveness seems to have replaced his rapidly disintegrating analogy for the time value of money as the point of the story. I suggest Shylock gets inappropriate pleasure conflating money-making with boinking sheep. "Or is your gold and silver ewes and rams?" My sexual allusiveness acknowledges his, threatening to force the innuendo into the open.

Whatever transpired, directly or indirectly, in the previous exchange, I become enraged. I interrupt Shylock even as he seems to return to the business I was so brusquely eager to conduct. I encroach upon his half line and drag Bassanio into the conversation with a half line of my own. "Mark you this Bassanio," I say, employing the same command Shylock used with me regarding Jacob's doings. I call Shylock a "devil" who twists scripture to suit his purpose, "an evil soul producing holy witness." As the discussion veers more deeply into the realm of the personal, I challenge him either to do business with me or refuse, but not to make it personal. I taunt him to lend instead to an enemy, "Who if he break,/ thou may'st with better face/ Exact the penalty." Shylock picks up my half line to complete it with "Why look how you storm!…." It might be argued these two lines are not shared because they amount to eleven syllables. If we assume the line has a feminine ending, Shylock's line reading becomes: "Why look how *you* storm!…." It equates my rant to his own. His treatment as a Jew caused his emotional tempest. What caused mine?

Then comes the final offer. "Tell ya what I'm gonna do…." Shylock spins the ridiculous pound of flesh offer, into which no rational businessman would enter were he not so provocatively goaded by the twists and turns of the previous scene. "Content in faith," say I, sealing the bargain. I take my own turn at the pun as I conclude the deal, "And say there is much *kindness* in the Jew" (emphasis mine). My double meaning creates the illusion I call him kind, when actually implying he's acting in a manner one would expect from a Jew. But Bassanio acquires some business sense, even as I begin to lose mine. "You shall not seal to such a bond for me." I seize this opportunity to prove my love for Bassanio, and answer the wager to which I have been goaded. Finally, I equate Shylock's recent benevolence with a propensity towards Christianity. My replacement of the word "Jew," with the less politically charged "Hebrew," softens the delivery, even as it equates the moneylender's people with unkindness. Bassanio perceives nothing but the most obvious of my meanings. Clearly these two men are not friends out of common interests or intellectual compatibility.

The only purpose for my next entrance is to deliver plot information about Bassanio's imminently sailing ship, and chivvy Lorenzo, Bassanio, and Jessica along to port (2.6). Anybody might have done it. By contrast, Shakespeare doesn't even allow me to appear in the following scene (2.8) in which I play a part; Salerio and Solanio recount the moment in which Bassanio bids me good-by and departs for Belmont. My physical presence is similarly barred from the next scene in which I play a part. I am inserted into it by means of a letter right after Bassanio has wrung success from the contest devised by Portia's father. But the letter first has the effect of forcing Bassanio to reveal himself a dissembler, an equivocator, and a debtor: "I have engag'd myself to a dear friend/ Engag'd my friend to his mere enemy." Bassanio's use of the word "engag'd" confirms my challenge to the footnote for "gag'd" in our first scene. As in that scene, I find myself identified with a material object. Previously I had equated my opened purse with my own person; now Bassanio equates me with my letter. "Here is a letter lady/, The paper as the body of my friend,/ And every word in it a gaping wound/ Issuing life blood." I can't help noticing the graphic depiction of hemorrhaging orifices in the object with which I am identified, and sense an allusion to gender. More obviously, the image, with words in place of quivers, recalls the martyrdom of St. Sebastian. The saint's renowned passivity intrigues. I have issued a challenge that will try Bassanio and Portia more thoroughly than the rather simplistic contest devised by the lady's father, from which they have only now emerged victorious. This newer, more complex trial will bring them back to Venice, and to me.

As the reading of my letter conjures me into that room, I drain the fun from the party. My prose departure from their heightened verse undercuts any lyricism there might have been in the scene. "[A]ll debts are clear'd between you and I, if I might but see you at my death; notwithstanding, use your pleasure,—if your love do not persuade you to come, let not my letter." Stacy Fischer's smart Portia catches the four-letter word trap in my missive. Her "Oh love!" is not a term of endearment, tossed by an ingénue to her hero, to hurry the nuptials and advance the story. Stacy takes those two monosyllables and separates them. "O!" *"love"*(emphasis mine), she says, playing a personal discovery. Does she sense my manipulation or something else? Whatever she discovers in the letter, her tone changes completely. She turns to the room in formal address: "dispatch all business and be gone!" Bassanio takes the opportunity to close the scene, promising from the "bottom of his gas tanks," "but till I come again,/ No bed shall e'er be guilty of my stay,/ Nor rest be interposer 'twixt us twain."

So I have been bound, gagged, narrated by others, and, most recently, milled into stationery. To add insult to injury, my next entrance is in chains in service to the plot. I seem to have kept my sense of humor, however, observing that because of my recent weight loss, the court will be hard pressed to find a full sixteen ounces of excisable flesh. I do manage, as well, to round the scene out with a useful piece of information. "Pray God Bassanio come/ To see me pay his debt, and then I care not." I want Bassanio to come back, not to save me but to watch me suffer for him. Very Christian. Oy!

My stated purpose moves beyond rhetoric and into open court action in my next scene. After thanking the Duke for the pains he has taken to try to stop the proceedings, I embrace the Christian paradox as a tactic: "I do oppose my patience to his [Shylock's] fury, and am arm'd/ To suffer with a quietness of spirit/ The very tyranny and rage of his." My weapon is suffering. My quietness and patience will battle Shylock's fury and rage. But the Shylock who appears in court doesn't correspond to my description. He calmly refuses to state reasons why he will not take payment for the overdue obligation with an annoying calm. We Christians, on the other hand, rage considerably. Under the pretense of calming the waters, I fan the flames of an already heated courtroom with my first overtly anti-Semitic statement:

> I pray you think you question with the Jew…
> You may as well do anything most hard
> As seek to soften that–that which what's harder?
> His Jewish Heart.

Shylock keeps his cool despite my vicious attack. He makes a cold legalistic argument, drawing an analogy between the pound of flesh for which he sues, and the practice of slavery indulged in by Venetian society. My pound of flesh belongs to him, he reasons, even as the "purchas'd slaves" of Venice are the exclusive property of those who own them.

In response to Bassanio's offer to submit to Shylock's knife in my stead, I counter-argue with the revelation that "I am a tainted wether of the flock," my metaphor harkening directly back to the spotted rejects from Laban's herd. I call myself a castrated male sheep, one that cannot reproduce. No peeled wands for me. But why am I tainted? Disease doesn't threaten my life. Decay seems unlikely. Shakespeare makes no mention of advanced age, and my friends are young. Corruption? My businesses practices tend toward generosity and humanitarianism. Moral corruption? How? "The weakest kind of fruit/ Drops earliest to the ground, and so let me." My corruption stems from a weakness. Both metaphors suggest a condition rather than a behavior. The grape is inferior and the wether impotent or sterile. Remarkably, I do not make the obvious ultra-Christian argument found in John 13:15: "Greater love hath no man than this, that a man lay down his life for his friends." To do so would reveal in words what I am trying to prove in deed; that my love is greater than Portia's, and greater than his for her. I suggest Bassanio is better employed writing my epitaph. I would prefer he spent the rest of his life mourning for mine.

As the trial proceeds, Portia scrambles to decide what to do next—a thoroughly dramatic novice's initial stumble—and grasps at a straw: "Then must the Jew be merciful." As Shylock, Steven Barkhimer's eyes widen into incredulous saucers as Portia reasons further and his rage now manifests itself for the first time. After a glance to Tubal, Shylock spits his monosyllables to the court, "My deeds upon my head! I crave the law." From thence onward, Portia seems predisposed to side with Shylock. In fact, she and Shylock begin to share lines as preparations for the penalty commence. The tone of the scene becomes official, procedural, and clinical. Addressing me as "You merchant," she asks me if I have anything to say. I ask for Bassanio's hand, and eventually say, "And when the tale is told, bid her be judge/ Whether Bassanio had not once a love." Were I Portia I would have offered to execute the sentence myself, and with my bare hands.

But I am not she. I am he, upon whom the sentence is to be executed. From the moment the learned doctor commands me to lay bare my bosom, an enormous vulnerability sweeps through me. I feel humiliated, taking my shirt off in the presence of so many sumptuously clothed people. As soon as the learned doctor and Shylock prepare to execute the penalty, the bald reality of it dawns on my Antonio. The actor in me knows I'm perfectly safe, but the thought of Shylock's knife cutting into my chest suffices to raise my heart rate. The rhythm of the dialogue leads inexorably towards the moment of penetration. The abortive call for an attendant physician raises the stakes further. The opportunity to say good-bye to Bassanio reprieves me momentarily, but raises the importance of what I have to say to him to vertiginous heights. I find it hard to part from him, and wonder if Shakespeare didn't deprive us of our previous parting scene in deference to this one. It is the moment of truth. When I bid him ask his wife if Bassanio had not once a love, I kiss him full on the lips. It is not a sexy kiss. Our mouths are closed. My purpose is not consciously erotic, but to underscore the momentousness of the farewell. I put my forehead against his when I say, "Repent but that you shall lose your friend/ And he repents not that he repays your debt." Tears come easily, as I pull away from him to say what I think are Antonio's most important words of the play: "For if the Jew do cut but deep enough/ I'll pay it instantly with all my heart."

Nat McIntyre's beautiful response as Bassanio captures nuances in the text, which may or may not have been originally intended, but were occasioned by my kiss. "Antonio, I am married to a wife/ Which is as dear to me as life itself," he says in a manner that just as easily removes gently any hope I may have harbored for anything beyond friendship as it sets the premise for what is to follow. "But life itself, my wife, and all the world, / Are not with me esteemed above thy life." Nat's completely heterosexual, if somewhat naïve Bassanio, consciously or unconsciously lets me down easy while simultaneously telling me he cares more for me than anything else in the world. Such a perspective can only come from a person thoroughly unaware of other possible constructions that could be placed upon his words and actions—an impulsive, excessive person who takes risks, wastes money and isn't entirely in control of his life. If he knew Portia were with him he might have spoken in the first person plural, looking to her for occasional nods of confirmation, and putting her in a terribly awkward position. He has

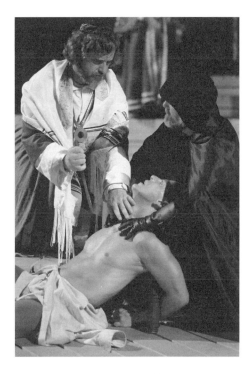

Fig. 7.1        From left to right: Steven Barkhimer (Shylock), Diego Arciniegas
                (Antonio), and William Gardiner (Gaoler). Carroll Photography

certainly crossed a line, but his fault is one of omission rather than commission. He didn't check with his wife. Portia confirms as much with, "Your wife would give you little thanks for that/ If she were by to hear you make the offer."

When Shylock demands sentence, the learned doctor does not mince words. "A pound of that same merchant's flesh is thine." The statement startles me. He restarts the rhythm and tone of inevitability with his repetition of the refrain, "The court awards it and the law doth give it." In the pause following Shylock's short line paean to Portia, "Most rightful judge!," the jailer places me in restraints. The learned doctor issues a monosyllabic order: "And you must cut this flesh from off his breast." I hold my breath and clench as the blade comes within inches of my chest. The learned doctor pulls Shylock back from the brink with "Tarry a little, there is something else." From there, of course, he outsmarts the plaintiff, citing the lack of a mention of blood in the bond. I know the doctor is punishing Shylock, daring him to spill Christian blood, but I am taking a considerable psychological beating as well. Shylock makes another pass. Another clench. He pauses. "Why doth the Jew pause?" I'm beginning to wonder about the partiality of the doctor. "Take thy forfeiture." This kind of rhetoric could push Shylock over the edge!

Does Venice have laws regarding incitement to violence? The doctor seems a little too convincing. Shylock concedes at last. The tension finally breaks.

A strange thing occurs at the moment of my reprieve. I start to laugh. I find the ensuing legal "gang bang" on Shylock exceedingly funny. I either laugh or cry as I get out of my restraints and put my shirt back on, but I am always on the verge of hysteria. Certainly relief plays an important part in how I feel, but more tellingly, I take amusement watching Shylock's suffering begin to approach my own. I don't follow the finer points of the institutionalized prejudice concerning aliens the learned doctor succeeds in digging out of the Venetian law books, but the death sentence strikes me as the funniest thing I ever heard. I barely hear the Duke pardon Shylock's life and give me half the Jew's wealth. I am too busy hugging Bassanio. When asked what mercy I can render Shylock, I ask the Duke to quit the fine. I accept half of Shylock's goods, but new ideas dawn on me even as I speak them, dropping in with each breath. I force Shylock to renounce his faith, converting to Christianity. I force him, additionally, to make his estranged daughter his sole heir and beneficiary. If this is a gentle rain from heaven, I wonder what weather Antonio could summon around the holidays.

I will "slubber" the details of the famous ring trick, only to focus on my unwitting participation in it; but not before remarking Bassanio's first impulse shouldn't have been to denigrate the value of the ring. Lies come far too easily to that boy! "My Lord Bassanio" I say, adding a measured and monosyllabic "let him have the ring" to my suspiciously formal address. I encourage him to weigh the judge's deserving and my love on the one hand against his wife's commandment on the other. In my defense, the equation balances deserving and love against a single commandment rather than the whole of Bassanio's wife's person. Bassanio relents and turns to me to say, "Come, you and I will thither presently/ And in the morning early will we both/ Fly toward Belmont." I wasn't there to witness it, but didn't Bassanio promise Portia: "No bed shall e'er be guilty of my stay,/ Nor rest be interposer 'twixt us twain.'"?

Wherever we spent the night of the trial, evening has come once again when Bassanio and I arrive in Belmont. Unbeknown to us, Portia arrived moments earlier. The welcome lacks warmth. Portia acknowledges it. "Sir, you are very welcome to our house:/ It must appear in other ways than words,/ Therefore I scant this breathing courtesy." But it doesn't appear in other ways. I say little during the protracted and unpleasant argument that ensues. Gratiano and some unknown woman drag their domestic squabble into the view of their betters and houseguests. The hosts, in turn, begin to quarrel. My first impression of the new Lady Bassanio is not particularly positive, even if I were predisposed to it. It turns out I am the cause of Bassanio and Portia's argument, not because of the debt Bassanio owes me, but because I urged him to give the ring away. I make my confession. "I am th'unhappy subject of these quarrels." Portia turns to me with a terse monosyllabic half line. "Sir, grieve not you—you are welcome not withstanding." She returns to the broil. I feel no more welcome than I did before.

Eventually, I insert myself into the marriage, if only to try to preserve it. "I once did lend my body for his wealth," I say to Portia, "I dare be bound again/

My soul upon the forfeit, that your lord/ Will never more break faith advisedly."
The tension in the antithesis between body and soul underscores the seriousness of
my intent. My last bond caused me considerable pain. I willingly hazard more by
offering my immortal soul for this one. Portia employs a term of trade to accept,
"Then you shall be his surety." She reverses the pun Shylock employed with
Bassanio, when the first bond was sealed. Instead of employing the more casual
sense of the term "assurance," to pun on the business concept of securitization,
Portia employs the financial term "surety" to stand for my assurance she should
maintain confidence in the marriage. She is talking business. Were she not a native
of Belmont, I would argue that the play's title rightfully belongs to her. Since she
did her best work within the jurisdiction of *La Serenisima*, I could still make the
argument. I recall her words, "Since you are dear bought I will love you dear."

After Portia discloses her identity, some of the troubling complications
occasioned by her disguise reveal themselves immediately. I imagine her hearing
the challenge I issued in open court regarding my love for Bassanio. I consider
the chance she took with my safety by impersonating a qualified legal expert.
Most awkward of all, I realize I owe her my life. I understand for the first time
all the implications of our newly concluded bond. She saved my life and I have
indentured my soul to her. Shylock himself could not have engineered the deal
more cleverly. And Portia is not even finished; more complications follow.

> [U]nseal this letter soon;
>  There you shall find three of your argosies
> Are richly come to harbor suddenly.
> You shall not know by what strange accident
> I chanced on this letter.

I notice that she, rather than just postponing the explanation, predicts I shall not
find out how this document reached her. It sounds like a warning. But still I open
the missive and read it. I look Portia in the eye. I distribute the pause evenly across
my short last line. "I AM DUMB," trying to convey speechlessness while giving
equal weight to some tacit promise.

The last decision I had to make as Antonio, how to exit, came as a surprise. I
had toyed with the idea of remaining alone onstage for the end of the play, while
the other couples exited, but it felt heavy-handed. I was searching for a way to
acknowledge the undercurrent of darkness I felt peering at me from underneath the
facile ending. I also had the problem of what to do with Solanio, who had no mate.
Eric Hamel's Solanio had insisted on accompanying me to Belmont. His argument
was that Solanio had stuck by Antonio, even when Salerio had not. He confessed
to me he had decided his Solanio was as obsessively preoccupied with Antonio
as Antonio was with Bassanio. He made reasonable arguments using proofs from
each of his scenes, the most convincing of which was his touching line reading for
"I think he only loves the world for him." I agreed to his character choices because
he had been applying the same methodology to Solanio that I had for Antonio. I
decided neither of us would leave the stage. When the concluding couplets of the

play rang out, as they skipped off to their newly wedded lives, the couples had to cross in front of me to exit. The bright lights began to fade and the lush symphonic music turned solemn, leaving me reading the letter center stage, and Solanio in a back corner looking at me. We both stood on grates above upward shafts of light that had previously been used to suggest light bouncing up from the canals in Venice. At the concluding note in the music cue, a long low cello strain, I would look up from my letter to the audience, and the lights would black out. I didn't exit the play; it left me and Solanio behind. A thought from William Flesch's essay that I referenced earlier again comes to mind. "The great hope that both theater and life create and inevitably disappoint is for an endless promise of human novelty. But in the end both playwright and person discover that the people they knew early on are not the cohort of the moment but the people they'll deal with till the end."

Perhaps the best way to initiate some sort of conclusion is to touch briefly on some of the choices of the other actors, most notably of those who played Bassanio, Shylock, and Portia. A bi-sexual or metrosexual Bassanio who flirts in exchange for loans (à la Joseph Fiennes in the film with Al Pacino) would have taken the play in a completely different direction, and changed the dynamics between himself and my Antonio. Nathaniel McIntyre's handsome and adorably goofy Bassanio never let it be known with any real certainty he was aware that my interest might be perceived as excessive. Stacy Fischer's astute Portia, equipped with considerably well-tuned "gay-dar," embraced her character's less innocent qualities, without ever compromising her status as an ingénue. When asked by Nerissa of her opinion of the French suitor "Monsieur Le Bon," she would adopt a sibilant affectation to say: "God made him, and therefore let him pass for a man … he is every man in no man, if a throstle sing he falls straight a-cap'ring." In the absence of a "show tune test," her Portia developed a screening methodology far subtler and more sensitive than that of her father. A less sophisticated, or a less threatened, Portia would have resulted in a more facile and superficial story. Steve Barkhimer's Shylock, funny even at his horrifyingly meanest, never lost touch with the character's Commedia dell'Arte origins, and still managed to endow him with a heart-breaking humanity. His Shylock wedded Harpagon to Willy Loman, while never upsetting the balance of the play. A Shylock who usurps the role of central character will always make the audience wonder why the play doesn't end at the courtroom scene. As the director, I, admittedly, had a hand in shaping these interpretations, but these consummate performers could never, and should never, be coerced into choices in which they could not whole-heartedly invest.

No conclusion would be complete without addressing the issue of homosexuality in the play. The question of whether Antonio consciously inserted himself into Portia and Bassanio's marriage, to my mind, is just as important as his perceived homosexuality, if not more so. A heterosexual pal can derail his best friend's marriage as easily as a homosexual lover; only the means differ. The subordination of the wife's needs to those of the friend remains the same. The question asked in this portion of the play concerns the obligations of love, after all, not sex. Unless and until some "Ur" Quarto is unearthed that includes a Bassanio/Antonio bed scene (thus giving new meaning to Shakespeare's famous "bed tricks"), no interpreter of Antonio ever has to play a moment that categorically defines his sexual preference. I believe it should be left for the audience to decide. I could imagine some actor portraying a completely heterosexual Antonio reasonably successfully.

My personal choice, however, was that if Antonio scored too low on the Kinsey scale, the play ran the risk of being reduced to yet another polemic about men being from Mars and women from Venus. I believe the story is more complex and layered than that. I chose to take Antonio at his word when he confessed he had "much ado" to "know himself." I chose to think my Antonio was physically attracted to Bassanio as well as consumed by an overpowering "man crush," but overcompensating in such a way that he wasn't completely aware or in control of his actions. This was one way I could hold together the character's considerable self-hatred with his passive-aggressiveness, and still connect to his more redeeming qualities. It also helped explain his obsession with the Christian paradox. Antonio hated himself because of the feelings he had for Bassanio. He made an uncharacteristically stupid decision to lend money he did not have, because of those feelings. If he raged at Shylock while making the bargain, it was because Shylock may have been intimating in his Laban story that he suspected Antonio of inclining towards "buggery," the term the Renaissance would have used. When the unexpected happened, and he forfeited the bond, he became unhealthily attracted to the idea of bleeding, if not dying, for the man he could not have. When he discovered the woman he wished to replace saved him, equilibrium was restored, without anyone present, except he and said woman, being any the wiser. But ultimately Antonio's story operates below the surface, because the playwright denies him or cannot supply him the words. The position in which he finds himself is one of abject desperation and perpetual unease rather than erotic titillation. I fear our current era risks romanticizing the homoeroticism of the play to the same extent it has insisted upon viewing Shylock's role through the prism of the Holocaust.

Having retraced the process I underwent in creating the role of Antonio, I believe any reader of this essay may be as qualified as I am to draw conclusions about attempting to perform this enigmatic character. I found asking questions and offering them up for the audience to answer far more satisfying than "telegraphing" my opinions in performance. Theseus' distinction between rational comprehension and emotional apprehension in *A Midsummer Night's Dream* proved to be the key for me. There is a truth in Shakespeare's language and structure that can be felt in performance as easily as, and in some instances better than, it can be comprehended with an extensive knowledge base prerequisite. In recent times we have come to believe in multiple kinds of intelligences. It would be silly to assume that bringing all of them to bear on our understanding of the plays would not bring new insight into the canon. More accurately, it might bring us closer to something the illiterate verbal Elizabethan audiences appreciated years ago. The difference between these two approaches describes the unnecessary fault line that runs between academic and performative approaches to Shakespeare.

# Chapter 8
# Letting Unpleasantness Lie: Counter-Intuition and Character in *The Merchant of Venice*

## Brett Gamboa

It has become customary to say that *The Merchant of Venice* can no longer be played as a comedy, since after the Holocaust audiences cannot tolerate the character of Shylock when presented as a comic villain. The theory rests on an assumption that in Shakespeare's time, and for some three centuries following, audiences accepted the comedy as a comedy, and on its own terms. I doubt, however, that audiences ever did—or ever could—accept the play on its own terms, because *The Merchant of Venice* is unfit for human consumption. By that I do not mean to say it is a bad play. On the contrary, it is a very great play, one that can succeed in ways that are extraordinary and even unique. Rather, I mean that the play is intolerable in an absolute sense: that the characters and the kind of comedy it relies upon can be met only with ambivalence, and that its resolution must always have proved more disturbing than satisfying. A play that cannot please may be considered unfit for audiences, something productions frequently confirm by not giving it to us. It is a rare production that doesn't work at smoothing out rough edges to the end of rendering the play palatable—rather than rendering *it*. And these rare exceptions generally darken the play and sully its Christian protagonists so much as to relieve the audience of any doubt about whom to side with. The ideas communicated in the resulting productions may therefore be bitter, but the audience will not be, since the productions suggest that others see things as we do. Such productions can comfort audiences by affirming a hierarchy of morality among characters that is sorely lacking in Shakespeare's text.

I suggest, however, that lessening the anxiety and eventual bitterness of the audience is a mistake, and that the more of *Merchant* that a given production delivers, the less pleasing—and yet the greater—the result will be. The play is ambiguous throughout and deeply unpleasant, but its success depends a great deal on its being allowed to remain so. And, ultimately, the success of a production might best be measured by how anxious and conflicted *we* are allowed to be.

Anxieties about the play's focus, genre, and resolution are longstanding. At least as far back as Edmund Kean actors have endeavored to present sympathetic Shylocks, and nineteenth-century productions routinely came in on Shylock's part by concluding with the trial in 4.1. Referring to the play simply as "Shylock" was a natural consequence of bending to the play's insistence that its villain was an unfortunately obscured tragic hero.[1] Since modern directors have restored the fifth act—a reunion in Belmont during which Portia tells Jessica and the man who stole her that all Shylock's wealth will be theirs—they must grapple with the problem of a play that continues to assert itself as a romantic comedy long after the audience has lost its appetite for one. In response, many have sought to manipulate the audience's reception of the comic characters or even to undermine the comedy itself. A common strategy for this is what Ron Rosenbaum refers to as the "sanitization" of Shakespeare's text.[2] Cutting or downplaying lines that morally compromise the Christians of Venice moderates the ugliness that otherwise leads an audience to resent their victory over Shylock. Alternatively, many directors choose to amplify the brutality of the Christians, allowing Shylock a less contested position at the play's center. They often affirm this position by having Shylock tone down his objectionable speeches and behavior, or by introducing into the plot excuses for his cruelty. Productions typically shape the fifth act so as to reconcile it to the darker mood occasioned by Shylock's fall in 4.1. It has become common, for example, to see Jessica sulking throughout the fifth act, mutely repentant for her Genoan excesses and for abandoning her father, or for Antonio to play the final scene as a "tainted wether of the flock" rather than as one triumphantly saved from death and newly enriched by Shylock's fall.[3] By loading the return to Belmont with sadness, regret and contention, productions can acknowledge and share in the audience's distaste for watching the Venetians in triumph. Their directors appear to assume that Shylock's humiliation has been irremediably cast over the mood of the drama, and that shifting the focus from Shylock to the happy couples is as irresponsible as it is sudden.

Still, scholars have suggested ways in which the play's generic tensions and offensive characters might be aesthetically productive. Marjorie Garber notes that the "ambivalence and ambiguity that emerge from a reading or staging of the play are not a sign of its failure, but rather of its signal success."[4] Garber is right, I think, though the gap between reading and seeing *this* play seems wider than it does for others, since, while reading can make ambiguity available, theater— which is built for the purpose—can actually work to tame ambiguities here. And even when directors take the play's problems as opportunities and are determined

---

[1]    It is not certain how often the play was produced under alternate titles in the nineteenth century. But in his reviews of Kean's performances at Drury Lane on January 27 and February 2 of 1814, Hazlitt mentions Kean "in the character of Shylock," but he also writes of seeing "Kean in Shylock." The reviews make no reference at all to Shakespeare's title. See *The Complete Works of William Hazlitt* (21 vols., London, 1930), V, 295-6.

[2]    Ron Rosenbaum, "Pacino Plays Shylock Like a Grouchy Tevya," *Jewish World Review*, 6 Dec., 2004. Web 5 Dec., 2010.

[3]    Sullen Jessicas and emotionally isolated Antonios no doubt made appearances before Trevor Nunn's 1999 production at the National Theatre, but Nunn's widely acclaimed production—and its adaptation for television—has influenced other productions so much as to make the characterizations standard.

[4]    Marjorie Garber, *Shakespeare After All* (New York: Pantheon Books, 2004), 283.

to preserve them, they struggle to maintain course. Lily Rabe, who played Portia in the Public Theater production directed by Daniel Sullivan,[5] commented on the tendency for directors to chasten the plot when asked whether *The Merchant of Venice* was a "controversial play":

> Yes, people are wary of *Merchant*. There is trepidation about this play, famously so, and I think that speaks volumes about Dan [Sullivan] and the Public that they didn't cut any of the pricklier lines, they didn't soften anything.[6]

Rabe voices the production's admirable objective to take the play as it comes, though at times the production in which she starred wasn't up to the task. This essay uses Sullivan's production as a basis for exploring how and to what ends *The Merchant of Venice* makes itself intolerable to directors and audiences, and how the play's unpleasantness is both aesthetically productive and difficult to preserve—difficult even when directors desire to maintain the play's deep-seated ambiguities. I am interested in what is lost when directors purposely smooth over the play's rough comedy, make changes that favor the audience's (presumed) sensibilities, and otherwise alter the audience's experience by what might be called insidious adaptations—impositions of mood or moral judgment of which directors and actors appear unaware, or compromises that occur and relieve the audience of anxieties even when actors and directors are working expressly against them. I will argue that *Merchant* operates, must always have operated, much like *All's Well That Ends Well*, thriving insofar as it creates anxiety in its audiences, the only parties aware of the gap between the play's generic and moral outcomes.

According to my thesis, then, Rabe's assertions about the production in which she starred must inevitably be mistaken. And for confirmation of this, we need look no further than her Portia. During her first appearance, Portia reviews her list of foreign suitors with Nerissa. She finds what seem legitimate faults in each before turning her attention to a new prospect, the "Prince of Morocco,"

> If I could bid the fifth [Morocco] welcome with so good heart as I can bid the other four farewell, I should be glad of his approach. If he have the condition of a saint and the complexion of a devil, I had rather he should shrive me than wive me.[7]

---

5   The Public Theatre production, starring Al Pacino as Shylock and Lily Rabe as Portia, opened on June 30, 2010 at the Delacorte Theatre in Central Park and ran until August 1, 2010 before being transferred—after changes in the playing company and a further period of rehearsal—to the Broadhurst Theatre for a three month run on Broadway.

6   Lily Rabe, Interview with Gemma Wilson, *Broadway.com*, 1 Nov. 2010. Web 1 Dec., 2010.

7   All citations from the play are to *The Norton Shakespeare*, ed., Stephen Greenblatt (New York: W. W. Norton & Co.) 1997.

After Morocco chooses the wrong casket Portia expands on the theme, expressing her hope that "all of his complexion choose me so" (2.7.79). The revelation that Portia is handsome, clever, rich, and racist, is never pleasant, so the lines are sometimes cut, as they were in this production. Like others before him, Sullivan seems to have been uncomfortable undermining his heroine at her introduction, forcing upon his audience the divided duty to admire the beautiful, well-spoken, and highly eligible heiress and to be morally repulsed by her. Going further, the production introduced a Morocco (played by Nyambi Nyambi) in line with the caricatures Portia described for her other suitors. The audience could not blame Portia for wanting a husband with some sense, so Nyambi's Morocco trilled his "r's" excessively and spoke with cartoonish intonation. The grossly sentimental performance guaranteed the audience's condescension and freed it from the belief that Portia should be fair to all comers. Eliding her comments about Morocco's complexion is a conventional way to clean up Portia's character, but this production used Morocco to justify her persistent aloofness and hints of mockery as signs of good judgment. While Rabe overlooks such signs of softening and adaptation, her comments suggest that the play is so full of "prickly lines" that she believes them all in place despite the absence of these. The production dodged an occasion for moral crisis—*our* moral crisis—yet one can continue to see the play as fully stocked with disagreeable parts.

Sullivan's production was celebrated, and at times very moving, but it interests me because it confronted the play's distasteful elements with rare nerve and still wilted before many of them. The results suggest how tricky the play is to preserve and how subtly it can work to put practitioners off. The production also helps demonstrate how preserving the play's objectionable and ambiguous aspects—especially its cast of mostly unpleasant, sometimes charming and usually offensive characters—might be dramatically advantageous, even vital. The ways in which Sullivan and his cast alternately achieved and fell short of their aim not to "soften anything," coupled with their efforts to cement Shylock's tragic hold throughout the final act, may also shed light on Shakespeare's conception of character. The results argue that each character's service to the plot and audience should be privileged over questions of his or her internal consistency. This idea has ramifications for acting these characters as well, most particularly for "character-based" or "method" acting, the latter a catchall term for the range of American acting schools derived from Stanislavski, of which Al Pacino, Sullivan's Shylock, is a noted exemplar. I hope to show not only how Sullivan and his actors succeeded in mining the play's unpleasantness to theatrically improving ends, but also how their failures point a way forward to other actors and directors seeking to confront the play and deliver to us more of its sweet uncleanness.

Sullivan's Venice was a gloomy and divided city dominated by commerce. The set was all in black, with three concentric circles set apart by iron gates or railings and a large abacus looming overhead. As the play began, three or four Jews—noticeably shut out of the inner rooms—peered through the gates at the prim, Edwardian-styled clerks working at their accounts within. By the time

Antonio entered to a wistful clarinet, the audience could guess at reasons for his sour mood even if he could not. This Venice was not a place for comedy. The cheerless tone persisted, perhaps excepting Bassanio's scenes in Belmont, as though the characters were bracing for the onset of Antonio's—then Shylock's—tragic circumstances in the fourth act.

The production was most memorable for Rabe's performance at Antonio's trial, and for everything that followed it. When Rabe stated in the interview that all the play's hardness was intact, she likely had these final scenes in mind. The trial was stunning and about as prickly as things get onstage, owing much to Rabe's fierce, unflinching Portia. In disguise as a doctor of laws, Portia is tasked with selling Shylock on a model of Christian courtesy ("The quality of mercy is not strained. / It droppeth as the gentle rain from heaven"), only to refuse to show him the mercy she espouses ("Thou shalt have justice more than thou desir'st" [4.1.179–180, 312]). Despite the fact that its sympathies for Shylock are heavily adulterated—because the Christian protagonists deride him on as many just as unjust grounds—audiences inevitably are made uneasy by Portia's hypocrisy. When she wins on a technicality, their uneasiness grows. The revelation that Shylock's bond allows him Antonio's flesh but no blood confirms Portia's victory but never quite feels like justice to an audience. We are glad to see Shylock no longer able to terrorize Antonio, but not to see him victimized by Portia.

His contract in doubt, Shylock offers to depart three times without harming Antonio: first for thrice the value of his bond, then for the principal alone, lastly with no repayment and no further claim on Antonio. All three times, everyone but Portia is willing to let him go. But Portia continues mining the law for means to impugn him until the audience is forced to conclude that she is exacting revenge in much the same spirit as Shylock had pursued Antonio. When Portia reveals that, by seeking Antonio's death, Shylock is subject to a law dictating that his wealth be divided among his enemies, and that his life is forfeit, the audience is more deeply troubled. Shylock now faces a penalty undeniably out of proportion to his actions. More strangely, we can imagine that Portia might have revealed this law earlier in the proceedings and thus ensured a more equitable outcome for everyone. That she wrapped her legal loophole in an enigma argues her desire to bait Shylock into further crimes—and to protract Antonio's suffering—solely for the chance to punish the Jew more severely.

When playing Portia in these moments, the temptation for actors to take their foot off the gas is great. It is likewise tempting for directors to put the onus of brutality on Gratiano, allowing Portia to temper her remarks without keeping the play from the assault that helps the audience to align with Shylock. Actors in the role of Portia may play the scene as if expecting the Duke to pardon Shylock when commanding him, "Down, therefore, and beg mercy of the Duke" (4.1.358); or they may convey a tense awareness that in posing as Daniels come to Judgment, they too might be flouting the law. But Rabe thrust Shylock onto his knees and growled out the order as if she hoped for the chance to stab Shylock herself. Many actors will shy from this kind of commitment to their own hypocrisy and bitterness, especially when filling roles for the resident ingénue. These likely do not want to erode the favor Portia has built up with the audience over three acts, the woman for whom rich men across the world will cross oceans. But Rabe was unrelenting. And Sullivan wisely moderated the role of Gratiano, letting his savagery intrude but always remain secondary to Portia's own. Gratiano can get more attention than Jesse L. Martin did in the role, but Martin's comparative restraint was a benefit to the production, and to Portia, though it did not raise her in the audience's esteem.

The production didn't defend Portia from Portia's actions in the trial, and she did not temper them herself. And this was not the character Rabe had been playing for ninety minutes. Rather, she played a character called for only momentarily by the drama, one unanticipated by the plot and deeply disturbing—as well as electrifying—to her audience. This energy is a function of the character, of course, but one Rabe assented to entirely, and entirely for our good. The play asks its audience to struggle through a comedy partly derailed by a character who transcends his generic boundary. This Portia made Shylock feel larger and even more transcendent. The result was a more profound sense of tragedy, for Shylock but also for us. Her insistence on the Jew's fall seemed harsher than is usual, and the play itself grew harsher because Portia fell along with him—some of her moral superiority and value was lost with Shylock's money. Given that the play repeatedly conflates people and money, the parallel between falls in esteem for Portia and Shylock was the more significant.[8]

Other Christians in attendance contribute to the ugliness of the trial scene, with Antonio, the Duke and Gratiano standing out as the most egregious offenders. We may not be surprised that Gratiano continues taunting Shylock even after losing his case, fortune, daughter and religion, but we might expect Antonio to show a Christian kindness after his delivery. Yet, given the chance to show mercy, Antonio takes after Portia, wrapping his olive branch in a crown of thorns. Antonio offers Shylock the chance to save his life only at the price of a compelled conversion, and the promise to leave all his wealth to the man who stole his daughter. As Diego Arciniegas writes in his account of playing Antonio, "If this is a gentle rain from heaven, I wonder what weather Antonio could summon around the holidays." And the Duke's offer of "mercy" echoes Portia's own, since he sanctimoniously pronounces a pardon for Shylock so that the Jew might "see the difference of our spirit," only to withdraw the promise after Antonio thinks up more degrading conditions. The play doesn't let up in turning punishment to abuse, and Sullivan wisely didn't permit his actors to let up either: the threats and abuse heaped on Shylock were given all possible sharpness, with no moments manufactured to make Shylock seem more deserving of his end. The production did not pause to notice that the punishments had grown excessive and that the Christians were adopting the bloodlust for which they had faulted Shylock. That is more difficult to do than it sounds, and it was mesmerizing.

---

[8]     See, e.g., the consistently sounded pun in 'pound of flesh' (1.3.145–46); also the reference to Portia as a 'golden fleece' (1.1.170; 3.2.240).

Fig. 8.1    From left to right: Lily Rabe (Portia), Byron Jennings (Antonio), Al Pacino (Shylock). Photo by Joan Marcus

The scene that followed the fourth act was even more gut-wrenching. Sullivan had several large Venetians muscle Shylock across the stage before thrusting him into a pool suddenly turned baptismal. They struck off his yarmulke, submerged him repeatedly, and then abandoned him in the water. At each step their hatred for him was palpable. One got the impression that the ferocity sustained during the trial came easier to a cast aware that the production and its Christians were destined for these depths. Tubal and a Jewish boy soon came to Shylock's aid, but they hurried off in fear of the Christians' return to the church. This left Shylock to retrieve his headgear and start a long, damp, solitary walk offstage in the direction of the departed Jews. It was an exit fit for a star, to be sure, but the scene was truly haunting.

The interpolated baptism was unquestionably a moving piece of drama and nearly every reviewer praised it. For audiences, however, the gain wasn't worth the loss. Most of the audience would likely disagree, based on the power of the scene and because the baptism allowed the production to confront problems of religious prejudice directly. It magnified the unpleasantness of the Venetians and the suffering of Shylock, intensifying our feelings about both. Still, however great Sullivan's courage in haunting the audience with his interpolation, its result was to provide clear definitions for things that the play leaves—more hauntingly—undefined. It is painful to know that the Christians forced Shylock to undergo a public baptism. But it is at least clear. This production effectively taught its audience that Shylock, even after his (manifestly violent) conversion, remained a Jew at heart: that he continued at odds with the Christians, that Tubal was still concerned about him. Those are comforting pieces of news when contrasted with possible alternatives—say, the chance that the Christians would invite Shylock over for pork chops and jokes about moneylenders like Tubal, to which he might be forced to attend and laugh along. And the chance that Shylock would adapt to his new circumstances, forgive Jessica, and decide all was well is equally distressing.

Whatever the outcome, the impact of a play that marginalizes and forgets its sudden—and suddenly sympathetic—center will be diminished by a scene that clarifies his fate, however powerful the scene. A miserable outcome for Shylock generates less anxiety in an audience that otherwise must remain alone in its awareness of one stranded on an island of gloomy possibilities. Since the play thereafter ignores what most interests us—the fate of Shylock—that anxiety deepens. In addition to the adverse effect of clarifying Shylock's end, the baptism scene also fixed the Venetians, who formerly had been shown alternating cruelty with kindness, as unequivocal villains. Rather than having overstepped their bounds in what we knew was a just cause, here the Venetians remove all ambiguity about their motivations and morality. Their characters, as well as Shylock's, are at this point set down in ink. The play gains significant energy from the fact that its generic good guys are not consistently good guys, and that its antagonist is clearly possessed of "senses, affections, passions" surpassing those of most of his rivals. But in using the staged baptism to cement these elusive, unprecedented moral conditions, the production dissipated that energy, allaying rather than adding to the audience's moral crisis. The *tragedy* was emphatically announced at this point, but its fixity made Shylock's position far less grave. The audience had hitherto been anxious over the "justice" shown to Shylock and the hypocrisy of those meting it out, but those feelings were weak in comparison to the outrage promoted by the fact that nobody else seemed to notice the inequity.

Put another way, by introducing the baptism the production declared who among its characters has integrity, and who has none. If a production concludes that Shylock is a tragic hero and that the others are hypocrites, then the audience's position is safe. Conversely, if it presents a range of unstable possibilities for protagonists and antagonists—something *Merchant* does from the start—and if it insists on the play's clear but shallow evidence to sanction its treatment of Shylock, then our position is far more conflicted. If that evidence proves him to be in the wrong but denies us the sense of justice and triumph that his accusers seem to experience, then our conflict is intensified. And in the theater, the drama that counts is always taking place in the audience. Sullivan's addition frightened the audience into a safer place, for suddenly we were no longer alone in our desire to rewrite the script.

The compromises that the baptism scene makes and forces the audience into making become clearer in the light of the production's fifth act. Sullivan's final act, beginning with Shylock forcibly baptized and ending with Jessica drowning her letter of inheritance in the baptismal pool, included the now standard sulking

Jessica and Antonio, but went much further toward darkening the romantic subplots. The return to Belmont begins famously with Lorenzo and Jessica in the night, recounting tales of mythical lovers who braved adversity to come together and mingling with it banter about their own elopement. The play thus takes up one of its several comic plots and starts carrying it through to completion. But the production would have none of it, staging the scene as a quarrel between lovers already frustrated with one another. The air of gloom and suspicion begun here carried over to the ring plot, so that the usual banter between the newlyweds turned grave. The restoration of the rings was preserved and the lines suggested that Portia and Bassanio, Nerissa and Gratiano, had reconciled their differences and gone off to bed, but Bassanio's jokes were strained and Portia's slowly forthcoming offer of forgiveness felt shallow and joyless. In the end, Nerissa and Portia left the stage without their husbands, apparently embittered over what they continued to understand as a real betrayal. They played the scene as though mindful of Bassanio's and Gratiano's admittedly alarming willingness to sacrifice their wives if doing so would save Antonio. Again, Sullivan confronted the play's ever-present underbelly, but he introduced it into the conscious minds of his characters and his audience. The production closed on Jessica, looking over the will her father left, clearly dissatisfied with her choice to abandon him, and possibly over choosing to wed Lorenzo too.

In the fifth act, to an even greater degree than in the baptism, the production acknowledged and legitimated the audience's discomfort with the plot and its characters. But by allowing the audience to see their own frustrations projected onto the characters, the play became more comfortable than it could have been if those characters had failed to notice. Again, our doubts and objections are more burdensome when it seems they are ours alone. The mistake was critical. The production allowed its audience to look upon a world dissatisfied and corrupt, and *aware* of its corruption, rather than depicting something truly horrifying, and genuinely tragic: that the play's characters had moved on with their lives, that they were comfortable enjoying a just and happy triumph over an unquestioned enemy. The play poses the possibility that Shylock is utterly forgotten other than as a means for filling Lorenzo's pockets. Antonio is rich again by Shylock, his argosies are come to harbor and all is well in the world. If everyone does live happily ever after, one thing is absolutely certain—the audience will not. Our tragedy is just beginning when the play appears not to notice its own generic complexities.

Readers are typically outraged by the play's fifth act. They want answers—and to the play's credit, none are forthcoming. Eventually they notice that plays rarely engage them as much as this one does in the fifth act, as they look on in disbelief that soon turns to dismay. I think the increase in frustration—and engagement— stems from their dawning awareness that the characters have blithely moved past the events of the previous scene though we cannot. Moreover, we cannot imagine or relate to anyone who could. The play counts on actors who are generous in one moment (Antonio to Bassanio) and cruel the next (Antonio to Shylock). It relies on Portia to alienate us by her prejudice against dark skin, but then cross the sea to rescue Antonio minutes later. These characters complement a plot that initially cannot make up its mind about which comedy it wants to be. Antonio, Bassanio, Portia, Launcelot, Jessica, and Lorenzo alternate in introducing the play's early scenes, each opening a familiar plot, each plot prescribing a different set of generic roles and duties to its protagonist's cast-mates. Shakespeare's final act cheerfully sets about resolving those plots, seemingly without mind to the troublesome fact that the intervening play has outgrown them.

When Jessica and Lorenzo depart the stage happy that Shylock's money is now theirs to spend, a conventional plot has been resolved, and just as we might expect. For audiences know that young lovers kept apart by old money-grubbing fathers (all of which pieces are present here) deserve not only to be married, but also to enjoy a handsome dowry. *Merchant* provides the right conclusion for the wrong play. Its audience can no longer be contented with what the rudiments of this plot promised, as they would be if Egeus from *A Midsummer Night's Dream* were forced to bestow his blessing and a large dowry on Hermia. Likewise, when Portia returns to Belmont, she plays the shrew over a "lost" ring, taunts Bassanio into jealousy of the Doctor she impersonated, and then forgives him with a kiss. But the audience can no longer be satisfied by the comic exchanges because the character, once again, has expanded beyond the bounds of her generic role, and because the play has unresolved concerns—in the minds of its audience—more critical than this light matter can resolve. Thus the play, like Antonio himself, gets off on a technicality, fulfilling all its explicit generic promises but leaving its audience unfulfilled. The essence of the play—an essence unforeseen when its scheme was laid out—seems to lack completion.

Sullivan's fifth act was not without merits, but it did the opposite of what it intended by sustaining and intensifying the bleak mood occasioned by the trial. Perpetuating the gloom was akin to admitting that the play itself was mistaken—in forgetting Shylock, and in continuing with a comic plot that must prove more bitter than sweet to its audience. The production showed the audience a troubling (but *intelligibly* troubling) world—one that knew its characters' real worth, even if the playwright had seemed to lose perspective. It asked us to notice and be impressed by the depth of Shylock's fall, but it also softened that fall, if not for him then certainly for us. Hardening the play's surface actually softened the production's impact on the audience, because the characters appropriated burdens that the play reserves for us alone. In this light, even the production's gloomy opening, well suited to the sadness and isolation of Antonio and Portia, was guilty, for it affirmed that, though comic in kind, this was a play whose comedy was tainted.

The effect of the softening in the last act was subtler and more profound than the sanitization of Portia, but it was ultimately quite like it in kind. Anyone familiar with the frustration at seeing Helena elated by finally winning Bertram, or at seeing a nun go off gleefully to marry a friar at the close of *Measure for Measure*, will understand the deep impact on an audience made possible when plays fail to notice the problems that audiences do. Isabellas who won't join hands with their Dukes make us think more than they make us feel, because they perform our anxiety for us. Shakespeare's plays are rare in their ability to generate dramatic tension within audiences, alongside and in addition to the conflicts they create among characters. A production that preserves Portia's racism alongside her charm, beauty, cleverness, and patient captivity to a dead father's whims, pushes the audience into conflict with itself; in the presence of such a figure the audience is like Camillo, a "hovering temporizer" who can "at once see good and evil / Inclining to them both" (*The Winter's Tale*, 1.2.304–306). Almost all the characters in *Merchant* force us into like positions.

It may be counter-intuitive that we should want moral crises in stage figures, and to experience like crises at their hands. But this is the only reasonable behavior for theater audiences. After all, all stage figures are animated by their fundamental pretensions, by the inherent dissonance between the actor and the figure he represents. This ongoing admission of his or her falsity is an essential component of any character's attractiveness, and it follows that those characters will be more attractive still when their hypocrisies are exposed. *The Merchant of Venice* is filled with characters that embody aspects unnatural to those in their generic positions, but its success argues that these are the characters worth having onstage. The play suggests that, for Shakespeare, stage character is built on inconsistency, on a kind of absence of uniform or coherent characteristics. Shakespeare's characters, when allowed to roam between advancing justice or injustice, participating in a comedy or a tragedy, gain complexity in much the way that actors do. In the end, their inconsistency is what likens them to "real" people, each kind and cruel depending on the point of comparison or the moment of measurement, than they would appear if more consistently drawn.

This brings me to Shylock, who is among the most inconsistently drawn figures in Shakespeare, and who owes his attractions to being so. I mentioned already the presumption that Shylock could once have been performed as a stereotypically comic villain and usurer, but that time has introduced new dignity and sensitivity to the role (this even though Shylock seems to have been the play's focal point, if one that elicited ambivalence, at least since the time of Macklin).[9] Whatever the history of change in characterization, and setting aside my doubts that any audience ever could have heard Shylock after losing Jessica and think about him principally as a comic usurer, it is usual in modern times to see Shylock at the center of a tragedy in which he stars. Many productions are quick to establish him from the first as a character best reflected by the abandoned father in 3.1. Actors will often work toward a consistent emotional template based on their most poignant lines—lines such as "If you prick us do we not bleed," and "…my turquoise. I had it of Leah when I was a bachelor" (3.1.54; 100–101) come to inform the whole performance. Such actors often sidestep or underplay lines that undermine this consistency and

---

[9]    Charles Macklin (1690?–1797) was an English actor who achieved great fame for his portrayal of Shylock in the eighteenth century. Macklin's prominence would suggest that Shylock was the most desirable role almost three centuries ago and, consequently, that it likely was not played as a simple stereotype even then.

productions look for ways to excuse or dampen what cuts against the character's ability to claim all the sympathy he can. Just moments before voicing his deep regard for his wife's first gift,[10] Shylock utters some of the more distasteful lines in literature, expressing his wish that Jessica "were dead at my foot and the jewels in her ear! Would she were hearsed at my foot and the ducats in her coffin!" (3.1.75–6). And it is easy to forget that Shylock begins his great speech on the humanity of Jews ("Hath not a Jew eyes?") by telling Salerio that Antonio's flesh will serve him "to bait fish withal"(3.1.45, 49–50). Each of the statements goes a long way toward justifying the epithets the Venetians attach to him, although, interspersed as they are with statements that affirm his humanity, an audience will struggle to come down firmly on one side. Or, rather, it will come down firmly on both sides.

Though Sullivan's production allowed Shylock to dominate the fifth act (an act in which he does not appear), it is to his and Pacino's credit that they didn't allow him to dominate the play, or to follow others in forging an emotionally consistent character from his disparate parts. Pacino's complex, even inconsistent, portrayal of Shylock may help explain the mechanisms behind the characters in the play, and, perhaps, generally in Shakespeare. As I've suggested, characters in this play work much like the play itself to force unwanted ambiguities and anxiety on the audience.

I suspect the world is not in need of someone to weigh in on whether Al Pacino is a great actor, but he was really special in Sullivan's production. Some of the cause is predictable and rests simply with his rare commitment to embodying a character. Pacino is emphatically present in nearly every moment he's on stage, seemingly sensitized to his surroundings in a way that has him always bristling with life. Each line or gesture is founded on a degree of conviction that allows us to mistake him for doing something other than acting in a play. And yet Pacino can speak more artificially—with more varied intonation than his cast-mates and more overt awareness of his audience—without coming off as artificial, because his conviction enables ours. But leaving aside Pacino's particular talents, his Shylock was remarkable because he didn't play the part for sympathy. He played it as inconsistently as it was written and chose not to overtake a play that was there for the taking. As Portia did during the trial, Pacino played his entire part as though he were ignorant of what would come next. He was (for Pacino) relatively tame and human—even realistic in his acting—but without softening lines that shifted his character toward a stereotype of a callous moneylender, and without gilding lines that were capable of winning him sympathy.

For example, Pacino worked through the series of questions about the humanity of Jews with ample passion but without pandering. He behaved wholly without regard to gaining leverage with his audience by means of the speech. He focused more on Salerio and Solanio than I can remember seeing from any other actor in

---

[10]   Note that in a play concerned with characters all of whom combine disagreeable with (nearly) redeeming qualities, the play takes pains to liken Bassanio and Shylock, both of whom lose rings that represent their wives' first gift.

the role, preferring engagement with them to lament or reverie. The choice kept the audience's focus on the play, and at the possible expense of increasing its sympathy for him. He neither prejudiced his audience for or against him, but rather gave it continual cause to switch sides. Eventually Shylock, and Pacino too, was like a coin that turned up heads and tails at once. The performance was immensely generous—by not rising above the plot Shylock helped to keep the play from resolving and its audience from fixing its judgment with respect to him or his enemies. His Shylock seemed perfectly unreasonable and inhumane in hating Antonio "for he is a Christian" and because he "lends out money gratis, and brings down / The rate of usance" (1.3.37–40), before appearing like another creation when at home with Jessica and Launcelot or when speaking with Tubal about his losses. It's not only that his mood was changeable; his mind was changeable too. Each scene saw him take up residence in a new place in the minds of his audience. He quickly and continuously redefined himself according to the play's dramatic action—playing the sympathy and the ugliness of 3.1, then entering the trial matter-of-factly, though with monstrous intent. In the end, Pacino helped deliver a plot rather than a character, preferring complexity to definition at every turn.

The Shylock that Pacino and Sullivan produced affirms the benefit of having characters that are supple enough to encompass contradictions. These are built more in service to the plot than they are loyal to a psychological or biographical back-story that aims to reconcile them to an actor's concept. They are useful, even "real," insofar as their artificiality is privileged. What is somewhat surprising is not that Shakespeare's characters function best this way, but that Pacino should help exemplify the need for such flexibility, considering that he comes from the Strasberg school, and is a name famously associated with method acting. Since America's introduction to Stanislavsky's early work with the Moscow Art Theatre, theater practitioners have largely privileged "emotional realism" in acting Shakespeare's plays, appearing to work from a premise that audiences cannot value, much less credit, acting that doesn't appear to flow from real emotion. As a result, actors like Pacino often rely on governing super-objectives, draw emotional through-lines for characters, and imagine and draw on biographies that allow them to make and render sensible the disparate actions called for in a given role.

But Pacino's performance managed to preserve the psychological intensity from moment to moment, while altering the back-story or seeming foundation for Shylock at will. In other words, he reflected the kind of commitment to character and truth presumably enabled—at least in part—by his technique, yet he employed the technique across what almost seemed a procession of several characters, each happening to share a name and parentage. He appeared to lack any super-objective as Strasberg might have defined it, preferring instead to chase something seen as vital in one moment, and something quite different in the next. These were not trivial changes. Rather, Pacino acted as though his core values and overarching objectives were feathers for every wind that blows, provided that those winds would keep the audience guessing. My definition of Strasberg's system is limited here, of course, and I do not overlook that it has helped produce actors capable of winning acclaim in complex roles for decades. But it is interesting to observe how different Shakespeare's characters often are from what we would have them be, and to consider the temptation for actors to be as consistent and uncompromised as the audience would like—or, rather, thinks they would like—them to be.[11] Pacino resisted that temptation in large part. His performance showed not only great depth, but also variation in a degree that suggested he was willing to jettison theories, and even his character, in favor of the plot. Because he did not build the character on a single axis, he stayed clear both of excessive sentimentality and pandering. The character still felt emotionally true, but true to the extremities of each moment rather than to a unifying persona. The performance substantiated my conception that *real* emotional realism shows emotional experience to be far less pure, far less amenable to the standard psychological through-line, than contemporary theories of acting and personality would let us believe. Pacino came off as more humble, both as an actor and a character, and yet no less large. Consequently, the star of the play always felt like one, but he did so by *not* standing out as one. This held until the baptism and its aftermath elevated the role of Shylock, a momentary triumph for him and for the audience, though, in granting him power over the play, the production finally sapped some of the play's power over us.

---

[11]    In addition to the foregoing examples from *The Merchant of Venice*, note the wide tendency for directors and actors to hedge against what complicates and compromises their characters in the minds of the audience. It is common, for example, to downplay Romeo's desire for Rosaline—or at least his attempt to "ope her lap to saint-seducing gold" (1.1.207). Variations on the theme include making the Casca of the storm scene consistent with the "fleering tell-tale" he is when Cassius and Brutus try to get information out of him on the Lupercal (*Julius Caesar*, 1.3.116); or having the Widow in *All's Well That Ends Well* not take Helena's money at every opportunity; or making sense of Hamlet's railing at Ophelia by having Polonius and Claudius announce their presence by coughing or knocking something over (3.1.130). The results of these choices comfort audiences and allow a less conflicted relationship to the characters, but the plays will always be worse for such decisions.

# Chapter 9
# Iago:
# In Following Him I Follow But Myself

## Dan Donohue

"To be a great actor, you need to play the great roles." I have heard that said many times by my teachers and mentors, and I believe it to be true. I would only qualify it by saying that I think the ideal of becoming a "great actor" should always feel like it is just out of reach. The actors I admire the most and try to emulate are those who, in spite of their past accomplishments, continue to push themselves to learn, to grow, and to improve. When I was offered the role of Iago in *Othello* for The Oregon Shakespeare Festival's 2008 season, I had no doubt that working on that character would test and measure my abilities as an actor. Great roles do that.

But clearly, Iago is not simply one of those "great roles." Iago, himself, is one of those "great actors." A masterfully skilled liar, Iago is without doubt a better actor than I am. In fact, it is striking to note just how many times the words "honest" and "honesty" are echoed throughout the play in relation to Iago.[1] For most characters, "Honest Iago" is spoken as a universally accepted understanding of who Iago is:

> A man he is of honesty and trust. (1.3.280)
> Honest Iago. (1.3.290)
> Iago is most honest. (2.3.6)
> Good night, honest Iago. (2.3.102)
> I never knew a Florentine more kind and honest. (3.1.38)
> O, that's an honest fellow. (3.3.5)
> This fellow's of exceeding honesty. (3.3.260)
> My friend, thy husband, honest, honest Iago. (5.2.153)

An audience of course hears the irony each time Iago is called "honest." But I am convinced that Shakespeare is not using that repetition simply to stir up a comic response. Iago is known as "Honest Iago" because he *behaves* that way. And the repeated use of the word serves as a challenge and a reminder to me to keep the performance *honest*. When an actor playing Iago wears his villainy on his sleeve, each reference to "Honest Iago" prompts the audience to laugh. From my perspective, hearing too many of those kinds of laughs is a warning sign that the actor is probably taking the play down the wrong path.

---

[1] All textual references are to William Shakespeare, *Othello*, ed., Julie Hankey. 2nd ed. (Cambridge: Cambridge University Press, 2005).

So I thought to myself—*If Iago is a better actor than I am, then in order to play him well, I need to work to bridge that gap.* For me, the opportunity to play that role would be like studying acting from a master teacher. It would be an opportunity to literally step into Iago's shoes and to follow in his footsteps. My challenge would be to be as honest in representing Iago as "Honest Iago" appears to the other characters in the play. The degree of success in bridging the gap between my own acting abilities and Iago's would be a measure of my growth as an actor. And that is why I eagerly accepted the offer to play him in 2008.

In my early observations of Iago's behavior, I saw him as savage, brutal, spiteful, and manipulative; and yet, he behaved like that in surreptitious ways. He was the epitome of a trusted soldier in wartime, but in peacetime, he is a kind of apothecary who deals in mental poisons. And he is surgical in his dismantling of Othello. Iago is also quite likely the smartest person in the room—any room. He probably sees himself that way, and he is probably right. He reveals no empathy for those he sets out to harm, and in the end, he has no remorse for what he has done to them. Iago seems to function without a moral compass.

That initial sketch was based on what Iago did and how he went about doing it. Those early general impressions were useful to me—but mainly as a starting point. To focus on Iago's outward qualities without fleshing out the mystery of what was inside of him was too simplistic, too judgmental, and too skeletal. Those kinds of simple judgments by themselves could reduce character work to cartooning. Iago would then become more of an archetype than a flesh-and-blood human being. And I was not interested in playing that version of the role.

Actors have an implied responsibility to represent the character they play fully and truthfully—whether the role is based on a historical or fictional figure. Of course, I had a point of view about the pain Iago inflicted on others. But when working on the role, I was careful not to dissociate myself from him because of what he did. I resisted judging him. If I distanced myself from the character, the audience would undoubtedly do the same. To play Iago fully and honestly, I needed to become friends with him, to find compassion for him, and even to love him—so to speak. My aim was to shine light on his behavior, and in doing so to provide the audience with a glimpse of his humanity.

Will most spectators disapprove of what Iago does? Yes. But I believe that an audience watching the play should be in danger of recognizing something of themselves in him. I am not suggesting a need to convince them that Iago is a lovable character, nor do I see any need to persuade them that he is a villain. Neither of those concepts is particularly helpful to me or to the audience. But we each share the same potential for good and evil. It is my job to make Iago human enough for that shared potential to be seen.

I have never been in a Shakespeare play where I thought there was more than enough time to rehearse it. And although I felt fortunate to have several months to prepare for *Othello* before rehearsals began, with a role as complex as Iago, the time still felt inadequate.

Prepping for rehearsals means learning as much as I can in advance about the play and the character I will be playing. My aim is to open my mind and imagination to the range and depth of possibilities that are in the role. There are countless helpful resources to draw from, but my main source of reference is, of course, the play itself. Reading and rereading the text and becoming as familiar with it as possible before rehearsals begin are fundamental to giving me that head start. And although I am bound to form opinions, I make every effort to keep an open mind, to let go of preconceived notions, and to remind myself that all discoveries need to be tested in the rehearsal hall.

Iago is not only one of Shakespeare's most complex and elusive characters; he is also the third longest role in the canon after Richard III and Hamlet. To make the best use of rehearsal time, it was important to me to have the text memorized before rehearsals began. I rarely make major discoveries in the rehearsal hall until I can put the script down and look into the eyes of my scene partners. That is when the important discoveries come; only then does the play begin to come to life.

Thankfully, the process of memorizing is not strictly technical. There are significant opportunities for discovery while meticulously combing through the text. As I work on my lines, I almost always speak the words aloud because the actual *sound* of the text is informative. Shakespeare gives each character a voice unique unto him or herself. A fingerprint. So I approach each character as if he, himself, were the author of what he was saying.

Countless questions emerge as I work through the lines. For example, when Iago says, "Thus, credulous fools are caught, …" I might ask myself—*Why does Iago choose to use the word* credulous? *Why doesn't he opt for a word like* naive *or* gullible? *Why does he speak that thought in verse and not in prose?* In addition to being a helpful way to memorize the words, those kinds of *why* questions are essential for making key discoveries about the character. The character's DNA is found in his words. To unlock the vital information that the words contain, posing those kinds of questions is crucial.

In life, words—even Shakespeare's words—are never completely adequate in expressing exactly what we are thinking or feeling. We actively search for just the right word, the perfect phrase, or the best metaphor as we struggle to connect with other people. In order to bring Iago to life, I needed to think of him in the same way. Iago must choose each word; he must coin each phrase; and he, himself, must be the architect of his speech. I meticulously pulled apart his text—line by line and word by word—as I asked myself questions about the choices he made in expressing himself through language.

But with the role of Iago comes that familiar and seemingly unanswerable question: *Why does Iago do what he does?* I was repeatedly asked that question by my colleagues and friends from the very first day I was cast. At first, my answer was, "Umm… let me get back to you on that." With Iago, there are many possible answers. But none of them seems to bring any consensus to spectators or scholars.

Nevertheless, in building Iago, my job was to decide—and to be very specific in doing so—what it was that motivated his behavior. It was an important question to ponder because the key to playing the role lay in the answer. So what was my answer? What was at the center of everything Iago did? For me, the most important piece of the puzzle and the key to unlocking my Iago resided in one word: *jealousy.*

Beyond anything else, I believe jealousy to be the fire that fuels Iago's behavior. He tells us that himself—twice. In Act I, scene 3, he says:

> I hate the Moor,
> And it is thought abroad that 'twixt my sheets
> He's done my office. I know not if't be true
> Yet I, for mere suspicion in that kind,
> Will do as if for surety. (1.3.372–77)

I wondered—*Do I believe him here or not?* In the above passage, the word *and* at the beginning of "*And* it is thought abroad..." was curious to me. Why did Iago choose to use the word *and* instead of *because*? *I hate Othello because he slept with my wife.* At first, I did not quite believe him. I heard Iago's *and* as the beginning of an afterthought—a cold and indifferent rationalization for hating the Moor rather than a true reason. Yet the more I explored this passage—and the play itself—the more Iago's use of *and* here seemed to me to be a clue that he was masking something. Perhaps he used the word *and* to separate his thoughts from the intensity of the feelings that went with them. Perhaps he used the word *and* to make light of a festering wound.

In that moment, as Iago, I struggled to keep my cool. Being alone with the audience for the first time, I did everything in my power to keep a lid on the disgust and rage I felt for Othello. I used the word *and*—after "I hate the Moor"— to separate and play down the pain I felt behind "it is thought abroad that 'twixt my sheets / He's done my office." At the end of that line, my Iago was unable to maintain his control, and he doubled over and retched at the mental image of his wife's assumed infidelity.

Unable to veil his pain for very long, Iago revisits those same feelings again in his very next soliloquy in 2.1. And there, for me, any doubts I may have had about his jealous motivation were dispelled. I believed Iago when he said:

> ...I do suspect the lusty Moor
> Hath leaped into my seat, the thought whereof
> Doth like a poisonous mineral gnaw my inwards;
> And nothing can or shall content my soul
> Till I am evened with him, wife for wife;
> Or failing so, yet that I put the Moor
> At least into a jealousy so strong
> That judgment cannot cure. (2.1.283–91)

The cadence of those words is relentless and perfect. When spoken aloud, they take on a deliberate, unbreakable rhythm. And there is a tightness to the passage. The vowel sounds are secondary to the consonants. Iago tries to maintain control of his jealousy, but it controls him. Jealousy is born out of pain. And this was the moment in our production where the audience got its clearest glimpse of the depth of Iago's pain.

In studying the script, what I found most convincing of all—even more than what Iago said or how he said it—was from Emilia in 3.4 when she spoke on the subject of men and jealousy.

> DESDEMONA: Alas the day, I never gave him cause.

> EMILIA: But jealous souls will not be answered so.
> They are not ever jealous for the cause,
> But jealous for they're jealous. 'Tis a monster
> Begot upon itself, born on itself. (3.4.156–61)

Emilia speaks of jealousy like someone with real experience who knows firsthand about jealous husbands.

Another convincing piece to the puzzle emerged in the encounter between Emilia and Iago in 3.3. This is the only moment in the play where we see Iago and Emilia alone together. Shakespeare affords us this one isolated glimpse of what their private home life might be like. Iago enters and finds Emilia by herself.

> IAGO: How now? What do you here alone?

> EMILA: Do not you chide; I have a thing for you.

> IAGO: You have a thing for me? It is a common thing—

> EMILIA: Ha!

> IAGO: To have a foolish wife. (3.3.306–11)

My immediate question was—*Why is Iago so curt with Emilia when he enters the scene?* Iago's "How now? What do you here alone?" may simply mean *Why are you not attending to Desdemona?* But to me, there is bite in the tenor of his words. Iago seems convinced that he has caught Emilia in a compromising situation. My subtext in playing the line was *Who are you standing here waiting for? Othello? Cassio? Or is there yet another man?*

Emilia hears his words as the familiar beginning of a quarrel. Knowing very well where Iago is headed, she quickly meets his pointed question with, "Do not you chide." To my ear, the tone suggests that the two of them have been down this road before. Emilia is once again responding to the pointed questions of a jealous man.

I also find it revealing that Iago chooses jealousy as the tool with which to destroy Othello. When leading him down that path, Iago clearly knows his way. My Iago sets out to inflict the greatest possible pain on Othello. What greater pain is there than jealousy? What greater justice is there than doing unto Othello what he believes the Moor has done unto him?

My early impression was that Iago's main source of jealousy was centered on his belief that Othello had been sexually intimate with Emilia. But as I continued to study the play, that impression began to evolve. I began to feel that Iago was actually more jealous of Emilia for stepping between him and Othello than he was of Othello for stepping between him and Emilia. To Iago, Othello was more of a partner and an object of love than Emilia was because Iago's self-concept was more entangled in his relationship with Othello than it was with her.

I also began to appreciate the range and scope of Iago's jealous feelings. He was not merely jealous of Emilia and Othello; he was also jealous of Cassio, of Desdemona, and perhaps of everyone else he encountered.

Being passed over for promotion had set off Iago's jealousy of Cassio. He was jealous of him—not so much because he was promoted to lieutenant—but because Cassio, like Emilia, had come between him and Othello. Iago was jealous of Desdemona for the same reason. In marrying Othello, she had usurped Iago's position as the person who was closest to the Moor. In Iago's mind, all of those people were to blame for his imagined loss of status with Othello. But, of course, the person who was most to blame—who had carelessly given away that vital piece of Iago's identity—was Othello himself.

In *The Psychology of Jealousy and Envy*, W. Gerrod Parrott writes that "at the heart of jealousy is a *need to be needed*."[2] To frame it in my mind that way was particularly influential in how I understood and approached the role of Iago. Parrott's observation illuminated for me Iago's peculiar need to draw near to Roderigo, Cassio, Desdemona, and especially to Othello after he hurt them. Frequently throughout the play, Iago creates chaos for others and then turns around to offer them his assistance in dealing with the trouble at hand. For instance, after he pours the pestilence into Othello's ear by suggesting that Desdemona has taken Cassio as her lover, he quickly takes advantage of the opportunity to move closer to the general. By taking on the role of the loyal soldier, the honest friend, and the trusted confidant, Iago quickly regains his position as Othello's right-hand man.

Fueled by intense jealousy, Iago's need to be needed and his correlative need to destroy made for a marriage of love and hate. My Iago internally savored each moment of Othello's destruction. Yet he still found pleasure in becoming so completely needed and even loved by him. It was part of his plan that he shared with the audience in 2.1 when he said:

> I'll …
> Make the Moor thank me, love me, and reward me,
> For making him egregiously an ass,
> And practicing upon his peace and quiet
> Even to madness. (2.1.292–96)

---

2    W. Gerrod Parrot, "The Emotional Experiences of Envy and Jealousy," in *The Psychology of Jealousy and Envy*, ed., Peter Salovey (New York: The Guilford Press, 1991), 17.

The power Iago gained from his closeness to Othello enabled him to strip the Moor of both his power and his identity and to have greater command in pacing Othello's ruin. Iago had become the general's general.

An earlier example comes after Iago skillfully orchestrates the "displanting" of Cassio. Although he, himself, has engineered Cassio's fall from favor, Iago quickly steps in to play the role of the loyal friend using words that are generous, supportive, and protective. He offers to assist Cassio in reclaiming his position as Othello's lieutenant. And by behaving as a trusted friend, Iago's "need to be needed" is satiated—at least for the moment. He is like an arsonist who sets a house ablaze and then warns everyone that the house is on fire. He becomes simultaneously both the destroyer and the hero. Out of the rubble of his chaos, he emerges as the savior.

Iago's victims pull him closer to them. They give him love. And they make him feel important, powerful, and necessary. Their dependence and trust strengthen his ability to manipulate them even more as he adds the finishing touches to his ever evolving plan—his architectural work of destructive art.

Shakespeare's Iago is, however, human. His schemes are loosely designed and untested: ". . .'Tis here, but yet confused; / Knavery's plain face is never seen till used" (2.1.293). Iago can predict an outcome in advance, but he cannot guarantee the result. I was infinitely more interested in playing an Iago who was continually forced to improvise rather than an Iago who was some sort of a clairvoyant who could clearly see how everything would eventually turn out. I thought of him as a man walking a tightrope—one false step away from losing everything.

Perhaps the best example of this tightrope act is in 3.3 when Iago first plants the seeds of doubt in Othello's mind. Can Iago know with absolute certainty what Othello's reaction will be? Not if Iago is human. That sense of incalculable possibility is what makes the scene so brilliant. Even a world-class bull rider is in danger of being thrown. No matter how well a rider may understand an animal, it is impossible to foresee exactly how the bull will react when the gate flies open. That dynamic makes it both exciting for the rider to experience and thrilling for the spectator to watch. Even an animal cannot be taken for granted. And take note: Othello is no simple beast. He is a man of exceptional power, complexity, and intellect. Iago is taking a tremendous risk, and the audience must realize that.

In building and performing the role of Iago, I paid particular attention to the character/audience relationship. Iago appears to unveil his genuine self to the audience by revealing his most intimate thoughts and feelings. He treats them as confidants. My first question regarding Iago's relationship with the audience was—*Why does Iago choose to speak to the audience at all?* In Shakespeare's plays, an aside or a soliloquy that is directed out to the audience is a familiar and accepted theatrical convention. Finding themselves alone, the characters in Shakespeare's plays often turn to the audience to reveal their private thoughts. Although spectators rarely think—*Why is that guy telling* me *all of this?*—as an actor, it is important for me to ponder that very question. *Why* am *I telling the audience all of this? Why* does *Iago choose to share his thoughts with them?*

Answering those questions by saying—*Because that's just something they do in Shakespeare*—is no help at all when it comes to playing those moments. A more helpful answer to *Why does Iago share so much with the audience?* is that *He* wants *something from them. But what does he want? What does the audience have that Iago needs?* To answer that question, I asked myself another one*: What is Iago's relationship with his spectators? Who are they to him?*

To me, in some ways, that relationship is not unlike the one he has with Roderigo. In 1.3 he describes it in this way:

> ...I mine own gained knowledge should profane
> If I would time expend with such a snipe
> But for my sport and profit. (1.3.368–70)

My Iago shared his inner thoughts with the audience because he found "sport" in taking them along for the ride and in making them complicit in what he was doing. His "profit"—that thing that he needed from the audience—was the pleasure he felt in showing off his intelligence, his cunning, and his ability to manipulate others. As witnesses to his thoughts, the audience fed Iago's sense of power—another key ingredient in his makeup. They validated him and helped to "plume up" his will.

But is Iago truly confiding in them? How much truth is he actually sharing? Should playgoers implicitly trust what he says to them? Well, probably not. As with all of Iago's other relationships, I feel that this one is manipulative as well. Though he may reveal more of who he is to the audience than he does to the characters in the play, at best I feel he offers them a guarded truth. A circuitous one. He enlists them as witnesses, but he shares only those particulars that reflect the Iago he wants them to see.

Ironically, the audience watches Iago lie to everyone onstage, and yet, they tend to want to believe that what he says to them is true. Iago's soliloquies and asides seem like gestures of intimacy and trust. In playing those moments, I extended my trust to the audience in hopes that they would reciprocate by extending their trust to me.

But no matter how much Iago shares and how much trust he gains, by the end of the play, most of the audience will be left feeling doubtful and uneasy about what they really know. In 5.2 Iago's final words have a particularly unsettling effect. I aimed those words at Othello. But I intended them for everyone—including the audience.

> Demand me nothing; what you know, you know.
> From this time forth I never will speak word. (5.2.301)

Iago's words were not intended to bring satisfaction to Othello nor to any other partial witnesses to his plots. The audience was no exception. Like Othello, they felt a connection with Iago. They trusted him. After all, he made them his confidants—didn't he? And he told them the "truth." Or did he? Iago's final line prompted everyone to question everything he had said. For a while, Iago may have treated the audience like friends and confidants. But he also treated Roderigo that way as he did Cassio, Desdemona, and Othello. And look what happened to them.

Another important part of the Iago–audience relationship—and one that was crucial to me—was maintaining control of the audience. Strange as it seems, considering all the pain he causes others, Iago can be a humorous character to watch. Playgoers are given a bird's-eye view of what Iago is up to. And as insiders, the irony is not lost on them. But if the audience is allowed to wander too far down that path, the laughs can take over, and the fragile ecosystem of the play can be destroyed. It can be tempting for an actor to be seduced by laughs. And *Othello* is a delicate play.

Determining the balance that is needed will differ from actor to actor. Some actors may not consider that balance at all and—as a result—may be seduced by the comic possibilities in the role. Others may veer too far in the opposite direction and—as a consequence—may snuff out all the moments of irony and humor that Shakespeare may have intended. But for me, it was important that Iago's comic moments were carefully rationed.

I found it helpful to think of each of Iago's soliloquies as an invitation to the audience to take a tour of his mind. But in playing Iago, I never let them forget that it was to be a carefully guided tour. If the tour were of Iago's home, he would only open doors to certain select rooms—sharing only what he wanted his guests to see. They would not be allowed to roam around on their own, to peek into his closets, or to rummage through his drawers. I felt that balance was important to maintain. Without it, the audience would be in danger of having too much fun with Iago. And that fun would be had at the expense of the play.

I found several moments in the play where the audience wanted to take over the tour. For instance, in 2.3 Iago sets out to displant Cassio. He succeeds in doing so, and the demoted lieutenant takes his leave—"Good night, honest Iago" (2.3.302). It was at that point in our production that the audience first gave in to their urge to talk back to me. Left standing alone onstage, I would hear them verbally react to what they had just witnessed. They were talking to themselves and grumbling to me, and I felt their desire to release the tension of the scene. A few of them would even begin to "hiss" as if they were responding to a stock character in a melodrama.

It was then, when our first preview audience turned on me with their disapproval, that I recognized that Shakespeare knew how audiences would likely want to react in that moment. And he had given Iago the words to rein them in:

> And what's he then that says I play the villain,
> When this advice is free I give, and honest …(2.3.304)

I delivered the line as a direct response to the audience's protestations. I used it to prevent them from taking over the moment and to discourage them from dismissing Iago as though he were a simple archetype. Shakespeare challenges the audience's preconceptions. And he gives Iago the words he needs to defend his own complexity. It was a crucial discovery for me, and I used that moment to set a clear boundary for the audience. Iago's subtext was—*Don't get ahead of yourselves. You don't know as much about me as you think you do. Remember. I am the one leading this tour.*

I feel it is critical that the characters manipulated by Iago—most notably Othello, Roderigo, Cassio, Desdemona, and Emilia—are *never* made to look foolish. My hope in playing each scene as truthfully as possible is that the audience will think—*I would have believed Iago too.* When an actor playing Iago wears his villainy on his sleeve, winks at the audience, or twirls a proverbial mustache, the play falls apart. If Iago fails to behave toward Othello in a credible way, the latter comes off as being foolish for believing him, and the emotional impact of the play is then lost. The audience is left thinking—*Othello was a fool. He should have known better than to trust Iago.*

Peter Macon, who played our Othello, said early on in rehearsals: "The smarter every character is, the better the play works." I completely agree. Nobody is a fool in this play, nor should anybody be treated like one. Iago is thought of as "Honest Iago"—not because the other characters are idiots but because he *behaves* in an honest way. And he is seamless in his behavior. To that end, I challenged myself to keep Iago's behavior within real-life parameters. As Iago, I never took anything for granted. And I was conscious of the risks I was taking each step of the way, knowing that at any given moment, all of my plans could fall apart.

There is no need to ignite a flare to alert the audience when Iago is lying. In real-life, bad liars get caught. Only in bad productions do we see the phenomenon of intelligent people believing terrible liars. In those moments when, as Iago, I lie to Othello, to Roderigo, and to Cassio or to any other characters in the play, my hope is to make the audience lose the sense that I am lying at all. Watching Iago work should be like watching a brilliant magician. The audience should be witness to all of his illusions without seeing the mechanisms that make them work.

As an actor, if your character is supposed to walk into a room, you simply walk into the room. There is no need to *act* as if you were walking into the room. The same is true for picking up a newspaper or shaking someone's hand. There is no need to *pretend* that you are shaking someone's hand or to *act* as if you are picking up a newspaper. Just shake the person's hand. Just pick up the newspaper. That simplicity makes the performance more honest. And that is the theme here.

So in thinking about Iago's deceptive behavior, I told myself—*Play one thing at a time. And make it simple.* In a scene where there are moments of deception, it is best for me—Dan, the actor—to be simply "Honest Iago." I keep in mind what Iago secretly wants, but I play the scene as if I were *really* trying to help the Moor. With that in mind, I would choose to play—*Protect my friend, Othello, from some painful news*—rather than playing—*Torture the person I want to destroy.*

Iago pretends, but he does not act like he is pretending. He acts, but he does not pretend like he is acting. Iago always tells the truth even when he is lying.

# Chapter 10
# "I lay with Cassio lately": Iago's Fantasy, the Actor and Audience Response to Othello in 3.3

## Michael W. Shurgot

To Othello's order that Iago "Give me a living reason she's disloyal,"[1] Iago responds with what many critics argue is his greatest risk: his narrative (ll. 426–41) of lying with Michael Cassio where, presumably, no one else could have heard or seen Cassio's supposed confession and manifestation of his love for Desdemona. Numerous commentators have examined this moment in 3.3 for what it reveals about Iago's complex and tortured character, especially his spontaneous daring, sinister audacity, and bizarre sexual desires and fantasies.[2] I wish to scrutinize further this short segment of 3.3 to argue three distinct but interrelated points: first, to unravel the convoluted sexual imagery of Iago's words as a means of further analyzing his character; second, to examine the challenge that Iago's sexual images pose to the actor playing him; and third, to speculate on how Othello's reaction to Iago's apparently convincing narrative might have heightened among Jacobean spectators, and probably does heighten among contemporary spectators, the racial tensions inherent within the play. I shall also consider arguments against these points as a means of strengthening my own position. While I realize that the segment I examine here is quite short (perhaps 3–4 minutes on stage), and while I do not assert that it is somehow the "key" to understanding either Iago's illusive motivations or his relationship with Othello, I shall argue that a scrutiny of Iago's language will deepen our understanding of his character and of the theatrical dynamics of these few moments in 3.3.

Essential to my approach to Iago as a *dramatis personae* is locating the performed "character" in the body of an actor, a "person" on the stage. Anthony B. Dawson writes that for the Elizabethans, person, deriving from the Latin *persona,* an actor's mask, is "primarily an embodied character, a real fiction, and bespeaks

---

[1]  3.3.425. All textual references are to David Bevington, ed., *The Complete Works of Shakespeare* (New York: Harper Collins, 1992).

[2]  See, for example, A. C. Bradley, *Shakespearean Tragedy* (1904; rpt. London: MacMillan & Co., 1964); Stanley Edgar Hyman, *Iago: Some Approaches to the Illusion of His Motivation* (New York: Atheneum, 1970); E.A.J. Honigmann, *Shakespeare: Seven Tragedies* (London: MacMillan, 1976); and Edward Pechter, *Othello and Interpretive Traditions* (Iowa City: University of Iowa Press, 1999).

the impossibility of splitting body from self or self from role."[3] Recent criticism's "materialist use of the word 'body,'" he adds, "tends to be one–dimensional, to textualize what is living and concrete" (2001, 15). Dawson further argues for a developing aesthetic in the Renaissance theatre of an "interiorized personhood based on at least the illusion of depth, and providing a paradigm for what we mean by 'character,' even by 'self'" (2001, 20). Performing then involves both *investing* the actor's body in his or her character and simultaneously *losing* that body in the depths of the character; spectators watch a variegated "rush of feeling" in actors' bodies for a set period of time during which characters develop and, especially in the tragedies, often change radically (2001, 21). J. Leeds Barroll emphasizes the importance of this process to our experience of character in a Shakespearean play:

> [I]n the final analysis the study of characterization, as opposed to the study of cultural presuppositions about personality in a specific historical period, is a study of artistic process. We suppose the dramatist attempted to solve the problem of characterization not by presenting 'very human' actions and reactions at random but by arranging an ordered series of behavioral phenomena related to some kind of sequence (or process) so as to convey to an audience that important fiction, the illusion of a 'person.'[4]

---

[3]     Anthony B. Dawson and Paul Yachnin, *The Culture of Playgoing in Shakespeare's England* (Cambridge: Cambridge University Press, 2001), 15. Dawson and Yachnin insist on the necessity of recognizing the embodied persons in the *dramatis personae* of a Shakespearean play:

> For both of us, the person (as opposed to the social formation) is the key category in theatrical performance and the pleasures it provides. . . . The single most important thing about persons is that they are present and palpable, and hence offer a challenge to those who want to read dramatic character purely in terms of the social formation.        While it is clear that characters occupy positions that can be described in terms of systems of domination, we seek to undermine the authority of such systems, both as explanatory tools deployed by critics and as thorough-going determinants of the behavior of persons, whether fictional or real. (7–8)

[4]     J. Leeds Barroll, *Artificial Persons: The Formation of Character in the Tragedies of Shakespeare* (Columbia: University of South Carolina Press, 1974), 101. Alan Sinfield, "From Bradley to Cultural Materialism," in "Forum: Is There Character After Theory?" *Shakespeare Studies* 34 (2006): 25–34, provides an excellent overview of recent critical arguments about character and character criticism. Sinfield acknowledges a sense of "interiority" in Shakespearean characters while arguing that this interiority is seldom sufficient or consistent. An equally sensible recent essay on character criticism is Michael Bristol's "How Many Children Did She Have?" in *Philosophical Shakespeare,* ed. John J. Joughin (London: Routledge, 2000), 18–33. Echoing L. C. Knights's famous essay in *Explorations* (London: Chatto & Windus, 1963), 1–39, Bristol insists on an eclectic engagement with Shakespeare's make-believe:

> Lady Macbeth's child cannot be fully accounted for, no matter how carefully the text of <u>Macbeth</u> is studied. This leaves critics with a dilemma: accept an ontological contradiction in the story or a fallacy in its  interpretation. There are no drop-dead arguments in favor of either way of doing things. . . . Full

Similarly, Arthur Sewell writes, "We can only understand Shakespeare's characters so long as we agree that we cannot know all about them and are not supposed to know all about them."[5] Sewell locates Shakespearean characters in the actors who play them and their effects on spectators:

> [I]n the creation of these [characters] Shakespeare's identification of himself is not with the character but with the actor. And this identification does not make him ask, What does it feel like to be Falstaff, Iago, Jaques, Richard III? But rather What effect is Falstaff, Iago, Jaques, Richard III, to make on his audience? A very different matter. This effect is the product of an address to the world, here and now made concrete in the address to the audience. ...And so, in Shakespeare's plays, the essential process of character-creation is a prismatic breaking-up of the comprehensive vision of the play; and each element of vision, so separated out, is in itself a unique illumination, finding its individual fulfillment in character. (1951, 15; 19–20).

Iago is among the most fascinating and frightening of what Barroll terms the Shakespearean "illusion of a 'person,'" and the thrust of my argument is that by scrutinizing some of Iago's most enigmatic language, locating that language in the body of the Iago actor on stage, and proposing the likely effects of that language on spectators' views of Othello we may further appreciate the theatrical dynamics of this short segment of 3.3.

Honigmann argues that when Othello exclaims "Would I were satisfied" (3.3.406), Iago "cannot resist torturing him with detailed sexual imagery ... and this becomes the play's turning point. Had he wished, Iago could have explained away all the hints that went before as misunderstandings; after his description of Cassio's dream he can no longer go back, he has to go forward. At this crucial point he takes a tremendous risk, an unnecessary risk, insured by nothing more substantial than Desdemona's handkerchief: he cannot help taking it, I feel, being impelled by an imperious devil within demanding his own kinky satisfaction" (1976, 80–81).

Honigmann asks how we can help thrilling at Iago's cruel artistry (1976, 22). Iago perfects what Stephen Greenblatt calls "improvisation," which he defines as

---

engagement in make-believe is part of a larger commitment to ethical and political reflection. (33)

Katherine Eisaman Maus, *Inwardness and Theatre in the English Renaissance* (Chicago: University of Chicago Press, 1995), argues persuasively for a sense of interiority among persons in the Renaissance. She establishes clearly in her first chapter the differences between her approach to interiority and individualism and that of critics such as Catherine Belsey, *The Subject of Tragedy* (London: Methuen, 1985), and Jonathan Goldberg, *James I and the Politics of Literature* (Baltimore: Johns Hopkins University Press, 1983). A useful review of these critical issues is Laurie Osborne's "Shakespeare and the Construction of Character," in *Shakespeare and Higher Education: A Global Perspective Shakespeare Yearbook* 12. eds., Sharon A. Beehler and Holger Klein (Lewiston: Edwin Mellen Press, 2001), 312–31.

[5] Arthur Sewell, *Character and Society in Shakespeare* (Oxford: Clarendon Press, 1951), 12.

"the ability both to capitalize on the unforeseen and to transform given materials into one's own scenario."[6] Samuel Crowl terms Iago a "freelancer, who picks up on what the immediate situation provides him and never thinks more than one move in advance."[7] Iago affects a "process of fictionalization that transforms a fixed symbolic structure into a flexible construct ripe for improvisational entry," thus constructing a narrative "into which he inscribes ... those around him" (Greenblatt, 234). James Bulman writes that Othello "makes Iago's task the easier by actually inviting him to supply those proofs by which he will confirm appearance as reality."[8] In his astonishing improvisational (i.e., theatrical) ability, Iago seems to manipulate Othello in 3.3 with amazing ease, perhaps damaging in the minds of many spectators (to say nothing of the critics) any vestige of the "noble Moor" or "Renaissance Complete Man" whom they saw in the opening scenes.[9]

As a framework for my analysis of Iago's sexual imagery in 3.3 I begin with Stanley Edgar Hyman's reading of Iago as a latent homosexual.[10] While Hyman argues that this is but one among several possible approaches to Iago's motivations, and that a character as complex as Iago cannot be reduced to either formulae or simplistic generalizations, nonetheless Hyman's analysis of this element of Iago's character is essential to my argument. Hyman's principal insight into Iago's language in his "story" to Othello is that Iago "has turned himself into a Desdemona for Cassio's sexual enjoyment on the surface of the spurious dream, and for Othello's in the latent content" (1970, 110–111). As Iago proceeds through his narrative, this imagery becomes increasingly obvious, bold, and lurid, suggesting that Iago is becoming subconsciously aroused by his narration of his (presumably) desired liaisons with both Cassio and (despite his avowed racism) Othello, rather than simply using this narrative to convince Othello that Cassio has slept with Desdemona. As he does in Macbeth's soliloquies, in which Macbeth's subconscious brings to his conscious speech images of the religious sanctions

---

[6]     Stephen Greenblatt, *Renaissance Self-Fashioning* (Chicago: University of Chicago Press, 1980), 227.

[7]     Samuel Crowl, *Shakespeare at the Cineplex* (Athens: Ohio University Press, 2003), 94.

[8]     James Bulman, *The Heroic Idiom of Shakespearean Tragedy* (Newark: University of Delaware Press, 1985), 118.

[9]     For the "noble Moor" argument, see especially Reuben A. Brower, *Hero and Saint* (Oxford: Oxford University Press, 1971); and Bulman, *The Heroic Idiom*. John Holloway, *The Story of the Night* (London: Routledge & Kegan Paul, 1961), argues for Othello as the "Renaissance Complete Man" (47–8).

[10]     In addition to Hyman's essay in *Iago: Some Approaches to the Illusion of his Motivation*, see two pioneering essays on Iago's homosexuality: Martin Wangh, "Othello: The Tragedy of Iago," *Psychoanalytic Quarterly* XIX (1950), 202–212; and Gordon Ross Smith, "Iago the Paranoiac," *American Imago* XVI (1959), 155–67. Both essays are reprinted in M. D. Faber, ed., *The Design Within* (New York: Science House, 1970), 157–68 and 170–182.

against regicide and murder that Macbeth defies, so here Shakespeare creates an inner life in Iago that the character seems not to fathom completely.[11] The more Iago's story supposedly conjures his own desired sexual unions with Cassio and Othello; the more lurid the details that Iago provides to feed his sexually hungry and frustrated imagination; and the more these details feed on themselves, the greater should be the risk for Iago that Othello will see through his fiction. Yet Othello never penetrates Iago's vivid homoerotic vision, supposedly based on memory, despite the irony that the actor playing Iago must convey emotionally and verbally his character's increasing sexual arousal if his playing of these lines is to be theatrically convincing. Indeed the skill required of the Iago actor here is precisely his ability to authenticate Iago's excessive auto-eroticism while pretending that Iago's spontaneous narration is "really" about Desdemona and Cassio. Thus emerges the theatrical irony that the more intensely conflicted the Iago actor can become during his performance, the more disturbing Othello's failure to penetrate Iago's mask will seem.

Iago's narrative of some sixteen lines, beginning with "I do not like the office" and ending with Michael Cassio's supposedly anguished cry "Cursed fate that gave thee to the Moor" (3.3.426–41), occurs 81 lines after Othello reenters at l.345 and following Iago's luckily getting the spotted handkerchief from Emilia. The initial fiction of Iago's narrative is that he is gratifying Othello's order for a "living reason" why Desdemona is disloyal. Since spectators have not heard Iago plan for his ensuing exchange with Othello, they assume that Iago is manufacturing spontaneously what Honigmann terms the "detailed sexual imagery" with which Iago tortures Othello. This imagery rapidly assumes a life of its own and reveals Iago's intense, underlying homoerotic desires. Iago is not on stage when Othello and Desdemona meet, Othello complains about a headache, and the handkerchief is left behind for Emilia to find and give to—or have it taken from her by—Iago. Iago is emboldened by having suddenly acquired this prize, which he immediately decides to "lose" in Cassio's lodging. When Othello reenters, Iago already knows that the "sweet sleep / Which thou owedst yesterday" will never return to Othello, and he hears Othello abandon his "occupation."[12] Iago believes that Othello will now believe anything that Iago tells him. Since Othello has abandoned what and who he was—the person who was the subject of his own narratives that won Desdemona—Iago now conspires to fill Othello's emotional and psychological

---

[11]  Michael Goldman, *Acting and Action in Shakespearean Tragedy* (Princeton: Princeton University Press, 1985), 94–111, analyzes superbly the complex imagery of Macbeth's soliloquies.

[12]  Michael Neill, "Changing Places in *Othello*," *Shakespeare Survey* 37, ed., Stanley Wells (Cambridge: Cambridge University Press, 1984), 115–31, esp. 127, superbly examines the "occupations" that Othello abandons throughout the play. Marjorie Garber, *Coming of Age in Shakespeare* (New York & London: Routledge, 1981), writes that when convinced of his wife's infidelity, Othello laments the passing "of his occupation, not his marriage. Everything is referred to the world of war, until the violence of his repressed sexual feelings takes the displaced form of murder" (136).

void. Iago sees that Othello is "Eaten up with passion" (407), and, repeating Othello's word "satisfied," asks "Would you, the supervisor, grossly gape on? / Behold her topped?" (411–12). Iago's word "supervisor" not only implies Othello looking down from above upon the adulterate lovers, but also mocks Othello as the once proud supervisor of the Venetian army and the savior of Cyprus.

Having suggested bringing the lovers together where Othello might grossly "gape" on them, Iago quickly scraps that idea as a "tedious difficulty," not only because he knows he could never create that scene, but also because his mind immediately rejects the image of Cassio in a heterosexual scene. What then? Iago suddenly needs a plan B, for he doubts that other mortal eyes might ever see them "bolster." [13] Iago's staccato rhetorical questions, "What then? How then? / What shall I say? Where's satisfaction?' (416–417), and his repetition of the animal imagery he had used in 1.1—goats, monkeys, wolves, even (like Michael Cassio, whom Iago suddenly recalls) drunken fools—suggest that Iago is biding time while his imagination searches for this alternative plan. Since "it is impossible" Othello should see Desdemona actually lying with, or under, Cassio, Othello's suddenly aroused imagination must be satisfied with "Imputation and strong circumstances" which Iago must now make so convincing that they shall "lead directly to the door of truth" (423).

The sexual punning that Iago begins with "office," suggesting the feminine "orifice" that he does not "like," continues in "Pricked to't by foolish honesty and love."[14] The "raging tooth" that troubles his sleep is arguably phallic, and, in the homoerotic reading, Cassio is the Jacobean dentist who shall soothe this raging member. In Iago's fantasy/narrative, he and Cassio are presumably alone, as apparently no one else heard or saw what Iago narrates. Given the often public nature of military quarters, Iago's narrative is all the more obviously his private fantasy, a fact that Othello, a military commander, does not notice. What Iago then narrates is presumably what he desires Cassio would actually say to him in a situation that Iago wishes would actually occur: lying privately with Cassio, a man, Iago admits, of "daily beauty in his life" that makes Iago ugly. Cassio's reputed initial assertion is "Sweet Desdemona, / Let us be wary, let us hide our loves" (434–35). As Hyman cogently argues, Iago becomes in his fantasy Desdemona, Cassio's supposed lover, thus (apparently) masking Iago's own

---

[13]　On Iago's word "bolster," and its erotic relation to his narration of Cassio's supposed fornication with Desdemona, see Michael Neill, "Unproper Beds: Race, Adultery, and the Hideous in *Othello*," *Shakespeare Quarterly* 40 (Winter, 1989), 383–412, esp. 200. Reprinted in Anthony Gerard Barthelemy, ed., *Critical Essays on Shakespeare's Othello* (New York: G. K. Hall & Co., 1994), 187–215.

[14]　3.3.428. Bruce Smith, *Homosexual Desire in Shakespeare's England* (Chicago: University of Chicago Press, 1991), finds primarily Iago's "militant maleness and his virulent contempt for women," not "sublimated homosexuality" in his sixteen line speech (62–3). Smith is certainly right to find Iago's contempt for women, not only in this speech, but elsewhere in the play, especially in 2.1. However, Iago's impromptu narration in 3.3 goes far beyond mere contempt for women.

barely hidden desire to be Cassio's "Sweet" and secret lover. Cassio's (i.e., Iago's) plural "loves" may be meant to suggest, for Othello's sake, either that both Cassio and Desdemona have multiple lovers; or (more probably), that they have met and will meet often and secretly, thus echoing and enlarging Brabantio's warning to Othello in 1.3 about Desdemona's deceit of him and thus possibly of Othello himself, during which Iago was on stage.[15] There is also a third possibility here: that Iago's using the plural "loves" suggests Iago's subliminal wish, perhaps at a level that Iago does not grasp, that he had twin "love[r]s": i.e., both Cassio *and* Othello. Iago is probably also trying to reinforce the point he made to Othello in 3.3.214–18 and remembering his deliberate pun on "country disposition": "I know our country disposition well; / In Venice they do let God see the pranks / They dare not show their husbands; their best conscience / Is not to leave 't undone, but keep 't unknown."[16]

Iago's narrative now progresses from words to deeds:

> And then, sir, would he grip and wring my hand,
> Cry 'O sweet creature,' then kiss me hard,
> As if he plucked up kisses by the roots
> That grew upon my lips; then laid his leg
> Over my thigh, and sighed, and kissed, and then
> Cried, 'Cursed fate that gave thee to the Moor.' (436–41)

In the subtext of these lines, Iago, supposedly narrating Cassio's secret liaisons with Desdemona, actually fantasizes his own desired liaisons with not only Cassio but also, as Hyman argues, with Othello himself. Almost against his will, as if animated by his own imagined eroticism, Iago's improvised description of his lying with Cassio cascades towards Cassio's cry "Cursed fate" and becomes the actual subject of Iago's narrative, the product of a sexually starved and vivid imagination that articulates for the first time in the play its deeply repressed sexual longings. Although, as Celia Daileader explains, Iago shares with the other men of the play a fear of "*sex out of bounds* [sic],"[17] as his narrative progresses Iago's sexual images become increasingly boundless and bizarre as they feed one another

---

[15] Peter L. Rudnytsky, "The Purloined Handkerchief in *Othello*," in *The Psychoanalytical Study of Literature*, eds., Joseph Reppen and Maurice Charney (Hillsdale, NJ: The Analytic Press, 1985), 169–90, writes of Brabantio: "Brabantio, it is clear, is an incestuously fixated father, unable to acknowledge his daughter's sexuality. Her choice of Othello, a black man and a foreigner, thus becomes a confirmation of his worst fears. . . " (180). As Edward A. Snow argues, in "Sexual Anxiety and the Male Order of Things in *Othello*," *ELR* 10 (1980), 384–412, Brabantio's inability and unwillingness to acknowledge Desdemona's sexuality also later infects Othello's view of her. Snow's essay is reprinted in Susan Snyder, ed., *Othello: Critical Essays* (New York: Garland, 1988), 213–49.

[16] Pechter, *Interpretive Traditions*, analyses thoroughly Iago's use of "country" in the play (88).

[17] Celia R. Daileader, *Eroticism on the Renaissance Stage* (Cambridge: Cambridge University Press, 1998), 37.

in his hyperbolically vivid imagination. In his attempt to persuade Othello with "living reason" that his wife has been and is unfaithful, Iago invents a brazen, graphic narrative of homoeroticism whose astonishing images Othello misses completely. The image of "pluck[ing] up kisses by the roots," combined with Iago's being "pricked" by "foolish honesty and love," and the raging tooth indicate Iago's extreme phallus-centered oral eroticism: Cassio engaging in homoerotic oral sex with Iago in which Iago's phallus, initially emerging in his narrative as his "raging tooth," metastasizes into several phalli, i.e., the "roots" that "grew" like multiple kisses upon his own lips, a bizarre displacement in which Iago's mouth and genitals are commingled into one organ.[18] In modern psychoanalytical terms, Iago's fiercely repressed sexuality suddenly explodes in an orgy of homosexual coupling in which his rooted phalli allow for multiple and simultaneous fellatic orgasms with both Cassio and Othello, the latter perhaps especially suited for Iago's desired couplings because of his "thick lips" that Roderigo mentions in 1.1, a phrase intended there to denigrate Othello but that we can perhaps imagine Iago's memory, here at the climax of his imagined orgasms, recalling as a sexually desirable physical feature. Iago's multiple ejaculations of his seminal fluids simultaneously into both Cassio and Othello is another version of what Janet Adelman identifies as his perverted attempt at insemination, of his "undoing the contours of the already-existing generative world."[19] Adelman adds that, "[P]art of the peculiar horror of this play is that Othello becomes so effective a receptacle for—and enactor of—Iago's fantasies. If Iago imagines himself filled with a gnawing poisonous mineral through what amounts to Othello's anal insemination of him [2.1.297–98], he turns that poison back on Othello: 'I'll pour this pestilence into his ear' [2.3.350]" (1997, 142). In my reading of Iago's imagery here in 3.3, he not only experiences pleasurable oral sex with Othello, thus fulfilling his homoerotic desire for Othello, but also projects his own envy and hatred—his poison—into Othello's body; as Adelman writes, "Othello really does change with Iago's poison, as he begins to experience himself as contaminated and hence to act out Iago's scenarios" (1997, 143). Iago's cascading sexual fantasy engages both his repressed *desire for* Othello, despite Othello's blackness; and simultaneously his *hatred of* Othello whose heterosexual activity with Desdemona Iago describes as

---

[18]    Wangh, "*Othello*: The Tragedy of Iago," writes that "A tooth is one of the commoner universal symbols of the penis in dreams," but also argues that Iago's saying he was troubled with a raging tooth suggests a censorship of and thus resistance to his homosexual excitement as well as the "wish for and fear of castration" (in Faber, ed., 163–64). Wangh adds that "kisses plucked up by the roots" can be "similarly understood as a phrase heavy with castration symbolism" (164). I see the plucking of multiple kisses "by the *roots*" as more obviously welcomed multiple phalli because the kisses are fantasized as "rooted" in Iago's lips. Hyman dismissed as "wretched" Wangh's interpretation of the tooth as phallic (120), but conversely Wangh's argument about the tooth as a phallic symbol is central to Iago's convoluted sexual imaginings in this speech.

[19]    Janet Adelman, "Iago's Alter Ego: Race as Projection in *Othello*," *Shakespeare Quarterly* 48 (Summer, 1997), 140.

bestial. Iago lectures Roderigo that we have reasons to "cool our raging motions" (1.3.333), but once his sexually overcharged imagination takes command, Iago's reason collapses in the chaos of his own sexual longings.[20]

Before returning to Othello, consider now my second point: the actor playing Iago and his relation to spectators. The actor has to make Iago's fantasy credible as a spontaneous speech that explodes from deep within his character's tortured psyche, while simultaneously suggesting to spectators Iago's awareness, at a conscious level, of the risk he is taking in order to provide Othello with the "evidence" that Othello requested of Desdemona's liaisons with Cassio. Shakespeare has thus created a fantastic challenge to the Iago actor who must convey to spectators this double awareness in Iago, yet not allow Iago's spontaneous and irresistible sexual imagery to become so powerful that it becomes utterly unbelievable and destroys the actor's performance of Iago's narration. Thus the striking theatrical paradox of this scene: the more deeply felt and convincingly performed the actor's impersonation of Iago's vivid sexual longings, the more incredulous will be Othello's failure to penetrate Iago's mask; and the greater the risk that this segment of 3.3 will dissolve into a grotesque parody of Othello's temptation and fall. Yet for all the risk for the Iago actor inherent in managing a convincing performance of this speech, its terror *during performance* depends entirely on precisely such a performance. As Hugh M. Richmond cogently observes, "Shakespeare systematically reinforces … detachment from the victims' perspective by the repeated soliloquies assigned to Iago alone, which serve … to continue the audience entrapment in the superior awareness of the manipulator."[21] As in Iago's soliloquies, so in his (i.e., the actor's) performance in 3.3: the more convincingly the Iago actor walks this performance tightrope strung between complete absorption in his character's cascading sexual fantasy and his desire to convince Othello of his wife's whoring, the more deeply spectators are enthralled in Iago's vision of Othello's frightening gullibility. Kent Cartwright explains the complex reactions of theatrical spectators to this scene:

---

[20]   Michael Neill, "Unproper Beds," terms Iago's "confession of [his] hidden thoughts" that erupts within his narrative the "monster at the heart of the psychic labyrinth" (399). Two recent essays in *Approaches to Teaching Shakespeare's Othello*, eds.,Peter Erickson and Maurice Hunt (New York: Modern Language Association, 2005) analyze further this "psychic labyrinth." Maurice Hunt, "Motivating Iago," writes that Iago's "wish to destroy Othello, and possibly Cassio too, stems from his need to remove temptations creating an unbearable inner conflict" (130). Nicholas F. Radel, "'Your Own for Ever': Revealing Masculine Desire in *Othello*," argues that by reporting Cassio's "supposed dream," Iago "introduces doubt into the normative system of male-male alliance" and "destabilizes normative homosocial bonding by exposing it as a location not only for negotiating social hierarchies but also for transgressing their boundaries. Iago understands the importance of place and position in normative male bonding, and he uses that knowledge to misread Cassio to Othello and, indeed, Othello to himself.… The villain also … colors the normative erotics of Cassio's relationship with Othello as a social transgression of place and appropriate male bonding in a way that also qualifies as sodomy" (68).

[21]   Hugh Macrae Richmond, "The Audience's Role in *Othello*," in *Othello: New Critical Essays*, ed., Philip C. Kolin (London and New York: Routledge, 2002), 94.

> *Othello* provides numerous examples of protagonists –Desdemona, Emilia,
> Roderigo—acting dense of mind, lost in thought, dumb to the implications of
> their own perceptions, or relieved by comforting rationalizations …. Here [3.3]
> the audience's perspective—its spectatorial distance—makes Othello guilty of
> complicity…. The bizarre fascination of the temptation scene is that it activates
> both spectatorial engagement (by making sympathy a subtext) and ethical
> detachment (by making judgment a text). We share sympathy with the very
> process of Othello's fall, even as the scene makes war upon that sympathy. [22]

The Iago actor's primary function in 3.3 is paradoxically to activate these dual,
contradictory reactions among spectators who marvel at his spontaneous descent
into this fantastic maelstrom of desire and deceit. Especially during this brief
segment of 3.3, the performance tightrope on which the Iago actor must balance
is on fire.

All of this, one assumes, to convince Othello that Desdemona has often slept
with Michael Cassio. Yet, as Richard Rudnytsky observes, Iago's shocking,
fictitious dream of Cassio actually proves nothing (1985, 184). In Iago's fantasy,
the sexual complexity of which he, the character, probably does not grasp[23] but the
actor must, Iago supposes that Othello will believe that Cassio is one heavy sleeper
who could perform all of the above sexual gymnastics—kissing hard, laying
his leg over Iago's (i.e., Desdemona's) thigh, sighing, and then crying "Cursed
fate that gave thee to the Moor!"—without awakening, and presumably without
arousing any suspicions in the army barracks where their liaison supposedly
occurred. Further, in addition to Iago's fantasy that he is Cassio's "thee" given
to Othello for his lover and thus desired by both men simultaneously (Hyman,
106–107), Iago assumes that Othello will believe that Desdemona apparently
accepts embraces from her lover even when that lover is asleep. The image of
an insatiable Desdemona, accepting even a sleeping lover, may seem comic,
if not ridiculous, but I would argue that in the state to which Iago has brought
Othello, this image from Iago's narrative evokes again for Othello the image of
Desdemona's "imagined monstrous sexual appetite."[24]

---

[22]  Kent Cartwright, *Shakespearean Tragedy and Its Double* (University Park:
Pennsylvania State University Press, 1991), 164.

[23]  Adelman analyzes thoroughly what she terms Iago's "injured I—his sense that he is
chronically slighted and betrayed, his sense of self-division—[that] produces (or perhaps is
produced by) fantasies of his body as penetrated and contaminated, especially by Othello….
To allow himself to be seen or known is tantamount to being stabbed, eaten alive. …[U]
nable to be gardener to himself, he will sadistically manage everyone else, simultaneously
demonstrating his superiority to those quats whose insides are so sloppily prone to bursting
out, and hiding the contamination and chaos of his own insides" (133). Writing of the
kisses in Iago's narrative, Neill, "Unproper Beds," remarks: "Yet this doubly fictive scene
of adultery is made to seem doubly adulterate by the homoerotic displacement of the kisses
that grow upon Iago's lips—kisses that themselves disturbingly mirror the one real adultery
of the play, the seduction of Othello in which Iago is at this very moment engaged" (400).

[24]  Karen Newman, "And wash the Ethiop white: Femininity and the Monstrous in
*Othello*," in *Shakespeare Reproduced*, eds., Jean Howard and Marion O'Connor (London:
Methuen, 1987), 133. Newman argues: "Desdemona is presented in the play as a sexual

Consider now my third point: Othello's response to Iago's narrative and the place of this short segment in the entire play. Pascale Aebischer writes that "the black actor's physical presence runs the risk of naturalising violence as black," and of "locking the black actor into his skin colour through the text's racism."[25] Othello's response to Iago's narrative is "O monstrous! Monstrous!" To what does Othello refer? Iago responds, "Nay, this was but his dream." Well, no, it was Iago's dream! As Greenblatt argues (1980, 234–35), Iago has improvised brilliantly, creating a narrative which is truly "monstrous" in its imaginative sexuality and frightening ability to convince Othello that his wife is a whore: "I'll tear her all to pieces" (3.3. 446). Thus Othello apparently means that Desdemona and her sexuality are monstrous; in his twisted logic, she must die, lest she betray more men. Othello has apparently accepted as true everything Iago has said; what does this fact say about the Moor, as a character, in the highly charged racial context of this play?

The presence of Africans in Elizabethan/Jacobean England has been well documented. Ruth Cowhig notes that there were sufficient numbers of blacks in sixteenth century Britain for Elizabeth to issue a warrant on 18 July, 1596, to "the Lord Maiour and to all Vice-Admyralls and other publicke officers" regarding the request of the merchant Casper van Senden of Lubeck to return English prisoners detained in Spain and Portugal in exchange for a "Lycense to take up so much blackamoores here in this realme and to transport them into Spaine and Portugall."[26] Elizabeth's warrant continues that this scheme seems desirable, blacks "being so populous and numbers of hable persons the subjectes of the land and Christian people that perishe for want of service" (Cowhig 1985, 60). Anthony Barthelemy stresses that the "importance of *Othello* as the dominant representation of an African on the stage cannot be overestimated.... *Othello* seems to have been always in revival. Not until *Orroonoko* was staged in 1695 was there a close rival to *Othello* for putting a dramatic representation of a black character before

---

subject who hears and desires, and that desire is punished because the non-specular, or non-phallic sexuality it displays is frightening and dangerous" (133). On the symbolism of the handkerchief, Newman writes that its "associations with the mother, witchcraft, and the marvelous, represents the link between femininity and the monstrous which Othello's and Desdemona's union figures in the play" (137). Pechter, *Interpretive Traditions*, scrutinizes the place of Othello's sense of Desdemona's love for him as "unnatural," and how the "intensely contradictory and incompletely resolved feelings raised by the opening scene," especially Brabantio's warning to Othello about Desdemona's deceit, return in 3.3 (83–4).

[25]   Pascale Aebischer, *Shakespeare's Violated Bodies* (Cambridge: Cambridge University Press, 2004), 110.

[26]   Ruth Cowhig, "Blacks in English Renaissance Drama and the Role of Shakespeare's Othello," in *The Black Presence in English Literature*, ed., David Dabydeen (Manchester: Manchester University Press, 1985), 6.

English audiences. Between 1604 and 1687, *Othello* was in production not less than fourteen times."[27]

*Othello* was seen by several thousand Jacobean spectators at its many performances. Especially at the Globe, a theatre of multiple perspectives, how might spectators have reacted to Iago's "monstrous" dream/fantasy narrative and Othello's response to it? While recovering actual responses is obviously impossible, I would argue that one probable response would have been to see Othello here as inescapably ignorant and ignoble, thus reinforcing Iago's assertion that Othello, being "of a free and open nature, / That thinks men honest that but seem to be so," will indeed "as tenderly be led by the nose / As asses are?" (1.3.400–101; 402–403). As Ania Loomba points out, "Othello is described in terms of the characteristics popularly attributed to blacks during the sixteenth century; sexual potency, courage, pride, guilelessness, credulity, easily aroused passions; these became central and persistent features of later colonial stereotyping as well."[28] Eldred Jones argues that several moments in the play, mainly in Iago's soliloquies, indicate Iago's contempt for Othello's mind,[29] and I would argue that while Iago's improvised narrative certainly tells us much about his own mind, in performance it also tells us much about Othello's. The "credulity" that Loomba mentions as characteristic of Renaissance Europeans' stereotyping of blacks seems inescapable here in Othello's inability to penetrate Iago's fiction, and I would argue that at a Jacobean performance this inability would have reinforced the assumed intellectual inferiority that marks Elizabethan and Jacobean stereotyping of Africans.[30] This segment of 3.3 thus exemplifies Dympna Callaghan's argument that "the sign of negritude" was always an "emblem of barbaric alterity beyond the parameters of civilization," and that "the theatrical necessity of Shakespeare's stage was to

---

[27]    Anthony Gerard Barthelemy, "Ethiops Washed White: Moors of the Nonvillainous Type," in *Black Face, Maligned Race: The Representation of Blacks in English Drama from Shakespeare to Sheridan* (Baton Rouge: Louisiana State University Press, 1987), 101.

[28]    Ania Loomba, "Sexuality and Racial Difference," in *Gender, Race, Renaissance Drama* (Manchester: Manchester University Press, 1989), 175. Reprinted in Barthelemy, *Critical Essays on Shakespeare's Othello*, 162–86.

[29]    Eldred Jones, "*Othello*—An Interpretation," in *Othello's Countrymen: The African in English Renaissance Drama* (Oxford: Oxford University Press, 1965), 86–109. Reprinted in Barthelemy, *Critical Essays on Shakespeare's Othello*, 39–54.

[30]    Jacquelyn N. McLendon, "'A Round Unvarnished Tale': (Mis)Reading *Othello* or African American Strategies of Dissent," in *Othello: New Essays by Black Writers*, ed., Mythili Kaul (Washington, D.C.: Howard University Press, 1997), 121–37, examines these stereotypes thoroughly. For example, McLendon writes: "Against the many arguments that Shakespeare emphasizes stereotypes only to explode them, we clearly see a *pattern* of inscribing blacks as devilish, suggesting that Shakespeare himself could not move beyond racial clichés" (129). Martin Orkin, "Othello and the 'plain face' of Racism," *Shakespeare Quarterly* 38 (Summer 1987): 166–88, while arguing that throughout the play Shakespeare "concentrates on the problem of the inevitable vulnerability of human judgment to hidden malice," concedes nonetheless that "The final image of a black man stifling or strangling a white woman, it might be argued, deliberately courts a racist impulse, which we know was likely to have been present in certain members of Shakespeare's first audiences" (176).

*produce* racial difference *and to control it nevertheless"* [sic].[31] As Iago dismantles Othello's marriage, his "cruel artistry" (Honigmann 1976, 22) becomes a means of enforcing that cultural order that demanded black inferiority and demonized inter-racialism.[32]

This moment might be even more divisive during a contemporary performance of *Othello.* Would not many well-educated black spectators be likely to recognize Iago's fiction here (the play's double time notwithstanding) and to recognize that what Greenblatt terms Iago's "improvising" talent is making a total fool of Othello, thus signifying the Moor's obvious intellectual inferiority? For all of Othello's nobility, is Othello at this moment much different from Roderigo, whom Shakespeare adds to Cinthio's story apparently to give Iago some practice with dupes before he destroys Othello? As Honigmann explains, in his dream/fantasy Iago takes a much greater risk than he has to. While his fantasy of a sexual liaison with Cassio may ignite spontaneously the lurid images that he uses, Iago may as well be deliberately testing the limits of Othello's credulity while simultaneously justifying his own racist view of Othello's ignorance. To the extent that black spectators in a contemporary staging perceive Othello's being led by the nose and made egregiously an ass, as Iago promises to do in his soliloquies, this moment in performance may be as much about racial prejudice and anger as it is about

---

[31]  Dympna Callaghan, *Shakespeare Without Women: Representing Gender and Race on the Renaissance Stage* (London and New York: Routledge, 2000), 91, 92. As Arthur L. Little, Jr. argues in "'An essence that's not seen': The Primal Scene of Racism in *Othello*," *Shakespeare Quarterly* 44 (Fall, 1993): 304–24, Othello's blackness and his attendant stereotypes become an "ocular proof that legitimizes an audience's guarded response to his blackness," and the "ocular sign of a cultural need to create and destroy monsters: create them so that they may not create themselves, destroy them so that they may not produce or multiply. In the nascent imperialism of early seventeenth-century England, this process is not merely birth control but ideological control. The black presence in Shakespeare's play makes visible and then amalgamates and critiques those impolitic fictions that become engendered and intermixed in the name of cultural order" (323).

[32]  Celia R. Daileader, *Racism, Misogyny, and the Othello Myth* (Cambridge: Cambridge University Press, 2005), argues that the "monstrous birth" that Iago labors to bring to light is the "inter-racial couple itself" (23). Daileader's chapter "White devils, black lust: inter-racialism in Early Modern Drama" summarizes superbly Jacobeans' pejorative attitudes towards and fear of miscegenation. Maurizio Calbi, *Approximate Bodies: Gender and Power in Early Modern Drama and Anatomy* (London and New York: Routledge, 2005), writes that Othello's gaining "access to the body of an aristocratic Venetian maiden is yet another step towards the attainment of the 'normative' body of white masculinity" (76). Regarding Othello's suicide as an attempt to resurrect his reputation among the white Venetians, Michael Neill, "'Mulattos,' 'Blacks,' and 'Indian Moors': *Othello* and Early Modern Constructions of Human Difference," *Shakespeare Quarterly* 49 (Winter 1998): 361–74, writes "In the reading of the Moor's body so successfully propagated by Iago, none of Othello's efforts to reinstitute the sustaining paradoxes of his mixed condition, as an 'honorable murderer' whose suicide triumphantly enacts and cancels out the contradictions that have been exposed in the designation 'Moor of Venice,' is sufficient to overcome the suggestion that such a creature can only constitute a kind of 'civil monster'" (373).

Iago's bizarre erotic imagination. John R. Ford argues that "our central dilemma with *Othello* is that both the resistance and the faith we need to understand its world are deeply infected."[33] So too with Othello; as the "noble Moor," or Holloway's "Renaissance Complete Man" (1961, 47) disintegrates before us, the racial implications of 3.3 become immensely uncomfortable in virtually every competent performance of the play.

As she revolts from realizing that Othello killed Desdemona on Iago's "word," Emilia screams at him: "O gull! O dolt! / As ignorant as dirt!" (5.2.170–171). Emilia's assertion here of Othello's ignorance is unequivocal, whether heard by Jacobean or contemporary spectators. She screams ferociously at an unspeakable, unimaginable horror, but she also echoes Iago's remarks about Othello's being easily duped, thus reinforcing spectators' perception that Othello really is as ignorant as his belief in Iago's "dream" implies: "As ignorant as dirt!" For Jacobean spectators, Iago's narrative and Emilia's scream may well have reinforced the racist stereotypes of blacks present in their culture, reinforced by treatises such as George Best's in Hakluyt's *Voyages* and by the roles allotted Africans in earlier Elizabethan drama.[34] While both black and white contemporary spectators might praise a black actor's portrayal of Othello, black spectators might very well find this scene a microcosm of *Othello* as a viciously racist play about white Europeans' too easy manipulation of a black man's mind. Othello's inability to decipher even the most grotesque images of Iago's sexual fantasy, offered as a spontaneous *recollection* of supposedly an actual past experience, is central to this chilling discrepancy.

Finally, consider some objections that one might raise against my analysis of Iago's language, its relevance to trying to fathom his seemingly inscrutable character, and the implications of this short segment in the larger play. Perhaps most obviously, in the midst of the intense verbal exchange between Iago and Othello, neither Othello nor spectators will concentrate on Iago's complex images. One can also cite Othello's own words: "This fellow's of exceeding honesty, / And knows all qualities, with a learned spirit, / Of human dealings" (3.3.274–76). Further, as Martin Orkin points out, none of the other characters have the "god-like vision" that would enable them to "penetrate the surface honesty of Iago" (1987, 176). Othello also laments, "Haply, for I am black / And have not those soft parts of conversation / That chamberers have, or for I am declined / Into the vale of years – yet that's not much –"(3.3.279–82). The next two lines are crucial: "She's gone. I am abused, and my relief / Must be to loathe her"(283–84). (Bevington, 4th ed., note to l. 283, p. 1145, glosses "abused" as deceived.) Othello thinks Desdemona "gone" some 40 lines *before* Iago recounts his "dream," and so Iago's narrative seems assured of complete success. There really is no risk; by this

---

[33]    John R. Ford, "'Words and Performances': Roderigo and the Mixed Dramaturgy of Race and Gender in *Othello*," in Kolin, ed., *Othello: New Critical Essays*, 152.

[34]    Virginia Vaughan, *Othello: A Contextual History* (Cambridge: Cambridge University Press, 1994), reviews the presence of Africans in Jacobean England, and includes George Best's "scriptural" account of the origins of black people from Hakluyt's *Voyages* (53).

point in the scene Othello will believe anything Iago says. Finally, one may argue simply that drama always produces disparate reactions among spectators, and that a production of *Othello* before a multi-cultural audience will inevitably create different reactions to any single scene in the play.

I would respond first by emphasizing the intensely rhetorical nature of Renaissance drama. Elizabethan and Jacobean spectators, as Hamlet reminds us, went to "hear" a play, and they would have been keenly alert to the extraordinary imagery of Iago's narrative. I would also argue that in such a long scene (3.3 is 495 lines in Bevington's 4th ed.), featuring primarily two characters, Jacobean spectators' attention would have been, and contemporary spectators' is, riveted on the language which produces such a rapid and frightening transformation in the "noble" Moor. Further, in a contemporary staging of *Othello* which, like *The Merchant of Venice,* features an alien in a central role, the cultural differences of black and white spectators would heighten their respective attention to the methods Iago uses to destroy Othello's faith in Desdemona and in Othello himself. I suspect that many black spectators leave a production of *Othello* today, regardless of the brilliance of the actor playing Othello,[35] agreeing with Emilia that Othello is "as ignorant as dirt" and hating that conviction.

Othello's belief in Iago's words, and the self-doubt resulting from his age, color, and supposed lack of aristocratic virtues, legitimately argue that by Iago's dream/narrative Othello will believe anything Iago says about anybody. But such arguments beg the question. The leap that Othello apparently makes from his own "weaknesses" to wholly believing Iago's narrative, its swiftness and apparent justification in Othello's long acquaintance with Iago notwithstanding, is all the more troubling because it is so indicative of Othello's gullibility. F.R. Leavis's familiar argument about Othello's "obtuse and brutal egotism," in which "self-pride becomes stupidity, ferocious stupidity, an insane and self-deceiving passion,"[36] is heightened by Othello's believing Iago's narrative. While I do not want to engage further Leavis and Holloway about the "promptness" or not of Othello's response to Iago's poison,[37] Othello's credence is immensely troubling. After Iago insists that his narrative was "but his [Cassio's] dream," Othello replies "But this denoted a foregone conclusion. / 'Tis a shrewd doubt, though it be but a dream" (3.3.442–44). (Bevington, 4th ed. glosses "shrewd doubt" as "suspicious circumstance"). Iago says his narrative may "help to thicken [perhaps unconsciously echoing the phallic tumescence of "raging tooth" and "roots"] other proofs / That do

---

[35]    Twice at the 1999 Oregon Shakespeare Festival I saw Derrick Lee Weeden play a brilliant Othello. The second time I saw the play, about ten seconds before Iago's narration began, I desperately wanted Othello (i.e. Weeden) to abandon the script and "see through" Iago's fantasy. I simply could not tolerate watching this magnificent Othello be completely fooled *again* by Iago's speech.

[36]    F.R. Leavis, "Diabolic Intellect and the Noble Hero," in *The Common Pursuit* (1952: repr. Harmondsworth: Penguin Books, 1962), 146–47.

[37]    Holloway argues his disagreements with Leavis about Othello's "promptness" to Iago's temptations in *Story of the Night,* 45–7.

demonstrate thinly," and Othello responds immediately with an image of horrible violence: "I'll tear her to pieces" (3.3.445–46). Even as Iago cagily admits that his other "proofs … demonstrate thinly," again taking a palpable risk, Othello is not so much "led by the nose, as asses are" but rather leads himself and Desdemona to their destruction by blindly accepting Iago's homoerotic fantasy as the final, conclusive "proof" of Desdemona's evil. While Martin Orkin is right that no other character in the play penetrates Iago's duplicity (1987, 176), it is likewise true that no other character has as much interaction with Iago as Othello does, and with no other character does Iago fashion such a grotesque fantasy.

Finally, to the argument that drama always produces disparate reactions, I would contend that this particular segment of 3.3 is probably far more divisive in performance than scholars may realize or actors may admit. While many scholars and, I assume, most actors cherish the image of the "noble Moor," Othello's credulity during and after Iago relates his erotic fantasy seems to vitiate Othello's nobility precisely when he needs it most. That Othello could accept Iago's narrative as fulfilling his own order for a "living reason" that Desdemona is disloyal is what is most "monstrous" about this scene, and what makes this short segment of 3.3 among the most racially divisive moments in Shakespeare's plays.

One way to address this proposition would be simply to test it among directors and actors. How have directors approached this scene? What have they told their actors about playing Othello? Have directors and actors asked the questions I do here, do they have answers for them, or do they assume that Iago's sixteen lines are intended to tell us more about Iago than about Othello? How have actors playing Othello "felt" during Iago's speech? What do actors believe Othello means by "O monstrous! Monstrous!"? In *The Masks of Othello*, Marvin Rosenberg writes "Up to the temptation scene, [Othello's] is as lofty an image of a hero as Shakespeare could produce, and so the great actors have made him, giving him their best. He is not simply a good, noble man—he is one of the finest, one of the noblest of men."[38] Rosenberg quotes Paul Robeson, who sees Othello as "intensely proud of his color and culture; in the end, even as he kills, his honor is at stake, not simply as a human being and as a lover, but as Othello. The honor of his whole culture is involved. 'It is the cause …'" (1971, 195). Rosenberg concludes that, given the seemingly indisputable and undeniable dignity of Othello, the cause of his downfall must be "betrayal by a friend so close, so trusted, that Othello has no choice but to listen to him" (1971, 203). Yet precisely this trust in Iago betrays the weakness in Othello's mind that Iago exploits so outrageously in his narration of "Cassio's dream." In performance, the cultural and racial differences that spectators bring to the theatre may deeply divide them as they witness this terribly difficult scene in which a white man virtually disables a black man's mind. Indeed, the more spectators marvel at the Iago actor, the more divisive this scene is apt to be.

This extremely divisive *potential* of Iago's narrative emphasizes what James Bulman terms the "radical contingency of performance—the unpredictable, often playful intersection of history, material conditions, social contexts, and reception

---

[38]   Marvin Rosenberg, *The Masks of Othello* (Berkeley: University of California Press, 1971), 202.

that destabilizes Shakespeare and makes theatrical meaning a participatory act."[39] No amount of critical exegesis or scholarly speculation can uncover how members of any one randomly assembled Jacobean audience reacted to Richard Burbage in blackface playing Othello. Now can we ever recover how any one of Burbage's many performances of Othello may have emboldened or diminished the dominant racial attitudes toward the intellectual capacity of Africans that England's participation in the lucrative slave trade indicates prevailed in early modern England. Contemporary voices suggest, however, that Othello's intellectual vulnerability to Iago in 3.3 is immensely disturbing. Virginia Mason Vaughan quotes black British playwright Kwame Kwei-Armah: "I feel I am yet to see . . . a version of *Othello* in which the character is not inextricably linked to the notion of a[n] unacceptably weak and intellectually vulnerable black male."[40] Vaughan also quotes the African-Anglo actor Hugh Quarshie, who asks: "[I]f a black actor plays Othello does he not risk making racial stereotypes seem legitimate and even true?" (2005, 104). Quarshie has also asserted that "Of all parts in the canon, perhaps Othello is the one which should most definitely not be played by a black actor."[41] Vaughan postulates that as *Othello* has been played for generations "[O]ne might argue that…the role of Othello has accrued significations that were not necessarily part of the original conception but which have solidified in contemporary readings" (2005, 105). Any contemporary production of *Othello* probably cannot now avoid these "significations," and regardless of the skill and power of the black actor playing the Moor, Othello's susceptibility to Iago's bizarre narrative seems to prove incontrovertibly the Moor's intellectual vulnerability.

Edward Pechter laments that "working on *Othello* means inhabiting a contaminated site; you want to say the right thing, but it comes out sounding terribly wrong" (1999, 181). The more thoroughly one grasps the grotesque sexuality of Iago's "dream," the less noble Othello appears for not deciphering it. That assertion may seem terribly wrong, but it also seems terribly right.[42]

---

[39]   James Bulman, ed., *Shakespeare, Theory, and Performance* (London and New York: Routledge, 1996), "Introduction," 1.

[40]   Virginia Mason Vaughan, *Performing Blackness on English Stages: 1500-1800* (Cambridge: Cambridge University Press, 2005), 105.

[41]   Hugh Quarshie, *Second Thoughts about Othello*. Occasional Paper # 7. (Chipping Camden: International Shakespeare Association, 1999), 5.

[42]   In his fine essay in this volume, "Iago: In Following Him I Follow but Myself" Dan Donohue details his own exploration of Iago for his brilliant performance of the role at the 2008 Oregon Shakespeare Festival. Donohue writes that "A character's DNA is found in his words," and he locates the center of Iago's elusive motivation in a searing jealousy that Donohue executed vividly on stage. Although Dan and I differ significantly about some aspects of the Iago-Othello relationship, and although my approach to Iago's language and its implications for Othello is primarily scholarly while Donohue's is primarily theatrical, our approaches are nonetheless complimentary. Together our essays explore and enlarge our understanding of the fascinating yet lethal tapestry of Iago's words, and how a superb actor like Donohue may convincingly play upon a stage the improbable fiction that is Iago's character.

# PART 3
# Beyond Naturalism:
# Then and Now

# Chapter 11
# Just Do It:
# Theory and Practice in Acting

Eunice Roberts

## Prologue

Especially among British actors, there is a reluctance to analyze or reflect upon their acting process. When asked, "How do you do it?" the response is frequently, "I just do it." In fact, it seems that actors are almost encouraged not to analyze their process: we might, for example, consider the following words from an acting teacher, a director and a playwright:

> To act is to do not to think. (Uta Hagen)[1]
> Acting is not a science. (Charles Marowitz)[2]
> It's not your job to explain it but to perform it. (David Mamet)[3]

I can trace the genesis of my own resistance to analysis of the acting process to my training in the 1970s at Bristol Old Vic Theatre School (BOVTS), which was largely based upon the acquisition of vocal and physical skills and not on one particular theory of acting. There was, however, a sense of tradition that one was part of a continuing line of actors learning a craft. The Bristol Old Vic Theatre had opened in 1766 and the Company formed in 1946.

Central to the training was a class with Rudi Shelley, who had at first been the movement instructor at the theatre but moved to the school when it opened in 1946. (He continued teaching until two weeks before his death at the age of 90 in 1998.) With Rudi, work was done on both the body and the voice. He believed that the body needed to be neutralized, so that there were no outstanding or inhibiting physical habits, such as throwing the shoulders back rather than dropping them correctly and lifting from the sternum. This "neutralization" was achieved through many exercises; one involved holding up medicine balls and throwing them from one student to another whilst speaking. Having worked on the body in order to make it a "blank canvas," our work then progressed onto the voice as an extension of that physicality. In acting classes Rudi spoke very little; he did not follow a system and

---

[1]   *Respect for Acting* (New York: Wiley Publishing, Inc., 1973), 67.

[2]   *Recycling Shakespeare* (London: Macmillan Educational, Ltd., 1991), 6.

[3]   *True and False: Heresy and Common Sense for the Actor* (London: Faber and Faber, 1998), 99.

avoided using terms such as "motivation," "character" or "action." Time was spent on breaking down scenes; the first scene of *The Seagull* was explored over many weeks. This would be done in many ways: as animals, in masks, all designed to make the students reach out beyond their own personal experiences and lose their personal inhibitions. By working the same scene over and over again, discoveries were made about the very things Rudi did not discuss: "motivation," "character" and "action." All these, of course, are very much rooted in the Stanislavski system but were not acknowledged as such. Instead, I discovered those terms from the practice of playing the scene, as opposed to talking about it. On leaving the school we were told that we had had a third of our training as an actor; the other two thirds would now take place working in the theatre.

In 1989, however, I worked for the first time with the company Actors From The London Stage (AFTLS), and it was in my continung work with them that the biggest influence on my practice occurred, not only with the work on stage but through a fundamental belief held by the Company about work in the classroom with students. The Company was founded in 1975 by an English professor from U.C. Santa Barbara, Homer Swander (known as Murph), and twice a year it tours a Shakespeare play to American universities. As has been the case from the beginning (and from 1989 to 2008 I have been a part of seven tours), the tour involves a group of five actors, with no director, stage manager or designer. Inevitably, this means the doubling and trebling of parts, sometimes simultaneously during a scene, as in the final scene of *Twelfth Night* when I doubled Viola and Sebastian. Working in this way also leads to actors having a responsibility for the whole play, so that a level of commitment and loyalty to the play develops that I had not experienced before. The constant factor through the rehearsal process is the text; that is what we turn to, *how* the story is told, and what binds the five of us together. Its changing rhythms, rhymes, shapes and sounds provide the anchor as, in the words of Homer Swander, "scripted signals become ... performed signs."[4] The words shape not only the character(s), but also the development of the play itself and therefore the performance. Thus our work on the text becomes our structure for the day.

Equally importantly, alongside the performances is work the actors take into the classrooms. This involves using the text, as well as demonstrating and discussing the choices that actors make. By having to discuss such matters with students, I found I was no longer in the position to say, "I just do it." I had to be able to analyze and verbalize my process; I therefore had to discover a way to articulate that process. As I worked more with the Company, I recognized for the first time that I had a way of working that I took from one rehearsal into another; it was becoming, without my ever saying so, *systematized*, and was being confirmed by taking the work into the classroom, not only with the Company but also on my own.

---

    [4]   "In Our Time: Such Audiences We Wish Him," *Shakespeare Quarterly* 35.5 (1984): 528–40, 537.

The growing self-awareness of the need to be able to verbalize my process led me to pursue a Masters degree in drama at the University of Kent, which culminated in a thesis titled *Practice as Research*. In taking up research for the thesis, I began by focusing on elements of the Company and in particular the moment of changing onstage from one role to another (necessitated by doubling). Developing the "neutral" body that Rudi had given me, working it as I changed back and forth between characters, had enabled me to cross the line between characters and provide clarity, so that one was not merged with the other; and the vocal qualities of each came with the extension of that physicality. It emerged that the work with AFTLS embodied the very tradition of the BOVTS training. But questions arose, such as: who are you as the actor as you move from one character to the other? Answering this meant exploring the nature of talking to yourself, but yourself as the "other." Researching this brought me to investigate and understand the concept of liminality, of being at a threshold. The idea not only became a major focus of the research, but also inspired the form the thesis took. The thesis included not only chapters of straightforward research, but also a solo performance piece (... *one, two, three* ...) and an analysis of the creation, rehearsal and performance of it. The piece is itself a form of research: a deconstruction of *Twelfth Night* that uses this meta-text as a way of investigating the actor playing multiple roles, not only of Viola and Sebastian but also the role of an actor itself. The following essay is adapted from a chapter that analyzes the creation and rehearsal of the piece, and is presented in the form of an "inner dialogue": a discussion between practitioner and researcher, along with a middle voice, thus reflecting the three voices in ... *one, two, three* ... The piece is appended at the end of the essay.

The two worlds of practice and theory have now come very close together in my process; what appeared to be abstract ideas of liminality, or the "writing pad," were of great practical use. But should actors change their reluctance to analyze? Is it a tool that is required in the practical process of acting? Actors may not refer to liminality, but the word does point to what is happening: a journeying from one moment to the next, one character to another, a transformation, stepping over the threshold from the waiting actor, to the actor in action—applying what has been embedded on the "slate" in rehearsal into the moment of performance.

§    §    §    §

Who is it that can tell me who I am?
I am that I am
I am not what I am
I am I, however I was begot
Simply the thing I am
Shall make me live.
You alone are you
I am I
Such as I am
Simply the thing I am.

I want to investigate my acting process when it no longer consists of the familiar building blocks: creating a character and motivation through "practice of the scene" with a set text. I want do so by creating my own text from texts worked on in the past when those very blocks were used. The verse above is composed of lines selected from texts worked on previously. What would happen if I were to remove words from their context? What new narrative would those words tell? And how would I then begin to analyse my process, not only with the words from a text but also with the theoretical language from my research?

Practice as research. There is a sense of duality here; a duality that is to have echoes throughout the work, in the piece itself, my part within it, and in this current writing. Of being "betwixt and between" in several ways: neither with a text nor without; combining the training at BOVTS with the more recent work of AFTLS and the need to verbalize my process. This duality of practice and research is a new territory for me.

> *But you know this territory; this is your practice you are researching, a practice that you trained for and with tools you have developed. You've separated yourself off, given yourself another voice ... talking about this is*

Over here

> *Doing it is here.*

The words: an investigation into the words. Where do they belong? Who do they belong to? Working with AFTLS my interest in the words themselves had taken on a new perspective; they were "the signposts" for telling the story. I wanted to know if I could remove them from their narrative and "De-contextualise" them.

> *"De-contextualise." Is that what I'm going to do? Do I use that word in the rehearsal room? No.*

According to Bert States, "One way of approaching the phenomenology of the actor is to consider him as a kind of storyteller whose specialty is that he *is* the story he is telling."[5] The methodology of the Company, and therefore my work, is both hermeneutic and heuristic.

> *I am a "storyteller." Am I "the story I am telling"? I do ask questions and I discover and am present; but do these words belong to me: hermeneutic/ heuristic methodology? Are they part of my world? They feel like a different language. Can those words guide me? "Methodology" I have that already, we have that in AFTLS, it is my "specified structure of working."*

---

[5]    "The Actor's Presence: Three Phenomenal Modes," in Philip B. Zarrilli, ed., *Acting (Re)Considered: A Theoretical and Practical Guide*, 2nd edition (London and NY: Routledge, 2002), 23.

The methodology of AFTLS isn't written down, there is no "one way" of doing it, and yet it has its structure, there are the basics, from which you ask questions.

> *We are on stage all the time. You see us before the play begins, we stand at the side, you see us as actors. We start with a "cast list" of the five of us saying all the parts we are to play; you understand that the story will be told with just the five actors. There is an area marked out: a square, or a circle around twenty feet, to focus the acting area. We then sit out of it, ready to step into it, to become one character, another character; to talk to yourself ... oh, let's not rush ahead here. Before that there is the rehearsal, the five of us, no director, no one ... but the play, the words. How those words tell the story: the rhythm, rhyme, shape, moving through the actor into the space.*

How am I to select the words I am going to use? I know they will be Shakespeare's; it is my practice. But, to take them and put them into some form of new narrative, to use the words themselves and to give a shape suggested by Andy Lavender's description of Neo-formalism: "to do with rhythm, space and image as primary sources of theatrical affect."[6]

> *"Neo-formalism." It's just the language, the language that's different.*

I talk about it.

> *I do it.*

I decide to look through the Shakespeare plays I have done, at first in any context but then just with AFTLS. I look for words, phrases that appeal to me, there is no analysis here, just a pure gut reaction; an intuition you might say. The list is endless. I place them in categories: night, day, weather, young, old, family, hatred, love, identity.

I bring together three actors who have just finished working together on *A Midsummer Night's Dream*: Caroline Devlin, Jan Shepherd and Christopher Staines. I hand them a sheet of words, from which they choose. They improvise, choosing words at random, not to make sense but to keep some sort of dialogue going. We continue in this fashion for a couple of hours, a narrative emerges, the speaker (actor) picks up on words that had been handed to them by the previous speaker (actor), a rhythm builds. One of the actors said, "It was on instinct, I had to make a choice which words to pick, how to say them." There was also a sense of performing, creating something to be listened to. From the listener's perspective there is a desire to create a narrative, to make sense, to give the words a situation; they are no longer words on their own.

I want to keep it simple, what did the words do themselves? But at this point I am in a vacuum, not just a "neutral" body from BOVTS but of not knowing what

---

[6]    Lavender, *Hamlet in Pieces, Shakespeare Reworked* by Peter Brook, Robert Lepage, and Robert Wilson (London: Nick Hern Books, 2001), 223.

it is that I am to create. I know that it will be a solo piece, in order to focus on my own analysis of my practice. I have the opportunity here, the time to investigate my process; it does not have to be commercial. It is still for an audience but one that is coming knowing that it is watching a piece of research—but also a performance.

An overriding topic came out of the words I had selected—identity.

> Who is it that can tell me who I am?
> I am that I am
> I am not what I am
> I am I, however I was begot
> Simply the thing I am
> Shall make me live
> You alone are you
> I am I
> Such as I am
> Simply the thing I am.

This was a nonsense rhyme in itself, but a major shifting point in the direction I am to go in. But why had this topic arisen? Why had I picked out those words? How, if I was to use those words, could I discover something about the practice of AFTLS itself? The work naturally questions identity, for you play not only multiple roles, but there are times when you can be two or three characters at once; an instance of three is at the opening of Act V in *Twelfth Night* when the same actor plays Orsino, Feste and Fabian. Talking to yourself when you are on stage and not there, yet still there, at one and the same time. There have been instances in the work when I have not had those moments; in *Romeo and Juliet, A Midsummer Night's Dream* and *Much Ado About Nothing,* I always felt cheated, for it is these moments, unique to the work, that excite me. People ask: "How do you do it?" And the answer is "You just do it." But how? How do you "Just do it"?

*You just do it*

One of the actors I had been working with earlier said, "I do have an idea of what I am doing, but worried at examining it too much, I might lose it."

So how do I with the words look at that moment, that moment of moving between one role and the other? Who is it? Is it anyone at all? The role you have left? The one you are moving to? The actor? And what is being thought in those moments? What and whose identity is it? Is it the moment of liminality?

*The moment of what? Liminality?*

Of being "neither here nor there," "betwixt and between," neither one thing nor another.

*I like that.*

Thinking of those moments I had done, was there anything that linked them? The instances that had stayed with me were in *The Winter's Tale*, which was the first time I had done the work and had played Hermione and Perdita, mother and daughter and then in *Twelfth Night*, playing Viola and Sebastian. Both of these had a strong sense of duality, of, as I described it, "the other side of being," for there was a strong attachment to the other, when being "the other."

In presenting my practice as a solo piece and exploring/researching the practice of AFTLS, was I running into a problem? For AFTLS is about being five, the interaction of a group of people, the dynamics of creating a production, of reacting to characters who are there and not there. So, how could I do it solo?

> *The one-handers. You've already done a solo piece within the work, two in fact. You are getting so wrapped up in justifying it, you are forgetting about being practical.*

When the work goes to America, two members of the company present what is referred to as one-handers. These come in many forms: a reading of T.S. Eliot's *Four Quartets*, *The Rhyme of the Ancient Mariner* or *Beowulf*. The next tour to go out was *Twelfth Night* and I, as an Associate Director, was to put it together, so if I imagined that I was on that tour, I could create a one-hander based on *Twelfth Night*.

I now had words from *Twelfth Night* and was looking at the exchange between Viola and Sebastian; that moment of liminality: Limen: "Threshold."[7] Threshold: The statistical point at which:

1. Two stimuli resemble each other so closely as to be confusable.
2. A stimulus is so weak that the presence cannot be detected except by chance.[8]

> *It's Viola and Sebastian, one resembles the other. I cross over from one to the other and back again. I play one and characters think I am the other. Identity is interchangeable and "confusable" and at points "becomes weak," in that it is not there and yet still there and through the narrative – it comes back.*

But liminality offers not only the moment of change, of crossing over from one to the other, but also a "threshold." Crossing over a line, stepping from one world to another, and that is what we do. We have the marked out area on the stage, a square or a circle; this can be done by literally marking it out with tape or salt, ribbon, books or the lighting (on a few occasions this has not happened). We sit at the side waiting to go on and then step over, step over the limen, to enter the play. The

---

7     Kenneth Pickering, *Key Concepts in Drama and Performance* (Basingstoke and NY: Palgrave Macmillan, 2005), 235.

8     Alan Bullock and Oliver Stallybrass, ed., *The Fontana Dictionary of Modern Thought* (Glasgow: William Collins Sons and Company Ltd., 1977), 636.

audience sees that moment of transition, when you are neither actor nor character, that split second; they then continue to watch as you change from character to character … even once more to character, back again and finally back to actor, to be sitting at the side, having crossed once more over the limen, "Neither on stage nor off stage."[9]

On all levels there is a sense of duality, of being this and that, neither here nor there and of course being both practitioner and researcher. But in AFTLS there is practice and theory, for there is the class work.

> *But that's different, it isn't theorizing; you discuss texts practically, get students on their feet, discovering how choices can be made from the text, always from the text.*

What's the difference? Here you are creating a piece of practice and then discussing it, reflecting on it, how you made the choices that you did.

> *There is a difference, for the theory in the classroom is presented practically, from a practitioner's point of view. As Murph told us "Put the students on their feet working with the word. Don't ever, ever let a class just sit there"*

And the main task is now—practice: to construct the piece.

> Do I stand there?
> I never had a sister.
> I had a brother
> I had a brother
> I had a brother

And so you create one.

I talk of constructing the piece, not writing, for that is what it is, in pieces. I have all the groups of words, the characters and themes. What is it I am to play with?

It is by placing myself in a room and beginning to "play" that something will emerge. I need to be in the rehearsal room and actively "Do it," not talk about it.

> *An empty space, a rehearsal room, but I have no script, just words, and a sense of being five. At the moment all is "bibble babble."*

> *I mentally mark out a square, a twenty-foot square. It is no longer an empty space; it is a blank space, within an empty space. Give yourself the framework.*

> *I stand outside of it, I try to get in, I walk around it, try to enter again. I can't enter the space. If I can't enter the space, I can't start … why not? I don't know what it is I am doing, I have no reason to enter. Who am I walking around? At the moment I am Eunice, the actor looking for what it is I am to do, without knowing what it is I am looking for. What am I and who am I as the actor?*

---

[9]    Pickering, *Key Concepts*, 234.

I have never asked myself this before; I have always been playing a part or parts in a play, knowing where I needed to look. Now I am "a blank," a "blank" within a blank space and with a blank page.

> An autonomous surface is put before the eye of the subject who thus accords himself the field for an operation of his own.[10]

But, I am not "a blank" for I have with me all my knowledge of working in the Company and I have the words.

> I had a brother
> I had a sister
> I had a Father
>     Mother
> I am … I am … I am …

*I enter the space. That way I may find the answer to my questions.*

*The words are on the floor. I pick them up, put them in my pocket, bring them out again, drop them, tear them up, keep one, throw one away.*

*I bring on two chairs. One in each hand, place one on top of the other, lift it off again, put it back, lift it off again … everything I do, I seem to repeat, a sense of going back and forth, of looking for something, in and out. It is also a way of confirming, of learning. I have no one to write anything down, it is imprinting itself on my memory.*

*I lift the chair off. I have one in one hand one in the other, they weigh on either side of me … they are equal. I swing from side to side.*

> I had a brother        I had a sister
> I am … I am … I am

There are times in rehearsal when things do—"just happen." Powerful theatrical moments have appeared in what seem to be a simple way. Alan Dessen, who was from 1998 to 2004 the Academic Director of AFTLS and has had a strong association with the Company from the beginning, seeing all but two shows, describes a moment from *A Midsummer Night's Dream* of 1991:

> Repeatedly the obvious liabilities (e.g. thirteen figures are onstage at one time in 5.1) were turned into assets … In a small but telling moment at the end of 1.2, Bottom called for a joining of hands to end the scene. Since Eunice Roberts was both Starveling and Snug, she provided a hand for the former (as did the four other mechanicals) and then, as the group was almost complete, a second hand

---

[10]   Michel de Certeau, *The Practice of Everyday Life*, Steven Rendall, trans. (Berkeley and Los Angeles: University of California Press, 1984), 134.

appeared to represent Snug's commitment as well. Early in the play, this brief gesture therefore set up the sixness of the five.[11]

I remember this moment "just happening" in rehearsal. It came about because in that moment I was two. There was no confusion over the fact that I was both Starveling and Snug; I already had one hand in the "joining," Eunice had another hand, so that joined too. Just as there was a "sixness of the five" there was a "doubleness" to the actor. I don't mean in any sense a split or a division; they are both in the actor at the same time, to be brought to the surface when called for. On the one hand this, on the other hand that, "That that is, is" (4.2.15). Viola and Sebastian, not only themselves but twins, "An apple cleft in two" (5.1.221).

I had Viola and I had Sebastian. In looking at that movement between them, that liminal moment, how could I represent it; not only to find out more about it, but how to make it physical on stage?

> *Look at the play, look at the play... that is always what you do when doing your practice—Why is it any different now?*

*Twelfth Night* itself offers up so many wonderful opportunities for looking at identity. In the rehearsal room you would be asking questions of the play—who / why / what, those Stanislavskian "Given Circumstances" from BOVTS, even though we didn't say that at the time. But here my questions were not to do with the play itself, but rather with the identity of myself as the performer, the doer. In the play people take on new identities, Viola becomes Cesario:

> I am not that I play. (1.5.185)
> So, if:
>     I am not that I play
> Who am I at that moment of playing?
>     I am not what I am. (3.1.143)
> Therefore what/who am I? Can I be:
>     A blank. (2.4.111)

For as Feste says:

> That that is, is ... for what is "that" but "that" and "is" but "is." (4.2.15)

So:

> I had a sister, I never had a brother
> I had a brother
> I had a brother.

I know that I have Viola on the one hand and Sebastian on the other, they are on either side of me, where they would sit naturally in rehearsal. When I first did the

---

[11]  Dessen, "Wonder and Magic in the ACTER Five Hander Comedies," *Shakespeare Bulletin* 10 (1992): 7–9; 9.

play I had, we had, this problem—how do you have them both on stage? You have to leave one to become the other and yet the first "other" is still there. It is difficult enough to do it in practice but to analyze it and write it down is even more difficult. I believe that the difficulty lies in the moment of bringing the other on, when you yourself in the first character are already on stage. Do you position yourself at the edge of the stage so you are there? Having done that and become the "other," you have then left the first "other" at the edge of the stage, they are where you left them; they do not walk independently, invisibly. At the same time there are no golden rules, there is no handbook of "How to do it" and each group finds new ways of working the old.

In the final scene of *All's Well That Ends Well* (2000) I was playing La Feu and Diana, and there was also Bertram, the Countess doubling with the Widow, and the actor playing the King, who was to remain on stage, about to enter as Parolles. The entrance of Parolles was achieved by all the actors in the scene looking upstage and being aware of a terrible odour as he entered; by reacting to this "invisible" odour walking downstage, we were able to bring him alongside the actor playing the King, so that he was then able to step back and forth between the two in the dialogue.

But to return to the moment when Viola and Sebastian meet on stage: Orsino, Olivia, and Antonio are already there, so they can help bring the "other" character (Sebastian) on. Once I leave one character and become the "other," the other actors on stage can look back to where the first "other" was. The audience appears never to have a problem with this, as long as you establish where the invisible "other" is. You hear time and again—I saw eight, twelve, thirteen people on stage.

I left Viola, became Sebastian, I saw Viola, they all looked between my present self and "other" and back again, just as you would if you had an actor in both. But I was in both, for I was Viola and Sebastian at one and the same time.

*I am there, I am there, "that that is, is." Now you see me, now you don't, but that's not true, for you do see me, you see me both present and absent, for in my absence there is presence.*

Presence and absence, "A natural perspective that is, and is not." (5.1.215). As Freud's grandson reassures himself in his *Fort/Da* game—gone and there, that his mother has not disappeared. So if we are clear about where the presence of the absence is on stage, the audience sees both.

April 27, 2005, a lecture by Patrice Pavis on "The Dramaturgy of the Actress" (at the point of writing unpublished); he talked of the theatre space—"Reduced space: a square of light, like a writing slate, a 'Wunderblock' from where all memories start and converge."

*A "square of light." A light goes on in my head.*

In this head

*No, in this head ... in ...*

my head. We have a "square of light" and I am working on a square now and with memories old and memories new. The memory of past productions is inside me, and my daily memories of the shifting piece.

My understanding, sitting there, listening to "Wunderblock," is that of a slate, where anything can happen. I can enter the acting space, unsure, not knowing what is to happen or why I am there. By the time I come to be doing the performance, there is of course nothing unsure about it, I am very certain in my uncertainty but in rehearsal I am standing in an empty room, on my writing slate, not knowing, allowing things to happen.

My first image of the "slate," "a square of light from where all memories start and converge," develops after reading "A Note Upon the 'Mystic Writing-Pad'": "If I want to put some fresh notes on the slate, I must first wipe out the ones that cover it."[12] At first I think this is like a rehearsal, having new ideas and trying them out but of course it isn't, for it is frequently out of the old ideas, the ideas that don't work, that solutions come; they do not get "wipe[d] out," there is an intermingling of old and new as with the "Mystic Writing Pad," layer built upon layer, even though not visible to the eye (or the audience) but still there:

> The surface of the Mystic Pad is clear of writing and once more capable of receiving impressions. But it is easy to discover that the permanent trace of what was written is retained upon the wax slab itself and is legible in suitable lights (Freud, 432).

In rehearsals things are tried one way and then another, the actor remembers. There is also the stage manager, writing moves down, not so much on a "Mystic Pad" but a permanent pad; a permanent pad written in pencil, however, to be retained or erased. I have no stage manager, no one marking down; I have to be doing that myself. I do have paper and pencil and write things down, but it is not always possible to get to that "pad" in order to make a note; what happens is a mental "pad," which becomes almost physical.

Freud talks of a "trace" of what was written being "retained upon the wax slab;" this is where the repetition of words, of phrases, is built up, being laid down in my actor memory. Derrida refers to it as "The multi layering of the writing pad."[13] At points I forget a thought I've had, of what I want to be happening; it is as if it has been wiped clean but those words/thoughts have been imprinted and by re-visiting them,

> I have one heart, one bosom
> the journey can start again.

---

[12]   Sigmund Freud, "A Note Upon the 'Mystic Writing Pad,'" in *The Penguin Freud Library*, vol II (London: Penguin, 1984), 430.

[13]   Jacques Derrida, *Writing and Difference*, Alan Bass, trans. (London and New York: Routledge, 2004), 281.

When I learn lines I do so (as many others do) by repetition, by building up, finding a mnemonic, a word that links to another, one imprinted on top of another; an echo of BOVTS playing a scene over and over again, discovering the needs of the text. It is very easy to do this with Shakespeare and in this rehearsal room I find myself isolating the layering of words, they are taking on a rhythm of their own; not so much, "What narrative can these words tell?" but by them becoming an entity in themselves. Pavis tells of how there is an "Underscore/Subscore" in an actor's work, not a subtext but what is there as a support:

> *The memory of the speaking actress ... is also linked to the kinaesthesia of language, to its rhythmic and driving fancy, to the pragmatism of the language concerned, to its support points which are physical as much as logical and mental—in short, to the whole (especially the kinaesthetic) subscore of concrete language.*[14]

In doing a solo piece, I have placed myself in an AFTLS framework but am shifting the boundaries within that. I want to be alone in order to discover what my own rhythms bring to the words, without the influence of others. What do I do to the words or the words do to me?

I start to build them up in layers, in the "wax underneath," remembering, wiping them away, remembering in the same way or perhaps not, as they have been indented with a new memory in the process. I become a physical "writing-pad." And that "writing-pad" becomes a character itself. Just as the words on the page inform you about your character, for they are the character, so these words, rhythms, are informing and creating this new "other."

I now:

had a brother      had a sister

I was secure when I was those "others" for they were already imprinted on my "writing-pad" in my memory. But it was these new "impressions" that I had to discover and investigate:

I am ... I am ... I am

The mnemonic rhythm builds up a kinaesthetic action within the words. I place the characters I know from the past on the sides of the stage they were on then, those areas are theirs, I can "reproduce them at any time I like," but even so, they are in a new situation, being informed by my new memory and situation. When I had done *Twelfth Night* before, I had a Father, who had since died and I had now a Mother whose memory was here and yet not here ... she is present and absent:

---

[14]   Patrice Pavis, "Underscore: The Shape of Things to Come," Ralph Yarrow and Barry Karlin, trans., *Contemporary Theatre Review* 6.4 (1997): 37–61; 46.

> She bore a mind that envy could not but call fair … she is drowned already with salt water, though I seem to drown her again with yet more … she is gone … yet here she is.         (2.1.28.30)

I cannot say these words in the way I had before, for they bring new memories with them. These lines belong to Sebastian, talking of his sister, yet with the thoughts of Eunice, the actor, informing Sebastian. I the actor did not impose this on Sebastian; it was not, "How do I feel about this?" not, "What would I do in that situation?" or "What *if?*"—"I am I; but *if* I were … ."[15] The words themselves had created the thought, through my history. Once they had been thought that way, said that way, they had then made their impression on my "writing-pad" in order to be reproduced. To be reproduced in this moment, until a newer impression was made. Though past impressions would never be erased completely.

The "Third Character" was becoming both the conscious and subconscious of the "others," the memory bank. It was the moment between thought and action, a liminal moment, "where anything could happen." A moment that on stage happens in an instant, is unseen, but this moment was becoming through the words a physical entity in itself.

In 1999 I had a conversation with Doug Scott, the first British man to climb Everest in 1975. He talked of the climb and the length of time it took from one thought to another, "The silence between the thoughts." That phrase had imprinted itself in my memory bank, on my "writing-pad." Now I was making it physical.

I stand at the edge, at the edge of the square; at the clean slate, but is it a clean slate? Can anything, anything happen? Is it not already imprinted in me what is to happen? I act forgetting, when I am remembering—remembering forgetting. To not be there … to be there:

> Do I stand there?
> Do I stand there?

Who is remembering and remembering when?

The pieces I am putting together are still apart, separate, there is Viola to my right, Sebastian to my left and this body in the middle, they and it feel disjointed, they are not working off each other, feeding through repetition, sound and shape. I am being too literal keeping to the words as they were before. I string them together, but there is still a distinction between who speaks when, I take that away, I change how they look on my pad and they become One, Two, Three. Three, that conscious and subconscious of the "others" have become a stream of consciousness, a "multi leveled flow … soliloquy, narration of mental process, direct interior monologue, indirect interior monologue."[16] Bringing them together:

---

[15]   Konstantin Stanislavski, *An Actor Prepares*, Elizabeth Reynolds Hapgood, trans. (London: Methuen, 1985), 65.

[16]   Bullock and Stallybrass, *Dictionary*, 605.

I am gone ......... I am not here. Yet there he was ...
there she was.

Remembered when required. They were listening to each other; the language was listening to itself.

I have my large black notebook, which becomes two books and I write all my thoughts into them as I go through the stages of the piece. Those thoughts are written on:

*This side of the book*

I read and research, and find through such material as "The Mystic Writing Pad" links with my practice that had not been there before and I write them into my notebooks:

Here

They go alongside each other:

Here    and    *There*

The two worlds are coming together, moving towards performance.

## Appendix[17]

... one, two, three ...
Say I do speak?...How say you to that?...My remembrance....I would it would make you invisible...My remembrance........is gone...I am gone, I am gone ...yet there he was, there he was... he was......let me see let me see let me see....I went from hence then leaving her...leaving her...yet there he was...he was...leaving her?...How say you to that...I have one heart one bosom one voice...that is...that is...that is...for what is that but that and is but is...A double dealer...primo secundo...My remembrance...Do I stand...there?...Do I stand ...there?...What is your name? What is your parentage? What are you?...I am ..I am...One heart one bosom one voice...one neck one chin...that is...that is...thy tongue thy face...that is that is...are you mad?..O say so and so be...No I am not mad...I am...gone... South....North...My remembrance...What are you?..What would you?..What I would...is in a dark room in a dark house as secret as' maidenhead......I am ....I am....In hideous darkness......What country friends is this?..This is a dark house...This is the glorious sun...I am ...I am...in a dark house...in the glorious sun..in the dark...in the sun...what country tell me where...I am in hideous darkness..Therefore I say again this house is dark......What should I do?..He is

---

[17]    Editor's Note: No part of this piece may be reproduced or performed without express written permission of the author.

gone...he is not here..yet there he was..he was...As I am man...What say you?..
As I am man...as I am woman...What are you mad?..I am not mad...else I am no
more mad than you are...I am a fellow..fellow, fellow of the strangest mind in the
world...But I am not mad...I am a foul way out... I have one heart one bosom one
voice one neck one chin that is..that is...Wherefore are these things hid? I say
remember, thou can'st not choose but know, I say remember...What country
friends is this...know'est thou this country...Who Governs here?..By whose
Authority? What country friends is this...My remembrance......my remembrance...
receiveth...receiveth as the sea...from the breach of the sea....in the glorious
sun....where like Arion on the dolphin's back I saw him hold acquaintance with
the waves so long as I could see......I saw him...saw him...leaving her...O so
long as I could see...receiveth as the sea...from the breach of the sea...Did she see
thee the while?..What country...south...north....south....north...I am gone.......I
am......Say I do speak?...Who Governs here?...By whose Authority?...What
country friends is this...what shall become of this...I am in....O my poor brother...
he is in...I am...one heart...one bosom......one...brother......I have one heart
one bosom...one...brother...By innocence I swear and by my youth I have one
heart one bosom ...I have one heart one bosom....and one truth...My brother he
is...my brother he is...perchance he is...not drowned...What country friends is
this?.. What should I do...As I am woman..Conceal me....Conceal me what I
am...O my poor brother.......I had a brother...she is...No lady...I am a
gentleman....She is... gone...Did she see thee the while...she...much resembled
me..and she is gone...she is...he is... not here...I am...I am...one heart one
bosom one....brother...I never had...I never had a brother...I had...I had...I had
a sister...a sister whom the blind waves and surges have devoured...my determinate
voyage is mere extravagancy...my stars shine darkly over me...Darkly over
me...I am in a dark house in a dark room...My stars shine darkly over me...my
father...my father left behind him myself and a sister both born in an hour...my
bosom...My bosom...I have one heart one bosom..My bosom is full of kindness
and I am yet so near the manners of my Mother...Of my Mother, I am gone...Yet
so near the manners of my Mother that upon the least occasion more mine eyes
will tell tales of me...I crave of you your leave that I may bear my evils alone....
Will you stay no longer...did he see thee the while...he is gone and she is gone,
yet she is no lady, she is a gentleman, so he is gone and he is gone...yet there he
was, there he was...he was...he...much resembled me...Wherefore are these
things hid?...Wherefore have they a curtain before them...As I am woman...as I
am man...as I am woman...as I am man...How have you made division of
yourself?..Who Governs here By whose Authority.I have the benefit of my
senses...I have one heart one bosom one voice one neck one chin one tongue one
face..two two grey eyes ...with lids to them..that is...that is......This is
madness...O say so and so be...this is not madness...They have laid me here in
hideous darkness, they have put me into darkness, this house is dark...Yet there he
was...there she was...he was...I had a brother, I never had a brother, I had a
sister...a brother, a sister...A sister whom the blind waves and surges have

devoured…I am yet so near the manners of my Mother…Of my Mother…a lady though it was said she much resembled me was yet of many accounted beautiful but though I could not with such estimable wonder overfar believe that…yet thus far will I boldly publish her…she bore a mind that envy could not but call fair… she is drowned already with salt water though I seem to drown her remembrance again with more…she is gone…yet here she is…what else may hap…………You are gone…you are now out of your text…in a dark house, in a dark room…out of your text…out of your…I might say…….element…My remembrance…….You must know of me….my mind… is a very opal……as I am man…he much resembled me..as I am woman……………………but she is gone…she'll none of me…but she is no lady…she is a gentleman…and he is gone…and he is gone… and I am …….gone to…….gone too…to thee……I have unclasped to thee the book even of my secret soul…my soul is in the house…in a dark house…I think his soul is in ……hell in….heaven…in hell….in heaven…no it doth walk about the orb like the sun…it shines everywhere in the glorious sun…This pearl she gave me I do feel't and see it and though tis wonder that enwraps me thus yet tis not madness…I am not mad or else the ladies mad…I am no lady I am a gentleman…I'll be sworn thou art…For though my soul disputes well with my sense that this may be some error but no madness…thy words are madness an improbable fiction…But no madness…yet doth this accident and flood of fortune so far exceed all instance all discourse that I am ready to distrust mine eyes ….Who Governs here…By whose Authority…That I am ready to distrust mine eyes and wrangle with my reason that persuades me to any other trust but that I'm mad or else the ladies mad…She is no lady …I am a gentleman, say that some lady…You are no lady…Say that some lady as perhaps there is hath for your love as great a pang of heart, if I did love …You can not love him…If I did love…more than I love these eyes, more than my life…was not this love indeed…She never told her love…But let concealment like a worm i'the bud feed on her damask cheek she pin'd in thought and with a green and yellow melancholy she sat like patience on a monument smiling at grief………I will smile…she much resembled me…if I did love, more than I love these eyes …with lids to them…two grey eyes…with lids to them…thine eye hath stayed upon some favour that it loves….hath it not… what is love, dream on the event…whoe'er I woo…mine eyes will tell tales of me…..I am ready to distrust mine eyes…for though my soul disputes well with my sense that this may be some error but no madness…This is silly sooth but no madness…But no madness…yet doth this accident and flood of fortune so far exceed all discourse that I am ready to distrust mine eyes there's something in't that is deceivable…….Put on this gown…give me my veil…for such disguise……….conceal me, conceal me what I am……………………I am… not that I play…………What say you to that?......I am not that I play…….Are you the lady of the house? …If I do not usurp myself I am…she may command me…I serve her…she is my lady…Are you a comedian?.....no…and yet…I am not that I play……….Are you the lady of the house?…I am no lady I am a gentleman…… and yet ….I am not that I play…I am not that I play…I prithee tell me what thou

think'st of me…That you do think you are not what you are…If I think so I think the same of you…Then think you right I am not what I am…I am not what I am……….Are you the lady of the house? …You have been mistook…let go thy hand…….Let go thy hand…hand…hand…let go thy hand…I have them at my fingers ends…How have you made division of yourself…a double dealer…my remembrance is very free and clear…Do I stand… there…he much resembled me…Do I stand there…she much resembled me…Do I stand …
…………there? I never had a brother;
Nor can there be that deity in my nature
Of here and everywhere. I had a sister,
Whom the blind waves and surges have devour'd:
Of charity, what kin are you to me?
What countryman? What name? What parentage?

…Do I stand there….

Of Messaline: Sebastian was my father;
Such a Sebastian was my brother too:
So went he suited to his watery tomb.
If spirits can assume both form and suit,
You come to fright us.

A spirit I am indeed,
But am in that dimension grossly clad
Which from the womb I did participate.
Were you a woman, as the rest goes even,
I should my tears let fall upon your cheek,
And say, 'Thrice welcome, drowned Viola.'

…He much resembled me…she much resembled me..I am…I am… in standing water between the elements of air and earth…for what is that but that and is but is.. one face …one voice…two persons…an apple cleft in two…primo…secundo… tertio…one…two…three….I am…I am…now…out of…my…text.

# Chapter 12
# Playing Sodomites:
# Gender and Protean Character in
# *As You Like It*

Lina Perkins Wilder

In his account of his travels in Italy at the beginning of the seventeenth century, Thomas Coryate famously reports having seen women players: "I was at one of their Play-houses [in Venice], where I saw a Comedie acted …. Here I obserued certaine things that I neuer saw before. For I saw women acte, a thing that I neuer saw before, though I haue heard that it hath beene sometimes vsed in London, and they performed it with as good a grace, action, gesture, and whatsoeuer conuenient for a Player, as euer I saw any masculine Actor."[1] Coryate's observation suggests just how little a coherent performance of gender identity might have mattered to some among early modern English audiences. Coryate does not seem to care about the naturalness of the actors' gender performance, which one would assume would be striking to an audience member used to seeing boys portraying female characters. His focus is rather on rhetorical technique. A "masculine actor," Coryate assumes, will be superior to a woman actor in his grasp of the rhetorical skills of "grace, action, [and] gesture"; Coryate is merely surprised that the women in Venice have mastered these skills.[2] Coryate's contemporary George Sandys, who also attended theatrical performances in Italy that included women, actually declares the women actors inadequate precisely because their characterization is too natural. Because these women are not playing a character far enough from

---

[1]    Thomas Coryate, *Coryats crudities hastily gobled vp in five moneths trauells in France, Sauoy, Italy, Rhetia co[m]monly called the Grisons country, Heluetia aliàs Switzerland, some parts of high Germany, and the Netherlands; newly digested in the hungry aire of Odcombe in the county of Somerset, & now dispersed to the nourishment of the trauelling members of this kingdome* (London, 1611), sig. T5r. On Coryate's reaction to women players, see Bruce R. Smith, *Homosexual Desire in Shakespeare's England: A Cultural Poetics* (Chicago: University of Chicago Press, 1991), 148–49.

[2]    In his introduction to *Twelfth Night* in the first edition of *The Norton Shakespeare*, Stephen Greenblatt asserts that Coryate's astonishment *does* have to do with the women players' ability "to hold their own in representing the female sex." Gender representation, however, is not Coryate's focus. "Introduction" to *Twelfth Night*, in *The Norton Shakespeare*, ed., Stephen Greenblatt et al. (New York: Norton, 1997), 1761.

themselves, Sandys feels, women actors are "too naturally passionated"[3] and lack the artistry required when a boy portrays a woman on the London stage.

Contemporary anti-theatrical treatises and many of the plays themselves suggest that coherent characterization, even in the category of gender, was not the rule in the London theaters.[4] The potential disjunction between male actor and female character receives particular emphasis when both male and female gender identities are performed by one actor—as, for example, by Rosalind/Ganymede in *As You Like It*. But while the disjunct nature of Rosalind/Ganymede's gender performance and her (or his) position in a theatrical culture that favored rhetorical mastery over coherent characterization might seem to work against a reading of this figure as a "character," in fact the opposite is true.[5] Gender ambiguity and other disjunctions in characterization produce Rosalind as a character whose Protean changefulness, in turn, shapes both her/his gender identity and her/his theatrical identity: as an embodiment of change, she/he is both mercurial boy actor and mercurial female character. Rosalind/Ganymede cannot be understood as "either" actor or character—the usual distinction made by critics who read this figure as opposed to notions of coherent characterization—but must be understood as, in some sense, both: in Yu Jin Ko's term, a "charactor."[6] In gender terms and in

---

[3]    George Sandys, *A Relation of a Journey Begun Anno Domini 1610*, 2nd ed. (London, 1615), 245–46. See also Smith, *Homosexual Desire*, 149.

[4]    See Tiffany Stern, *Rehearsal from Shakespeare to Sheridan* (Oxford: Clarendon Press, 2000), 46–123.

[5]    Readings of Rosalind in character terms include: Louis Martin, "As She Liked It: Rosalind as Subject," *Pennsylvania English* 22, nos. 1–2 (Fall-Spring 2000 ): 91–96; Clare R. Kinney, "Feigning Female Faining: Spenser, Lodge, Shakespeare, and Rosalind," *Modern Philology* 95, no. 3 (February 1998 ): 291–315; Margaret Boerner Beckman, "The Figure of Rosalind in *As You Like It*," *Shakespeare Quarterly* 29, no. 1 (Winter 1978 ): 44–51.

[6]    See Yu Jin Ko, "Rosalind-as-Ganymede: *Charactor* of Contingency," in his *Mutability and Division on Shakespeare's Stage* (Newark: University of Delaware Press, 2004), 77–91 ; see also Michael Keevak, "The Playing of Sodomy in *As You Like It*," *Studies in Language and Literature* 9 (June 2000): 48–9. (Keevak's argument has to do not with the nature of character but with the nature of sodomy, which he finds to be less subversive than theatrical performance as a whole; see 56.) Arguments against reading Rosalind as a character almost always draw an opposition between the functions of actor and mimetic character, an opposition that can also be read in gender terms. See Lesley Anne Soule, "Subverting Rosalind: Cocky Ros in the Forest of Arden," *New Theatre Quarterly* 7, no. 26 (May 1991): 126–36; see also the longer version of her argument in Lesley Wade Soule, *Actor as Anti-Character: Dionysus, the Devil, and the Boy Rosalind* (Westport, CT, and London: Greenwood Press, 2000). Soule excludes the possibility of an actorly "character" taking place by noting that Rosalind in the Forest or Arden "has no significant motivation or objective. Her arrival in the Forest of Arden is the completion of a character action, not the beginning" ("Subverting Rosalind," 130). Since the conception of character invoked here is anachronistic, however, it is difficult to maintain as a historicist argument. On actors as anti-characters, see also Tracey Sedinger, "'If Sight and Shape Be True': The Epistemology of Crossdressing on the London Stage," *Shakespeare Quarterly* 48, no. 1 (Spring 1997): 63–80, esp. 77–8; Douglas Green, "The 'Unexpressive She': Is There Really

terms of character, Rosalind/Ganymede is an exercise in what Eunice Roberts, in this volume, calls "liminality" or "duality"—the sense that performing this figure places the performer between two states and also requires him (or, later, her) to inhabit both states. Again borrowing Roberts's language, I would suggest that there is a "twoness" in Rosalind/Ganymede's gender identity that speaks both to the quality of gender in the play and to the construction of character.

For boy actors in early modern London, the conjunction of gender and professional characteristics makes "liminality" a matter of course. In the common imagination in early modern London, boys are changeable;[7] women are changeable; and actors are changeable.[8] Rosalind/Ganymede is all three.[9] For sixteenth- and seventeenth-century anti-theatrical polemicists, this multiplicity, this gender

---

a Rosalind?" *Journal of Dramatic Theory and Criticism* 2, no. 2 (Spring 1988): 41–52. Even the comparatively conservative reading given by Beckman must rely on the mystery of *discordia concors* to make sense of Rosalind as a "harmon[ious]" whole (46).

[7] On change, boys, and actors, see also Soule, "Subverting Rosalind," 131–32. Soule does not discuss Rosalind/Ganymede's own comment on this affinity, which includes women; see below.

[8] In addressing the complexities of Rosalind/Ganymede's gender performance, I focus on the performance conditions of the Elizabethan and Jacobean theater (i.e., boy actors as women) rather than those that prevail currently in North America and Europe. On the shifting dynamics of androgyny and of *As You Like It*, see Jan Kott, "The Gender of Rosalind," trans. Jadwiga Kosicka, *New Theatre Quarterly* 7, no. 26 (May 1991): 113–25.

[9] The scholarship on gender in *As You Like It* is too copious to be accounted for here, but some examples include: Janet Adelman, "Male Bonding in Shakespeare's Comedies," in *Renaissance Essays in Honor of C. L. Barber*, eds., Peter Erickson and Coppélia Kahn (Newark: University of Delaware Press, 1985), 73–103; Gilchrist Keel, "'Like Juno's Swans': Rosalind and Celia in *As You Like It*," *CCTE Studies* 56 (1991): 5–11; William Kerrigan, "Female Friends and Fraternal Enemies in *As You Like It*," in *Desire in the Renaissance*, eds., Valeria Finucci and Regina Schwartz (Princeton: Princeton University Press, 1994), 184–204; Leah Marcus, "Shakespeare's Comic Heroines, Elizabeth I, and the Political Uses of Androgyny," in *Women in the Middle Ages and Renaissance: Literary and Historical Perspectives*, ed., Mary Beth Rose (Syracuse: Syracuse University Press, 1986), 135–53; Susanne L. Wofford, "To You I Give Myself, For I Am Yours': Erotic Performance and Theatrical Performatives in *As You Like It*, in *Shakespeare Reread: The Texts in New Contexts*, ed. Russ McDonald (Ithaca: Cornell University Press, 1994, 147–69); Lisa Jardine, *Still Harping on Daughters: Women and Drama in the Age of Shakespeare* (Sussex: Harvester Press; Totowa, NJ: Barnes and Noble, 1983), 9–36; Lesley Anne Soule, "Subverting Rosalind: Cocky Ros in the Forest of Arden," *New Theatre Quarterly* 7 (1991): 126–36. On crossdressing, see Sedinger, "If Sight and Shape Be True," passim; Marta Powell Harley, "Rosalind, the Hare, and the Hyena in Shakespeare's *As You Like It*," *Shakespeare Quarterly* 36, no. 3 (Autumn 1985): 335–37; Nancy K. Hayles, "Sexual Disguise in *As You Like It* and *Twelfth Night*," *Shakespeare Survey* 32 (1979): 63–72; J. W. Binns, "Women or Transvestites on the Elizabethan Stage?: An Oxford Controversy," *Sixteenth Century Journal* 2 (1974): 95–120; M. C. Bradbrook, "Shakespeare and the Use of Disguise in Elizabethan Drama," *Essays in Criticism* 2 (1952): 159–68; F. H. Mares, "Viola and Other Transvestist Heroines in Shakespeare's Comedies," in *Stratford Papers, 1965–67*, ed., B. A. W. Jackson (Hamilton, Ont.: McMaster University Library Press, 1969): 96–109.

ambiguity, is subversive: actors, such polemicists argue, are nothing other than "sodomites." For all its offensiveness, this opprobrious term captures something of the hybrid state I am describing here. By naming the layered boy-woman-boy "Ganymede"—"Jove's own page" and an early modern euphemism for an object of homosexual desire (1.3.123)—this play embraces rather than rejects the charge of sodomy.[10] As a figure of ambiguous gender and desire, Rosalind/Ganymede identifies the actor's profession with a failure to abide by rules that govern stable gender identities; of this, the play constructs a separable "character." Character, identity, and gender are all destabilized as, in *As You Like It*, characters become the very gender-bending actors who portray them.[11]

Indeed, changeability is the characteristic that links Rosalind and Ganymede and also defines the actor's performance. Rosalind/Ganymede describes for Orlando how she cured another man of love melancholy:

> He was to imagine me his love, his mistress; and I set him every day to woo me. At which time would I, being but a moonish youth, grieve, be effeminate, changeable, longing and liking, proud, fantastical, apish, shallow, inconstant, full of tears, full of smiles; for every passion something, and for no passion truly anything, as boys and women are for the most part cattle of this colour—would now like him, now loathe him; then entertain him, then forswear him; now weep for him, then spit at him, that I drave my suitor from his mad humour of love to a living humour of madness, which was to forswear the full stream of the world and to live in a nook merely monastic.

Male actors—and, according to Coryate, female actors as well—are defined by their skill in evoking a series of contrasting passions. For "boys and women," however, such changeability is supposedly natural, a key element in a common gender identity. To behave like an actor, changing like Proteus from liking to loathing to entertaining to forswearing to weeping to spitting, is to behave like a woman. In Rosalind/Ganymede's case, "natural" changeability—"natural" for actor and character both—is identical with performance. What complicates this further is the fact that both changeable woman and changeable boy are objects of desire. The declared purpose of Rosalind/Ganymede's performance as Orlando's "love, his mistress" and as "moonish youth" is to cure him of sexual desire. The

---

[10]    Quotations from *As You Like It* follow *Oxford Complete Works*, 2nd ed., eds., Stanley Wells, Gary Taylor, et al. (Oxford: Clarendon Press, 2005).

[11]    Ko makes a similar point in *Mutability and Division on Shakespeare's Stage*, especially as regards the role of the boy-actor: "Let us for a moment stop considering Rosalind-in-disguise exclusively as a girl playing at being a man; let us rather visualize a boy-actor in-play as a woman *and* as a rollicking stage antic loosed by disguise who undercuts the interpretive codes on which role-playing depends. ...The ambidexterity of this figure, in my understanding, allows for a dynamic exchange between a psychologically real social character called Rosalind and an irrepressibly ebullient interlocutor whose theatrical outbursts bring alive the play's irreverent energy. This combined stage persona is the figure I call *charactor*" (85).

actual result, however, is the opposite. Orlando insists on making the charade a reality: "I can live no longer by thinking" (5.3.48), he tells the playacting Rosalind/ Ganymede. Orlando does not wish to end the game but to make it real. When Rosalind "magically" provides an acceptable, or acceptably clothed, object for his desire, she performs precisely the act feared and condemned by anti-theatrical polemicists: she transfers the gender-bending "sodomite" that is the boy actor from a play-world to a social context that, as the play's ending gives way to the epilogue, begins to look increasingly like the real world. The play produces a separable "character" out of the sexual qualities that anti-theatrical polemicists condemn in the actor. This is a subversive act both in gender and in theatrical terms.

## Proteus and the Sodomite

The antitheatricalists' two-pronged complaint against players and those who transgress gender roles is well known. Philip Stubbes, to take a familiar example, condemns

> Playes and Enterludes, where suche wanton gestures, such bawdie speeches: suche laughyng and flearyng: suche kissyng and bussyng: suche clippyng and culling: such winckyng and glauncing of wanton eyes, and the like is vsed, as is wonderfull to beholde. Then these goodly Pageantes beyng doen, euery mate sortes to his mate, euery one brynges an other homewarde of their waie very freendly, and in their secrete conclaues (couertly) thei plaie the Sodomits, or worse. And these be the fruits of Plaies and Enterludes, for the most part.[12]

For Stubbes, theatrical performance—the "goodly Pageantes" of the stage— inspires private, imitative performance. What is imitated is not just behavior—the "kissyng and bussyng...clippyng and culling" and "winckyng and glauncing of wanton eyes" practiced on the stage—but a role. Inspired by what they behold, spectators return home to "plaie the Sodomits." The "sodomite" embodied in the cross-dressing boy actor becomes a role, a playable character, not limited to the confines of the plot (or for that matter the stage or the theater) but escaping into private spaces.[13]

The behavior described as "sodomy" in this context is, of course, ambiguous. Many critics attest to the fact that what anti-theatrical polemicists or indeed law courts understood as "sodomy" was not limited to anal penetration or to the broader category of male homosexual behavior. Acts characterized as sodomy include both the legally defined "nonreproductive erotic acts," more specifically "penetration by the penis"; "carnal knowledge between men, between man and

---

[12]   Philip Stubbes, *Anatomy of Abuses* (London, 1583), sig. N4v–5r.

[13]   Keevak notes, following Goldberg, that "Stubbes's only other use of the term sodomites refers to adulterous husbands and wives, not to men alone," but for my purposes the ambiguous sex of these "mates" does not matter: as ambiguously gendered figures, they have more in common with Rosalind than not. "The Playing of Sodomy," 41.

beast, or between woman and beast"; idolatry; and theatricality.[14] In John Bale's "Thre lawes," for example, Sodomismus appears in company with Idolatry, a figure who switches genders: "sometime thou wert a he," an observer objects, to which she replies, "Yes, but now Ich am a she." The solution to this conundrum is that Idolatry cross-dresses:

> Then art thou like to Clisthenes,
> To Clodius and Euclides,
> Sardanapalus and Hercules
> Which themselves oft transformed
> Into a woman's likeness
> With agility and quickness;
> But they had Venus' sickness,
> As writers have declared.[15]

Both the costumes and the lovesickness adopted by these figures suggest that Idolatry herself is a sodomite, and it is to this that Sodomismus himself responds with desire. After hearing Idolatry declare her skill with "oil and holy water," Sodomismus can hardly restrain himself from "falling to mutton"—having sex with Idolatry on the stage.[16] Sodomismus himself works by inspiring both homosexual and heterosexual desire, voyeurism (Cham's "scorning" of his father Noah's nakedness), masturbation, idolatry, and bestiality.[17]

What sodomy amounts to is not a single, easily identifiable act but one among many, a multiplicity consonant with the character's costume:

> The fellow is well decked,
> Disguised, and well necked,
> Both knavebald and piepicked:
> He lacketh nothing but bells.[18]

"Disguised" as a priest, Sodomismus combines the (from a Protestant perspective) threatening hypocrisy of the Catholic Church with that of the stage. Even if notions of identity in the period allowed, such a broad "category of acts" as

---

[14]  Sedinger, "If Sight and Shape Be True," 75–6. On the epistemological problem of "sodomy," see also Alan Bray, *Homosexuality in Renaissance England* (London: Gay Men's Press, 1982); Gregory W. Bredbeck, *Sodomy and Interpretation: Marlowe to Milton* (Ithaca and London: Cornell University Press, 1991); Janet E. Halley, "Bowers v. Hardwick in the Renaissance," in *Queering the Renaissance*, ed., Jonathan Goldberg (Durham and London: Duke University Press, 1994), 15–39.

[15]  John Bale, "A comedy concernynge thre lawes, of nature, Moses, & Christ," in *The Dramatic Writings of John Bale*, ed., John S. Farmer (London: Early English Drama Society, 1907), 17–18.

[16]  Bale, "Thre lawes," 18, 19.

[17]  Bale, "Thre lawes," 21–22. See also Sedinger, "If Sight and Shape Be True," 76.

[18]  Bale, "Thre lawes," 23.

Sodomismus embodies could hardly be said to represent a single "character." But this is the figure given physical form by Sodomismus (and by Sodomismus's lusty relationship with the gender-bending Idolatry) and "play[ed]" by Stubbes's theatergoers. Stubbes does not allow even the indeterminate category of sodomy to remain closed: his friendly play-goers "play the sodomites, or worse"; what in Stubbes's judgment might be "worse" than a sodomite is left to the reader's imagination.[19]

But the fact that Stubbes imagines the "sodomite" (or worse) as a role that might be played complicates this view somewhat. Imagining "sodomite" as a theatrical role does not by any means contradict the prevailing reading of sodomy: a theatrical role is, for the most metatheatrically minded of Shakespeare's characters (or charactors), made up of "actions"—plural—"that a man might play," and correct playing consists in "suiting the action to the word, the word to the action" (*Hamlet* 1.2.84; 3.2.16–17).[20] While Hamlet evinces acertain distaste for the trappings of his first theatrical role, that of a melancholic mourner ("inky cloak," "dejected haviour of the visage," etc.; 1.2.77, 81), he also manages to perform that role, and he even manages to embody a role to which his playing skills initially seem less well fitted: that of revenger. His first attempts at this role are either misread or, even to himself, laughable. Polonius is determined and Claudius willing to believe his "antic disposition" (1.5.179) the result of love melancholy; and when, following the Player's speech, Hamlet tries on the revenger's ranting anger, he finds it untenable:

> Bloody, bawdy villain!
> Remorseless, treacherous, lecherous, kindless villain!
> O, vengeance!—
> Why, what an ass am I? Ay, sure, this is most brave,
> That I, the son of the dear murderèd,
> Prompted to my revenge by heaven and hell,
> Must, like a whore, unpack my heart with words
> And fall a-cursing like a very drab,
> A scullion! (2.2.582–90)[21]

Here, rather than inhabiting the role that his father's Ghost has assigned him, Hamlet switches from angry invective to self-criticizing commentary. Embodying

---

[19]   Stephen Orgel suggests that the one "worse" than a sodomite is "the passive partner in the act." *Impersonations: The Performance of Gender in Shakespeare's England* (Cambridge: Cambridge University Press, 1996), 159.

[20]   Sedinger's reading of Rosalind's cross-dressing culminates in a rejection of "a reading based on a depth-psychology model that might impute unconscious desires to either" Orlando or Phebe, both of whom, it has been speculated, "really" desire something outside the heteronormative marriage in which the play ultimately situates them. Alongside the "depth-psychology model," Sedinger implicitly rejects a character-based reading of the play. "If Sight and Shape Be True," 77.

[21]   Quotations from *Hamlet* follow the second edition of the *Oxford Complete Works*.

the contrasting passions with which London audiences were so impressed, Hamlet interrupts himself, unable to sustain the wrathful vein in which he begins. In part, this is a problem of character—that is, an inward disposition to go with all this "show": without the central required action of revenge, angry words suggest not a revenger but a female figure whom Hamlet variously describes as a "whore," a "very drab," or a "scullion." That is, when Hamlet attempts to create a coherent character, one who suits his actions and words to the central motivation of revenge, and when this characterization fragments, Hamlet's gender identity also becomes fragmented. The reading given in the *Second Quarto* further suggests that this inadequate impersonation results not only in a failure to suit the action to the word but also in a loss of gender coherence. In the *Second Quarto*, Hamlet is not a "scullion" (a menial female kitchen servant) but "a stallion": a male prostitute. Cursing like a whore, Hamlet, like Rosalind, becomes the very figure whom anti-theatrical polemicists condemn: a "stallion," a sodomite.[22]

Like Hamlet—with whom she is an almost exact contemporary, both plays having been written around 1600—Rosalind adopts a deliberately deceptive mode of behavior, a fictitious "character" defined not by stability or coherence but by changefulness and inconsistency. Hamlet puts on an "antic disposition"; Rosalind adopts the guise of a mercurial youth who then pretends to be an even more mercurial woman. Rosalind's "disposition"—a word she uses to describe her elusive gender identity—is, like Hamlet's, enigmatic. In her changefulness, Rosalind suggests the comic side of a model of acting described by Joseph Roach (and evoked by Hamlet) in which the ability successively to embody contrasting passions gradually develops into a total identification between actor and role. The ability to embody contrasting passions is associated in the period with the figure of Proteus (as in the celebration of Richard Burbage as a "delightful Proteus"); the identification between actor and role with fairy changelings. But even the Proteus metaphor suggests a kind of self-abandonment, "not only the power of self-alteration, but also the more mysterious Delphic power of self-abdication in favor of the role. ...[H]e who can assume any shape is in danger of losing his own."[23] As a "changeling Proteus," Rosalind epitomizes a kind of characterization

---

[22]     Ultimately, Hamlet does adopt both the action and the manner of a revenger. As he takes his revenge, Hamlet masters the same adjectival fury that earlier eluded him: "Here, thou incestuous, murd'rous, damnèd Dane, / Drink off this potion. Is thy union here? / Follow my mother!" (5.2.77–9) The questions surrounding Hamlet's motivation for revenge at this moment do not change the fact that Hamlet has adopted without self-criticism the language and mode of behavior that he rejected in earlier scenes—has become, by his own lights, the theatrical type known as a revenger.

[23]     Joseph Roach, *The Player's Passion: Studies in the Science of Acting* (Newark: University of Delaware Press; London: Associated University Presses, 1985), 41, 49. Roach finds the "changeling" metaphor first in the late seventeenth century; on the possibility that the metaphor is current in Elizabethan England and later, see my "Changeling Bottom: Speech Prefixes, Acting, and Character in *A Midsummer Night's Dream*," *Shakespeare* 4, no. 1 (March, 2008): 52–6.

defined not by depth and consistency but by multiplicity, changefulness, and a threatened loss of self that is also a transformation of bodily shape.[24] For Hamlet, identifying with multiple "characters" or roles (mourner, revenger) causes unease and even self-alienation: in the role of a mourner, he shrugs off the significance of his own behavior as a series of mimetic actions; experimenting with his new role as revenger, he imitates the passionate rhetoric of the player's speech but then loses countenance and interrupts himself, denying and destroying the effectiveness of his own characterization and falling into actorly sodomy. Rosalind, however, inhabits multiple roles, multiple emotional and social positions, both simultaneously and successively, with pleasure rather than self-criticism and (until the plot requires her to rein in her multiplicity) almost without a sense of conflict. Further, Protean imagery abounds in her self-characterizations.[25] "Playing the sodomit[e]," Rosalind/Ganymede inhabits an ambiguous physical form that changes seamlessly from one passion to another, from one gender to another. To Hamlet, a loss of gender coherence is reason for self-condemnation. It is no mistake that, when Hamlet accidentally becomes a whore and a stallion, he is attempting to embody a figure who could not be more monolithic in his heteronormative masculinity. Laertes, the more efficient revenger, prepares himself for his role in part by purging every last bit of gender ambiguity from his makeup—or at least attempting to do so, as when he insists while weeping for his sister that "[w]hen these [tears] are gone, / The woman will be out" (4.7.161–2). But for Rosalind, gender ambiguity is a source of pleasure.

## Gendering the "Person Personated"

Hamlet and Rosalind both act a part. In both cases, there is some question as to whether the adopted character is natural or false, and in both cases, the question derives from the fact that actions are at best an equivocal indicator of inward disposition. An act, like a performance, may be real or false, an "act" or one among many "actions that a man might play."[26] The tired question of whether Hamlet's madness is real or feigned speaks to the real difficulty of the epistemological problem presented by Hamlet's mad actions; the related question of identity in

---

[24] For Thomas Heywood in the *Apology for Actors*, to take an early instance, the rhetorician's "action" consists not only of "a naturall and a familiar motion of the head, the hand, the body," but also "a moderate and fit countenance sutable to all the rest"; by such changes in physicality, the actor must "qualifie euery thing according to the nature of the person personated." Thomas Heywood, *An apology for actors Containing three briefe treatises. 1 Their antiquity. 2 Their ancient dignity. 3 The true vse of their quality* (London, 1612), sig. C4r.

[25] Ko also characterizes Rosalind's "wit" as protean. See *Mutability and Division on Shakespeare's Stage*, 83.

[26] On the double nature of the word "performance," see Diana Taylor, "Translating Performance," *Profession* (2002): 44–50.

Rosalind's case is reflected in her obsession with gender-significant clothing, on the one hand, and the state and reactions of her own body on the other. (Hamlet is also concerned with his clothing, which indeed for him is among the "actions" whose potential falseness he derides and which is central to the play's notions of identity: in the play's first moments, the sentry's challenge is a clothing metaphor, "Stand and unfold yourself" [1.1.2].[27]) It is difficult, however, to identify either the "truth" of the body or the "falseness" of clothing with character or actor; these categories overlap for Rosalind as they do for Hamlet.

The practice of costuming is, of course, a key part of the perceived "hypocrisy" of the theater and becomes especially problematic in the case of crossdressing boy actors. Thomas Heywood defends the practice of crossdressing on the grounds that costume is a penetrable disguise:

> To do as the Sodomites did, vse preposterous lusts in preposterous habits, is in that text [i.e., the Bible] flatly and seuerely forbidden: nor can I imagine any man, that hath in him any taste or relish of Christianity, to be guilty of so abhorred a sinne. ...[N]or do I hold it lawfull to beguile the eyes of the world in confounding the shapes of either sex, as to keepe any youth in the habit of a virgin, or any virgin in the shape of a lad, to shroud them from the eyes of their fathers, tutors, or protectors, or to any other sinister intent whatsoeuer. But to see our youths attired in the habit of women, who knowes not what their intents be? who cannot distinguish them by their names, assuredly knowing, they are but to represent such a Lady, at such a time appoynted?[28]

Backwards or "preposterous" clothing and actions are to be condemned, Heywood suggests; actors' costumes are not, because they are not accompanied by sexual behavior that reverses gender roles or bodily positions for the male participants. (The "pre-post-erous" pun, suggesting the perceived reversal of male sexual submission, is a common one.) Heywood dismisses the charge of sodomy and focuses on the less common charge that female costumes are tantamount to disguise and specifically to the kind of disguise meant to fool "fathers, tutors, or protectors"—the very authority figures so often gulled by cross-dressed female characters on the stages of early modern London. The charge against which Heywood defends the theater is, in effect, that the boy actors in female costumes are doing what female characters often do: just as Rosalind's "doublet and hose" prevent her father and her lover from recognizing her and her true gender, so the audience will be unable correctly to read the gender or social identity of a cross-dressed boy actor. Heywood argues rather that the costume is merely incidental: we know the actors' "intents" and can even "distinguish them by their names"; moreover, we know that the disguise is only a temporary expedient, part of a play to be staged "at such a time appoynted." In Heywood's reading, actors are always

---

[27]   Quotations from *Hamlet* follow the third-series Arden edition of the 1604 *Quarto*, eds., Ann Thompson and Neil Taylor (London: Thomson Learning, 2006).

[28]   Heywood, *Apology*, sig. C3r–v.

legible as actors, and there is a clear division between the "assuredly know[n]" male gender of the actor and the temporary, costumed gender of the represented "Lady." This distinction prevents theatrical crossdressing from becoming "preposterous," either in terms of propriety or in sexual terms. The "character," as such, is a flimsy expedient; the actor is what is really important: he's the one whose name is recalled by the audience; the "Lady" is just a nameless lady. But the actual dynamics of cross-dressing in the Elizabethan and Jacobean theater render such simple binary divisions untenable.[29] Costumed character and actor are not nearly as easy to distinguish as Heywood makes out, nor can the "sodomite"'s crossdressing be so easily distinguished from the cross-dressing of the actor.

Rosalind does not adopt a single gender identity along with her male-gendered clothing. Primarily this is a function of her onstage audience and their degrees of initiation into the secret of her "true" gender.[30] While she is "suit[ed] ...all points like a man" (1.3.115), Rosalind sometimes "passes" for a man, sometimes does not. In her first appearance as Ganymede, Rosalind stands outside her own gender performance both as boy and as woman: "I could find in my heart to disgrace my man's apparel and to cry like a woman. But I must comfort the weaker vessel, as doublet and hose ought to show itself courageous to a petticoat; therefore, courage, good Aliena!" (2.4.3–8). Rosalind/Ganymede's gender performance consists of two deliberate and opposite possibilities: "cry[ing] like a woman" and behaving with the courage appropriate to "man's apparel" or "doublet and hose." The simile ("like a woman") already begins to suggest the winking interplay of natural and performed characteristics that will become Rosalind's and Ganymede's identity. She/he does not present tears as a natural reaction—what a woman, because biologically female, could not help but produce—or even as a reaction that must be suppressed. Crying "like a woman" is merely one of a number of options, all of them apparently to be "f[ou]nd" in Rosalind's "heart." The heart—which one might expect to be a source of a more stable, less ambiguously gendered, identity—is the location for performance options, not inward truths. Since crying does not match the preferred gender of the moment, another option must be chosen. Weeping, like any other gender signifier, is a "like[ness]," an imitation. (That crying on cue is an actor's skill is indicated by the advice given to Bartholomew the page in the Induction to *The Taming of the Shrew*. The page is told to "bear himself with honourable action / Such as he hath observed in noble ladies / Unto their lords," and one part of this "honourable action" is tears: "And if the boy have not a woman's gift / To rain a shower of commanded tears, / An onion will do well for such a shift, / Which, in a napkin being close conveyed, / Shall in despite force a watery eye" [*The Taming of the Shrew*, "Induction," 108-110, 122–26].) Rather than "find[ing] it in [her/his] heart to cry like a woman," Rosalind/Ganymede

---

[29]   On the epistemology of cross-dressing, see Sedinger, "If Sight and Shape Be True," passim.

[30]   On the epistemological significance of Rosalind's different onstage audiences, see Sedinger, "If Sight and Shape Be True," 74–5.

extracts the "courage" appropriate to her/his clothing. The clothing is mentioned twice, by way of emphasis. But if Rosalind/Ganymede is defined at this moment by her/his "man's apparel," Celia/Aliena is represented in equally artificial terms. She is "petticoat" to Ganymede's "doublet and hose," her female gender as much a matter of clothing in this metonymic construction as is Rosalind/Ganymede's. Doublet, hose, petticoat, and courage are *all* a matter of "show" in this moment.

But whether Rosalind contrasts her clothing with something "within which passeth show" (*Hamlet* 1.2.85) is less clear. The "doublet and hose" motif recurs as a marker of gender performance and gender identity, especially in the gender-performance-straining context of heterosexual love: "Good my complexion! Dost thou think, though I am caparisoned like a man, I have a doublet and hose in my disposition?" (3.2.190–192) Rosalind asks, impatient at Celia's delay in revealing the identity of the man who has been posting love poems around the forest. In one sense, Rosalind's "complexion" reveals her inner "disposition"—female, when the context suggests a return to heteronormativity now that a potential male partner has entered the forest—while clothing does not. But the suggestion that Celia might expect to find Rosalind's male clothing contained in her "disposition" makes it more difficult to separate this putative stable gendered identity from the gender roles that Rosalind impersonates. When the word "disposition" appears again in the play, it is as a marker of a changeable and put-on "character" rather than an authentic inward state: "[N]ow I will be your Rosalind in a more coming-on disposition," she tells Orlando (4.1.105–106). For Robert Burton, similarly, "disposition" is a transient rather than a lasting state: "*Melancholy* ... [i]n Disposition, is that transitory *Melancholy*, which goes and comes vpon every small occasion of sorrow, neede, sicknesse, trouble, feare, griefe, passion, or perturbation of the Minde[.]" Burton contrasts this "disposition" with the lasting and pathological melancholy of "Habite."[31] While the *OED* defines "disposition" primarily as a *permanent* mental or physical state, and does not give any instances before the eighteenth century in which "disposition" indicates a temporary "mood" or "humour,"[32] it seems that Burton, at least, uses the word to mean precisely that. Rosalind's "disposition" seems to include both an inward and authentic gender identity and an actorly construction of gender identity through clothing—a doubleness that also infects Hamlet's use of the word. Again, while Rosalind's blush, which indicates her female "disposition," seems like the mark of an unfeigned femininity, it is in fact a reaction constructed by the actor.

When she hears that the verse-writer is Orlando, her reaction is also bound up with her clothing: "Alas the day, what shall I do with my doublet and hose?" (214–215) This moment is a crisis in the plot: having assumed male clothing,

---

    [31]    Robert Burton, *The anatomy of melancholy vvhat it is. VVith all the kindes, causes, symptomes, prognostickes, and seuerall cures of it. In three maine partitions with their seuerall sections, members, and subsections. Philosophically, medicinally, historically, opened and cut vp. By Democritus Iunior. With a satyricall preface, conducing to the following discourse* (Oxford, 1621), sig. A8v.

    [32]    *OED*, "disposition," 7b; emphasis added.

Rosalind finds herself playing a male role in the presence of a potential male lover. But rather than abandoning her "doublet and hose"—either to reveal the body underneath (which would collapse the illusion of female gender, since the body belongs to a male actor) or to replace doublet and hose with clothing appropriate to a woman (which would continue the illusion)—Rosalind chooses rather to layer her gender performance with yet another gender, making complex erotic play out of what is now unmistakably actorly "sodomy."

Whether Orlando's reported description of Rosalind as a boy "[o]f female favor" who "bears himself / Like a ripe sister" (4.3.87–8) suggests that he recognizes her as a woman—always a question students ask about this play—or whether this adjectival femininity is a remnant of her impersonation of "Rosalind" remains unclear. That is, while on one level Rosalind/Ganymede's performance of the character of "Rosalind" collapses the intervening character of Ganymede and reveals Rosalind's "real" identity along with her "real" gender, on another level this "Rosalind" suggests that the original Rosalind is also a matter of performance. This, too, is a product of Rosalind's elaborate gender performance for Orlando's benefit: "Nay, you must call me Rosalind" (3.2.418). To call Rosalind "Rosalind" in this context is both to call her by her "true" name and to call her by a name that Rosalind/Ganymede attaches to a new, composite character.

The discussion among Orlando, Rosalind, and Celia about "Rosalind"'s likely actions gradually elaborates not one but a series of "Rosalinds," each of whom both is and is not the palimpsest Rosalind/Ganymede/Rosalind:

> *Orlando*: Virtue is no hornmaker, and my Rosalind is virtuous.

> *Rosalind*: And I am your Rosalind.

> *Celia*: It pleases him to call you so; but he hath a Rosalind of a better leer than you.

> *Rosalind*: Come, woo me, woo me, for now I am in a holiday humour, and like enough to consent. What would you say to me now an I were your very, very Rosalind? …Am I not your Rosalind?

> *Orlando*: I take some joy to say you are because I would be talking of her.

> *Rosalind*: Well, in her person I say I will not have you.

> . . . . . . . . . . . . . . . . . . . . . . . . . . . . . . . . . . . . . . . . . . . . . . . . . . . . . . .

> *Orlando*: I would not have my right Rosalind of this mind, for I protest her frown might kill me.

> *Rosalind*: By this hand, it will not kill a fly. But come, now I will be your Rosalind in a more coming-on disposition; and ask me what you will, I will grant it. …No, no, Orlando, men are April when they woo, December when they wed. Maids are May when they are maids, but the sky changes when they are wives. I will be more jealous of thee than a Barbary cock-pigeon over his hen,

more clamorous than a parrot against rain, more newfangled than an ape, more giddy in my desires than a monkey. I will weep for nothing, like Diana in the fountain, and I will do that when you are disposed to be merry. I will laugh like a hyena, and that when thou art inclined to sleep.

*Orlando*: But will my Rosalind do so?

*Rosalind*: By my life, she will do as I do. (4.1.59–68, 83–7, 102–106, 138–50)

The sheer number of versions of "Rosalind" in this exchange is bewildering. There is the "Rosalind" whom the audience knows to be speaking these lines and "Ganymede" who in the fiction of the moment speaks them; as well as the "Rosalind" whom he pretends to be, but there is also "my Rosalind," "my right Rosalind," "your Rosalind," "your very, very Rosalind," "your Rosalind in a more coming-on disposition," Rosalind "now ...in a holiday humour," and "a Rosalind of a better leer than you." (Here, Rosalind's "disposition" is unmistakably temporary and actorly.[33]) Orlando's attempts to understand this elaborate performance are muddled: "Will *my* Rosalind do so?" he asks, attempting to differentiate between the Rosalinds the conversation has created and the Rosalind he maintains as an ideal. Orlando's idealized "Rosalind" is not the "real" Rosalind any more than is the flighty "Rosalind" created by Rosalind/Ganymede for Orlando's benefit. The very notion of a "real" Rosalind seems less and less tenable as the scene progresses, particularly since the only one who insists on the absolute authenticity of his "Rosalind"—Orlando—is imagining a Rosalind who least resembles the figure onstage who sometimes bears that name.[34]

The animal analogies further emphasize Rosalind's changefulness and even suggest that she lacks a coherent species, let alone gender. One of the animals to which she compares "Rosalind" was thought to be a hermaphrodite (the hyena);[35] a pair of animals (the "Barbary cock-pigeon" and "his hen") reverses the presumed future gender relationship between Rosalind and Orlando, casting Orlando as the hen to Rosalind's cock. These "preposterous" reversals keep the sexual implications of Rosalind/Ganymede's multiplicity clearly in view. The implications for Rosalind's gender identity are not, however, the only point of this series of analogies. As, in turn, a male pigeon, a parrot, an ape, a monkey, the goddess Diana, and a hyena, Rosalind is precisely Protean. These changes are not

---

[33] The *OED* includes Rosalind's "coming-on disposition" under definition 7a, "state or quality of being disposed, inclined, or 'in the mind' (*to* something, *to do* something)," a definition which suggests the temporary quality of her "disposition" in this moment.

[34] For an argument that male actor and playwright cause Rosalind the (female) character to disappear, see Green, "The 'Unexpressive She.'"

[35] On Rosalind's self-comparisons to hares and hyenas—both proverbially non-heteronormative and possibly hermaphroditic, bisexual, or homosexual figures—see Marta Powell Harley, "Rosalind, the Hare, and the Hyena in Shakespeare's *As You Like It*," *Shakespeare Quarterly* 36, no. 3 (Autumn1985): 335–37.

literal animal transformations, of course, but the fact that the analogy glancingly suggests that Rosalind is going to turn into a series of different animals (and one goddess) gives her changing passions a Protean cast. Changing in her passions, Rosalind is not just a Proteus figure but the "delightful Proteus" that is the actor, a creature of constant and unstable transformation whose changefulness, in this case, is a product of her/his gender identity both as boy and as woman.

This double awareness must be borne in mind when considering the "revelation" of Rosalind's gender identity in the penultimate act. From one perspective, by fainting at the sight of the "bloody napkin," Rosalind reveals her true biological sex. Oliver seems to express doubt about her gender identity:

> Be of good cheer, youth. You a man? You lack a man's heart.
>
> *Rosalind*: I do so, I confess it. Ah, sirrah, a body will think this was well counterfeited. I pray you, tell your brother how well I counterfeited. Heigh-ho!
>
> *Oliver*: This was not counterfeit. There is too great testimony in your complexion that it was a passion of earnest.
>
> *Rosalind*: Counterfeit, I assure you.
>
> *Oliver*: Well then, take a good heart, and counterfeit to be a man.
>
> *Rosalind*: So I do; but, i'faith, I should have been a woman by right.
>
> *Celia*: Come, you look paler and paler. Pray you, draw homewards. Good sir, go with us.
>
> *Oliver*: Thatwill I, for I must bear answer back
> How you excuse my brother, Rosalind.
>
> *Rosalind*: I shall devise something. But I pray you commend my counterfeiting to him. Will you go? (4.3.165–83)

Especially since it involves a faint that is read as being opposed to martial masculinity, Rosalind's "counterfeit" evokes the counterfeit death of Falstaff in *1 Henry IV*. Fainting itself is a performance, a fact ironically revealed in Rosalind's insistence that her reaction was "counterfeit," just as Falstaff's "counterfeit" death, performed as it is next to the "truly" dead Hotspur, suggests the falseness of all stage deaths. In both cases, it is not possible to sort out a binary opposition between "counterfeit" and natural behavior and thus between false "acts" and true actions, between playacting and action that is not done in play. As a character gendered female, Rosalind herself does not counterfeit fainting, but she does counterfeit adolescent masculinity. The boy actor playing Rosalind does, however, counterfeit to faint, just as, being a boy, he may "counterfeit to be a man"—that is, an adult male rather than an adolescent. The counterfeit faint must at least on some level seem real; in fact, the implied stage direction calls for the same display of actorly skill that attracts Polonius's admiration for the Player in *Hamlet*, a change of color. Changing color is what marks Rosalind/Ganymede as something other than the man she "counterfeits" to be: "This was not counterfeit. There is too great testimony in your complexion that it was a passion of earnest." Coloring is a mark of authenticity, both for the "passion" that moves Rosalind/Ganymede in this moment and, by implication here and explicitly elsewhere, for Rosalind/Ganymede's "true" female gender. Celia notes earlier that Rosalind blushes when Orlando's name is mentioned, and Rosalind offers this fact as evidence of her female "disposition." But the facts are that the change of color, like weeping, is an actorly skill (and the skill of "hypocritical"—acting—women) and that the actor in this case is not a woman but a boy. If he "should have been a woman by rights," this shape-changing boy only speaks to his own skill in transformation. Fainting and turning pale at this moment, he changes in his passions just as the Protean actor is meant to change. Unlike Proteus, however, he also changes gender. He is not just hawk, then hound, then bear, like the Puck in *A Midsummer Night's Dream* (another Proteus figure), but male "cock-pigeon," then parrot, then ape, then monkey, then female goddess, then ambiguously gendered hyena. In this changeful state, his gender ambiguity and his actorly skill are one and the same.

The plot demands, finally, that Rosalind's "true" character and true gender be revealed. How to reveal her true gender identity presents difficulties. Celia's solution is more conundrum than anything else: "You have simply misused our sex in your love-prate. We must have your doublet and hose plucked over your head, and show the world what the bird hath done to her own nest" (4.1.191–94). In the scene of revelation that Celia proposes, Rosalind's clothing takes on a double role: the "doublet and hose" are of course male, but the act by which they are removed and the underlying body revealed would be more appropriate for the skirts worn by a woman. Neither doublet nor hose can be with any comfort "plucked over [the] head"; even if this could be accomplished, the body thus revealed would be that of a young man rather than a woman. The act of revelation thus preserves the ambiguity it claims to remove.

To resolve her gender indeterminacy and engineer a comic ending, Rosalind requires not just riddles but also magic and even a literal *deus ex machina*. Even the poetry of Hymen, however, is not without its surprises in the earliest printed texts of the play:

> *Hymen from Heauen brought her*
> *Yea brought her hether.*
> *That thou mightst ioyne his hand with his,*
> *Whose heart within his bosome is.*[36]

The magical or divine solution to Rosalind's gender indeterminacy becomes instead a textual crux: the daughter, clearly female in the first lines—the pronoun

---

[36]   *Mr. VVilliam Shakespeares comedies, histories, & tragedies Published according to the true originall copies* (London, 1623), sig. S1v; emphasis added.

"her" is repeated—switches gender in the final line.[37] Joined together are not a "he" and a "she" but "his hand" and "his hand." The crux is "resolved" by nearly all editors so that the hands joined in marriage belong to a man and a woman, but the fact remains that in the text as given, Hymen directs the Duke to join two men in holy matrimony.

The play's resolution, finally, is encapsulated in Rosalind's and Touchstone's word "if": "I'll marry you if ever I marry woman, and I'll be married tomorrow" (5.2.107–109); "Much virtue in 'if'" (5.4.100–101).[38] Touchstone's disquisition on the word "if" allows Rosalind the time to change into the clothing that allows her/him to be legible as female. "If" shapes character not as a coherent whole but as a series of suppositions. Even at the end of the play, Rosalind need not wholly embrace any of her multiple identities; rather, she must merely (and temporarily!) assume one that will allow the plot to conclude.

"If" takes us to the epilogue, where Rosalind/Ganymede escapes the borders of the plot not merely as actor but as the layered and successive combination of characters and actor, male and female, reality and representation:

> It is not the fashion to see the lady the epilogue; but it is no more unhandsome than to see the lord the prologue. ...I am not furnished like a beggar, therefore to beg will not become me. My way is to conjure you; and I'll begin with the women. I charge you, O women, for the love you bear to men, to like as much of the play as please you. And I charge you, O men, for the love you bear to women—as I perceive by your simpering none of you hates them—that between you and the women the play may please. If I were a woman I would kiss as many of you as had beards that pleased me, complexions that like me, and breaths that I defied not. And I am sure, as many as have good beards, or good faces, or sweet breaths will for my kind offer, when I make curtsy, bid me farewell. (Epi.1–3, 9–21)

The character's indeterminate gender becomes shorthand, in this final moment, for the unclear boundary between character and actor. This actor's appearance after the play has been completed is a transgression against social but also theatrical decorum: "It is not the fashion to see the lady the epilogue"—that is, "in the person of the Epilogue." Even the Epilogue loses any precise gender identity as the boy actor acknowledges his character's gender (or the first gender he has impersonated, at any rate) but—in a sleight of hand rarely acknowledged in readings of this speech—entirely fails to state whether "the lady" is now speaking. The actor simply acknowledges that Epilogues are not usually played by ladies. The speech prefix to the epilogue is "Rosalind," but of course her identity, gendered and otherwise,

---

[37]    Ko suggests that the unexpected male pronoun is a cue for Rosalind to unmask and show that Rosalind is in fact the boy Ganymede. *Mutability and Division on Shakespeare's Stage*, 88.

[38]    See Sedinger, "If Sight and Shape Be True," 72–3; Maura Slattery Kuhn, "Much Virtue in *If*," *Shakespeare Quarterly* 28 (1977): 40–50.

has been muddied throughout the play. Similarly, the Epilogue speaks from a radically ambiguous gender identity. Not only does the ambiguously gendered, multiplicitous Rosalind reappear after her gender identity has supposedly been resolved by marriage to Orlando, but she (or he) reappears in yet another character, equally if not more ambiguous in gender terms. The Epilogue may or may not be the play's "lady" but certainly is no longer a "woman"—or is far enough from being easily identifiable as a woman that her (or his) femininity can be dismissed or winkingly reinvoked with an "if." Which gendered form of "curtsy" the actor would have made is not specified. ("Curtsy" was not then an exclusively female term.[39]) Does he make a male bow that reinforces the speaker's denial of female gender but jars with the gown he is now wearing (or is he still wearing the gown? Prospero, in another famous epilogue, traditionally has started to remove his costume), or does he make a female curtsy appropriate to the clothing but not to the speaker's refusal to kiss men? This figure retains enough of the role of "Rosalind" to recall her self-declared status as a magician and to "conjure" the audience to be pleased with the play. But at the same time the actor is very much visible. As the actor's gender becomes the subject of discussion, so does the (gender) difference between the actor and the character. The easy binary opposition of male actor and female character, however, cannot be maintained while that teasing "if" remains.

A "delightful Proteus," Rosalind/Ganymede constructs character from the changeful materials of the actor's craft: not only quickly changing passions but also quickly changing gender. The mark of actorly skill—the ability quickly to change from one thing to the next—is explicitly linked in this play to the feature of the actor most feared and condemned by anti-theatrical polemicists: his sexual attractiveness and his lack of allegiance to a coherent gender identity. As Proteus, Rosalind/Ganymede is also a "sodomite." Like the "sodomites" who perform their role outside the public space of the theater, Rosalind/Ganymede escapes the plot of the play in which she/he originates. Her escape from the plot resembles that of clowns and others who stand apart from the representational *locus* of early modern theater and step into the presentational *platea* to interact directly with the audience. But her escape from representation is deeply bound up with the mechanics of the represented world, even if only in opposition to them. In *The Merchant of Venice*, *Twelfth Night*, but especially in *As You Like It*, crossdressing—and the "charactors" it produces—allows audiences and characters alike to toy with the idea of other endings than marriage. Complex gender identities are key among the many factors in Shakespeare's comedies that work against the easy conclusion of the comic plot. Any character who engages in gender play, then, has every opportunity to be more than simply a structural, plot-based expedient. The comic plot seeks to focus wandering desires on a single, heterosexual, marital object; cross-dressing, like other forms of mistaken and layered identity, redirects and (by the rules of the comic plot) misdirects desire. While the plot resolves Rosalind's multiplicity into one socially-conservative function, the complex figure that is Rosalind/Ganymede

---

[39]   Kott assumes that it is. See "The Gender of Rosalind," 113.

actually escapes the plot, emerging after the play has concluded to reassert her/his gender ambiguity, her/his Protean and "sodomite" character.

For Joseph Roach, the actor's changeable passions lay the groundwork for coherent characterization, a "self-abdication in favor of the role" that is at once admirable and dangerous to the actor's own identity. Roach's argument provides a partial answer, *avant la lettre*, to the position taken by Tiffany Stern and others that the celebration of changing passions by early modern theatergoers indicates that coherent characterization was neither sought nor achieved by early modern actors.[40] The figure of the "sodomite," a separable character "play[ed]" not only on the stage but beyond it, emphasizes the centrality of gender and sexuality to such threatening self-transformations. (Roach does not include gender in his survey of early modern protean acting.) For early modern observers, acting introduces not just Protean change but a potential change in the (not then entirely fixed) categories of sex and sexuality.

---

[40] See Tiffany Stern, *Rehearsal from Shakespeare to Sheridan* (Oxford: Clarendon Press, 2000), 64; see also my "Changeling Bottom," 58–9.

# Chapter 13
# "Stops" in the Name of Love: Playing Typological Iago

## Travis Curtright

The critical argument over early modern acting styles originates with the distinction between "naturalism" and "formalism," an opposition that I would like to dispute by examining how Iago may be played as a type character.[1] The influence of typological character—passing through Menander, Plautus, Terence, and Cicero to poets in early modern England—has long been recognized, an influence that comes not only from playwrights, but also from classical rhetoric, its figures of speech, and a variety of ethical or poetic treatises.[2] So, too, we are assured that characters based on early modern social roles, allegory, or types do not possess the "interiority" or "subjectivity" often attributed to them.[3] "Types" are not sufficiently "rounded" or multidimensional to capture a Hamlet or an Iago. If Shakespeare began with types, he must have transformed them, "stretching character," creating

---

[1]    "The critical debate about early-modern acting styles," writes Yu Jin Ko, *Mutability and Division on Shakespeare's Stage* (Newark: University of Delaware Press, 2004), 42–3, "still largely centers on, but remains divided about, the question of whether the acting leaned more or less towards one of the two poles labeled long ago as 'naturalism' and 'formalism,' though related if not entirely interchangeable binary oppositions between 'inwardness' and 'rhetorical character,' 'representation' and 'presentation,' or 'identification' and 'alienation' come into play as well."

[2]    On Theophrastus' relation to classical rhetoric, and influence upon Shakespeare's England, see Benjamin Boyce, *The Theophrastan Character in England to 1642* (Cambridge: Harvard University Press, 1947), 11–52; on figures and character, see Charles McDonald, *Rhetoric of Tragedy* (Amherst: The University of Massachusetts Press, 1966), 87, 33n, who points out how grammar school exercises in *ethopoeia* are sufficient to present the idea of type. For a reading of a poetic treatise with reference to character, see my "Sidney's Defense of Poetry: Ethos and the Ideas," *Ben Jonson Journal* 10 (2003): 101–115, where I address rhetorical and poetic objectives of type in Sidney's articulation of "character" and the "ideas."

[3]    See Francis Barker, *The Tremulous Private Body* (New York: Methuen, 1984), 24–5, 31–2, 52, 59, 68; Catherine Belsey, *The Subject of Tragedy: Identity and Difference in Renaissance Drama* (New York: Methuen, 1985), 18, 26–34, 40; on roles over individual identity, Beatrice Gottlieb, *The Family in the Western World from the Black Death to the Industrial Age* (New York: Oxford University Press, 1993), 262.

a space for later and more complex representations of "subjectivity."[4] Hence, how one plays a character indicates how one theorizes character, but more particularly, the implication that type should be considered distinct from more individual and natural portrayals.

Even so, I will argue that type as an indication of rhetorical or formal acting style does not adequately account for how type may be performed. "Modern concepts," argues Edward Burns, "like 'the stereotype'" or "E.M. Forster's 'flat characters'" involve a misunderstanding of the ancient traditions out which typology emerges. Burns writes of the ancient "character sketch" that it "derives from its schematization of the social codes of character—dress codes, typical behavior, common physical types, and so on—a flexible basis for the articulation of character as social interaction, as implicated in the knowledge of a particular world."[5] As a flexible basis for the portrayal of specific traits, I will argue a performance of type need not be "rhetorical," but can be natural, even like our more modern notions of character. To show how type character may be played with a natural acting style, I will sketch one possible realization of the flatterer type by retracing the links between Plutarch's description of a flatterer and how that account could function as a resource for playing Iago. By first examining Shakespeare's Iago in light of Plutarch's description of a flatterer, and then reviewing how figures of "auricular defect"—"stops" or pauses—could aid a performance of 3.3, I will propose playing Iago according to type *and* in a natural acting style. Though "stops" are part of the conventional rhetoric of flatterers, even a strategy of "dilation" crucial to the play's narrative, they correspond with the later, distinctly modern directions for playing Iago written by Edwin Booth and even to more contemporary accounts. These resonances will suggest how oratorical conventions may contribute to a naturalistic performance.[6] Playing Iago

---

[4]    For Catherine Belsey, *Ibid.*, 32–3, "the half century before the revolution" presents the "intersection of the two modes, illusionist and emblematic," with Shakespearean characters like Iago "moving between the two modes." Similarly, E.A.J. Honigmann, *Shakespeare: Seven Tragedies Revisited: The Dramatist's Manipulation of Response* (Palgrave: New York, 2002), writes:

> Placing his tragic hero upon the rack, and thus making him act against his nature (as it was previously exhibited), Shakespeare achieved an effect that we may observe in his other plays as well. All the complex comic characters behave incongruously, from Petruchio's Kate to Caliban, as do the tragic heroes: arriving on the literary scene just as English drama advanced from Faustus, from type to individual, Shakespeare stretched character by exploring its inexhaustible diversity, and so prepared the way for later pluralistic theories. (13)

Though Belsey and Honigmann have very different approaches, both believe a more modern sense of character emerges from type, especially by deviation from it.

[5]    Edward Burns, *Character: Acting and Being on the Pre-Modern Stage* (New York: St. Martin's Press, 1990), 32.

[6]    On the significance of "stops," see Patricia Parker, "Shakespeare and Rhetoric: 'dilation' and 'delation' in *Othello*," in *Shakespeare and the Question of Theory*, eds. Patricia Parker and Geoffrey Hartman (London: Routledge, 1985), 54–74

according to type, in other words, may be both "formal" and "natural" because the assumed differences between rhetorical and more modern notions of character seem reconcilable in the flatterer figure.

## I.

In locating an important source behind the character of Iago, Paul Jorgensen recommends that Iago's "honesty" be looked for in "the widespread and urgent Elizabethan problem: How may one know the honest man from the knave?"[7] Warnings about knaves, dissemblers, and flatterers often particularly described their tactics, providing an itinerary of identifiable traits, which Iago would seem to represent. More recently, Robert Evans has focused attention on Iago in light of Plutarch's distinction between flatterers and true friends from Philemon Holland's translation of Plutarch's essay on how "To Discern a Flatterer from a Friend."[8] Rather than simply identifying the flatterer with comely, ingratiating speech, Plutarch amplifies the similarities between a true friend and a flatterer who plays one. It is a "hard matter" to "discern a flatterer from a friend" because it appears "there is no difference between them."[9] Plutarch means there is no difference in outward behavior, for the "right flatterer" is covert, "his own craftmaster, and can skill how to handle the matter artificially" (41).[10]

That assessment of covert sycophancy corresponds with other depictions in which the flatterer possesses what Christy Desmet calls the capacity to use "effectively the gestures and props of an actor," thereby playing a friend or advisor in a credible manner. Indeed, the flatterer's ability to deceive contributed to an

---

[7]    Paul A. Jorgensen, "Honesty in Othello," *Studies in Philology* 47 (1950): 557–67, 557. In a note, Jorgensen writes "Probably the most nearly definite usage of honest or honest man was in its habitual antithesis to knave. Cf. Wilson's *The Pedlar's Prophecy* (1595)" (557). To Jorgensen's *Pedlar*, Robert Evans adds eight books that are written before 1600, which "include essays dealing with character-types relevant to the issues of flattery, false friendship, true friendship, and how to distinguish a flatterer from a friend." Robert Evans, "Flattery in Shakespeare's *Othello*: The Relevance of Plutarch and Sir Thomas Elyot," *Comparative Drama* 35 (2001): 1–41, 39n.

[8]    In proposing Holland's Plutarch as a source text for Shakespeare's *Othello*, Evans argues: "It is possible, in fact, that Holland's translation may have been in existence several years earlier than this date of publication [1603] would suggest, since a version of the text was entered on the Stationers' Register on 18 April 1600 by the publisher W. Ponsonby, while the same translation was later entered on the Register on 5 July 1602 by G. Bishop and others. When the book finally did appear in print in 1603, the publisher was A. Hatfield. It seems possible, then, that Holland's translation may have existed in manuscript several years before it finally appeared in print. Indeed, it may have existed in manuscript at least four years before our first recorded performance of *Othello* in November 1604" (3).

[9]    Here and throughout I quote from *Plutarch's Moralia: Twenty Essays translated by Philemon Holland*, ed. E.H. Blakeney (London: Dent, 1911). For the lines cited, see p. 41. Hereafter, page numbers are cited parenthetically.

[10]    False friendship and flattery are interchangeable terms in Plutarch's essay.

early modern preoccupation with his "rhetorical gestures."[11] As Evans shows, Plutarch's flatterer *plays* a friend by pretending to find lies, comely discourse, and superficialities detestable; such a posture is necessary to conceal deception. In fact, the flatterer's "whole study is to win the name and reputation of a man that hateth vice" (63). Plutarch writes that flatterers "have learned forsooth to knit and bend the brows" and "look with a frowning face and crabbed countenance," mixing "glavering glozes" with "rough reprehensions and chiding cheeks." These histrionics are supposed to create a persona that is "rough, violent, and inexorable in all dealings with others," employing what we may think of as "display candor" for the purpose of deception.

Iago's own use of display candor is the most obvious element of his relationship to the flatterer type, epitomized best, perhaps, by his statement—"For I am nothing if not critical."[12] Iago makes this confession before exchanging "praises" with Desdemona about the nature of women, employing the "rough reprehensions" and "chiding cheeks" that indicate a man unafraid to speak harshly despite decorum. Even "deserving women," Iago ultimately claims, "suckle fools, and chronicle small beer" (2.1.159–60). Although Desdemona responds to Iago's words by calling him a "profane and liberal counsellor," Cassio interprets the matter differently. He parses Iago's harsh words: "He speaks home, madam, you may relish him more in the soldier than in the scholar" (2.1.165–66). Honigmann glosses "home" as "directly, to the point," which is a polite way of describing the "rough, violent, and inexorable" manner that Plutarch's flatterer takes up to "win the name and reputation of a man that hateth vice." Iago uses display candor to suggest to others that he is in possession of a kind of virtue. A.C. Bradley writes of Iago: "In fact, he was one of those sterling men who, in disgust at gush, say cynical things which they do not believe, and then, the moment you are in trouble, put in practice the very sentiment they had laughed at. On such occasions he showed the kindliest sympathy and the most eager desire to help." Iago here represents a "blunt, bluff soldier" who "spoke his mind freely," though he was "not seldom rather rough and caustic of speech."[13] Iago's display candor, then, appears to have taken in at least partially Bradley himself. Bradley finds Iago's words a sign of "cynicism," an outlook that disguises hidden, meritorious qualities like "sympathy." Yet the situation is almost the precise opposite. Iago plays the honest man of rough speech, a pretense Cassio mistakes for a candid and unlearned soldier.

For Plutarch, a flatterer behaves in a rough manner in imitation of the honesty that constitutes a true mark of friendship. Such a teaching on candor in friendship

---

[11]     Christy Desmet, "The Persistence of Character," in *Shakespeare Studies*, vol. 34, ed. Susan Zimmerman (Cranbury, NJ: Associated University Presses, 2006), 52.

[12]     Here and throughout I refer to the *Arden Shakespeare: Othello*, ed. E.A.J. Honigmann (London: Thomson Learning, 2001). Hereafter cited internally. For the lines cited, see 2.1.119. See, too, Evans, "Flattery in *Othello*," 10, who demonstrates a connection between these lines and Thomas Elyot's treatment of flattery in *The Book Named The Governor*.

[13]     A.C. Bradley, *Shakespearean Tragedy: Lectures on Hamlet, Othello, King Lear, Macbeth* (New York: Penguin Books, 1991), 201.

is an ancient commonplace; for Cicero, too, good will intrinsically relates to honesty, telling the truth without fear or favor.[14] "It is characteristic of true friendship both to give and to receive advice," writes Cicero, and to do so with "all freedom of speech"; as a result, "nothing is to be considered a greater bane of friendship than fawning, cajolery, or flattery."[15] Here honesty exists in tandem with the ability to give "good advice," but advice includes persuasion as well. A speaker's projection of good will in giving advice constitutes an ingredient of *ethos* as well as of friendship. Within the Ciceronian tradition, an emphasis upon *honestas* in friendship finds its parallel in oratory, for both friend and orator enact the role of "good man."[16]

That persuasive, flatterer type—the pose of a "good man" and the practice of display candor—Plutarch combines with a specific area in which flatterers are prone to play the false friend and give harmful, though persuasive, advice: In matters of love. In a passage that Evans identifies as a "thumb-nail summary of the plot" of Iago's persuasion of Othello in 3.3, Plutarch writes that flatterers excel

> in amatorious and love matters .... : there you shall have them most of all to come over those whom they flatter and lay on load; to them they will join close, and set them on flaming fire. For if they see brethren at some variance, or setting nought by their parents, or else to deal unkindly with their own wives, and to set no store by them, or to be jealous and suspicious of them; they never admonish, chastise, or rebuke them for it, that they may amend, but rather they will kindle more coals between, and increase their anger and discontentment on both sides .... (66)[17]

---

[14]   Cicero, *De Amicitia*, trans. William Armistead Falconer (Cambridge, MA: Harvard University Press, 1959), 6.20–22.

[15]   Ibid., 25.91–2.

[16]   Cicero specifically relates *honestas* to friendship and giving advice in *De partitione oratoria,* trans. H. Rackam (Cambridge, MA: Harvard University Press, 1942), XXV.88–90; see, too, *De Oratore*, trans. E. W. Sutton and H. Rackham (Cambridge, MA: Harvard University Press, 1960), II.lxxii.333; and *Rhetorica ad Herennium,* trans. H. Caplan (Cambridge, Massachusetts: Harvard University Press, 1954), III.ii.3. For the relationship between a "good man" and oratory, see *Quintilian: The Orator's Education*, Bk 12, trans. Donald A. Russell (Cambridge: Harvard University Press, 2001) 12.1.1ff, where a good man (*vir bonus*) is also skilled in speaking.

[17]   On 3.3 and Plutarch, however, Evans writes: "Indeed, the excruciatingly hesitant way in which Iago first plants a suspicion and then pretends to dismiss it suggests the process Plutarch describes when he remarks that the false friend's 'conterfeit liberty of plain dealing and plain speech may be very well likened to the wanton pinches and bitings of luxurious women who tickle and stir up lust and pleasure of men by that which might seem to cause their pain.' [Plutarch, 67]. There is, indeed, an almost erotic quality to Iago's seduction of Othello here, especially since the ensign is alternately coy and blunt in the ways he speaks" (15). If "seduction" and an "erotic quality" are at work in Iago's words, Othello does not understand them in such a manner. As I argue, Othello is aware that the "stops" of Iago are "custom's tricks," and, therefore, they are signs of courtly rhetoric, not erotic seduction.

In matters of love, Plutarch believes the flatterer will use the rhetoric of friendship in order to "set brethren at variance" or, more relevant, to "deal unkindly" with wives. That template, using friendship as persuasion to turn one against a spouse, not only is Iago's work, but also part of his genealogy as a flattering type.

## II.

Flatterers introduce a division between seeming and being, inner and outer, what is intended and what is conveyed through speech, a set of oppositions that requires attention for performance. In 3.3, Iago's own advising of Othello employs figures of "auricular defect," a rhetorical approach that may be viewed as an enactment of the wiles of false friendship described by Plutarch. Iago observes Cassio's departure from Desdemona with the exclamation, "Ha, I like not that." Othello replies, "What dost thou say?" And Iago rejoins: "Nothing, my lord; or if – I know not what" (3.3.34–6). Iago's initial "Ha" is a *praecisio*, which Thomas Wilson calls "A Stop, or Half Telling of a Tale." It occurs "when we break off our tale before we have told it."[18] That "half telling" George Puttenham describes as *aposiopesis*, "another auricular figure of defect," which occurs when "we begin to speak a thing and break off in the middle way, as if either it needed no further to be spoken of, or that we were ashamed or afraid to speak it out."[19] The rest of Iago's and Othello's exchange displays a series of "stops" that indicate how performing a typological Iago could occur:

> Iago:     I did not think he [Cassio] had been acquainted with her.
>
> Othello:  O yes, and went between us very oft.
>
> Iago:     Indeed?
>
> Othello:  Indeed? Ay, indeed. Discern'st thou aught in that?
>           Is he not honest?
>
> Iago:     Honest, my lord?
>
> Othello:  Honest? Ay, honest.
>
> Iago:     My lord, for aught I know.
>
> Othello:  What dost thou think?
>
> Iago:     Think, my lord? (3.3.94–107)

---

[18]    Thomas Wilson, *The Art of Rhetoric* (1560), ed. Peter E. Medine (University Park: The Pennsylvania State University Press, 1994), 205.

[19]    George Puttenham, *The Art of English Poesy:  A Critical Edition*, eds. Frank Whigham and Wayne A. Rebhorn (Ithaca: Cornell University Press, 2007), 250.

Iago's interrogative stops combine the display candor of the flattering type with conventional figures of persuasion, indicating a rhetorical acting style. Tiffany Stern has added to the picture of such style by suggesting "study"—referring both to "private learning" and to "learning with a teacher"—as a term better suited than "rehearsal" to describe how a Shakespearean actor would prepare.[20] Study would be the means of suiting the word to the gesture, and here the actor followed "the classical rhetorical tradition," which emphasized "action," or the "physical side," including gesture and facial expression, and "pronunciation," including cadence and figures of speech.[21] In particular, stops or pauses, speculates Stern with Simon Palfrey, were determined less by the punctuation observed in the actor's part-text, and more by that "private 'study' and 'instruction'" where the actor would determine how pauses would facilitate rhetoric's art of persuasion.[22] Pronunciation and gesticulation, too, were part of the process in which "passions" and "humors"—or transitions from one passion to another—would be identified.[23] Palfrey and Stern note how players "were famous," in particular, "for contrasting words and stops with magnificent grandeur."[24] Like new or long words, stops could provide opportunities for performative flourish, displaying "passion," and the players' rhetorical training or study made them keen observers of such chances.

The context provided by Stern and Palfrey helps explain the exchange between Iago and Othello cited above in which stops and directions for emotional expression are associated through figures of speech. In reply to Othello's questions, Iago says: "Nothing, my lord; or if – I know not what." That stop is the *aporia*. According to Puttenham, the *aporia* should be called "the doubtful." He explains: "because oftentimes we will seem to cast perils and make doubt of things, when by a plain manner of speech we may affirm or deny him."[25] Likewise, in reply to Othello's question—"Honest? Ay, honest"—Iago's rejoinder, "my Lord for aught I know," illustrates *epitropis*, a figure in which Puttenham describes speakers who for "manner sake," and to avoid troubling "the judge or hearer with all that we could say," rest content with "having said enough already."[26] In the uses of any, or some, of the tropes for suggestive stops, we find connections between linguistic feature, what Stern calls "pronunciation," and passion or emotion, all of which prescribe how an actor may play a character, such that Iago feigns doubt, or awkward embarrassment, or shame.

Each of the emotional prompts from the figures, too, corresponds to the type of a flatterer, who plays the role of a friend. Stern and Palfrey argue: "[R]hetorical

---

[20]   Tiffany Stern, *Rehearsal from Shakespeare to Sheridan* (Oxford: Clarendon Press, 2000), 64.

[21]   Ibid., 72.

[22]   Simon Palfrey and Tiffany Stern, *Shakespeare in Parts* (Oxford: Oxford University Press, 2007), 318–20

[23]   On passions and performance, see Ibid., 311–317.

[24]   Ibid. 319.

[25]   George Puttenham, *Arte of Poesie*, 311. The editors gloss *him* as *it*.

[26]   Ibid., 311–312.

tropes and figures of speech, and the generic 'types' that underlie particular characters (e.g., the Vice in Iago or Richard III)" are matters "fundamental" for performance.[27] Type characters and figures, in particular, could have been associated together as early as Theophrastus, whose sketches, Desmet writes, may have been "intended as models for dramatic figures" or for providing "orators with a handy reference for gauging audiences."[28] The repetition of some words— such as "indeed," "honest," and "think"—call attention to themselves, not simply as cues or tropes of repetition, but as directions for performance according to type, detailing where and how Iago should feign good will, and show good will as part of the "honest advice" that may turn Othello from Desdemona. Because the flatterer feigns friendship, Iago attempts a pose of reluctance through his use of stops, hesitating to broach a topic that would bring pain to Othello, all the while, however, that reluctance "kindles more coals." Reticence as insinuation combines with Othello's belief in his ancient's "honesty," thereby increasing the significance of stops and illustrating how Plutarch's "candid" flatterer may perturb people in "amatorious and love matters." The withholding tactics of Iago work in conjunction with the display candor exhibited elsewhere by him to persuade Othello: "This honest creature," claims Othello of Iago, "sees and knows more— much more—than he unfolds" (3.3.246–7). The implication of Plutarch's flatterer was that he could play a friend with such authenticity that a difference between friend and knave was hard to determine, and that dilemma may find its way into performance by following the figures of withholding.

## III.

In the way that feigned friendship appears authentic, playing Iago according to the flatterer's type indicates a more "naturalistic" acting style and returns us to the question of the introduction: whether the divide between natural and formal acting styles rightly diminishes the possibility for interplay between illusionist and emblematic dramaturgy. Already, we have seen how the figures above, though oratorical conventions, are precisely meant to cover artifice. One should pretend doubt, for example, to increase an audience's curiosity in what you have to say, as the distinction between persuading and playing collapses. As Polixenes claims in *The Winter's Tale*, "over that art / Which you say adds to nature is an art / That nature makes."[29]

The natural acting style implicit in the figures of Wilson and Puttenham listed above becomes transparent when they are compared to the directions of the famous Shakespearean actor, Edwin Booth. Booth wrote out directions for the Horace Furness *Variorum Othello* (1886) because Furness was of the opinion that "in the interpretation of Shakespeare's plays, our first appeal, and perhaps our last,

---

27  Palfrey and Stern, *Shakespeare*, 9.

28  Desmet, "Persistence," 50.

29  *The Winter's Tale* in *The Complete Works of Shakespeare*, 5th ed., ed. David Bevington (New York: Pearson Longman, 2004), 4.4.90–2.

should be made to the dramatic instinct, as it has been termed, with which eminent Actors are especially endowed."[30] We know Booth himself favored a romantic Othello, and his own directions encourage "reflections" that "help the actor to *feel* the character he assumes."[31] Booth's modern, naturalistic sense of identifying with the character should stand in contrast to a formalistic performance based upon type and figures of speech.[32] Yet Booth's instructions beside the figures discussed above show more correspondence rather than deviation:

Iago:     Indeed?

[Puttenham: "we begin to speak a thing and break off in the middle way, as if either it needed no further to be spoken of, or that we were ashamed or afraid to speak it out."]

[Booth: "Contract the brows, but do not frown,--rather look disappointed, and merely utter in surprise, 'Indeed'!]

Othello:   Indeed? Ay, indeed. Discern'st thou aught in that?
             Is he not honest?

Iago:     Honest, my lord?

[Puttenham: *Aporia*, "the doubtful"]

[Booth: "Hesitatingly."]

Othello:   Honest? Ay, honest.

Iago:     My lord, for aught I know.

[Puttenham: *Epitropis*, "this manner of speech is used when we will not seem, either for manner sake or to avoid tediousness, to trouble the judge or hearer with all that we could say . ...."]

[Booth: "With indifference."][33]

---

[30]   *A New Variorum Edition of Shakespeare: Othello*, new Dover edition, ed. Horace Howard Furness (New York: Dover Publications, Inc., 1963), vii.

[31]   Ibid., 27.

[32]   That assumed divide between Booth and earlier performance holds for more modern acting styles as well. "The enactment of 'character,'" writes W.B. Worthen, in "The Rhetoric of Performance Criticism," *Shakespeare Quarterly*, 40. 4 (Winter, 1989): 441–55, may have been a more "collaborative or even collusive activity" than modern acting methods because "the seam between actor and character may have been visible"; hence, "to naturalize" the playing of parts according to "Stanislavskian attitudes" will obscure "certain potentialities of Shakespearean characterization" (455) by negating the presence of an audience.

[33]   For Booth's notes, see *A New Variorum Edition of Shakespeare: Othello,* 167–69.

The final "Think, my lord?" of Iago, Booth recommends, should be stated with "embarrassment." That embarrassment indicates the pain and awkwardness of Iago, performing like one of "exceeding honesty," a friend that, Othello believes, "knows all qualities, with a learned spirit, / Of human dealings," yet is not sharing that insight (3.3.262–4). Both the figures and Booth's directions attempt to portray reticence as a part of friendship, which we have seen Plutarch describe as an identifying mark of the flatterer.

The unexpected similarities between Booth's directions, Puttenham's figures, and Plutarch's type, indicate where and how type provides a region of possibility—full of distinctive sayings, typical behaviors, gestures, feigned emotions, and so on—that the text particularizes, and which may function as prompts for performance, ranging from early modern theatre to Booth's directions. Type remains the "flexible basis" for disclosing character, as Burns noted, but performance constitutes an elaboration of those basic traits. When Martin Rosenberg first explained his disagreement with rhetorical character, or "formalism," he thought actors would "exaggerate movement," use "inflated delivery" and "conventional posture," a proposal too restrictive, especially considering the size of the Globe and other theatres, which were small enough to accommodate an "expressive face to help communicate the emotion the playwright intended."[34] Yet the figures prompt a feigning of emotion too. Statues do not pretend doubt or friendly concern, but the flatterer type, and the tropes that correspond to its performance, prescribe just that. The figures of withholding correspond with the teachings of persuasive oratory, and those instructions are not at variance with Booth's "naturalistic" performance.

As with figures, or *pronuntio*, so, too, with gesture, *actio*: Booth's focus on the "contracted brow" above illustrates both correspondence and divergence between type and individual performance in a way that particularly resonates with Plutarch's description. After Iago responds—"Think, my lord?"—Othello wonders about Cassio, saying of him and then of Iago:

> And when I told thee he was of my counsel
> In my whole course of wooing, thou criedst 'Indeed?'
> And didst *contract and purse thy brow together*
> As if thou then hadst shut up in thy brain
> Some horrible conceit. If thou doest love me
> Show me thy thought. (3.3.109–119, my emphasis)

"In a highly gestured theatre," writes Stern, "non-verbal byplay could significantly affect the way the audience responded to a drama: fools like Tarlton and Reade were famous for the facial additions they made to their parts."[35] Booth, as we have seen, thought the "contracted brow" should show "disappointment," as if Iago were disappointed to have confirmed, in part, his suspicions about Cassio

---

[34]    Marvin Rosenberg, "Elizabethan Actors: Men or Marionettes?", *PMLA* 69 (1954): 920.

[35]    Stern, *Rehearsal*, 105.

and Desdemona. In Holland's translation, too, Plutarch teaches that flatterers "have learned forsooth to knit and bend the brows," especially as they perform the role of true friend; likewise, Othello wonders why Iago did "contract and purse thy brow together," concluding that the expression is the result of some "horrible conceit" that Iago will not share. For Plutarch, such a sign indicated false or pretended candor, the means by which a flatterer could assume the posture of a man who hated vice. If so, irritation, or indignation, would be the emotion feigned by Iago, as if he were angry over hearing confirmation of his suspicions, rather than Booth's more moderate "disappointment." Yet either response shows how the flattering type is manipulating oratorical conventions. Thomas Wilson's *Art of Rhetoric* (1560) considers "gesture" as a "certain comely moderation of the countenance and all other parts of the body," agreeing with Cicero, that the "gesture of man is the speech of his body." A persuasive body entails such things as "the head to be holden upright, the forehead without frowning, the brow without bending"; in short, all that a serene ethos would convey.[36] Plutarch's flatterer is the near opposite with a contracted brow. Othello remarks upon those brows, providing what we might think of as a stage direction for a natural acting style in the performance of Iago's "Indeed." For Plutarch, such uncomely expressions are necessary to counteract the "glavering glozes"—that hypocritical smooth speech—by which flatterers may be easily identified. That disguise is necessary because covert sycophancy requires something other than statuesque delivery, or a serene *ethos*, as a means of persuasion. Describing the flatterer, Plutarch writes, "he carrieth himself like a grave tragedian, and not as a comical and satirical player, and under that visor and habit he counterfeiteth a true friend" (42). For Plutarch, the "knit brows" show seriousness of thought and authentic concern. Covert sycophancy requires a natural acting style.

In fact, Iago's words suggest that Othello is foolish for preferring Desdemona to his ancient as confidant and friend, but it is Iago's manner and delivery that Othello ultimately finds convincing. Before Othello turns against Desdemona, Othello confesses to Iago the reason why he finds him persuasive:

> I think thou dost [love me].
> And for I know thou'rt full of love and honesty
> And weigh'st thy words before thou giv'st them breath,
> Therefore *these stops of thine* fright me the more.
> For such things in a false disloyal knave
> Are tricks of custom, but in a man that's just
> They're close delations, working from the heart,
> That passion cannot rule. (3.3.120–127, my emphasis)

Othello specifically recognizes "these stops" of Iago as performative "tricks," but what are "tricks of custom" in a "false disloyal knave" become marks of truth in an honest man. "In a man that's just," Othello judges, such "stops" are "close

---

[36]   Wilson, *Art of Rhetoric*, 243–44.

delations, working from the heart, / That passion cannot rule." Othello, once again, directs our attention to a naturalistic acting style in his ancient: Iago does not play a part, using oratorical methods, but is true. The irony, of course, is that the knave plays the just man in a natural way; that is the flatterer's type, a combination of emblematic and illusionist modes. "Characters," writes Peter Lichtenfels, "always use their most effective strategy for change, and therefore actors always have to take active responsibility for the words and silences within the text to realize or 'play' the characters' actions." Though Shakespeare writes the "words and silences," Lichtenfels concludes, "an actor has to choose them."[37] Lichtenfels writes in explanation of how contemporary actors approach Shakespearean drama, yet he suggests a model of performance wherein the playwright provides a framework for delivery, even for stops or silences, which corresponds to Stern's emphasis upon rhetorical instruction.[38] Like Booth, Lichtenfels might find Iago's stops as opportunities to add to performance. In the case of Iago, the framework for stops employed by Shakespeare may have come from the flatterer type, but that type which now appears to coincide with directions for naturalistic performance.

An actor today, then, may choose to follow those cues of the flatterer type that Othello recognizes, but in a way that provides audiences a more authentic depiction of deception, a truer picture of how Iago uses false words. Considering Iago's manipulation of Cassio, Booth provides an overall recommendation applicable to the exchange above and consistent with Plutarch's description of flatterers: "The more sincere your manner," Booth writes, "the more devilish your deceit."[39] Booth's view, too, remains. Dan Donohue, reflecting upon his performance of Iago at the 2008 Oregon Shakespeare Festival (in an essay in this volume), makes a similar finding: "Iago is known as 'Honest Iago' because he behaves that way." Indeed, Iago's powers of manipulation mean that Iago is a "great actor." The challenge for an actor who plays a great actor in this case is to make the audience think, as Donohue puts it, "*I would have believed Iago too.*" That assessment of credulity explains and updates Booth's own recommendation for a "more devilish" deceit. Yet what Booth and Donohue note is not a modern version of character anachronistically applied to Shakespeare but the display candor of a flatterer at work.

---

[37]  Peter Lichtenfels, "Shakespeare's Language in the Theatre" in *Reading Shakespeare's Dramatic Language: A Guide*, eds. Sylvia Adamson, Lynette Hunter, Lynne Magnusson, Ann Thompson, Katie Wales (London: The Arden Shakespeare, 2001), 162.

[38]  See Ellen J. O'Brien, "Mapping the Role:  Criticism and Construction of Shakespearean Character" in *Shakespearean Illuminations:  Essays in Honor of Marvin Rosenberg* (Newark:  University of Delaware Press, 1998), 13–32, who argues that character is the product of a player's labor, which is guided by the role found in the playtext, a role "shaped by the nuances of every word, metrical feature, rhetorical structure, spatial arrangement, and so on" (17); she concludes that "mapping the role is a form of close reading" (19).

[39]  *Variorum Othello*, 146.

## IV.

A union of formal and natural elements in the playing of Iago as a flatterer would have ramifications, too, in terms of audience response, a topic too large to investigate fully here, but one which I would like to raise in hopes of suggesting how a performance of Iago as Plutarch's flatterer may fashion a unique way for audiences to experience, or identify with, Othello's dilemma. As in the case of acting style, audience response includes a sharp natural versus formal distinction, a divide that a typological Iago played with naturalism would defy. Considering Iago, Peter Holland notes that the "vice figure" tradition includes a particular "dramatic trajectory that has strong similarities with the audience's dynamic in its response to *Othello*." When type is employed, Holland acknowledges a "certain staginess, a conscious theatricality," a design which may indicate that "the mode of Jacobean performance of such realist roles" like that of Iago is better referred to as "quasi-Brechtian *presentation*" rather than "Stanislavskian *representation*." Holland calls this a "participatory mode" for audiences, distinct from psychological or novelistic portrayals, where character is "prescriptively separate from and observed by the audience."[40] In opposition to Holland's account of the connection between formal acting style and audience participation, I would cite Harold Bloom as exemplifying the contrary tradition of audience isolation; Bloom writes that "a Shakespearean audience is like the gods in Homer: we look on and listen, and are not tempted to intervene."[41] A formal versus a natural distinction in acting style emerges in correspondence to the division between audience participation and isolation.

Yet we have seen how type may incorporate an acting style that would not seem "unnatural" because the appeal from friendship, though duplicitous, should appear as credible. The division between flattering type and displays of friendship, then, would entail subsequent distinctions, where Iago's soliloquies, for example, might retain some of Holland's "staginess," but the dramatic and deceptive dialogues, paradoxically, would be played as "authentic." In this way, rather than isolating audiences, or appropriating them through participation, playing a typological Iago would propose a version of what S.L. Bethell originally called "dual awareness." For Bethell, "the mixture of conventionalism and naturalism demands a dual mode of attention," which allow audiences a variety of responses to character, just as Falstaff, in Bethell's analysis, evokes "amusement" and is "morally reprehensible."[42] By analogy, audiences could find Iago "amusing" as

---

[40]　Peter Holland, "The Resources of Characterization in *Othello*" in *Shakespeare Survey Volume 41: Shakespearian Stages and Staging*, ed. Stanley Wells (Cambridge University Press, 1989), 129–30.

[41]　Harold Bloom, *Shakespeare: The Invention of the Human* (New York: Riverhead Books, 1998), 7.

[42]　S.L. Bethell, *Shakespeare and the Popular Dramatic Tradition* (Westminster: P.S. King & Staples, 1944), 27.

stage villain, orchestrating and articulating his plots, but "morally reprehensible" in the enactment of his deceits.

Alternatively, because type may convey naturalism, audience awareness could extend not just to the illusion of the person over the conventions by which the illusion occurs, but also to the feigned persona of the type character. Deceiving types, flatterers like Iago, enact a persona as part of a type character, as a friend is played by a knave, with the persona of friend "read" by audiences. Flattering types show not just an actor playing a character, but also an actor playing a character who plays *another* character, as Booth might play an Iago who plays an honest friend for Othello. As audiences focus on the drama of courtship between Orlando and Rosalind, knowing Rosalind is dressed as Ganymede, that a boy plays a "girl" who plays a "boy" who then plays a "girl" in the performance; so, too, they attend to the drama of deceiving Othello, finding Iago's portrayals of friendship credible, though they know he is other than his self-presentation, just as they know he is other from the actor's body who plays both flattering character and the corresponding role of "honest friend" that the type employs.

In this last understanding, where Iago's persona of "friend" receives emphasis, Iago's relationship to the flatterer type becomes part of the dynamic of audience response, less as an interaction with a character's "staginess" and more in terms of the believability of his displays of friendship. An audience dynamic in response to a natural display of friendship would create for the playgoer the dilemma faced by Othello, who thinks his wife "honest" but finds Iago "just" as well (3.3.88–9).[43] Though such a theatre experience would only occur in select places like 3.3 and suffer an obvious and great diminishment in those scenes where Iago's villainy becomes transparent, it would increase the ultimate anguish audiences experience on behalf of Othello. In those brief moments when Iago is particularly persuasive, we know what Othello does not about his ancient, but we see—and may even feel—the power of Iago's rhetoric and his performance of friendship at the same time. Indeed, Donohue comments of his experience that "the audience watches Iago lie to everyone onstage, and yet, they all seem to want to believe that what he says to them is true." That kind of audience response dramatizes the problem, to borrow from Plutarch, of how to discern a flatterer from a friend.[44]

---

[43]     Audiences went to the theater, write Palfrey and Stern, *Shakespeare*, 317, "to feel newly amazed, not only at an actor's or playwright's facility, but at their own capacity to feel apparently impossible 'contraries' at one time, as though the theatre was introducing its 'rapt' spectators to new possibilities of feeling."

[44]     Compare Donohue's position here to the anxieties over dissimulation that scholars like Jorgenson and others have claimed early modern audiences brought to the theatre. In addition to the work of Evans, Desmet and Jorgenson on flattery, for a general statement on the ubiquity of concerns over flattery and dissembling, see Katharine Eisaman Maus, *Inwardness and Theater in the English Renaissance* (Chicago: The University of Chicago Press, 1995), 5–8.

# Chapter 14
## *Henry V*'s Character Conflict

### James Wells

As every novice Shakespearean learns, the old character criticism, established and practiced by A.C. Bradley, suffered a crushing and undignified end when L.C. Knights posed the loaded question, "How many Children Had Lady Macbeth?" to suggest the potentially absurd upshot of Bradley's psychological studies of character. As Michael Bristol reminds us in his recent impenitent apology for character criticism, the question became a "byword for asinine literal-mindedness" that confuses fictional characters and real people.[1] Bristol is unapologetic for his "guilty secret" of wanting the answers to Knights's and other like questions and insists on getting us to admit that our understanding of real people informs our understanding of make-believe ones. However, his study finally does center on differentiating between the two. And, as the critical energy of our field flows back to questions of "character," this difference between fictional and non-fictional characters (both in terms of "figures that appear in plays" and "the personalities of those figures") should remain at the forefront of our studies. Otherwise, we risk similar ridicule for making a mistake on paper we would never make in the theatre.

However, such distinctions turn out to be harder to define than they might at first seem, especially in Shakespeare's plays. In fact, I want to suggest that discussions of character and its problems breed and swarm around Shakespeare not mainly because, as is commonly held, Shakespeare created characters that are so lifelike;[2] but rather because so many of his plays show a chronic fascination with how qualities or what we might call character traits of real human beings take on new dimensions because they occur in a fiction, particularly dramatic fiction,

---

[1]    Michael Bristol, "How Many Children Did She Have?" *Philosophical Shakespeares*, ed., John J. Joughin (London: Routlege, 2000), 18–33; esp. 18. See also L.C. Knights, "How Many Children had Lady Macbeth? An Essay in the Theory and Practice of Shakespeare Criticism.," in *Explorations: Essays in Criticism Mainly on the Literature of the Seventeenth Century* (1963; rept. New York: New York University Press, 1964), 1–39.

[2]    For example, Stephen Greenblatt's desire in "The Circulation of Social Energy" to answer theoretically the practical question of how the "textual traces" in Shakespeare's play get "so much life" is very close to Harold Bloom's insistence that "[i]t is not an illusion that readers (and playgoers) find more vitality both in Shakespeare's words and in characters who speak them than in any other author, perhaps in all other authors put together." (Stephen Greenblatt, *Shakespearean Negotiations* [Berkeley: University of California Press, 1988], 2; Harold Bloom, *Shakespeare: The Invention of the Human*, [New York: Riverhead Books, 1998], 10).

where palpably real human bodies with identities of their own become fictionalized as characters in plays. For example, Hamlet, a character in a play, claims an untheatrically real interior self, "that within which passes show," as the basis of his identity. Coriolanus repeatedly asserts his unwillingness (and complains of his inability) to act or be other than he is, yet is cast into positions that require him to do both. Lear vows to keep the "the name and all th'additions to a king," yet gives over the "sway, revenue, execution of the rest"—the prerogatives without which the name and additions lose meaning. In all three cases, Shakespeare has endowed the title figure of his plays with primary character traits that in significant ways contradict the experiences the audience has with them as characters in plays. On a fundamental level of audience experience, Hamlet has no untheatrical or interior self, Coriolanus cannot exist without acting, and a stage Lear always only has the name and additions of a king. For Lear, to give over the rest is as superfluous as it is impossible. However, the traits these characters possess and the principles they articulate still fall within the range of behaviors that are eligible for dramatic imitation, for there is no action that a man might play that a character might not. In other words, Shakespeare confuses the distinction between fiction and non-fictional character by making characters that are too lifelike but only in a very particular way that counters or ironically fulfills our experience of them as characters in a play. And this experience of confusion is central to fully experiencing the plays and their characters.

Such mirthful distress is crucial to the critical history of *Henry V*. We would be hard-pressed to find a play where issues of character—not in terms of the "illusion of personhood" but in the sense of "ethical makeup"—have been more polarizing. A critical history that is too long to recount (or even footnote in a useful way) has generally divided on the question of whether Shakespeare depicts Henry as the "mirror of all Christian kings" (2.Chorus. 6) and a national hero; or as a scheming Machiavel who bullies and manipulates his way to success under the cover of piety.[3] We would be equally hard-pressed to find a play where the dialogue points more self-consciously to the artificiality of the character that is being performed. On the most obvious level, the Chorus repeatedly and redundantly alerts the audience to an artificiality of which it is already aware and bemoans the inadequacy of the representation it attempts. Although these primary issues appear unconnected, the play links them in a fundamental way in that the issues of Henry's personal or moral character result directly from the issues of dramatic character. By linking the issues of the King's character (or ethical makeup)—both those that audiences face when confronting Henry and those that Henry faces himself—to issues of what it means to be a character in a dramatic fiction, the play intensifies paradoxes that define dramatic characters in the audience's experience.

The difference between fictional and non-fictional characters has hardly been a major concern for the dominant modes of Shakespeare criticism that emerged

---

[3]    All quotations from *The Life of Henry V* follow Annalisa Castaldo's edition from *The New Kittredge Shakespeare* (Newburyport MA: Focus Publishing, 2007).

in the 1980's and still holds sway today. We might even say that the discoveries and foci of those modes have obscured the difference between the two. If we risk taking a few procrustean shavings here and there, we can generally say that the driving principle behind this critical turn has been a preoccupation with reality. Much criticism has focused on looking at literary fiction in order to reveal, in the words of Jonathan Dollimore, "the real historical conditions in which the actual identity of people is rooted."[4] Of course, when many modern critics examine real conditions, the idea of the "real" no longer holds the weight it once did. The reality of existence consists of our participation in institutions and discursive constructs that the forces of history, culture, or power impose on us. Reality is at least factitious, if not outright fictional. In fact, when Dollimore and other movers in our field such as John Drakakis exhumed the long-deceased corpse of Bradley's character criticism in order to have another go at it, they did not censure it for confusing fictional and real people but for misrepresenting what it means to be human.[5] Far from seeing character criticism as dead, both critics inveighed against the persistence of the philosophy of humanist essentialism supporting Bradley's criticism.[6] In the introduction to his influential collection *Alternative Shakespeares*, Drakakis argues that when Bradley locates the center of tragedy in character, he "presupposes the autonomy of each individual character"—a presupposition that allows him to ignore the way "the family, the state, and all those cultural and social institutions in which human beings are necessarily involved ...might conceivably *determine* character."[7] This criticism issues from the materialist opposition to what Dollimore classifies as "the humanist belief in a unified, autonomous self."[8] Bradley's problem, it turns out, was not confusing fiction and nonfiction but thinking there was such a thing as character at all.

We may observe the opposing activities of pursuing reality and insisting on its illusion being simultaneous being performed in the shift from conceiving humans as "beings" to thinking of them as "subjects." And the difficulty of distinguishing dramatic characters from human subjects emerges from this very move. In both the psychoanalytical and political fields out of which the concept developed, those who endorse the theory of subjectivity urge us to admit that integrated self-hood, free will, and individuality are fictions, or, at least, dearly and tenaciously held illusions. More specifically, many of the terms that are often used to define

---

[4]   Jonathan Dollimore, *Radical Tragedy: Religion, Ideology, and Power in the Drama of Shakespeare and his Contemporaries,* 2nd ed. (Durham: Duke University Press, 1998), 153.

[5]   See John Drakakis's "Introduction" to *Alternative Shakespeares* (London: Routledge, 1985), 6–7; and Dollimore, 153.

[6]   Dollimore, 1998, argues that the "[r]ejection of his speculative character analysis in Shakespeare has tended to obscure the extent to which Bradley's metaphysic of tragedy has remained dominant" (53).

[7]   Drakakis, 7.

[8]   Dollimore, (xxviii).

subjectivity are identical to those that might be used to describe characters in plays. Subjects are constructed by external forces, written upon, performed, and contingent, terms and phrases that make humans sound as if they are actors performing roles that have been written by authorities, if not actual authors.

Adding to the confusion is the suggestion some critics make that dramatic fictions are not only just as suitable as other, often non-fictional texts for studying real human subjects but also preferable to them. In *The Subject of Tragedy*, Catherine Belsey argues that dramatic fiction is the most fit place to study the "history of the subject" because it "tends to throw into relief the problems and contradictions which are often only implicit in other forms of writing."[9] In *Notorious Identity*, Linda Charnes defends her decision to study subjectivity in plays because, "in the Renaissance, drama is the dominant mode in which the provisional, performative, and contingent nature of subjectivity can literally be observed."[10] Charnes's assertion raises the question of why, if human identity really is "provisional, performative, and contingent," we could observe those qualities any more "literally" in dramatic characters than we can in humans offstage. How could we only figuratively be the selves that we supposedly are?

The point of these questions is not to deride either of these authors[11] or to challenge in any substantial way modern theories of subjectivity.[12] Theories of subjectivity have helped make visible the forces of society that influence non-fictional human experience, forces that were less available under the more flattering theories of the individual that Dollimore and Drakakis attack. And, to a certain extent, Charnes is correct because the qualities of human existence on which those who study subjectivity focus indeed are figurative or at least resemble

---

[9]    Catherine Belsey, *The Subject of Tragedy: Identity and Difference in Renaissance Drama* (London: Methuen, 1985), 49.

[10]   Linda Charnes, *Notorious Identity: Materializing the Subject in Shakespeare* (Cambridge: Harvard University Press, 1993), 9.

[11]   However, I think that Bert O. States's point in "Performance as Metaphor" in which he exposes a "habit" in performance criticism of "using words … in a metaphorical way and then forgetting they are metaphors" might be applicable to subjectivity studies (*Theatre Journal* 48 [1996] 1–26), 2.

[12]   Those interested in challenges to various forms of subjectivity might look at the following essays: Richard Levin's "Bashing the Bourgeois Subject," *Looking for an Argument: Critical Encounters with the Criticism of Shakespeare and his Contemporaries* (Madison, NJ: Fairleigh Dickinson University Press, 2003), 114–123, which argues that a popular version of subjectivity often attacked is merely a distorted straw man invented by those with a political ax to grind; and David Aers, "A Whisper in the Ear of Early Modernists; or Reflections on Literary Critics Writing the History of the Subject," in *Culture and History 1350-1600*, ed., David Aers (Detroit: Wayne State University Press, 1992), 177–202, which argues that the specific version of early modern subjectivity adduced by Belsey and others is historically inaccurate. For a compelling essay challenging the idea of using poetry or any other fiction to study historical subjectivity, see Amittai Aviram's 'Lyric Poetry and Subjectivity" (*Intertexts* 5.1 [2001]: 61–86).

figuration because they are secondary rather than primary (as I will argue below). Still, one could wonder, if theatre merely allows to be observed in literal fashion what is figurative in human subjects, what we could really hope to learn from studying it that we do not already know? The point of posing these questions is to show why, given a critical climate where human identity has been defined in such theatrical terms, the difference between dramatic and human subjects has not been an issue and how, had it been one, this difference might have been hard to address.

As in any recovery program, if that indeed is what we are in, the first step is admitting that we have a problem. And the problem defining the difference between dramatic characters and human beings may reside in dramatic characters themselves as much as it does in recent critical trends. From a certain definitional standpoint, dramatic characters really are identical to human beings. They look, talk, act, and, in almost every way, exist, much, if not exactly, as the real humans they imitate. In fact, there is no abstract or definitive characteristic of either that does not buckle easily under the slightest deconstructive pressure. Nevertheless, despite the theoretical equivalency between the two, audiences reading plays or sitting in theaters have no fundamental trouble telling them apart. This strange practical dissonance arises from the mimetic essence of dramatic and all other fictions and how we experience them. This experience takes the form of a paradox of recognition. In order to apprehend what we have accepted as imitation, we have simultaneously to recognize in the imitation the object being imitated and then dismiss that object as mere artifice. We carry out in unison two contradictory mental operations: treating the object as real—else recognition could not occur—and rejecting it as artificial—else it could not be distinguished from the object it imitates.

Maynard Mack's terms "engagement" and "detachment," which Kent Cartwright has more recently developed more extensively in relation to Shakespeare's plays, seem to capture the experience of imitation, especially as it occurs in dramatic character. Mack says engagement results from artistic "forces drawing the spectator to identify with the faces in the mirror," and the detachment from "those which reminded him that that they were mere reflections." Mack further claims that Shakespeare's theatre often holds the two psychological states in balance by provoking one or the other response.[13] Although Mack and Cartwright both stress the alternating quality of these opposing functions and point to places where plays encourages one or the other, they both at times suggest something more material to the argument at hand—that engagement and detachment can occur simultaneously. Fiction, like all imitation, combines engagement and detachment since much of the paradox of recognition requires both involvement in the illusion and repulsion from it.

---

[13]    Maynard Mack, "Engagement and Detachment in Shakespeare's Plays," in *Essays on Shakespeare and Elizabethan Drama in Honor of Hardin Craig*, ed., Richard Hosley (Columbia: University of Missouri Press, 1962), 277.

The experience of dramatic character differs from that of other kinds of fiction or imitation only in the degree to which it involves audiences in the paradox of recognition. Drama intensifies the paradox of imitation because it is the only form of art whereby the object of imitation (i.e. human bodies) is the same as the medium, unlike, say, writing, painting, drawing, and sculpture, where object and medium are materially distinct. We must look at real human bodies, which have identities of their own, and perceive them as fictions. No matter how realistically performed, dramatic character simultaneously combines engagement and detachment, by which the illusion of the character draws us in and the bodily presence of the actor pushes us away. However, this experience is much more involved and paradoxical than this simple opposition implies because the body that repels us is the same as the one that provides the occasion for the illusion in the first place. In the end, this heightened experience of conflict is what differentiates our perceptions of fictional characters from non-fictional human subjects. While, as the theory of subjectivity suggests, human identity may in fact resemble dramatic character in that subjects are divided, performed, constructed, scripted, over-determined, and so forth, these conditions are deferred under all but the most stressful circumstances. In almost all cases, when we encounter real human beings, we experience them as unified and acting of their own accord. Even if they appear divided or over-determined, we still do not experience them as fictions.[14] In drama, the audience constantly experiences (can never leave experiencing) characters in plays as paradoxes of self-alienation for whom the reality and palpability of the persons on whom their existence depends renders them unreal. This paradoxical experience holds whether the audience is consciously thinking about it or not. The unbroken quality of dramatic experience invalidates and makes redundant the commonplace that metadramatic moments in plays remind us that we are watching a play.[15] A more appropriate way of thinking of how Shakespeare is using such moments is to say that they redouble or intensify by recreating on-stage and in the audience the manifold paradoxes that issue from the fundamental paradox of dramatic imitation.

---

[14]   This secondary nature of our subjectivity helps us understand how Charnes is in fact correct when she suggests that our subjectivity is figurative rather than literal. Still, we must wonder what we can accomplish by examining drama in terms of human subjectivity because we already know about them what we hope to discover, i.e. that they literally embody a more figurative essence of human existence. In other words, theoretically speaking, have we really gotten beyond the Globe Theatre's *Totus Mundus Agit Histrionem*?

[15]   When in his seminal work, *Imaginary Audition* (Berkeley: University of California Press, 1989), Harry Berger takes to task metadramatic readings that confuse actor and character, he has in mind something much different than the experiential paradox I am discussing here. His complaint is against those readings that suggest that the character knows something that only the actor could: "A character in a play cannot know he is a character in *that* play being performed in *that* theater" (99). In the experiential paradox of theatre the knowledge or awareness that Shakespeare is intensifying belongs entirely to the audience and not to the fictional characters within the play.

This intensified paradoxical experience of recognition certainly helps shed light on the persistent questions of character in *Henry V*. Those familiar with the issue will recall Norman Rabkin's pivotal account of the protagonist's character issues (noted above) in which he argues against both sides as well as against the middle ground position between the two extremes and for the play as a combination of radically incongruous characters: "[I]n *Henry V* Shakespeare created a work whose ultimate power is precisely the fact that it points in two opposite directions, virtually daring us to choose one of the two opposed interpretations it requires of us."[16] (For an illustrative model of Henry's condition, Rabkin borrows Ernst Gombrich's gestalt figure of the Rabbit/Duck, which, Gombrich claims, offers "alternative readings" that "we cannot experience ... at the same time."[17] "Experience," however, seems to be the wrong word for what cannot occur at the same time. Although we may not be able to *see* both rabbit and duck at once, the totality of the gestalt he describes seems to be one of simultaneity rather than exclusivity of experience. In other words, when we come to apprehend the way the optical illusion works, we *experience* both rabbit and duck even though we may only be looking at one (or neither).

Given Rabkin's reliance on an optical illusion for his conceptual framework, it further seems odd that he ultimately locates Henry's embodiment of incongruous characters in reality rather than in an internal property of fiction. That is, he concludes by positing Henry's complexity first in "Shakespeare's recognition of the irreducible complexity of things" (*things,* he implies, of life more than dramatic fiction) and then in our lived reality, "the simultaneity of our deepest hopes and fears about the world of political action."[18] Both may in fact be correct; I certainly suspect that Shakespeare must have grasped the complexity of life, and I identify

---

[16]   Norman Rabkin, "Either/Or: Responding to *Henry V*.," in *Shakespeare and the Problem of Meaning* (Chicago: University of Chicago Press, 1981), 34.

[17]   Rabkin, 35.

[18]   Rabkin, 62, By comparison, we are not, in retrospect, surprised when Stephen Greenblatt moves from the theatricality of *Henry V* to that of "[r]oyal power," which, he argues, "is manifested to its subjects as in a theatre." ("Invisible Bullets: Renaissance Authority and its Subversion, *Henry IV* and *Henry V*," in *Political Shakespeare: New Essays in Cultural Materialism*, eds, Jonathan Dollimore and Alan Sinfield [Ithaca and London: Cornell University Press, 1985], 44). Reading reality in theatrical terms is a first principle of New Historicism. Those familiar with Rabkin's other work will remember his earlier appeals to reality as the foundation of literary paradox. In his introduction to *Shakespeare and the Common Understanding* (New York: The Free Press, 1967) Rabkin is anxious lest his fascination with paradox and pleasure be confused with what others might call "pernicious aestheticism which sees literature as laudably unconcerned with finding answers to life's problems" (19). Rabkin holds that instead of "turning away from life's problems," the sometimes illogical complexity of art mirrors "the nature of our ability to understand and come to terms with reality" (20). Still, I do think it denies the complexity of life to suggest that art and drama have their own set of experiences and problems and that Shakespeare is creating new experiences for the audience out of these problems.

with those who have hopes and fears about political leaders. But what Shakespeare demonstrates in *Henry V* and throughout his plays is the appreciation for the irreducible complexity of his artistic medium and the talent for optimizing the possibilities of that complexity. Henry's oppositional qualities (to which Rabkin points) result from Shakespeare's exploitation of qualities inherent in dramatic characters, particularly as they are refracted through Henry's personal character in this play.

From the outset, the play urges us to think about Henry's character precisely in terms of how it is presented in the play; or, we should say, of how it fails to materialize because the nature of drama cannot produce it. As is well-known, the opening Chorus does not promise to give us Henry's greatness but advertises the impossibility of giving us Henry "like himself" without "a muse of fire ...A Kingdom for a stage, princes to act, / And monarchs to behold the swelling scene," or without a stage reality that more nearly approximates the illusion the play purports to create (1.1.1–4). Only then could the "warlike Harry, like himself, / Assume the port of Mars" (1.1.4–5). However, the Chorus does not seem completely confident that gaining the more ideal theatrical components he mentions would result in the desired end. The terms through which he renders Henry's actual greatness denigrate his figure even as they elevate it. The Chorus does not guarantee that the Henry presented on the ideal stage would become the God of War but would merely "assume" his "port." "Assume" is an ambiguous verb, which Shakespeare in other plays uses to imply equally sincere and insincere stances in adopting or putting on traits. In *Hamlet*, Shakespeare stresses this same tension operating here. When Hamlet famously instructs his mother, "Assume a virtue if you have it not" (3.4.167), his hope is that her habitual feigning might create real virtue, that "assuming" in one sense might lead to "assuming" in the other. "Port," as "bearing, "demeanor," or "manner," likewise divides on the same opposition between true and feigned actions that a man might play. Further, it is difficult to distinguish from the Chorus's grammar whether what the actor would imitate is actually Henry or his ability to assume ports. The realized point is that even if the stage could produce all these desired ingredients, Henry would still merely look like Mars. By deflating Henry in the very terms it uses to build him up, the Chorus rehearses the paradox of dramatic character according to which, even in the most ideal conditions, the Henry on-stage could never be more than a stage Henry.

Therefore, the Chorus stipulates the participation of the audience whose "imaginary forces" and "thoughts must deck [their] kings" (1.1.28). The reason behind this requirement is the disparity between the "flat unraisèd spirits" of the actors and the kingly subject that at least one of them will represent, whom, a mere fifty lines later, the Archbishop reports to be filled with "celestial spirits." The proximal occurrences of the term "spirit," used divergently to describe first the impoverished actor playing Henry and next the glorious character being produced by the actor, is indicative of the way the play aligns issues of personal character with those of dramatic character. The ensuing depiction of Henry reveals the Chorus's apology as more than conventional stage modesty. The play takes seriously and literally the idea and the problem of presenting an ideal king in a medium that by nature degrades its subjects and whose debasing quality is magnified in inverse proportion to the greatness of the subject it is presenting. Instead of doing what the Chorus says cannot be done by trying to represent Henry as great as he was, the play reproduces and redoubles the uneasy combination of actor and character that is already part of the audience's experience of him. This doubling of his experiential condition occurs in the way Henry's performance of his greatness always undoes itself. And the way it always undoes itself is by revealing itself as a performance, one which Henry enacts often whether he wants to or not.

Henry's entrance into the play brings to the fore the cohabitation of these contrary animating forces of actor and character. While Canterbury claims that Henry is angelically freed from "th'offending Adam," the unprecedented contribution the Archbishop makes toward the French campaign to forestall the loss of church lands suggests that he at least thinks that the king is venal (1.1.29). However, when Henry appears on stage to assess the legitimacy of his claim to the French throne, his actions, taken in isolation, are beyond reproach. He is a model of piety who admonishes the Archbishop against the very kind of tendentious response his contribution would have suggested:

> And God forbid, my dear and faithful lord,
> That you should fashion, wrest or bow your reading
> Or nicely charge your understanding soul
> With opening titles miscreate, whose right
> Suits not in native colours with the truth. (1.2.13–17)

Yet readers as far back as Bradley have noted that Henry seems far from exemplary or even innocent. The entire situation feels like a setup. Henry knows precisely what Canterbury will say because the Archbishop has already shown his hand. That the Archbishop would express misgivings, even under Henry's strong admonition, is unthinkable. Still, Henry *does* nothing (at least that the audience sees in the scene or in anything that has been reported to us) to deserve this suspicion. Rather, circumstances have inescapably rendered Henry's actions a performance, regardless of whether they are sincere or not. In fact, the more upright he acts—the more sincerely he performs his piety—the more his sincerity and insistence sound like cant. Henry's situation has become like that of the actor playing him, unable to establish the reality of the role he plays. The King cannot step out of a theatrical existence even when he models probity. To call him a model of probity, however, is not to defend his character. After all, Henry may indeed be behind the Commons' urging the bill that would have taken Church lands and so prompted the Archbishop's offer. Rather, it is to suggest that the play sets it up so that his status as a character in a play undermines the greatness of his character in the very realization of that greatness.

The same self-subversion occurs in Henry's discovery and handling of the traitors in act two. By almost any measure, what Henry accomplishes is nothing short of amazing. He discovers treason, captures the traitors, allows the traitors to determine their own punishment, and elicits gratitude from them for having been discovered. However, he negates his magnanimity in the act of executing it. As in his first appearance, the scene is once again a setup. Circumstances have been manipulated in Henry's favor so that Cambridge, Grey, and Scroop forfeit Henry's mercy by their own choice. The difference here is that the audience sees Henry manipulating the circumstances. Before Henry and the traitors join them, Exeter assures a worried Bedford that the three "shall be apprehended by-and-by" (2.2.2), and Bedford notes the King has foreknowledge by "interception which [the traitors] dream not of" (2.2.7). Henry further amplifies his duplicity when he insistently performs his own moral character in the long speech where he sanctimoniously calls out the traitors (particularly Scroop) for appearing "dutiful" and seeming "grave," "learned," and "religious" (2.2.126–30). From the lips of someone who has just tricked people into their deaths by withholding knowledge, this moralizing lecture lacks a certain moral force. Shakespeare has made Henry potentially look petty when performing actions that are otherwise worth our admiration. And this incongruous union of the petty and the grand is an intensified rehearsal of the experience of Henry *qua* character that the audience would already be having of him. Henry is a squeaking Cleopatra boying his own greatness. Or he is a magnified instance of Fluellen's Welsh substitution of the unvoiced bilabial plosive ("p") for the voiced ("b"), an overbearing Alexander for whom every articulation of "big" will always come out as "pig."[19]

A telling iteration of what we might now simplistically rename Henry's "character conflict" occurs in his speech during the battle at Harfleur, where he famously rallies his troops "once more unto the breach" (3.1.1). While the thrust of the speech is encouragement, its substance is advice on how to be an effective soldier. Yet fittingly, the instructions are rife with theatricality; they must "*imitate* the action of a tiger," "*[d]isguise* fair nature with a hard-favored rage," "*[l]end* the eye a terrible *aspect*" (apparently by letting "it pry through the portage of the head like a brass cannon") and, "bend up every *spirit* to its full height" (3.1.6–11).[20] These instructions offer no appreciable distinction between how a person becomes an effective soldier in real life and how an actor might impersonate one in a play. They serve equally well as the encouragement of a general rallying his troops and the instructions of a stage-director or lead actor rallying his players. In fact, the advice might be taken for how to be a soldier in the play they are already in (albeit for a performance that is never seen because the battle takes

---

[19]    Scholars critical of Henry's character fail to recognize how Fluellen's supposed mistake is the product of blowing hot and cold with the same breath. Harold C. Goddard cannot hear beyond the Welshman's accent to hear the genuine affection that he has for his titular countryman, the Prince of Wales, believing Fluellen's comparison to be Shakespeare's final "comment [implicitly negative] on the rejection of Falstaff." (Harold C. Goddard, "Henry V," in *The Meaning of Shakespeare* [Chicago: The University of Chicago Press, 1951], 251).

[20]    Italics mine.

place off stage). Henry's exhortation recreates his basic problem in the play; the performance of greatness turns out to be simply a performance. And, apropos the mixture of reality and illusion that is part of the experience of dramatic character, Henry claims that if his men imitate well enough they can prove they really are the legitimate sons of the heroic English they appear to be: "Dishonor not your mothers; now attest / That those you called your fathers did beget you" (3.1.22–3).

Henry's use of legitimacy as a motivation in battle presents a suitable point for moving from the concerns that the audience has with Henry's character to those that Henry has as a character in the play—concerns which, likewise, intensify the paradoxical experience of dramatic character. Throughout most of the play, Henry's motives and interior thoughts are inscrutable. He discourses frequently and at length on a number of issues—the responsibility for misbegotten war, the motives for treachery, a general's ability to control the fury of his troops— but the rhetorical ends and dramatic context of these comments compromise their reliability as marks of real interior character. However, one theme emerges repeatedly and in numerous permutations—legitimacy: the legitimacy of his claim to the French throne; of his friend's loyalty; of his soldiers' commitment to battle; even of his own word (presented once-removed while in disguise and over which he quarrels when Williams disputes it). Given this preoccupation, it should come as no surprise that when, in his two-part soliloquy on the eve of Agincourt, Henry finally does reveal what is (and perhaps has been) on his mind: he is concerned with self-legitimacy on two fundamental levels. The second part of the soliloquy addresses the possible repercussions of his questionable legitimacy as King that results from the irregular way Henry IV came to power. He prays that the "God of battles" overlook "the fault / [his] father made in compassing the crown" (4.1.291–92), else Henry's whole enterprise threatens to founder. The God of battles will not "steel" the hearts of his soldiers (4.1.247). Henry fears that his claim to the French throne, which is based upon divine-right heredity through Edward II, might not hold up in battle if his claim to the English throne rests on shaky grounds. Although the struggle for legitimacy that dominated both *Henry IV* plays has been largely absent from the action and dialogue of this one, that same struggle turns out to have been hanging invisibly in the air throughout.

In an elementary way, Henry's concern with self-authenticity is appropriate for how the play is recreating on stage the experience of the audience. Because Henry is a fiction, his legitimacy can never be more than an illusion, even if Henry could buck history and prove to be unquestionably legitimate in the play. This doubling of audience experience would occur in any play where legitimacy is at question, in the same way that a recurring disguise motif would engage experiences that the audience is having with characters simply because they appear in a play. *Henry V* has shown itself especially attuned to this gap between representation and thing represented when the Chorus brings to the foreground the regrettable lack of a princely equivalent to legitimate Henry's princely role. By worrying over his own legitimacy, Henry is merely staging a more political form of the experience the audience is already having with him.

However, the play amplifies the experiential paradoxes of the audience in a much more complex, particularized, and powerful way than merely presenting a character whose authenticity is in question. How it does so emerges in the first part of Henry's soliloquy, which involves the legitimacy of kingship itself on a more existential level. In this part, Henry laments the predicament of kingship, which he categorizes as "ceremony." In the opening part, Henry isolates ceremony as the feature that distinguishes kings from "private men" and bemoans its artificiality and inutility (4.1.195). Ceremony consists of the trappings and suits of "place, degree, and form," of "the farced title," and of the "the intertissued robe of gold and pearl" (4.1.204, 220–221). Kingship's ceremony inspires only fear, not love. Like Falstaff's "honor" in *1 Henry IV*, ceremony cannot "command the health" of his self or of "the beggar's knee" (4.1.214). But the larger problem is that the ceremonial nature of kingship renders reality unreal. The "homage sweet" of the subject is turned into poisoned flattery by the ceremonial nature of kingship. The existence of a king is illegitimate, even for a legitimate king.

This problem is evident in an episode at the beginning of the sequence of events that, in part, prompts Henry's complaint here. When the King suggests to Erpingham that a "good soft pillow" better suits his "good white head," the old Lord responds, "Not so my liege. This lodging likes me better / Since I may say, 'Now lie I like a king'" (4.1.14, 16–17). Although his response might contain an element of truth, it simultaneously performs a double meaning latent in the word "lie." Erpingham's response antiphonally keeps step with the ceremonial expectation created by the king's comment. By stating a preference for his current discomfort because it equates him with his king, Erpingham is both uttering the lie that ceremony creates and telling the truth about ceremony—that it involves king and subject in a confederacy of deception. The King himself acknowledges this tacit conspiracy later in the scene when, disguised as a common soldier serving under Erpingham, he reports that his commander thinks their estate is "[e]ven as men wrack'd upon a sand" and countenances his deceit by observing that "it is not meet" that Erpingham should tell "his thought to the King," for fear that "it might dishearten his army" (4.1.92–93, 101). His Crispin's Day speech gives voice to a version of Erpingham's noble lie when Henry claims universally that no matter how "vile" a soldier might be, "[t]his day shall gentle his condition" (4.3.63–4). Although soldiers who fight valiantly can be knighted, and, thereby, "gentled," a character like Pistol, who tellingly is the only soldier the audience sees "fighting" the enemy at Agincourt, certainly marks the limits of Henry's claim. Therefore, by telling a lie that turns out to be a truth (or vice-versa), Erpingham provides a miniature form of the King, whose sincere performance always reveals itself as a performance.

Although Henry never says exactly why he debases himself by donning Erpingham's cloak under the cover of night, we can reasonably infer that the inevitability of Erpingham's kind of flattery plays a large part in it. The only way Henry can experience a reality free from ceremony is to wear a disguise. Yet, as should be obvious, such reality is dearly bought. Disguise merely recreates the problem of engaging reality that it is meant to solve. Henry can only experience reality if he is no longer himself. Henry's inability to have a direct encounter with reality as King constitutes a further intensification of the paradox of dramatic character, especially as it occurs in a history, which can only reproduce Henry's reality with the alienating presence of another.

Materialist and new historicist critics present a similar argument for how the play undoes the grandeur it purports to show but regards Henry's unraveling in a strictly political light. Alan Sinfield's essay from *Alternative Shakespeare* classifies the contradictions in Henry's character as the inevitable result of an ideology that tries to cover up its own mechanisms of power. Sinfield claims that the play attempts to present power as consolidated into the one "unified . . . individual human subject" of Henry V, but that the presence of detracting voices in it betrays the "inherent contradictions" that emerge "even as" that play attempts consolidation.[21] The opposing conclusion that Stephen Greenblatt draws from similar observations forms the basis of the well-rehearsed debate within materialism over subversion and containment. Greenblatt's famous essay "Invisible Bullets" argues that Henry's power throughout *1* and *2 Henry IV* and in *Henry V* rests ironically on a "theatricality" that should undermine it. Greenblatt argues that "the subversive doubts the play continuously awakens serve paradoxically to intensify the power of the king and his war, even while they cast doubts upon his power."[22] Greenblatt extends this reading of Henry's character to the content of theatre in general, which, despite being subversive, remains "contained" within a state-sponsored theatre. Where Sinfield and Greenblatt agree is in their equation of theatre and reality. For both, to borrow from Sinfield, the "indeterminacy" of "theatrical representation" always reflects the indeterminacy of "political and social process."[23] Whether or not such an equation—so fundamental to materialism—errs in general, it is certainly wrong in the case of *Henry V*. It mistakes a function of fiction for an effect of politics and, in so doing, denies the experiential difference between fictional and non-fictional character.

Such a denial closes off the game in which *Henry V* is inviting audiences to participate, a game which requires that we preserve this experiential distinction. This game we have been tracking throughout receives further intensification through Henry's own confusion of these experiences. This confusion and intensification emerge in the way that Henry handles ceremony's tendency to vitiate reality by repeatedly treating ceremony as if it were real. In fact, *Henry V* presents a series of episodes in which Henry treats foregone conclusions as if they could have turned out otherwise. This treatment is certainly true of the question of the Salic Law he puts to the Archbishop. It also underscores his behavior with the Dauphin's insult, which he claims is an impetus for a war he has already determined to fight. It

---

[21]    Alan Sinfield, "History and Ideology: The Instance of *Henry V*," in *Alternative Shakespeares*, ed., John Drakakis (London: Routledge, 1985), 211.

[22]    Greenblatt, 43.

[23]    Sinfield, 215.

likewise describes the way he deals with Cambridge, Grey, and Scroop and their capital crimes. By setting up a scenario in which it appears that the traitors have created their own fate, Henry bestows the appearance of chance on their certain ends. Ironically, however, Henry creates the illusion of arbitrariness that normally attends reality by manipulating the ceremonial expectations carried by the scene at hand. Henry has ostensibly assembled the group so that by commission he can officially transfer power from his self to these three regents who will rule in his absence. In the same way that Henry can depend on Erpingham to follow his lead, he anticipates the solicitous responses the three traitors will have to his suggestion that he put himself in danger by freeing the man "[t]hat rail'd against [his] person" (2.2.58). The surprise for the traitors occurs when the scene turns out to be anything but the ceremonial transfer of power it has been set up to be.

Although Henry enters it in disguise, his quarrel with Williams is perhaps the closest he gets to an unmediated contact with reality. However, Henry's problem that develops in this exchange is that reality fails to live up to ceremony. Henry becomes upset when Williams unceremoniously dismisses both Henry's assurance that he will not be ransomed and the disguised Henry's presumption that earning the distrust of a foot soldier might matter to the king: "That's a perilous shot of an elder-gun that a poor and a private displeasure can do against a monarch. You may as well go about to turn the sun to ice with fanning in his face with a peacock's feather. You'll never trust his word after! Come, 'tis a foolish saying" (4.1.163–66). Henry's trouble here is the same one that ceremony creates and the same that exists for all characters in a play—the inability to force the veracity of his own word from his position of disguise (even though that disguise was necessary to elicit veracity from others). In other words, Henry fails to convince others of a nature that transcends ceremony.

Henry's ironically real treatment of ceremony plays out most conspicuously in his courtship of Katherine. The play seems to make it clear that the courtship is unnecessary if Henry's end is marriage; Katherine, who was a peace offering in Act 3, is a spoil of war in Act 5. Yet, despite the obvious political nature of their match, Henry presses Katherine to admit love for him as her motive for marriage. Although Henry does not reveal his motive, his wooing functions as an attempt to make real the ceremonially over-determined scene in which he finds himself. However, Kate is thoroughly and consistently unyielding—not just to his request for marriage but also to his attempt to impart a sense of reality to the proceedings. She regards his earnest protestations of his love as duplicity, telling him "the tongues of men are full of deceits" (5.2.112) and that he has "fausse French enough to deceive de most sage damoisell dat is en France" (5.2.185–86). Although both of Katherine's responses might be purely conventional echoes of the demurs offered even by willing brides, their effect is to uphold the ceremonial nature of the scene that Henry is trying hard to dispel. The same might be said of her consent to marriage in which she noncommittally defers to her father: "Dat is as it sall please de roi mon père" (5.2.207). Although Katherine's respectful response is almost exactly the same as that of the perhaps more willing Margaret to

Suffolk's scheming invitation for her to marry the King in *1 Henry VI*, it preserves ceremony by refusing to indulge Henry's attempt to get her to match his emotional heights. Henry's attempt to kiss Kate pushes the tension between ceremony and reality to the breaking point. The appeal to "custom" in Kate's demurral provides an attempt to preserve the ceremony of the scene. "Custom" and the English equivalents "fashion" and "manners" are the functional equivalents of ceremony in that they constrain desire and render reality less than real. Henry, therefore, insists on his immunity from such constraints, claiming that "nice customs curtsy to great kings" and that the two of them "cannot be confined within the weak list of a country's fashion" (5.2.225–26). They, he claims, "are the makers of manners" (5.2.226–27). Henry, in the end, grounds his right to kiss his fiancée in the more general prerogative of "great kings" to operate outside the strictures of custom and above the whispers of the prying populace. Yet Henry cannot assert this creative power over custom without the risk of looking pushy, if not flagrantly malfeasant.

Henry's habit of treating ceremony as real provides a further intensification of the paradox of dramatic character. To the audience, drama consists of characters who, by definition, do not know they are in plays and, therefore, treat unreal and predetermined situations as if they are real, as if they might be open to chance. This general paradox is already redoubled in history plays, where the predetermined nature of the content replicates that of the form. But Henry's case is special because his wonted rehearsal of his dramatic condition affects the audience's assessment of his character. The harder Henry pushes to confer a sense of reality back onto his personal and situational fiction, the more he exposes himself to charges that he is pushy, manipulative, and insincere; i.e., the more he appears the consummate player-king. But, at the same time, in keeping with the dizzying intersection between dramatic and personal characters that the play has dramatized, the more he treats ceremony as real, the more he underscores his own artificial nature as a dramatic character and reveals himself to be what he already is.

In most of the foregoing discussion, the conflicts in Henry's character that intensify the paradoxical experiences of dramatic characters have been confined to theoretical experiences that an audience has while reading a play with the foreknowledge that the text is meant to be embodied on stage. However, actual theatres provide even greater opportunities for intensifying these experiences than do the venues of the reader's imagination. This equivalence may come as a surprise given the tendency of directors to assign motives and to varying degrees emphasize either Henry's nobility or his duplicity, often at the expense of the other. Whether Henry appears grand or grandiose, the audience would still experience this intensification because it would still behold the king contending with the formidable burden of ceremony, even as he dispatches the appreciably less redoubtable French foe. If the production presents Henry as greater than he is in the text (a greatness that, admittedly, is hard to gauge), the audience will still experience the disparity that the Chorus advertises in the beginning. Such a disparity is undeniable at a point such as the Crispin's Day speech, in which Henry reaches rhetorical heights only to fall, as Sharon Tyler reminds us, on "the small cast representing the English army—not quite four or five …'foils' or 'four swords and bucklers,' but still the ears only of a few."[24] If the production emphasizes Henry's duplicity, the audience gets to experience the disparity from the other end, from the conflict between the Chorus's claims and stage realization of those claims. Neutralizing this intensified experience altogether could only result from cutting swaths of text large enough to remove Henry entirely from the play. As long as Henry appears in these highly ritualized scenarios and says what Shakespeare wrote for him, he continues to stoke the audience's experience of him as markedly less than his role.

The Royal Shakespeare Company seems to have created its 1975 Centenary production with the principle of intensification in mind. Fiscal necessity prompted the director to employ a stripped-down, ascetic approach to the staging. The play began with characters still dressed as actors in rehearsal clothes on a stage stripped of scenery and which not only exposed the machinery of the theatre but also exaggerated it. These choices, as Tyler points out, reinforced the participatory role of the audience in decking the kings.[25] Such a deliberately dressed-down production kept the viewer in contact with the dissonant combination of actor/ character that defines Henry. By temporarily keeping Henry out of costume, the production intensified the experience of having him in it. Yet the production went one step further and connected ethical character to costume by making Henry essentially earn his role. Only after Henry acted in a decisively king-like manner by announcing war with France did the production supply the accoutrements of theatrical illusion. The director Terry Hand recounts, "As Henry lifts into decision, the first costume arrives on stage, the lights come up."[26] In this RSC rendition, Henry had to perform his character before he could become "like himself" and assume whatever port the play was willing to vouchsafe him. Nevertheless, while the production insisted on an artificiality that detracted from Henry's assumption of royalty, it endowed him with a compensatory power over his theatrical environment by making it look responsive to his actions. On stage, this Henry made things happen closer to the way we are accustomed to thinking about Prospero. Thus, the RSC's production recreated on stage a theatrical phenomenon indispensable to theatre according to which characters whose moves are scripted by the writer and controlled by the actor are experienced by the audience as if they are willed by the character. Although such recuperating illusions might seem to be what Greenblatt classified as containment, they, once again, intensify the paradox of character.

The version of *Henry V* produced for the inaugural 1997 season of Shakespeare's new Globe Theatre in London gives us a different take on the way the conditions

---

[24]   Sharon Tyler, "Minding True Things: The Chorus, The Audience, and *Henry V*," in *The Theatrical Space*, ed., James Redmond (Cambridge: Cambridge University Press, 1987), 74.

[25]   Tyler, 74.

[26]   Sally Beauman, *The Royal Shakespeare Company's Centenary Production of* Henry V (Oxford: Pergamon, 1976), 19.

of dramatic character affect our assessment of it. In keeping with the new Globe's mission of approximating original practices and conditions of the Shakespearean stage (and taking its cue from the Chorus's repeated exhortations to the audience to engage the play with their imaginations), the production exploited every chance to invite audience participation. In his careful study of how this performance was received, Yu Jin Ko notes the unusually "collective intensity of response" the audience displayed.[27] Audiences answered the Chorus's rhetorical question about the wooden O's capacity to contain the "very casques that did affright the field at Agincourt" with a resounding "Yes!" and recited the final lines of the speech at Harfleur in unison with Henry. Yet Ko notes that during the "wordy interludes" that constitute the battle of Agincourt, the theatre audience exhibited a palpable "loss of energy and deflation of defeated expectations."[28] Such disappointment is to a certain extent part of the play's program. The same Chorus who exalts Henry's war prowess warns viewers from the beginning of the play's inevitable failure to produce either Henry's greatness or war's ferocity. That the audience responded with ennui and disaffection in the revelatory fourth act might ironically be a testament to the level of engagement that the Globe's environment made possible. However, the more germane lesson here stems from the way circumstances beyond the control of the company led a number of reviewers to find fault with the play. Ko cites several reviewers who were "unwillingly taken out of the moment more frequently than is usual even for reviewers" by the extraneous noise of fidgeting viewers and who, "to varying degrees and with different spins, drew some connection between that experience [of the audience's static] and disappointment of epic expectations."[29] When critics judge the production according to the conditions of the theater, they unknowingly create a parallel with how audiences in general measure Henry's character. In Shakespeare's play Henry is repeatedly called into account by the theatrical circumstances of his existence that are beyond his control and that leave him besmirched whenever he tries to control them.

The influence that the fictional nature of dramatic characters has on the audience's experience of the personal characters as they are formed and occur in plays should be among the most important factors we consider as we return to character criticism. Ironically, the materialist investment in subjectivity as a means of seeking to understand drama according to the historical conditions of theatre ignores this fundamental condition of theatre. The energy behind theories of subjectivity, the ardor with which they have been embraced, and the fervor with which they have been pursued in studying drama all suggest the rather simplistic assumption that a better understanding of human beings would lead to a better understanding of theater. In the end, characters and humans alike are bodied texts. Dramatic characters imitate human subjects; so, it is reasonable to

---

[27]   Yu Jin Ko, "A Little Touch of Harry in the Light: *Henry V* at the New Globe," *Shakespeare Survey* 52 (1999): 107–119, 116.

[28]   Ko, 117.

[29]   Ko, 118.

assume that a more accurate understanding of the objects imitated will yield a better understanding of drama. But this assumption is no more complete than its counterpart: that understanding theatre or a particularly accomplished play better will help us understand ourselves. The better-known formulation of this idea is the belief that the theatre contains universal truths, a belief materialists rightly dismiss as naïve. What is true in general for dramatic character is even more pressing for Shakespeare who, if *Henry V* is any indication, is aware of the complexities of creating fictional characters and consistently exploits them in a way that intensifies the experiences that they already offer. Not all character criticism should resemble the kind of study I have undertaken of *Henry V*, in which problems of dramatic character merge with personal character. However, emphasizing that fiction and non-fiction differ, and that fictional character has a set of experiential possibilities unavailable to human subjects, is essential to avoid falling into the trap that has ensnared both old character criticism and its materialist detractors and could result in a character criticism that is genuinely new.

# Bibliography

Adelman, Janet. "Male Bonding in Shakespeare's Comedies." In *Renaissance Essays in Honor of C. L. Barber*, eds. Peter Erickson and Coppélia Kahn. Newark: University of Delaware Press, 1985.

———. "Bed Tricks: On Marriage as the End of Comedy in *All's Well That Ends Well* and *Measure for Measure*." In *Shakespeare's Personality*, eds., Norman Holland, Sidney Homan, and Bernard J. Paris. Berkeley and London: University of California Press, 1989.

———. *Suffocating Mothers: Fantasies of Maternal Origin in Shakespeare's Plays, Hamlet to The Tempest*. New York and London: Routledge, 1992.

———. "Iago's Alter Ego: Race as Projection in *Othello*." *Shakespeare Quarterly* 48 (1997): 377–90.

Aebischer, Pascale. *Shakespeare's Violated Bodies*. Cambridge: Cambridge University Press, 2004.

Aers, David. "A Whisper in the Ear of Early Modernists; or Reflections on Literary Critics Writing the History of the Subject." In *Culture and History 1350-1600*, ed. David Aers. Detroit: Wayne State University Press, 1992.

Auerbach, Erich. *Scenes from the Drama of European Literature*. New York: Meridian Books, 1959.

Augustine, Saint. *On Christian Teaching*. Trans. R.P.H. Green. Oxford: Oxford University Press, 1997.

Aviram, Amittai, F. "Lyric Poetry and Subjectivity." *Intertexts* 5.1 (2001): 61–86.

Axton, William. "'Keystone Structure' in Dickens' Novels." *University of Toronto Quarterly* 37.1 (1967): 31–50.

Aylett, Robert. *Divine and Moral Speculations*. London: Abel Roper, 1654.

Babula, William. "The Character and the Conclusion: Bertram and the Ending of *All's Well That Ends Well*." *South Atlantic Review* 42.2 (1977): 94–100.

Bale, John. "A comedy concernynge thre lawes, of nature, Moses, & Christ." In *The Dramatic Writings of John Bale*, ed. John S. Farmer. London: Early English Drama Society, 1907.

Barker, Francis. *The Tremulous Private Body: Essays on Subjection*. London and New York: Methuen, 1984.

Barroll, J. Leeds. *Artificial Persons: The Formation of Character in the Tragedies of Shakespeare*. Columbia: University of South Carolina Press, 1974.

Barthelemy, Anthony Gerard. "Ethiops Washed White: Moors of the Nonvillainous Type." In *Black Face, Maligned Race: The Representation of Blacks in English Drama from Shakespeare to Sheridan*. Baton Rouge: Louisiana State University Press, 1987.

———. ed. *Critical Essays on Shakespeare's Othello*. New York: G.K. Hall & Co., 1994.

Barton, John. *Playing Shakespeare.* New York: Methuen, 1984.

Bate, Jonathan, ed. *The Romantics on Shakespeare.* New York: Penguin, 1992.

Beauman, Sally. *The Royal Shakespeare Company's Centenary Production of Henry V.* Oxford: Pergamon, 1976.

Beckerman, Bernard. *Dynamic of Drama: Theory and Method of Analysis.* New York: Knopf, 1970.

Beckman, Margaret Boerner. "The Figure of Rosalind in *As You Like It.*" *Shakespeare Quarterly* 29.1 (1978): 44–51.

Belsey, Catherine. *The Subject of Tragedy: Identity and Difference in Renaissance Drama.* London: Methuen, 1985.

Benson, George. *A Sermon Preached at Paules Crosse.* London: H. Lownes, 1609.

Berger, Harry. *Imaginary Audition.* Berkeley: University of California Press, 1989.

Berry, Cicely. *The Actor and the Text.* New York: Applause Books, 1992.

Berry, James D. "Wopsle Once More." *Dickensian* 64 (1968): 43–47.

Bethell, S.L. *Shakespeare and the Popular Dramatic Tradition.* Westminster: P.S. King & Staples, 1944.

Binns, J. W. "Women or Transvestites on the Elizabethan Stage?: An Oxford Controversy." *Sixteenth Century Journal* 2 (1974): 95–120.

Bloom, Harold. *The Western Canon.* New York: Harcourt Brace, 1994.

———. *Shakespeare: The Invention of the Human.* New York: Riverhead Books, 1998.

Bogart, Anne and Tina Landau. *The Viewpoints Book: A Practical Guide to Viewpoints and Composition.* New York: Theatre Communications Group, 2005.

Boyce, Benjamin. *The Theophrastan Character in England to 1642.* Cambridge: Harvard University Press, 1947.

Bradbrook, M.C. *Elizabethan Stage Conditions: A Study of their Place in the Interpretation of Shakespeare's Plays.* Cambridge: Cambridge University Press, 1932.

———. "Shakespeare and the Use of Disguise in Elizabethan Drama." *Essays in Criticism* 2 (1952): 159–68.

Bradley, A.C. *Shakespearean Tragedy: Lectures on Hamlet, Othello, King Lear, Macbeth.* 1904. Reprint, New York: Penguin, 1991.

Brathwait, Richard. *The Arcadian Princesse.* London: Th. Harper, 1635. . *A Survey of History.* London: N. and I. Okes, 1638.

Bray, Alan. *Homosexuality in Renaissance England.* London: Gay Men's Press, 1982.

Bredbeck, Gregory W. *Sodomy and Interpretation: Marlowe to Milton.* Ithaca and London: Cornell University Press, 1991.

Bristol, Michael. "Vernacular Criticism and the Scenes Shakespeare Never Wrote." *Shakespeare Survey* 51 (2000): 37–51.

———. "How Many Children Did She Have?" In *Philosophical Shakespeare*, ed. John J. Joughin. London: Routledge, 2000.

———. "… And I'm the King of France." In *Presentist Shakespeares*, eds. Hugh Grady and Terence Hawkes. London and New York: Routledge, 2007.

————. "'A System of Oeconomicall Prudence': Shakespearean Character and the Practice of Moral Inquiry." In *Shakespeare and the Eighteenth Century*, eds., Peter Sabor and Paul Yachnin. Aldershot: Ashgate, 2008.

Brooks, Cleanth. *The Well Wrought Urn*. New York, Harcourt Brace, 1947.

Brower, Reuben A. *Hero and Saint*. Oxford: Oxford University Press, 1971.

Browne, Thomas, Sir. *Religio Medici and Other Works*. Ed. L.C. Martin. 1643. Reprint, Oxford: Clarendon Press, 1964.

Bruster, Douglas. *Shakespeare and the Power of Performance: Stage and Page in the Elizabethan Theatre*. New York and London: Cambridge University Press, 2008.

Buber, Martin. *I and Thou*. Trans. Ronald Gregor Smith. Edinburgh: T. and T. Clark, 1959.

Bullock, Alan and Oliver Stallybrass, eds. *The Fontana Dictionary of Modern Thought*. Glasgow: William Collins Sons and Company Ltd., 1977.

Bulman, James. *The Heroic Idiom of Shakespearean Tragedy*. Newark: University of Delaware Press, 1985.

————, ed. *Shakespeare, Theory, and Performance*. London and New York: Routledge, 1996.

Burns, Edward. *Character: Acting and Being on the Pre-Modern Stage*. New York: St. Martin's Press, 1990.

Burton, Robert. *The anatomy of melancholy vvhat it is. VVith all the kindes, causes, symptomes, prognostickes, and seuerall cures of it. In three maine partitions with their seuerall sections, members, and subsections. Philosophically, medicinally, historically, opened and cut vp. By Democritus Iunior. With a satyricall preface, conducing to the following discourse*. Oxford, 1621.

Calbi, Maurizio. *Approximate Bodies: Gender and Power in Early Modern Drama and Anatomy*. London and New York: Routledge, 2005.

Callaghan, Dympna. *Shakespeare Without Women: Representing Gender and Race on the Renaissance Stage*. London and New York: Routledge, 2000.

Carlell, Lodowick. *The Passionate Lover,* Part I. London: Humphrey Moseley, 1655.

Cartwright, Kent. *Shakespearean Tragedy and Its Double*. University Park: Pennsylvania State University Press, 1991.

Cavell, Stanley. "Recounting Gains, Showing Losses: Reading *The Winter's Tale*." In *Disowning Knowledge in Seven Plays of Shakespeare*. Cambridge: Cambridge University Press, 2003.

Charnes, Linda. *Notorious Identity: Materializing the Subject in Shakespeare*. Cambridge: Harvard University Press, 1993.

Cicero. *De partitione oratori.,* Trans. H. Rackam. Cambridge, MA: Harvard University Press, 1942.

————. *Rhetorica ad Herennium*. Trans. H. Caplan. Cambridge, MA: Harvard University Press, 1954.

————. *De Amicitia*. Trans. William Armistead Falconer. Cambridge, MA: Harvard University Press, 1959.

———. *De Oratore*. Trans. E.W. Sutton and H. Rackham. Cambridge, MA: Harvard University Press, 1960.

Cohen, Eileen Z. "'Virtue is bold': The Bed-trick and Characterization in *All's Well That Ends Well* and *Measure for Measure*." *Philological Quarterly* 65 (1986): 171–86.

Coleridge, Samuel Taylor. *Selected Poetry and Prose of Coleridge*. Ed. Donald A. Stauffer. New York: Random House, 1951.

———. *Coleridge's Writings on Shakespeare*. Ed. Terence Hawkes. New York: Capricorn Books, 1959.

Coryate, Thomas. *Coryats crudities hastily gobled vp in five moneths trauells in France, Sauoy, Italy, Rhetia co[m]monly called the Grisons country, Heluetia aliàs Switzerland, some parts of high Germany, and the Netherlands; newly digested in the hungry aire of Odcombe in the county of Somerset, & now dispersed to the nourishment of the trauelling members of this kingdome*. London, 1611.

Cowhig, Ruth. "Blacks in English Renaissance Drama and the Role of Shakespeare's Othello." In *The Black Presence in English Literature*, ed. David Dabydeen. Manchester: Manchester University Press, 1985.

Crowl, Samuel. *Shakespeare at the Cineplex*. Athens: Ohio University Press, 2003.

Curtius, Ernst Robert. *European Literature and the Latin Middle Ages*. Trans. Willard R. Trask. Princeton: Princeton University Press, 1953.

Curtwright, Travis. "Sidney's Defense of Poetry: Ethos and the Ideas." *Ben Jonson Journal* 10 (2003): 101–15.

Daileader, Celia R. *Eroticism on the Renaissance Stage*. Cambridge: Cambridge University Press, 1998.

———. *Racism, Misogyny, and the* Othello *Myth*. Cambridge: Cambridge University Press, 2005.

Davies, John. "Against Aesop the Stage-player." In *The Scourge of Folly*. London: Edward Allde, 1611.

Davies, Michael. *Hamlet*. Character Studies Series. New York: Continuum Books, 2008.

Dawson, Anthony B. and Paul Yachnin. *The Culture of Playgoing in Shakespeare's England*. Cambridge: Cambridge University Press, 2001.

de Certeau, Michel. *The Practice of Everyday Life*. Trans. Steven Rendall. Berkeley and Los Angeles: University of California Press, 1984.

de Grazia, Margareta. Hamlet *without Hamlet*. Cambridge: Cambridge University Press, 2007.

Decker, Dan. *Anatomy of a Screenplay*. Chicago: The Screenwriters Group, 1998.

Dekker, Thomas. *The Blacke Rod, and the White Rod*. London: John Cowper, 1630.

Derrida, Jacques. *Writing and Difference*. Trans. Alan Bass. London and New York: Routledge, 2004.

Desmet, Christy. *Reading Shakespeare's Characters: Rhetoric, Ethics, and Identity*. Amherst: University of Massachusetts Press, 1992.

————. "The Persistence of Character." *Shakespeare Studies* 35 (2006): 46–55.

Dessen, Alan. "Wonder and Magic in the ACTER Five Hander Comedies." *Shakespeare Bulletin* 10 (1992): 7–9.

Dodd, William Nigel. "Character as Dynamic Identity: From Fictional Interaction Script to Performance." In *Shakespeare and Character: Theory, History, Performance and Theatrical Persons*, eds. Paul Yachnin and Jessica Slights. Basingstoke, U.K.: Palgrave, 2009.

Dollimore, Jonathan. *Radical Tragedy: Religion, Ideology, and Power in the Drama of Shakespeare and his Contemporaries,* 2nd ed. Durham: Duke University Press, 1998.

Donnellan, Declan. *The Actor and the Target.* St. Paul: Theatre Communications Group, 2002.

Drakakis, John, ed. *Alternative Shakespeares.* London: Routledge, 1985.

Eliot, T. S. "Shakespeare and the Stoicism of Seneca." In *Selected Essays.* New York: Harcourt, Brace, 1950.

Enders, Jody. "Of Madness and Method Acting." In *Death by Drama and Other Medieval Urban Legends.* Chicago: University of Chicago Press, 2002.

Erickson, Peter and Maurice Hunt, eds. *Approaches to Teaching Shakespeare's* Othello. New York: Modern Language Association, 2005.

Erne, Lukas. *Shakespeare as Literary Dramatist.* Cambridge: Cambridge University Press, 2003.

Evans, Robert. "Flattery in Shakespeare's *Othello*: The Relevance of Plutarch and Sir Thomas Elyot." *Comparative Drama* 35 (2001): 1–41.

Farley-Hills, David, ed. *Critical Responses to Shakespeare's* "Hamlet," Vol 2: 1790–1838. New York: AMS Press, 1996.

Field, Catherine. "'Sweet practicer, thy physic I will try': Helen and Her 'good receipt' in *All's Well, That Ends Well*." In All's Well That Ends Well*: New Critical Essays*, ed., Gary Waller. New York: Routledge, 2007.

Fisch, Harold. "Character as Linguistic Sign." *New Literary History,* 21.3 (1982): 592–606.

Fitz-Geffry, Charles. *Compassion towards Captives.* London: Leonard Lichfield, 1636.

Flesch, William. *Generosity and the Limits of Authority: Shakespeare, Herbert, Milton.* Ithaca: Cornell University Press, 1992.

————. "The Ambivalence of Generosity: Keats Reading Shakespeare," *ELH* 62:1 (1995): 149–69.

————. "The Bounds of the Incidental: Shakespeare Reading by His Own Light." In *Something Understood: Essays and Poetry for Helen Vendler*, eds. Stephen Burt and Nick Halpern. Charlottesville: University of Virginia Press, 2009.

Flessner, Robert F. *Dickens and Shakespeare: A Study in Histrionic Contrasts.* New York: Haskell, 1965.

Ford, John R. "'Words and Performances': Roderigo and the Mixed Dramaturgy of Race and Gender in *Othello*." In Othello*: New Critical Essays*, ed. Philip C. Kolin. London and New York: Routledge, 2002.

Freeman, Neil. *Shakespeare's First Texts*. Vancouver: Folio Scripts, 1999.

———. *Once More unto the Speech, Dear Friends: Monologues from Shakespeare's First Folio with Modern Text Versions for Comparison*. Vol 1. New York: Applause Theatre Books, 2006.

Freinkel, Lisa. *Reading Shakespeare's Will: The Theology of Figure from Augustine to the Sonnets*. New York: Columbia University Press, 2002.

French, A. L. "Beating and Crying: Great Expectations." *Essays in Criticism* 24 (1974): 147–68.

Freud, Sigmund. "A Note Upon the 'Mystic Writing Pad.'" In *The Penguin Freud Library*, Vol. 2. London: Penguin, 1984.

Fumerton, Patricia. *Cultural Aesthetics: Renaissance Literature and the Practice of Social Ornament*. Chicago: University of Chicago Press, 1991.

Gager, Valerie L. *Shakespeare and Dickens: The Dynamics of Influence*. Cambridge: Cambridge University Press, 1990.

Garber, Marjorie. *Coming of Age in Shakespeare*. New York and London: Routledge, 1981.

———. *Shakespeare After All*. New York: Pantheon Books, 2004.

Garrick, David. *The Letters*, eds. . David M. Little and George M. Kahrl. 3 Vols. London: Oxford University Press, 1963.

Gayton, Edmund. *Pleasant Notes upon Don Quixote*. London: William Hunt, 1654.

Gillette, William. *The Illusion of the First Time in Acting*. Publications of the Dramatic Museum of Columbia University, 2nd Series, 1915.

Goddard, Harold C. *The Meaning of Shakespeare*. Chicago: University of Chicago Press, 1951.

Goldberg, Jonathan. *James I and the Politics of Literature*. Baltimore: The Johns Hopkins University Press, 1983.

Goldman, Michael. *Acting and Action in Shakespearean Tragedy*. Princeton: Princeton University Press, 1985.

Gottlieb, Beatrice. *The Family in the Western World from the Black Death to the Industrial Age*. New York and Oxford: Oxford University Press, 1993.

Green, Douglas. "The 'Unexpressive She': Is There Really a Rosalind?" *Journal of Dramatic Theory and Criticism* 2.2 (1988): 41–52.

Greenblatt, Stephen. *Renaissance Self-Fashioning*. Chicago: University of Chicago Press, 1980.

———. *Shakespearean Negotiations*. Berkeley: University of California Press, 1988.

———. Introduction to *Twelfth Night*. In *The Norton Shakespeare*, ed. Stephen Greenblatt et al. New York: Norton, 1997.

Hagan Jr., John. "Structural Patterns in Dickens's *Great Expectations*." *ELH* 21.1 (1954): 54–66.

Hagen, Uta. *Respect for Acting*. New York: Wiley Publishing, Inc., 1973.

Halley, Janet E. "Bowers v. Hardwick in the Renaissance." In *Queering the Renaissance*, ed. Jonathan Goldberg. Durham and London: Duke University Press, 1994.

Hamilton, Alan. "Laurence Olivier at Seventy-Five." *The Times of London*, 17 May 1982.

Harley, Marta Powell. "Rosalind, the Hare, and the Hyena in Shakespeare's *As You Like It*." *Shakespeare Quarterly* 36.3 (1985): 335–7.

Hawke, Ethan. Introduction to *William Shakespeare's* Hamlet. Screenplay by Michael Almereyda. London: Faber and Faber, 2000.

Hayles, Nancy K. "Sexual Disguise in *As You Like It* and *Twelfth Night*." *Shakespeare Survey* 32 (1979): 63–72.

Hazlitt, William. *Characters of Shakespeare's Plays*. Oxford: Oxford University Press, 1916.

Heywood, Thomas. *An apology for actors Containing three briefe treatises. 1 Their antiquity. 2 Their ancient dignity. 3 The true vse of their quality.* London, 1612.

Hill, Aaron. "Prologue, spoken by a young Gentleman, At a Play, called the *Tuscan Treaty.*" In *The Works*. London: n.p., 1753.

Hill, John. *The Actor.* London: R. Griffiths, 1750.

Holford-Strevens, Leofranc . "Polus And His Urn: A Case Study in the Theory of Acting c. 300 B.C.– c. A.D. 2000." *International Journal of the Classical Tradition* 11 (2005): 499–523.

Holland, Peter. "The Resources of Characterization in *Othello*." *Shakespeare Survey* 41 (1989):119–32.

Holloway, John. *The Story of the Night.* London: Routledge & Kegan Paul, 1961.

Honigmann, E.A.J. *Shakespeare: Seven Tragedies.* London: MacMillan, 1976.

———. *Shakespeare: Seven Tragedies Revisited: The Dramatist's Manipulation of Response.* New York: Palgrave, 2002.

Hyland, Peter. "'A Kind of Woman': The Elizabethan Boy-Actor and the Kabuki Onagata." *Theatre Research International* 12.1 (1987): 1–8.

Hyman, Stanley Edgar. *Iago: Some Approaches to the Illusion of His Motivation.* New York: Atheneum, 1970.

Inchbald, Elizabeth. "Remarks." In Measure for Measure*; A Comedy, in Five Acts; As Performed at the Theater Royal, Covent Garden.* London: Longman, Hurst, Rees, and Orme, 1773.

Jameson, Frederic. *Postmodernism, or, The Cultural Logic of Late Capitalism.* Durham: Duke University Press, 1991.

Jardine, Lisa. *Still Harping on Daughters: Women and Drama in the Age of Shakespeare.* Sussex: Harvester Press, 1983.

Johnson, Samuel. *The Complete Works of Shakespeare: The Dr. Johnson Edition.* 1765. Reprint, Philadephia: Gebbie, 1896.

Jones, Eldred. "*Othello*—An Interpretation." In *Othello's Countrymen: The African in English Renaissance Drama.* Oxford: Oxford University Press, 1965.

Jorgensen, Paul A. "Honesty in *Othello*." *Studies in Philology* 47 (1950): 557–67.

Joseph, B. L. *Elizabethan Acting.* Oxford: Oxford University Press, 1964.

Junius, Fanciscus. *The Painting of the Ancients.* London: Richard Hodginksonne, 1638.

Keats, John. *Selected Letters*, Ed. Robert Gittings. New York: Oxford University Press, 2009.

Keel, Gilchrist. "'Like Juno's Swans': Rosalind and Celia in *As You Like It*." *CCTE Studies* 56 (1991): 5–11.

Keevak, Michael. "The Playing of Sodomy in *As You Like It*." *Studies in Language and Literature* 9 (2000): 48–9.

Kerrigan, William. "Female Friends and Fraternal Enemies in *As You Like It*." In *Desire in the Renaissance*, eds. Valeria Finucci and Regina Schwartz. Princeton: Princeton University Press, 1994.

Kiefer, Frederick. *Writing on the Renaissance Stage: Written Words, Printed Pages, Metaphoric Books.* Cranbury, NJ: Associated University Presses, 1996.

Kierkegaard, Soren. *Fear and Trembling* and *The Sickness unto Death,* Trans. Walter Lowrie. Princeton: Princeton University Press, 1954.

Kinney, Clare R. "Feigning Female Faining: Spenser, Lodge, Shakespeare, and Rosalind." *Modern Philology* 95.3 (1998): 291–315.

Knights, L. C. "How Many Children Had Lady Macbeth?" In *Explorations: Essays in Criticism, Mainly on the Literature of the Seventeenth Century.* London: Chatto and Windus, 1946.

Ko, Yu Jin. "A Little Touch of Harry in the Light: *Henry V* at the New Globe." *Shakespeare Survey* 52 (1999): 107–19.

———. *Mutability and Division on Shakespeare's Stage.* Newark: University of Delaware Press, 2004.

Kolin, Philip C., ed. Othello*: New Critical Essays.* London and New York: Routledge, 2002.

Kott, Jan. "The Gender of Rosalind." Trans. Jadwiga Kosicka. *New Theatre Quarterly* 7.26 (1991): 113–25.

Kuhn, Maura Slattery. "Much Virtue in If." *Shakespeare Quarterly* 28 (1977): 40–50.

Langer, Suzanne. *Problems in Art: Ten Philosophical Lectures.* New York: Scribner, 1957.

Lavender, Andy. Hamlet *in Pieces, Shakespeare Reworked by Peter Brook, Robert Lepage, and Robert Wilson.* London: Nick Hern Books, 2001.

Le Loyer, Pierre. *A Treatise of Spectres.* London: Val. Simmes, 1605.

Leavis, F.R. *The Common Pursuit.* 1952. Reprint, Harmondsworth: Penguin Books, 1962.

Lee, John. *Shakespeare's* Hamlet *and the Controversies of Self.* Oxford: Oxford University Press, 2000.

Lehnhof, Kent R. "Performing Woman: Female Theatricality in *All's Well, That Ends Well*." In All's Well That Ends Well*: New Critical Essays*, ed. Gary Waller. New York: Routledge, 2007.

Levin, Harry. *The Question of* Hamlet*.* New York: Oxford University Press, 1959.

Levin, Richard. "Bashing the Bourgeois Subject." In *Looking for an Argument: Critical Encounters with the Criticism of Shakespeare and his Contemporaries.* Madison, NJ: Fairleigh Dickinson University Press, 2003.

Levinas, Emmanuel. *Totality and Infinity: An Essay on Exteriority.* Trans. Alphonso Lingis. Pittsburgh: Duquesne University Press, 1969.

———. *The Theory of Intuition in Husserl's Phenomenology.* Trans. André Orianne. Evanston: Northwestern University Press, 1973.

———. *Ethics and Infinity: Conversations with Philippe Nemo.* Trans. Richard A. Cohen. Pittsburgh: Duquesne University Press, 1985.

———. "Dialogue with Emmanuel Levinas." In *Face to Face with Levinas,* ed. Richard A. Cohen. Albany: State University of New York Press, 1986.

———. "Signature." In *Difficult Freedom: Essays on Judaism.* Trans. Seán Hand. Baltimore: The Johns Hopkins University Press, 1990.

Levine, Laura. *Men in Women's Clothing.* Cambridge and New York: Cambridge University Press, 1994.

Lewes, G. H. "Fechter in *Hamlet* and *Othello.*" *Blackwood's Magazine* 40 (December, 1861), 745.

Lewis, Cynthia. "'Derived Honesty and Achieved Goodness': Doctrines of Grace in *All's Well That Ends Well.*" *Renaissance and Reformation* 14 (1990): 151–56.

Lewis, David."Truth in Fiction." In *Philosophical Papers.* Vol. I. Oxford: Oxford University Press, 1983.

Lichtenfels, Peter. "Shakespeare's Language in the Theatre." In *Reading Shakespeare's Dramatic Language: A Guide,* eds. Sylvia Adamson, Lynette Hunter, Lynne Magnusson, Ann Thompson, and Katie Wales. London: The Arden Shakespeare, 2001.

Linklater, Kristin. *Freeing Shakespeare's Voice: The Actor's Guide to Talking the Text.* New York: Theatre Communications Group, 1992.

Lipsius, Justus. *Two Bookes of Constancie.* London: Richard Johnes, 1595.

Little, Arthur L. Jr. "'An essence that's not seen': The Primal Scene of Racism in *Othello.*" *Shakespeare Quarterly* 44 (1993): 304–24.

Lloyd, Robert. *The Poetical Works.* London: T. Evans, 1774.

Loomba, Ania. *Gender, Race, Renaissance Drama.* New York and Manchester: Manchester University Press, 1989.

Lording, Barry. *Ram-Alley.* London: G. Eld., 1611.

Mack, Maynard. "Engagement and Detachment in Shakespeare's Plays." In *Essays on Shakespeare and Elizabethan Drama in Honor of Hardin Craig,* ed. Richard Hosley. Columbia: University of Missouri Press, 1962.

Mamet, David. *True and False: Heresy and Common Sense for the Actor.* London: Faber and Faber, 1997.

Mansfield, Katherine. *Journal of Katherine Mansfield.* Ed. J. Middleton Murry. New York: Alfred A. Knopf, 1927.

Marcus, Leah. "Shakespeare's Comic Heroines, Elizabeth I, and the Political Uses of Androgyny." In *Women in the Middle Ages and Renaissance: Literary and Historical Perspectives,* ed. Mary Beth Rose. Syracuse: Syracuse University Press, 1986.

Mares, F.H. "Viola and Other Transvestist Heroines in Shakespeare's Comedies." In *Stratford Papers, 1965–67,* ed. B.A.W. Jackson. Hamilton, Ont.: McMaster University Library Press, 1969.

Marowitz, Charles. *Recycling Shakespeare.* London: Macmillan Educational, Ltd., 1991.

———. *The Other Way: An Alternative Approach to Acting and Directing.* New York: Applause, 1999.

Martin, Louis. "As She Liked It: Rosalind as Subject." *Pennsylvania English* 22.1–2 (2000): 91–96.

Maus, Katherine Eisaman. *Inwardness and Theatre in the English Renaissance.* Chicago: University of Chicago Press, 1995.

Mazer, Cary. "The Intentional-Fallacy Fallacy." In *Staging Shakespeare: Essays in Honor of Alan C. Dessen,* eds. Lena Cowan Orlin and Miranda Johnson-Haddad. Newark: University of Delaware Press, 2007.

———. "Miss Julie at the University of Pennsylvania: A Case Study in Shared Student-Faculty Theatre Research." *New England Theatre Journal* 20 (2009): 104–11.

McCandless, David. "Helen's Bed-Trick: Gender and Performance in *All's Well That Ends Well*." *Shakespeare Quarterly* 45 (1994): 449–68.

McDonald, Charles. *Rhetoric of Tragedy.* Amherst: University of Massachusetts Press, 1966.

McLendon, Jacquelyn N. "'A Round Unvarnished Tale': MisReading Othello or African American Strategies of Dissent." In Othello*: New Essays by Black Writers*, ed. Mythili Kaul. Washington, D.C.: Howard University Press, 1997.

Meisner, Sanford. *Sanford Meisner on Acting.* New York: Vintage, 1987.

Nashe, Thomas. *The Unfortunate Traveller and Other Works.* Ed. J.B. Steane. London: Penguin Books, 1985.

Neeley, Carol Thomas. "Epilogue: Remembering Shakespeare, Revising Ourselves." In *Women's Re-Visions of Shakespeare,* ed. Marianne Novy. Urbana and Chicago: University of Illinois Press, 1990.

Neill, Michael. "Changing Places in *Othello*." *Shakespeare Survey* 37 (1984): 115–31.

———. "Unproper Beds: Race, Adultery, and the Hideous in *Othello*." *Shakespeare Quarterly* 40 (1989): 383–412.

———. *Issues of Death: Mortality and Identity in English Renaissance Tragedy.* Oxford: Oxford University Press, 1997.

———. "'Mulattos,' 'Blacks,' and 'Indian Moors': *Othello* and Early Modern Constructions of Human Difference." *Shakespeare Quarterly* 49 (1998): 361–74.

Newman, Karen. "And wash the Ethiop white: Femininity and the Monstrous in *Othello*." In *Shakespeare Reproduced,* eds. Jean Howard and Marion O'Connor. London: Methuen, 1987.

Nicholson, Samuel. *Acolastus.* London: John Baylie, 1600.

Nussbaum, Martha C. *Women and Human Development: the Capabilities Approach.* Cambridge: Cambridge University Press, 2000.

Nuttall, A.D. *A New Mimesis.* London and New York: Methuen, 1983.

O'Brien, Ellen J. "Mapping the Role: Criticism and Construction of Shakespearean Character." In *Shakespearean Illuminations: Essays in Honor of Marvin*

*Rosenberg*, eds. Jay L. Halio and Hugh Richmond.Newark: University of Delaware Press, 1998.

Orgel, Stephen. *Impersonations*: *The Performance of Gender in Shakespeare's England.* Cambridge: Cambridge University Press, 1996.

———. "What is a Character?" In *The Authentic Shakespeare and Other Problems of the Early Modern Stage.* London: Routledge, 2002.

Orkin, Martin. "*Othello* and the 'Plain Face' of Racism." *Shakespeare Quarterly* 38 (1987): 166–88.

Osborne, Laurie. "Shakespeare and the Construction of Character." In *Shakespeare and Higher Education: A Global Perspective, Shakespeare Yearbook 12*, eds. Sharon A. Beehler and Holger Klein. Lewiston: Edwin Mellen Press, 2001.

Overbury, Thomas Sir. *Characters: together with poems, news, edicts, and paradoxes based on the eleventh edition of A wife now the widow of Sir Thomas Overbury.* Ottawa: Dovehouse Editions, 2003.

Parker, Patricia. "Shakespeare and Rhetoric: 'dilation' and 'delation' in *Othello*." In *Shakespeare and the Question of Theory,* eds. Patricia Parker and Geoffrey Hartman. London: Routledge, 1985.

Parrot, W. Gerrod. "The Emotional Experiences of Envy and Jealousy." In *The Psychology of Jealousy and Envy*, ed. Peter Salovey. New York: The Guilford Press, 1991.

Pavis, Patrice. "Underscore: The Shape of Things to Come." Trans. Ralph Yarrow and Barry Karlin. *Contemporary Theatre Review* 6.4 (1997): 37–61.

Pechter, Edward. *Othello and Interpretive Traditions.* Iowa City: University of Iowa Press, 1999.

Pickering, Kenneth. *Key Concepts in Drama and Performance.* Basingstoke and New York: Palgrave Macmillan, 2005.

Plutarch. *Plutarch's Moralia: Twenty Essays*. Trans. Philemon Hollan., Ed. E.H. Blakeney. London: Dent, 1911.

Pope, Alexander. *The Works of Shakespear: In Six Volumes.* 1725. Reprint, Charleston, S.C.: Nabu Press, 2010.

Puttenham, George. *The Art of English Poesy: A Critical Edition, eds.* Frank Whigham and Wayne A. Rebhorn. Ithaca: Cornell University Press, 2007.

Quarles, Francis. *The Virgin Widow.* London: R. Royston, 1649.

Quarles, John. *The History Of the Most Vile Dimagoras.* London: J. M., 1658.

Quarshie, Hugh. *Second Thoughts about* Othello. Occasional Paper No. 7. Chipping Camden: International Shakespeare Association, 1999.

Quinney, Laura. "Enter a Messenger." In *William Shakespeare's Antony and Cleopatra,* ed., Harold Bloom. New York: Chelsea House, 1988.

———. *William Blake.* Cambridge: Harvard University Press, 2009.

Quintilian. *Quintilian: The Orator's Education.* Trans. Donald A. Russell. Cambridge: Harvard University Press, 2001.

Rabe, Lily. "Interview with Gemma Wilson." Broadway.com, 1 Nov. 2010. Web 1 Dec., 2010.

Rabkin, Norman. *Shakespeare and the Common Understanding.* New York: The Free Press, 1967.

————. *Shakespeare and the Problem of Meaning.* Chicago: University of Chicago Press, 1981.

Richmond, Hugh Macrae. "The Audience's Role in Othello." In Othello: *New Critical Essays,* ed. Philip C. Kolin. London and New York: Routledge, 2002.

Roach, Joseph R. *The Player's Passion.* Ann Arbor: University of Michigan Press, 1993.

Rodenburg, Patsy. *Speaking Shakespeare.* New York: Palgrave Macmillan, 2002.

Rokison, Abigail. *Shakespearean Verse Speaking: Text and Theatre Practice.* Cambridge: Cambridge University Press, 2009.

Rosenbaum, Ron. "Pacino Plays Shylock Like a Grouchy Tevya." *Jewish World Review,* 6 Dec., 2004.

Rosenberg, Marvin. "Elizabethan Actors: Men or Marionettes?" *PMLA* 69 (1954): 915–27.

————. *The Masks of* Othello. Berkeley: University of California Press, 1971.

Rowe, Nicholas, ed. *Hamlet, Prince of Denmark.* Vol. 5, *The Works of William Shakespear*: in six volumes, adorned with cuts. London: Jacob Tonson, 1709.

Rudnytsky, Peter L. "The Purloined Handkerchief in *Othello.*" In *The Psychoanalytical Study of Literature,* eds. Joseph Reppen and Maurice Charney. Hillsdale, NJ: The Analytic Press, 1985.

Russell, D. A. and M. Winterbottom, eds. *Ancient Literary Criticism: The Principal Texts in New Translations.* Oxford: Oxford University Press, 1972.

Rutter, Carol. *Clamourous Voices: Shakespeare's Women Today.* New York: Routledge, 1989.

Rylance, Mark. "Meet the Real Shakespeare." *The Times of London,* 14 August 1998.

Said, Edward. "The Problem of Textuality: Two Exemplary Positions." *Critical Inquiry* 4.4 (1978): 673–714.

Sanders, Eve Rachele. *Gender and Literacy on the Shakespearean Stage.* Cambridge: Cambridge University Press, 1998.

Sandys, George. *A Relation of a Journey Begun Anno Domini 1610,* 2nd ed. London, 1615.

Schultz, Stephen C. "William Poel on the Speaking of Shakespearean Verse: A Reevaluation." *Shakespeare Quarterly* 28 (1977): 334–50.

Searle, Leroy F. "Hamlet, Oedipus, and the Problem of Reading." *Comparative Literature* 49.4 (1997): 316–43.

Sedinger, Tracey. "'If Sight and Shape Be True': The Epistemology of Crossdressing on the London Stage." *Shakespeare Quarterly* 48.1 (1997): 63–80.

Sewell, Arthur. *Character and Society in Shakespeare.* Oxford: Clarendon Press, 1951.

Sinfield, Alan and Jonathan Dollimore. "History and Ideology: The Instance of *Henry V.*" In *Alternative Shakespeares,* ed. John Drakakis. London: Routledge, 1985,

————. "When is a Character Not a Character?" In *Faultlines: Cultural Materialism and the Politics of Dissident Reading.* Berkeley: University of California Press, 1992.

————. "From Bradley to Cultural Materialism." In "Forum: Is There Character After Theory?" *Shakespeare Studies* 34 (2006): 25–34.

Skura, Meredith Anne. *Shakespeare the Actor and the Purposes of Playing.* Chicago: University of Chicago Press, 1993.

Smith, Bruce R. *Homosexual Desire in Shakespeare's England: A Cultural Poetics.* Chicago: University of Chicago Press, 1991.

Smith, Gordon Ross. "Iago the Paranoiac." *American Imago* 16 (1959): 155–67.

Snow, Edward A. "Sexual Anxiety and the Male Order of Things in *Othello*." *ELR* 10 (1980): 384–412.

Snyder, Susan, ed. Othello*: Critical Essays* New York: Garland, 1988.

Solomon, Robert. *Continental Philosophy since 1750: The Rise and Fall of the Self.* Oxford and New York: Oxford University Press, 1988.

Soule, Lesley Anne. "Subverting Rosalind: Cocky Ros in the Forest of Arden." *New Theatre Quarterly* 7.26 (1991): 126–36.

Soule, Leslie Wade. *Actor as Anti-Character: Dionysus, the Devil, and the Boy Rosalind.* Westport, CT: Greenwood Press, 2000.

Spencer, John. *Kaina kai Palaia: Things New and Old.* London: W. Wilson and J. Streater, 1658.

Spolin, Viola. *Improvisation for the Theater.* Evanston: Northwestern University Press, 1963.

Stanislavski, Constantin. *Creating a Role.* Trans. Elizabeth Reynolds Hapgood. New York: Theatre Arts Books, 1961.

————. *An Actor Prepares.* Trans. Elizabeth Reynolds Hapgood. London: Methuen, 1985.

States, Bert O. *Hamlet and the Concept of Character.* Baltimore: The Johns Hopkins University Press, 1992.

————. "Performance as Metaphor." *Theatre Journal* 48 (1996): 1–26.

————. "The Actor's Presence: Three Phenomenal Modes." In Philip B. Zarrilli, ed. *Acting (Re)Considered: A Theoretical and Practical Guide*, 2nd edition. London and New York: Routledge, 2002.

Stern, Tiffany. *Rehearsal from Shakespeare to Sheridan.* Oxford and New York: Oxford University Press, 2000.

————. *Documents of Performance in Early Modern England.* Cambridge: Cambridge University Press, 2010.

Stern, Tiffany and Simon Palfrey. *Shakespeare in Parts.* Oxford and New York: Oxford University Press, 2007.

Strasberg, Lee. *A Dream of Passion: The Development of the Method.* New York: New American Library, 1988, 121.

Stubbes, Philip. *Anatomy of Abuses.* London, 1583.

Styan, J. L. *The Shakespeare Revolution.* Cambridge: Cambridge University Press, 1977.

Swander, Homer. "In Our Time: Such Audiences We Wish Him." *Shakespeare Quarterly* 35.5 (1984): 528–40.

Taylor, Charles. *Sources of the Self: The Making of the Modern Identity.* Cambridge, MA: Harvard University Press, 1989.

Terry, Ellen. *Four Lectures on Shakespeare.* London: M. Hopkinson, 1932.

Thomson, Peter. "Rogues and Rhetoricians: Acting Styles in Early English Drama." In *A New History of Early English Drama,* eds. David Scott Kastan and John D. Cox. New York: Columbia University. Press, 1998.

Tillyard, E. M. W. *The Elizabethan World Picture.* New York: Macmillan, 1944.

———. *Shakespeare's History Plays.* New York: Macmillan, 1946.

Tucker, Patrick. *Secrets of Acting Shakespeare: The Original Approach.* New York: Routledge, 2002.

Tyler, Sharon. "Minding True Things: The Chorus, The Audience, and Henry V." In *The Theatrical Space,* ed. James Redmond. Cambridge: Cambridge University Press, 1987.

Vaughan, Virginia Mason. *Othello: A Contextual History.* Cambridge: Cambridge University Press, 1994.

———. *Performing Blackness on English Stages: 1500–1800.* Cambridge: Cambridge University Press, 2005.

Wangh, Martin. "*Othello*: The Tragedy of Iago." *Psychoanalytic Quarterly* 19 (1950): 202–212.

Watson, John Selby, Trans. *Quintilian's Institutes of Oratory.* London: Henry G. Bohn, 1856.

Weimann, Robert. *Shakespeare and the Popular Tradition in the Theater: Studies in the Social Dimension of Dramatic Form and Function.* Baltimore, Md.: The Johns Hopkins University Press, 1987.

Weingust, Don. *Acting from Shakespeare's First Folio: Theory, Text, and Performance.* New York: Routledge, 2006.

Welsh, Alexander. *Hamlet in His Modern Guises.* Princeton and Oxford: Princeton University Press, 2001.

Werner, Sarah. "Performing Shakespeare: Voice Training and the Feminist Actor." *New Theatre Quarterly* 12.47 (1996): 249–58.

Whigham, Frank. "Reading Social Conflict in the Alimentary Tract: More on the Body in Renaissance Drama." *ELH* 55 (1988): 333–50.

Wilder, Lina Perkins. "Changeling Bottom: Speech Prefixes, Acting, and Character in *A Midsummer Night's Dream.*" *Shakespeare* 4.1 (2008): 52–6.

Wilson, Thomas. *The Art of Rhetoric.* Ed. Peter E. Medine. 1560. Reprint, University Park: The Pennsylvania State University Press, 1994.

Wilson, William A. "The Magic Circle of Genius: Dickens's Translations of Shakespearean Drama in *Great Expectations.*" *Nineteenth-Century Fiction* 40 (1985): 154–74.

Wofford, Susanne L. "To You I Give Myself, For I Am Yours': Erotic Performance and Theatrical Performatives in *As You Like It.*" In *Shakespeare Reread: The Texts in New Contexts,* ed. Russ McDonald. Ithaca: Cornell University Press, 1994.

Worth, George J. "Mr. Wopsle's Hamlet: 'Something Too Much of This'." *Dickens Studies Annual: Essays on Victorian Fiction* 17 (1988): 35–46.

Worthen, W.B. "The Rhetoric of Performance Criticism." *Shakespeare Quarterly* 40.4 (1989): 441–55.

———. *Shakespeare and the Authority of Performance.* New York: Cambridge University Press, 1997.

Wright, Thomas. *The Passions of the Minde.* London: Valentine Simmes, 1604.

Yachnin, Paul and Jessica Slights, eds. *Shakespeare and Character: Theory, History, Performance and Theatrical Persons.* Basingstoke, U.K.: Palgrave, 2009.

Zamir, Tzachi. "Love as Performance." In *Double Vision: Moral Philosophy and Shakespearean Drama.* Princeton: Princeton University Press, 2007.

# Index